Violent Attachments

Violent Attachments

J. Reid Meloy, Ph.D.

JASON ARONSON INC.
Northvale, New Jersey
London

Production Editor: Judith D. Cohen

This book was set in 11 point Century by Lind Graphics of Upper Saddle River, New Jersey, and printed and bound by Haddon Craftsmen of Scranton, Pennsylvania.

Library of Congress Cataloging-in-Publication Data

Meloy, J. Reid.
  Violent attachments / by
J. Reid Meloy.
    p. cm.
  Includes bibliographical references and index.
  ISBN 0-87668-537-8
  1. Violence–Psychological aspects. 2. Homicide–Psychological
aspects. 3. Object relations (Psychoanalysis) 4. Attachment
behavior. I. Title.
  [DNLM: 1. Homicide. 2. Love. 3. Object Attachment.
4. Psychopathology. 5. Violence. WM 460.5.02 M528d]
RC569.5.V55M44 1992
616.85'82–dc20
DNLM/DLC
for Library of Congress   92-10469

Manufactured in the United States of America. Jason Aronson Inc. offers books and cassettes. For information and catalog write to Jason Aronson Inc., 230 Livingston Street, Northvale, New Jersey 07647.

This book is dedicated to
the shadow of violence
in our dreams

Contents

PART I:
CLINICAL THEORY AND RESEARCH

    Infant Research and Object Relations
    Animal Research and Psychobiological Regulation
    Attachment Pathology and Violence
    Premises of Clinical Investigation

    Empirical Research
    Psychodynamics and Structure
    Narcissistic Traits
    Hysterical Traits
    Paranoid Traits
    Psychopathic Traits
    Conclusions

PART II:
CLINICAL DIAGNOSIS AND TREATMENT

Acknowledgments

The Athenian orator Demosthenes once observed, "Envy is a disease, whereas gratitude has a place among the Gods." My gratitude extends to a number of people who have helped me as I wrote this book. Most notable, and often forgotten, are those writers listed in the reference section, without whom many of my own ideas would not have been born. My moments of envy are for those who personally knew some of these great minds of psychology and psychiatry. I extend a personal thank you to Dr. Bill and Rosemary Wilkins, whose hospitality and interest in my work sustained me in a most comforting manner. I would also like to thank my parents, Rev. John and Janet Meloy, who taught me the great pleasure inherent in work and accomplishment, and passed along that often forgotten genetic endowment that made them a reality in my life.

A very important source of intellectual stimulation and friendship for me during these past two years has been my fellow Rorschach researchers: Drs. Carl Gacono, Phil Erdberg, Lynne Kenney, Joanna Berg, Jacqueline Singer, Carey Weber, Judith Meyers, Nancy Kaser-Boyd, Marvin Acklin, Charles Peterson, and Donna Peaslee. The contributions of Drs. Amy Lamson, Glen Lipson, Glen Gabbard, Robert Hare, and Stephen Hart have also made this a stronger book.

Friends in the legal community have also helped in ways they may not even recognize. In particular, the Honorable Patricia Cowett and attorneys Kate Elkin, Mark Pettine, Jack Earley, and Kerry Wells have provided me with enormously useful experiences and guidance. Students at the University of San Diego School of Law and residents, predoctoral interns, psychology fellows, and psychiatry fellows at the University of California, San Diego, School of Medicine have often asked questions that stimulated my thoughts. Hundreds of workshop participants throughout the country have also helped me formulate ideas through their attention and curiosity.

I owe a special thanks for the tireless promotion of my work to Drew and Konni Leavens and Specialized Training Services. They have helped me through the years, and our collaboration continues. In the "home" office, the camaraderie of Douglas Smith and the Mental Health Conditional Release Program staff has been most welcome. And a special thanks to Marilyn Clarke and Cecilia Ancheta for their superb clerical and organizational skills. Joyce Eisen, Esti Stevens, Bortai Shaw, Dr. Benjamin Bensoul, Dr. Ansar Haroun, Dr. David Schein, and Dr. David Keenan, my administrative team, have been steady emotional companions and loyal friends.

A book such as this could not begin to be written without the case histories that bring to life the theory and research. Eleven individuals are specifically found in the cases in this book, and although their names cannot be revealed, their lives have contributed to psychological science. I thank them.

A special note of gratitude to Judy Cohen, my production editor, and Norma Pomerantz for their hard work and support of this project as it took final form and Dr. Jason Aronson for his confidence in my ideas.

Last, but never least, I want to thank Sally for her steady love, and Katie, my lovely stepgranddaughter who, at the seasoned age of 9, found the Egon Schiele painting for me on the cover of this book. She pointed to it and said, "That's violent attachment!" She was right.

Introduction

Attachment, Object Relations, and Violence

T he wish to injure or intentionally kill the object of one's love is a paradox. Yet physical violence as a behavioral manifestation of the psychopathology of attachment is common parlance to the mental health professional. Two-thirds of homicide victims are family members, friends, or acquaintances of the perpetrator (Uniform Crime Reports 1989). It has been reliably estimated that a woman is beaten every 15 seconds in the United States, usually by her male partner (Geffner and Rosenbaum 1990). Twenty to 25 percent of families will experience one or more instances of domestic violence (Sedlak 1988). And approximately 14 percent of women report having been raped by their husbands (Russell 1982).

Homicide deaths of infants are three times greater than for toddlers, and in a survey of twenty-five countries, infanticide tended to be as high as, or higher than, the rate for adult homicide (Straus 1987). The extremely high adult homicide rate among the nonwhite population of the United States is well documented (Rosenberg and Mercy 1986), but gross racial comparisons are confounded by differences in socioeconomic status (Straus 1987). And although homicide mortality for adults doubled between 1960 and 1980, the infant homicide rate remained essentially constant (Straus 1987). Most child homicides (filicides) are committed by women, and the few filicidal men appear to be severely mentally impaired. Their homicides are usually the result of isolated explosive disorder (Campion et al. 1988).

Recent epidemiological research has found an important but modest correlation between mental disorder and violence (Swanson et al. 1990). Mentally ill individuals are rarely violent toward others, but when they are, the victims are usually family members or acquaintances. Most matricides, for instance, appear to be committed by schizophrenic males living alone with their mother (Campion et al. 1985). In one carefully designed study, the modal diagnosis for insanity acquittees who committed homicide was paranoid schizophrenia, and these subjects were significantly more likely to kill a parent or child, and less likely to kill a spouse or nonfamily member, than were the matched personality-disordered controls (Packer 1987).

Cornell and colleagues (1987) found in their sample of seventy-two adolescents charged with homicide that 68 percent of the victims were family members or acquaintances. Among those that killed a family member, the most likely victim was the father, killed by a gun after an extended history of interpersonal conflict. The adolescents who murdered an acquaintance usually used a knife and were motivated by either affective violence (Meloy 1988a) or did it in the course of another criminal act.

This litany of violence can numb the senses and foster a curious yet detached attention to only the statistics. We minimize or deny the affectional paradigms and psychodynamics that existed between the aggressor and the victim. The numbers dampen our wish for insight, and our thoughts resist an attempt to comprehend the meaning of such inexplicable yet troublesome antisocial behavior. The remarkable fact, however, is that most violence among human beings is perpetrated within a bond or an attachment. And attachment theory, a conceptually elegant and empirically researched behavioral system, has rarely been applied to understanding human violence (Bowlby 1984, Symonds 1984, Zeanah and Zeanah 1989).

My intent in this book is to theoretically and empirically investigate violence, particularly homicide, using the conceptual tools of both attachment theory and object relations theory. The genesis of Bowlby's work (Bowlby 1953, 1958, 1969, 1973, 1980) was psychoanalysis, and despite the ethological and biological dimensions of attachment theory, Bowlby (1969) personally acknowledged his debt to the British object relations school, and to one of his supervisors, Melanie Klein. It seems wise that the sociobiological domain of attachment theory should remain closely linked to the developing intrapsychic formulations of object relations theory, as some recent authors have done (Horner 1984, Osofsky 1988). It also fosters comprehension of a complex behavior such as homicide from a biopsychosocial perspective and guards against the reductive mistake of attempting to understand, and thereby grossly distorting, an overdetermined behavior by considering only one domain of inquiry.

I have adopted an approach in this book that is unusual for studies of violence. Instead of applying attachment and object relations theory to more commonly perceived modes of violence, I have selected idiosyncratic and in some cases bizarre forms of homicidal violence that, despite their rarity, heavily implicate a psychopathology of attachment. For instance, the phenomenon of erotomania, the delusional belief that one is loved by another, leads to approach behavior in certain cases, and occasionally to violence. This unusual pattern of proximity seeking, a core element of attachment, is all the more curious because the object sought does not positively reinforce the attachment. Fantasy or, more technically, the intrapsychic representation of the love object, is the central motivator for this behavior. Extreme idealization of the object will often be followed by extreme devaluation, both of which are gross distortions of reality and set the stage for violence.

My reasons for choosing such forms of violence are threefold: first, these patterns of violence are outside the range of normal human observation and are naturally compelling by virtue of their novelty. Our conscious psychological link to these individuals may be nothing more than a reluctant acknowledgment that we are all members of the same species. The challenge, however, is to sustain empathy for the individuals who commit such extreme forms of violence and to examine the adaptive aspects of their behavior. Second, these forms of violence are outliers. They are remote and removed. Statistically these patterns of violence are two, if not three, standard deviations from the mean *of violent behavior*. Such anomalies, from the standpoint of science, shed light on the still imperceptible changes and milder psychopathology that may exist, unnoticed, at the center of a distribution. Extremes can be sensitive indicators of changes at the mean. By analogy, suppose we are watching children on a teeter-totter: If we only focus on the fulcrum, little movement will be seen. If we look at the children at either end of the teeter-totter, however, we see their alternating up-and-down movements very clearly, along with their expressions of glee! To return to psychology for an example, the developmental sequelae observed 40 years ago by Spitz (1945) in a small sample of institutionally raised infants inspired the clinical research on normal attachment, separation, and loss a decade later.

Third, I have personally evaluated, and in some cases treated, the perpetrators and victims of these patterns of violence. I have been involved in the formal evaluation of some of these individuals for the California Superior Court. In other cases the data have been gathered as part of an ongoing research project concerning the Rorschach and psychopathy (Meloy and Gacono, in press). And for several patterns of violence, such as individuals who have formed an attachment to the psychopath, I have provided psychotherapy for the victims. My own proximity-seeking to this topic and these cases is driven by a professional urgency to understand why such acts occur, seemingly uniquely between human beings (the phrase "He behaved just like an animal" often strikes me as exceedingly unfair to animals and their often civilized ways). Data gathering stimulates theory, and theory extends understanding of data.

My personal motivation is to understand my own psychopathology, both the ontogenetic roots of my own occasional homicidal feelings, predatory fantasies, and identifications with the nonhuman, and the phylogenetic basis upon which I share these intrapsychic capacities with other *homo sapiens.* And sometimes, through a counter-transferential hint of understanding, I glimpse an answer to the question, Why not, but for the grace of God, go I?

The nature of the cases within this book, which have been disguised to protect the privacy of the individuals involved, also brings a certain forensic perspective to the material. *Forensic* is derived from the Latin *forensis,* meaning forum, and is the application of a subject to the law or a legal issue. The act of violence, or homicide, invariably engages the criminal law, and throughout the book I will explain forensic concepts or problems that apply to certain theoretical or empirical aspects of violent attachment.

In an earlier book, *The Psychopathic Mind: Origins, Dynamics, and Treatment* (Meloy 1988a), I ventured a social and psychological prediction that psychopathy would eclipse the field of narcissistic psychopathologies as we ended the twentieth century. I am now even more certain that this prediction has merit, but see it in a broader context. Psychopathy is, among other things, a disorder of profound detachment. From this conscienceless, detached psychology emerges a heightened risk of violence, most notably a capacity for predation. On the other end of the continuum, however, is the disorder of extreme attachment, an intense, pathological, and intrusive bond that also may heighten the risk of violence in adult humans. Ironically, the evolutionary adaptiveness of normative attachment was postulated to be protection from predation (Bowlby 1969). I am concerned that both psychopathic detachment and pathological attachment, and their correlates of violence, may signal pervasive disturbances of attachment in our larger society, generally imperceptible because of their close proximity to what we perceive as normal.

Reality testing, self and object representations, and defensive operations within an attachment paradigm provide the framework for understanding violent and homicidal behavior in this book. Because the psychopathology discussed is rather unusual, I have organized the book into two parts: clinical theory and research, and clinical diagnosis and treatment. Each problem in the first section—erotomania, catathymia, attachment to the psychopath, and assassination—has its corresponding chapter in the second section. The appendices extend my work into the forensic areas of the insanity defense and erotomania, and a weapons history assessment method, which addresses a common form of "hard object" attachment.

It is my final hope that the reader will discover in this clinical and forensic investigation a partial answer to the question posed by Henrik Ibsen in *Peer Gynt:*

> The thought perhaps—the wish to kill,
> That I can understand, but really
> To do the deed. Ah no, that beats me.

Part I

CLINICAL THEORY AND RESEARCH

1

Normative Attachment and Object Relations Theory

The genesis of attachment theory can be traced to the early work of James Robertson, John Bowlby, and Mary Salter Ainsworth at the Tavistock Clinic and Tavistock Institute of Human Relations in London. Stimulated by the ethological work of Lorenz (1935), young researchers such as Robertson and Bowlby (1952), Bowlby (1953), and Ainsworth and Bowlby (1954) published seminal papers concerning mother–child separation.

The fundamental premise of attachment theory is the presence of a biologically rooted and species-characteristic attachment behavioral system that brings a child close to its caretaker. A behavioral system includes external, observable behavior and intraorganismic components (Ainsworth et al. 1978). It may be environmentally stable or labile (Bowlby 1969). Although variations exist in attachment behavior, influenced by genetic constitution, culture, and individual differences, it is phylogenetically deeply rooted and widely distributed among birds and mammals. In altricial mammals such as humans, attachment in infants occurs slowly through a prolonged period of sensitivity. It begins with primitive biological approach behaviors, such as attractions to warmth and touch, and progresses to more specifically directed psychobiological and socioemotional exchanges between the infant and the maternal object, such as responses to certain vocalizations and facial expressions (Hofer 1983).

Attachment behavior follows a predictable course in the human infant and toddler. At birth the infant uses signaling behaviors, such as sucking and crying, to solicit the attention of a caregiver, any caregiver, and to promote proximity to a person. Bowlby (1969) called this first phase "orientation and signals without discrimination of figure," a period that Ainsworth and colleagues (1978) renamed "the initial preattachment phase." The object relations corollary of this phase is that of "normal autism" (Mahler 1979), during which the infant establishes a homeostatic equilibrium outside the mother's womb. These behaviors are only expressed and not goal directed, but gradually the infant is able to differentiate one person from another and convert his signaling into a vector, with both magnitude and directionality.

Bowlby (1969) called this second phase "orientation and signals directed towards one (or more) discriminated figure(s)." Ainsworth and colleagues (1978) labeled it "attachment-in-the-making." Lasting from the eighth week to 6 months, this phase is a corollary of Mahler's (1979) stage of "normal symbiosis," and probably is most akin to de Bary's (1879) original biological meaning for the word *symbiosis:* a commensual, or mutually dependent, living arrangement among certain species.

At approximately 6 to 7 months of age, locomotion and directed reaching and grasping develop, facilitating the infant's activity and effectiveness. His proximity keeping can now be "goal-corrected" (Bowlby 1969), and there is evidence that this behavior corresponds with the first inner representation of the maternal object, or primary caregiver (Ainsworth 1989). Bowlby (1969) termed this third phase "maintenance of proximity to a discriminated figure by means of locomotion as well as signals," and Ainsworth and colleagues (1978), with characteristic brevity, called it "the phase of clear-cut attachment." The infant now has formed an attachment, and this achievement is accompanied by separation distress when the primary object leaves the infant. During the first year of life, the infant internally organizes these care-giving rhythms into what Bowlby (1969) called "working models" of the environment, objects, and self. Object permanence has been attained, but not object constancy, a milestone yet to be reached. Object permanency is the perceptual-mnemonic ability of the infant to evoke a memory of the actual object in its absence (Rinsley 1982) and to differentiate actual objects from the manipulation of them (Piaget 1954).

Phase three concurs with Mahler's (1979) stage of separation and individuation, and its first three subphases – differentiation, practicing, and rapprochement. During this period, which extends through the second year of life, the infant's sensory and perceptual development stimulates the child's exploration from the secure base of the mother (Bowlby 1988), while intrapsychically self and object representations are differentiated. The practicing period, from 10 months to approximately 16 months, is the high-water mark for the child's sense of omnipotence. As he walks alone and upright, with mother in his available reach, he shares in a "symbiotic dual unity" of grandiosity with his maternal object (Mahler 1968, p. 23). His elation is only matched by his mother's smiling, clapping, and laughter.

The third subphase of rapprochement, at the approximate age of 18 months, is marked by the toddler's growing uneasiness concerning separateness from mother. The harshness of reality, contact with hard objects, the experience of unpleasant feelings separate from mother, the awkwardness of mobility, all collude to deflate omnipotence, and hence self-esteem. Shame and depression are the germinating affective experiences that convey the importance of the love of the separate, internalized object in the intrapsychic life of the toddler. It is the dawn of socialized emotional experience, and the child's task is to relinquish omnipotence without undue shame or separation anxiety.

Intrapsychically, the genotypic defense of splitting, and its phenotypes such as projection, introjection, idealization, and devaluation, are still predominant. The maternal object is alternately idealized and feared. The child's behavior, within the "set-point" (Bowlby 1969) of proximity to the mother, alternatively seeks approval from, and asserts a will against, the maternal object. This set-point, also termed environmental homeostasis (Bowlby 1973), is an attachment control system that maintains a child's relation to the mother between certain limits of distance and accessibility.

In the early stage of separation-individuation, the danger situation was loss of the object. At this end point of separation-individuation, the rapprochement crisis, the danger situation is loss of the *love* of the object (Horner 1984, Mahler 1968). There is also a continuation of part-object relations, in which there is not yet an integration of good and bad self-representations (as a whole self) and good and bad object representations (as a whole object). The demarcation during separation-individuation is between good and bad self-object representations (Kernberg 1976).

The maternal object, however, is not the only attachment figure for the child. By the second year of life, the child has developed multiple attachments, but they are not equally treated. Studies have demonstrated that attachments can be arranged in a hierarchical order, and that the child who has developed a strong primary attachment is more likely to direct his social behavior to other objects as well (Bowlby 1969). Bowlby (1969) refers to this bias toward one primary attachment as *monotropy.*

In normative development, the third and fourth years of life are marked by substantial changes in attachment behavior, defensive operations, and object relations. The child becomes capable of what Bowlby (1969) termed a "goal-corrected partnership." Characterized by flexibility and reciprocity, and facilitated by language development, this fourth phase of attachment finds the child able to grasp the parents' motivations and plans. He can more skillfully persuade the parent, and acceptable compromises are reached. Separation distress lessens because the child has internalized the maternal object as a constant for the first time. Locomotion has advanced to confident walking and running, and the distance from the secure base of the parent has expanded.

Object relations have markedly changed. In this fourth subphase of separation-individuation, what Mahler (1979) termed "object constancy," the maternal object is now available to the child as a whole and constant mental representation. Despite variations in feelings toward the mother from moment to moment, the child has integrated both the positive and negative characteristics of the maternal object into an evocative representation available in the absence of the actual mother. The child has "the capacity to feel and use the psychological presence of the primary love object even when he or she is not present or, if present, not approving" (Solnit 1986, p. 2). Object constancy is the "intrapsychic paragon of safety" for the child (Meloy 1988a, p. 56) and the bedrock of socialization. Affects toward the primary attachment, or maternal object, although discordant, can be experienced contemporaneously. There is an empathic deepening of the perception of the object as not just a source of want-gratification, but as a whole, real, and meaningful person separate from the child. In Kohutian terms, the selfobject as a two-dimensional extension of the self has attained a three-dimensional[1] separateness and is a source of affect regulation within the child.

Kernberg (1976) saw this stage of object constancy as an integration of libidinally and aggressively invested self-representations, and a likewise integration of object representations. Ambivalence toward the self and object is experienced and tolerated. This cognitive perspective taking (Ainsworth 1989) allows the child, for instance, to both love mother and be angry at her at the same time. With this consolidation of different affective states within each self and object representation begins the tripartite structuring of the personality into id, ego, and superego. No longer is the psychic structure composed of only dyadic self and object representations and their respective, polarized affects.

The structuring of the personality during this stage of development is fostered by repression, a defense that supersedes, but does not eliminate, splitting as the genotypic organizing mechanism. The id

---

1. The three-dimensionality of perception of the maternal object has an empirical correlate in the Rorschach test. The only three-dimensional determinants, Vista and Form Dimension, find their validation in feelings of remorse and capacity for insight, respectively (Exner 1986a): both operations indicative of object constancy and oedipal organization. These determinants are not found in most character-disordered or schizophrenic patients' Rorschachs. Vista responses, on the other hand, are expected in depressed patients, and Form Dimension responses are expected in adult normals.

integrates primitive aggressive and libidinal drives and their affect states, which, prior to this period, were dissociated or split object relations that had free access to consciousness at various times (Kernberg 1976). These unacceptably primitive self and object representations, which may have been experienced as anhedonic, unpleasant, anxiety producing, or dangerous, together with their affect complexes, are repressed and are no longer freely available to awareness. The child's fear of being trapped in an identity-bearing introject (Searles 1986) dissipates at the expense of conscious access.

Likewise the superego emerges as an independent structure. The early sadistic superego forerunners (Jacobson 1964) and early ego ideal formations integrate, modulating both the attacking and idealizing functions of these objects, which originally protected the good relationship with mother. This leads to a greater receptivity and capacity to internalize the realistic parental directions during the oedipal period (Kernberg 1976).

So goes normative object relations and attachment during the first years of the child's life. If most, but not all, has gone well, the child grows into the oedipal period with the integration of contradictory images of self and others into a object world of whole and real evocative representations; the activation of higher level defenses, such as repression, sublimation, rationalization, and intellectualization; and a capacity to test reality, both perceptually (the discrimination of internal from external stimuli) and conceptually (realistic insight and meaning) (Kernberg 1984, Meloy 1985). The behavioral experience of a safe and secure attachment history has been internalized as a reasonably expectant and secure model. The child and mother representations are now an integrated and whole self–maternal object unit with predominantly hedonic, nurturant, and soothing affective components.

INFANT RESEARCH AND OBJECT RELATIONS

Although the stimulus for attachment research continues to be observation of infants and children, such has not been the case with object relations theory. The latter has primarily been derived from clinical reconstruction and subsequent theoretical formulations based upon psychoanalytic work with adult patients, and empirical measurement of adult object relations through the use of the Rorschach (Kissen 1986, Kwawer 1980, Lerner and Lerner 1988).

Fortunately, a remarkable amount of infant research by psycho-analytically oriented clinicians has been published during the past decade, with a particular focus, for our purposes, upon object relations (see Zelnick and Buchholz 1990). This research has both confirmed, and in some cases, challenged, traditional psychoanalytic assumptions concerning early intrapsychic life.

The points of view that diverge from classical psychoanalytic theory include several findings. First, self and object differentiation appears to emerge within the first several months of birth, heralded by much earlier interpersonal abilities in the realm of perceptual acuity and stimulus seeking (Stern 1985, Trevarthen 1979). Second, these internalized mental "schema" (Stern 1983) involve the represen-tation of engagement-disengagement with the maternal object (Beebe and Stern 1977), a synchrony that initially is a pairing of the infant and mother as an open, biological system (Sander 1983). This negotiation and modulation during the first 6 months of life necessarily contains a personal expectation of how things are likely to be from one moment to the next (Stern 1985). Third, infant research holds the dyad as the unit of analysis. The infant does not exist without the maternal object (Winnicott 1965). Interactive exchanges are coordinated between the infant and mother, and unmet expectancies are repaired through their mutual efforts. This "forecasting of future experience . . . the proto-type for the formation of future relationships" (Aber and Slade 1987, p. 10) is supported by a parallel line of research being conducted by Bruhn (Bruhn, in press, Bruhn and Davidow 1983, Davidow and Bruhn 1990) concerning earliest memories of the primary parental objects in adults as expectable templates for characterological be-havior in adulthood. In one study, 81.7 percent of delinquents and 95.8 percent of nondelinquents were correctly classified based upon early memories *alone* (Davidow and Bruhn 1990). The congruence of psy-choanalytically oriented infant research with attachment research and theory is found in the emphasis Bowlby (1969) placed upon the dynamism of internal working models, the central issue of maternal availability in infancy, and the notion of the infant and mother as an adaptive, evolutionary, and biologically based system.

ANIMAL RESEARCH AND PSYCHOBIOLOGICAL REGULATION

Psychobiological research has extended our understanding of attachment to include its role as a regulator of various neurochemical, metabolic, sleep–wake, cardiovascular, and endocrine systems in a wide variety of mammalian infants, including humans.

Hofer (1983, 1987) has systematically measured, in an impressive series of research papers, the nature of attachment and separation in infant rats, with important implications for humans. His findings indicate that early attachment can be delineated into various mother–infant interactions that regulate diverse physiological and behavioral systems in the infant. For instance, one biological experiment led to the finding that higher concentrations of dopamine and norepinephrine were present in the brains of pup rats following separation from their mothers (Stone et al. 1976). The behavioral hyperreactivity, as a consequence of this separation, could be prevented through the administration of reserpine at the time of separation. Further analysis of the various sensory modalities that could reduce this hyperreactivity revealed that tactile or olfactory aspects of the mother–infant interaction, when presented alone, could prevent it. Thermal aspects of the mother also modified behavioral reactivity (Stone et al. 1976).

Other research has supported the hypothesis that separation of the infant from the mother, the prototypical separation distress experienced by all mammals, has both an acute phase and a chronic, slow-developing despair phase. The behavior of the *acute* phase includes agitation, vocalization, and searching. The accompanying physiological responses include increased heart rate, cortisol levels, and catecholamines. The *chronic* phase behavior includes decreased social interaction, mouthing and rocking, hypo- or hyperresponsiveness, variable food intake, and sadness. The physiology of the chronic despair phase includes decreased body weight, sleep disturbance, decreased REM, decreased core temperature, decreased oxygen consumption, decreased heart rate, increased ectopic beats, decreased growth hormone, and decreased T-cell activity (Hofer 1984). Most remarkably, the chronic phase proceeded independently in separated infants when the acute distress phase was completely prevented through the use of surrogates (Hofer 1983). These independent psychobiological processes also appear to be generally consistent across mammalian species.

Hofer (1987) theorized that this biologically open regulation system in the infant precedes social attachment behavior and is a better explanation of the evolutionary adaptiveness of attachment than is fear of predators (Bowlby 1969). He saw this maternal biological regulation between mother and infant as a superordinate organization that could be termed "symbiosis."

The attachment object thus begins as a totality of sensory cues experienced by the infant that regulates his biology, which then combines into a highly specific gestalt as the sensory capacities mature. Stimulation reinforces at appropriate times, and these regulators become internalized. Sensorimotor direction shifts to developmentally more mature associative, symbolic, and affective representations, and social attachments become multiple and flexible (Hofer 1983, 1987).

Convergent animal research concerning the immunological consequences of maternal separation has demonstrated that psychological disturbance can alter the immune system of the primate infant (Coe et al. 1989). Studies collectively support the potentially long-lasting effects of early life trauma on immune responses (Kelley 1980, LaBarba 1970, Laudenslager et al. 1982). Retrospective studies on children that have developed leukemia, juvenile rheumatoid arthritis, and other autoimmune diseases, for instance, indicate that stressful life events over a 2-year time period may contribute to the onset and course of the disease (Laudenslager and Reite 1984). And epidemiological studies of humans have suggested that abbreviated duration of breast-feeding is correlated with an increased predisposition for diabetes and some forms of cancer (Davis et al. 1988).

I have outlined in Table 1-1 the various outcomes of early normative attachment that can be postulated from both the theoretical and empirical literature. The outcomes are organized according to social, psychological, and biological functions.

This list of functional outcomes is not intended to be comprehensive, but predicts and organizes the expected psychopathology of abnormal attachment. Attachment is both psychosocially protective and biologically self-regulating. Deviations from normative attachment in infancy and childhood may have important pathological sequelae in adulthood.

ATTACHMENT PATHOLOGY AND VIOLENCE

Bowlby (1969) identified, and Rutter (1981) and others measured, three psychosocial states following the disruption of early attachment between the ages of 15 and 30 months. The *protest state* is marked by the infant's acute distress at the sudden loss of mother. It is characterized by vocalization, agitation, and searching (Hofer 1987). The *despair state* is marked by both preoccupation and hopelessness. The child withdraws and becomes less active. From an evolutionary perspective, such behavior furthers safe hiding from predators and conserves metabolic energy until reunion with the maternal object occurs (Hofer 1987). Prolonged separation leads to *detachment*, the third state. There is an appearance of recovery from despair, but when the mother returns, there is an absence of normal attachment behavior. The child is apathetic. After a series of such experiences, the child stops bonding to others, becomes increasingly self-absorbed, is preoccupied with nonhuman objects, and does not display emotion (Bowlby 1969). The ensuing superficial sociability and detachment may be a prelude to the development of an antisocial pattern of behavior (Ainsworth 1962, Horner 1984) and psychopathic character (Meloy 1988a).

In contrast to the initially acute *states* of separation response, Bowlby (1988a) also identified two enduring patterns of attachment that predict disturbed, or pathologically developed *traits* in the child. A number of prospective research studies of socioemotional development during the first 5 years of life have empirically confirmed his theories (Ainsworth 1985, Grossmann et al. 1986, Main and Westen 1981, Sroufe 1985, Waters and Deane 1985).

Anxious resistant attachment is the first pattern of disturbed

Table 1-1.

Normative Early Attachment and Its Outcomes:
A Biopsychosocial Model.

Paradigm	Functional Outcome
Social	Protection from predators
	Maternal proximity
	Familial bonding
	Promulgation of familial and kinship networks
	Normative parenting of next generation
Biological	Maternal–infant regulation
	Behavioral activity level
	Neurochemical regulation
	Metabolic regulation
	Sleep-wake states
	Cardiovascular regulation
	Endocrine regulation
	Immune regulation
Psychological	Whole, real, and separate mental representations of self, others
	Mature defensive operations
	Repression
	Intellectualization
	Sublimation
	Reality testing
	Adequate perceptual discrimination
	Abstract concept formation
	Mature affects and emotions
	Intersubjective-empathic feelings
	Unconscious modulation of feelings
	Conscious control of feelings
	Conscience-superego maturity
	Internalized prohibitions
	Social imperatives

attachment behavior, in which the child is uncertain whether the primary parent will be responsive when solicited. There is a marked proneness to separation anxiety (Bowlby 1960), a tendency to cling to the parent, and generalized anxiety concerning exploration away from the parent. Bowlby (1988a) noted that this pattern is promoted by inconsistent availability of the parent, unexpected separations, and threats of abandonment used to control the child.

Anxious avoidant attachment is the second pattern of disturbed attachment behavior, in which the child has lost all confidence that help will be forthcoming. The child attempts to live in a pseudo-autonomous manner and chronically displays the pattern of detachment that is evident as an acute state during individual separation episodes (see above). Bowlby (1988a) theorized, and empirical evidence supports, that such attachment behavior is the result of constant rejection by the maternal object when approached for comfort or protection.

Complete failure to make an attachment in infancy, whether due to the absence of a maternal object or biological predisposition, may lead to affectionless (Bowlby 1946, Horner 1984) or primary (Meloy 1988a) psychopathy. One of the paradoxes of the psychopathic character, however, is his need to repetitively and aggressively engage with objects despite an absence of any history of attachment, and despite a profound emotional detachment from others. Our Rorschach research suggests that a partial answer to this paradox is found in the odd pairing of both narcissistic mirroring and symbiotic merging object relations in the psychopathic character (Gacono 1990). At first glance such pairings seem contradictory, but probably reflect both the borderline personality organization (Kernberg 1984) and the inherent relational conflicts that predispose this character pathology to a greater frequency of violence (Hare and McPherson 1984).

The psychopathic character, moreover, is particularly suited for predatory violence, a psychobiological mode of violence that is planned, purposeful, and emotionless (Meloy 1988a). This form of violence is contrasted with affective violence, which is a reaction to a perceived threat and is preceded by heightened levels of autonomic arousal (Meloy 1988b). In both modes of violence there is proximity seeking. In predatory violence, the perpetrator seeks out the victim. In affective violence, the victim has usually sought proximity to the perpetrator and has been perceived as a threat. Both modes of violence have somewhat distinctive neurochemical and neuroanatomical correlates and are independent of the perpetrator's reality testing at the time of the violence (Meloy 1988b).

Proximity seeking, however, does not mean that an attachment or bond has existed prior to the violence. The introduction of attachment as a biopsychosocial aspect of certain patterns of violence, whether they be predatory or affective, adds another dimension to the nature of the relationship between the victim and the perpetrator. The psychodynamic meaning of this relationship and its homicidal aspects are the focus of this book.

PREMISES OF CLINICAL INVESTIGATION

Several premises underscore the clinical investigations in this book and have been suggested by my brief review of the literature. First, attachment is a biopsychosocial behavioral system that ensures the proximity of the child to its maternal object, and in adulthood, proximity to other objects that carry a certain emotional valence for the individual. In a social context, it can be observed in normal or pathological patterns of proximity seeking toward the object.[2] In a psychoanalytic context, it is the mental representation of an object that is imbued with certain affects and maintains an enduring and relational, but not necessarily reality based, quality in the mind of the individual. Both intrapsychic representation and behavioral proximity seeking are necessary points of departure for our investigation of attachment and its relation to homicide.

---

2. One researcher refers to the individuals who engage in this pathological form of proximity seeking as "delusional or quasi-delusional followers," an apt expression (Mary Rowe, personal communication, Sept. 20, 1991). In California, "stalking" is a criminal offense (Penal Code § 646.9). It involves two elements: willful, malicious, and repeated following, and a credible threat with intent to place the person in fear of death or great bodily injury.

Second, early disruptions of attachment, or the complete absence of attachment, may lead to certain social, psychological, and biological changes in the individual that may be manifest as characterological traits in adulthood.

Third, such characterological traits may predispose an individual to violent or homicidal behavior, given certain precipitating situational or environmental factors[3] (Meloy 1987).

Fourth, the intrapsychic aspects of violent attachments appear to constellate around the rapprochement subphase of separation-individuation, or earlier periods of development. The most *progressed* intrapsychic operations that accompany homicide within a bonded relationship are very similar to the preoedipal defenses, object relations, and affects seen in the later stages of separation-individuation. The most *regressed* intrapsychic operations that accompany homicide within a bonded relationship would be developmentally symbiotic or autistic – that is, clinically psychotic. A psychotic or borderline level of personality organization (Kernberg 1984) is a corollary of most homicidal attachments.

This last premise is the object relational key to understanding extreme violence in attached relationships and is also the bridge between the representational world and overt behavior of the violent individual. In a sense, preoedipal personality organization permits, or releases, the acting out of homicidal or violent impulses. Such personality organization may be an *acute state* in which a particular disinhibitor, such as extreme stress or an ingested chemical, causes regression from a more mature, oedipal level of organization to a preoedipal level of personality. The acuity of the stressor and the predispositional vulnerability of the individual's personality would determine the degree of regression. For instance, a borderline personality organized individual who ingested a small amount of a sympathomimetic drug, such as methamphetamine, might experience a paranoid delusional

---

3. Although my focus in this book is upon intrapsychic structure and function, it is not my intent to devalue the enormous significance of social and situational factors in the genesis of violent behavior. It is also not my intent to be sanctimoniously reductive, but only to recognize the boundaries of my own professional competence. I leave this area of research and theorizing to the social psychologists and sociologists.

psychosis: a complete biochemically induced regression to a psychotic level of personality organization. The propensity for homicide would increase.[4] By contrast, an oedipally organized individual ingesting a similar amount of methamphetamine might be frightened by his ego-dystonic suspicious mentation, terrified by auditory hallucinations, and attempt to rigidly control the regression through help seeking.

Personality organization is not only subject to acute states of regression, but also exists as a dynamic, and chronic, constellation of *traits* organized at a particular level. Such traits may predispose the expression of violent impulse in attachment paradigms through several structures and functions.

Reality testing, that is, the ability to discriminate between interoceptive and exteroceptive stimuli, may be impaired or absent. At a borderline level of personality organization (Kernberg 1984), reality testing is impaired because there is confusion concerning the location and source of the cognitive-affective stimulus: it prompts the patient to wonder if feelings are within him or someone else. Boundaries are maintained, but the introjective-projective oscillation that occurs to stabilize a chronically unstable organization leads to confusion regarding the source of psychological content. At a psychotic level of personality organization, reality testing is lost. There is no confusion concerning the source of stimuli, because there is no demarcation between external and internal space (Grotstein 1978). The oscillation of the primitive defenses, such as projective and introjective identification, has given way to the collapsing and expanding phenomena of hallucinations and delusions. Violent impulses at borderline levels of personality organization are most prone to expression when coupled with the projective dynamics of paranoia (Meissner 1978). Violent impulses in attachment paradigms at psychotic levels of

---

4. Unpublished data from homicide investigations in San Diego County, California, indicate that methamphetamine-related intentional killings have distinctive characteristics: they are initially ritualistic and then become quite disorganized, involve two or more weapons, and the victim is "overkilled," suggesting a high degree of paranoid and psychotic rage experienced by the perpetrator (Tom Streed, personal communication, February, 1991).

personality organization are often imbued with grandiosity and religiosity that have reached delusional proportions.

Mental representations of self and objects, and their affect complexes, are split and polarized at a borderline level of personality organization (Kernberg 1975). The intrapsychic representation of self and others as part-objects, for instance, aggravates the perception and interpretation of affects. The defense of splitting, to maintain the separateness of dissonant part-objects and reduce anxiety, fosters the exaggeration and polarization of experience. Irritation with the self or other is experienced as rage, dislike becomes hatred, and criticism is felt as a deeply hurtful narcissistic wound. Such extremes of perception increase the risk of the expression of violent impulse. At a psychotic level of personality organization, fusion of self and object representations transmutes the destruction of the object into the destruction of the self. Both conceptual and perceptual self and object boundaries (Meloy 1985) have dissolved, and with the dedifferentiation of internal space is the perception of actual objects as part of an undifferentiated psychotic mass. (I am using the term *dedifferentiation* in the analogous biological sense: a reverting of cells to a more primitive or general state. Likewise my term *mass* refers to a gathering of incoherent parts or objects into the formation of one psychological body; in the psychotic sense, it is a body with infinite proportions.) In homicidal violence, psychosis links the actual victim to the perpetrator through a teleological event. In one matricide, for example, the adult son murdered his mother to save the world from a nuclear holocaust. He delusionally believed that this would be the last murder on earth, he would be executed with worldwide television coverage on CNN, and this would usher in a millennium of peace.

These four premises are the cornerstone of this book: attachment is a biopsychosocial behavioral system, early disruptions of attachment manifest as characterological traits in adulthood, such traits may predispose an individual to violence, and the intrapsychic aspects of these violent attachments are organized at a borderline or psychotic level of personality.

2

Violence and Erotomania[1]

> You know a few things about me, dear sweetheart, like my
> obsession with fantasy; but what the rabble don't yet understand
> is that fantasies become reality in my world.
>
> —John Hinckley, Jr.
> [cited in Caplan 1987, p. 62]

On February 16, 1988, Richard Farley, an unemployed computer technician, shot his way into a Sunnyvale, California electronics firm that had recently terminated him. Over the course of 5½ hours, he fired more than 100 rounds of ammunition, killing seven people and wounding three others, including Laura Black, a young woman who had consistently rejected his romantic overtures for several years. Two weeks earlier, Black had finally secured a temporary restraining order against Farley and had expressed relief to a friend that her ordeal might finally be over. On February 17, 1988, the Santa Clara County Superior Court of the State of California made the temporary restraining order permanent.

Violent behavior toward self or others as the *denouement* of unrequited love is as old as antiquity. Yet the empirical and psychodynamic understanding of such behavior remains elusive. In this chapter

---

1. Reprinted with permission from the *Bulletin of the Menninger Clinic*, vol. 53, no. 6, pp. 477–492, copyright © 1989, The Menninger Foundation. This revision of the article has been expanded.

I will summarize the current status of empirical research in this area and then seek to develop, in light of attachment and object relations theory, a fuller understanding of such behavior: the wish to injure or kill the once loved, and now hated, object of affection.

EMPIRICAL RESEARCH

The psychiatric and psychological literature has focused on the obviously more pathological form of unrequited love called de Clerambault's syndrome, or delusional erotomania, which was first described by Esquirol (1838). The French psychiatrist Gatian de Clerambault (1921) carefully defined this delusional disorder and classified it as either pure or secondary (the latter superimposed on a preexisting paranoid disorder; see also Fenichel 1945). Erotomania has historically been conceptualized as a female delusional disorder wherein a woman believes that a man, usually of higher social status, is passionately in love with her. In fact, no such relationship exists, and the love object has had, at most, only brief contact with the delusional individual (Hollender and Callahan 1975, Seeman 1978).[2] Recent reports, however, suggest that men also develop this disorder; examples are often found in a forensic context because male erotomania is more likely to result in violent acting out (Goldstein 1986, 1987a, Taylor et al. 1983). There are no epidemiological data concerning the gender prevalence of erotomania, and controversy continues as to whether it is a predominantly female disorder (Meloy 1990, Segal 1990). Until recently all published reports have been anecdotal case studies, and it

_____

2. Erotomania in the female was implicated in the recent and extraordinarily controversial nomination proceedings of Judge Clarence Thomas for the U.S. Supreme Court. On October 14, 1991, testimony was presented that Professor Anita Hill's sexual harassment allegation was, in fact, only her *fantasy* that Thomas was sexually attracted to her, and her allegations were the result of unrequited love. This was an intriguing, but unconvincing attempt to characterize women, once again, as emotionally unstable and vulnerable to romantic delusions concerning males of higher social status. In fact, the first patient admitted to England's York Retreat in 1796 was a woman named Margaret Bradford. Her diagnosis was "unrequited love."

is unscientific to draw prevalence conclusions without random sampling from a large psychiatric or normal population. Segal (1990) speculated, perhaps correctly, that the increasing prominence of women in the professions, business, and the arts may contribute to a corresponding increase in erotomania among men.

Some experts think that two recent cases of violent acting out that received national attention were forensic examples of de Clerambault's syndrome. First, Prosenjit Poddar, who murdered Tatiana Tarasoff, developed a delusional fixation on her as a love object. After a New Year's Eve kiss, followed by her active discouragement of his love, Poddar planned to create a disaster from which he would rescue her and which would result in her recognition that she loved him. His plans ran amok, he stabbed her to death, and the civil suits resulting from her murder changed the parameters of privilege in the doctor-patient psychotherapy relationship (Blum 1986, *Tarasoff* v. *Regents of the University of California* 1976, Winslade and Ross 1983). Second, John Hinckley, Jr., tried to assassinate President Ronald Reagan on March 30, 1981, after his repeated failure to romance movie actress Jodie Foster. He neatly scripted a note to her just prior to the shooting: "Jodie, I would abandon this idea of getting Reagan in a second if I could only win your heart and live out the rest of my life with you" (Caplan 1987, p. 21).

Although not included in *DSM-III*, de Clerambault's syndrome appeared in *DSM-III-R* (1987) as the erotomanic subtype of delusional (paranoid) disorder with the central theme of "an erotic delusion . . . that one is loved by another" (p. 199). This delusion usually focuses on idealized romance or spiritual union rather than sexual attraction, and the fixated object is often of higher social or economic status. The delusion must be present for at least one month; auditory or visual hallucinations are not prominent; and other behavior is not conspicuously odd or bizarre. Organic factors, of course, must be ruled out.

Dietz (1988a), and Dietz and colleagues (1991a,b), who gathered data from an empirical study of letters sent to celebrities and politicians and from other case studies, reported several findings from a sample of 65 erotomanic individuals: erotomania should not be considered a rare disorder; it is not a predominantly female disorder; the most likely recipient of violence is the person perceived to be standing in the way of the desired object; and fewer than 5 percent of erotomanic individuals are violent. Dietz also noted that erotomanic individuals do not necessarily remain fixated on one object, but may shift to other targets. The mobility and tenacity of erotomanic persons tend to make their celebrity love objects accessible to them. If there is a common thread among female celebrity victims, it may be that their public demeanor is affectionate and caring enough to invite approach. Such a finding was tragically confirmed in the shooting death of 21-year-old actress Rebecca Schaeffer on July 18, 1989. The vivacious and wholesome star of the TV sitcom "My Sister Sam," Becky Schaeffer became the sudden fixation of her assailant, Robert John Bardo, in 1986: "From the first moment I saw her I was attracted to her spunk and her beauty . . . at the time, I didn't consider myself obsessed. I just considered myself in love. I definitely think it was an obsession now"[3] (*The Oregonian*, July 18, 1990, p. A10). Dietz (personal communication, May, 1988) also reported that of the 214 subjects who wrote to celebrities, 16 percent had erotomanic delusions. Eleven subjects believed they were married to the celebrity. Among the 100 subjects who wrote to senators and congressmen, 5 had erotomanic delusions and 2 believed they were married to the politician.

Prior to Dietz's study, the empirical literature has been limited to case examples of erotomania, with a gradual recognition that the disorder is not confined to women and is less rare than was once assumed (Doust and Christie 1978, Enoch and Trethowan 1979, Evans et al. 1982, Feder 1973, Freud 1911, Goldstein 1987a, Greyson and Akhtar 1977, Pearce 1972, Raschka 1979, Sims and White 1973). Two recent papers, moreover, have furthered our understanding of this disorder. In a thoughtful review of the literature, Segal (1989) drew five conclusions: there is a specific syndrome of erotomanic delusion without schizophrenia; the *DSM-III-R* category of Delusional (Paranoid) Disorder properly includes an erotomanic subtype; the eroto-

---

3. Bardo was convicted in Los Angeles County Superior Court for the first degree murder of Rebecca Schaeffer. In California the prosecution must prove premeditation, deliberation, and malice aforethought for this form of homicide.

manic syndromes described by Kraepelin (1921) and de Clerambault (1921) are clinically identical; the psychodynamic motivation for the disorder is probably unmet narcissistic needs; the delusions are persistent and may diminish in intensity, transferring to a new object; and neuroleptics and forced separation from the love object are the only, minimally effective, treatments. Segal (1989) also found that the typical patient described in the literature, whether male or female, led a withdrawn, socially vacuous, and probably lonely life; few were married and many had no sexual contacts for years at a time; most worked in semiskilled jobs; and some were notably unattractive. He recognized the adaptive nature of erotomania for these individuals: ". . . it may provide solace for a few lonely souls, who might otherwise spend their lives in unrelieved isolation and solitude" (Segal 1989, p. 1265).

Rudden and colleagues (1990) conducted a clinical study of the largest sample to date of erotomanic patients, comparing them with a sample of patients with other delusional disorders. The erotomanic sample ($N = 28$) was similar to the other delusional sample ($N = 80$) on most variables, except the erotomanic subjects were more often female, had a significantly higher number of manic symptoms, were more frequently treated with lithium, and had a lower percentage of relatives with schizophrenia. Twenty-five percent of the erotomanic patients had an additional schizoaffective disorder, 7 percent had a bipolar disorder diagnosis, and 43 percent had a diagnosis of one of the schizophrenias. Erotomania as a sole diagnosis occurred in only 25 percent of the patients with erotomanic symptoms. This latter subgroup had the highest level of social and occupational functioning.

Rudden and colleagues (1990) drew several conclusions from their research. Patients with erotomanic symptoms are a diagnostically heterogeneous group, with affective symptoms being a prominent part of the clinical picture. The few patients with only erotomania had a better clinical course, with far fewer hospitalizations and no accrual of symptoms over time. The chronicity of erotomanic delusions is not necessarily linked to lower social functioning, and the course of the disorder is not uniform.

The relationship of erotomania to cultural-social attitudes between men and women is just beginning to be explored (Meyers and Meloy, 1992). The linkage, moreover, is a natural one in that behaviors by the love object in one culture may be completely misconstrued by an individual from another culture. I have encountered two cases of erotomania where traditional Islamic cultural factors, or at least the process of acculturation, has played a role, and will detail these in Chapter 5. My review of the world literature revealed only one published case of erotomania in a Saudi woman (El-Assra 1989). This paranoid schizophrenic patient developed a sudden erotomanic delusion to a ward psychiatrist. She became preoccupied with him and insisted that he had married her. She wrote him numerous love letters and poems, among them:

> It has been a long time since I last had a lover
> My heart weeps for its deepest wounds
> Oh my heart! life smiles upon everyone
> But I search for a doctor to treat my bleeding heart . . .
> Life may make us sad
> Yet God will not abandon the ambitious . . .
> Even the doctor is cruel to the patient's heart
> He wants me when it suits him, then walks away.
>   [El-Assra 1989, p. 554]

El-Assra (1989) concluded that the hospital environment, relatively free when compared to community life in Saudi Arabia, was a factor in the development of erotomania; but religion, unlike psychiatric disorders in Saudi Arabia, had little impact on the etiology and course of this patient's disorder.

PSYCHODYNAMICS AND STRUCTURE

Erotomanic delusional disorder is clinically quite obvious because of its psychotic nature. These patients, even when faced with substantial evidence to the contrary, remain convinced that their fixated object passionately loves in return. It is clinically critical, however, to consider erotomania in the absence of the delusional belief that the love object feels the same way. In other words, such individuals may pursue their love object, yet be aware that the love object does not reciprocate. This argument was raised in the Hinckley trial by the prosecution psychiatrists and psychologist, who maintained that there was no evidence that Hinckley delusionally believed Jodie Foster loved him. His bizarre behavior was fueled, they contended, by the frustration of knowing she did *not* care for him, and he therefore pursued a course of events designed to bring him to her attention (Low et al. 1986). This differential diagnosis between delusional erotomania and what I would call nondelusional or *borderline erotomania* is clinically significant and also has legal implications concerning pleas of insanity. The former implies the presence of psychosis; the latter indicates a gross disturbance of attachment or bonding but not necessarily a loss of reality testing.

I selected the term *borderline* because it captures the intense and tumultuous attachment problem of this nondelusional form of erotomania. Other writers have developed the relationship between separation, loss, and erotomania, but always in the context of delusional thinking (see Evans et al. 1982 for a formulation of erotomania as a variant of pathological mourning in some patients). Borderline erotomania implies a *level* of personality organization (Kernberg 1984). Although certain erotomanic individuals may fulfill the criteria for the diagnosis of borderline personality disorder in *DSM-III-R*, I am not implying that all nondelusional erotomanic individuals should be so diagnosed.

Implicit within this distinction between delusional and borderline erotomania is the nature of the attachment between erotomanic persons and their objects. In delusional erotomania there has usually been no actual historical attachment (although one of the cases in Chapter 5 will prove to be the exception). The attachment, or cathexis, is directed toward an object *concept* (Meloy 1985) in the patient's mind embellished with meaning and emotions that have no basis in reality. This fantastic object concept may be perceptually supported by external stimuli that are sought out by the erotomanic individual: photos of the love object, responses to fan mail, public appearances by a celebrity love object, or arranged private encounters – perhaps unknown to the erotomanic person's target. In extreme cases the erotomanic delusion includes beliefs of union or merger with the love object that suggest an intrapsychic loss of representational boundaries between self and other object concepts. Such beliefs are usually accompanied by a loss of perceptual distinctiveness between self and others. In common parlance, the individual is psychotic. My evaluation of a 38-year-old erotomanic male illustrates this phenomenon during the mental status examination:

> The patient does report, at times, hearing Linda's voice (the love object). Although he denies the voice is heard like a sound, he does believe that she is communicating with him in an extrasensory fashion. He also reports seeing her face in a "vision" and reports incidents of mistaken identity (Capgras's syndrome) on the street when he was sure he saw her. He reports one incident of dissociation from his own body and also reports the experience of autoscopy, the visual seeing of himself. He reports that he believes Linda's husband, George, is controlling her mind. This control, however, is "not magical, but influential."

In contrast to delusional erotomania, borderline erotomania usually involves some history of actual emotional engagement with the object. This relationship may vary from a friendly glance and smile to a terminated relationship that included emotional and sexual dimensions. *The degree of disturbance is the discrepancy between the attachment behavior of the love object and the intensity of the erotomanic person's own emotional attachment to the love object.* Borderline erotomanic individuals view separation as abandonment, and rejection by the object evokes abandonment rage.

Rejection, in the mind of the delusional erotomanic person, may be conceived in autistic fantasy without any actual precipitating behavior by the object; on the other hand, rejection in the mind of the borderline erotomanic person is usually a grandiosely elaborated and distorted childhood abandonment fantasy that is recapitulated in the present by the object. Such actual rejection may represent the culmination of a pattern of selecting love objects who are unable or un-willing to respond to the erotomanic individual's affections, what Kernberg (1988) called pathological, or masochistic, infatuation.

My clinical experience with the erotomanic patients I have eval-uated in forensic settings indicates that there is often a *DSM-III-R* personality disorder, usually diagnosed as narcissistic, histrionic, antisocial, borderline, or paranoid, or a combination thereof. If there is a true erotomanic delusion, then there will usually be both an Axis I and an Axis II diagnosis. Delusional erotomanic symptoms usually appear in patients with schizophrenia or affective disorder (Rudden et al. 1990).

Kernberg's (1984) model of personality organization helps to elucidate this clinical phenomenon. The erotomanic individual is usu-ally organized at a borderline level, with distinctive defensive opera-tions and identity issues, and with only marginally adequate reality testing.

The genotypic defense of splitting (Freud 1938, Grotstein 1980) underscores the blatantly contradictory perceptions and affect states of the person with erotomania: the love object is initially idealized, then ragefully devalued; intense love and intense hatred exist concur-rently but are experienced only in alternate, extreme affect states; and the narcissism and grandiosity of the violent act betray the defensive projection of devalued parts of the self *into* the victim (Klein 1946). This final defensive maneuver of projective identification is most apparent in the omnipotent control and devaluation of the victims during the act of violence itself. Richard Farley, the eroto-manic man who killed and injured the people in the electronics firm, stated that he wanted only to wound his unrequited love so that she would know the suffering *her* behavior had caused.

The delusional erotomanic person will also exhibit defenses char-acteristic of borderline disorders but, as Kernberg (1984) noted, at a psychotic level of personality organization these defenses protect the patient from experiencing further disintegration of boundaries be-tween self and object, both intrapsychic perceptual representations and actual interoceptive-exteroceptive sensory-perceptual experi-ence. In such circumstances, the more fixed and false the erotomanic belief, the more regressed to a psychotic level of personality organization the erotomanic individual has become. Paradoxically, the intensity of attachment to the actual object may lessen (evidenced by less proximity-seeking behavior) as the erotomanic individual retreats to more autistic levels of relatedness to fantasied object concepts and percepts (Meloy 1985).

> A 26-year-old black male with paranoid schizophrenia was rejected by his girlfriend. During the ensuing 12 months he attempted suicide on three occasions and constantly telephoned her home, telling her mother that she was dead. During his course of inpatient treatment in a forensic hospital, he became acutely psychotic. He developed the somatic delusion that his girlfriend had entered his body, and his skin enveloped her like a glove in perfect symmetry. When he looked to the left, he looked through her eyes; when he looked to the right, he looked through his eyes. His incessant telephoning and suicide attempts completely stopped.

Identity disturbance in erotomanic individuals is evidenced by their intense yet tumultuous attachment to their love objects. They yearn for affection, yet may eventually wish to destroy the love object, or at least devalue the person's life. Klein's (1957) notion of envy is paramount here: the motivation to destroy the good object in the face of inevitable frustration. These contradictory self-concepts of lover and destroyer *directed toward the same object* are symptomatic of poorly integrated identity and are kept apart through splitting defenses such as denial and dissociation. Other erotomanic individuals may, through aspiring narcissism, seek a twinship alliance (Kohut 1971) by their acts of violence and eventual identification in history with the famous, unrequited love. Erotomanic individuals pursue a narcissistic wish to be like the love object to enhance their own grandiosity. This desire for identification was illustrated in the Hinckley case during the testimony of Park Dietz, one of the government-appointed psychiatrists:

> On June 7, 1981, I interviewed Mr. Hinckley, and I asked him if he had been trying to impress Jodie Foster, and he said, "Well, it is a combination of things: To impress her, almost to traumatize her.

That is the best word. To link myself with her for almost the rest of history, if you want to go that far." [Low et al. 1986, p. 44]

The erotomanic individual's reality testing is usually not completely lost but is clearly more impaired if an actual delusion of love is apparent. More often the reality testing is marginal at best and is exemplified in the erotomanic person's intentional blending of fantasy and reality: Richard Farley would surreptitiously take photographs of his love object at her aerobics class and then show them to friends, stating that they were taken during a skiing trip together in Colorado. Prosenjit Poddar would audiotape conversations with Tatiana Tarasoff and then splice the tapes to produce false utterances of love and affection (Blum 1986). This conscious manipulation and unconscious denial of certain realities is typical of borderline defensive operations in general and of borderline erotomania in particular.

Erotomanic individuals with a borderline level of personality organization also have distinctive characterological traits such as narcissism, hysteria, paranoia, and psychopathy that may contribute to their propensity for violence toward the love object. The clinician should be alert to these traits during the evaluation and treatment of the erotomanic patient.

NARCISSISTIC TRAITS

Reik (1963), Hollender and Callahan (1975), and Segal (1989) thought that narcissism played a significant role in shaping erotomanic delusions. This "felt quality of perfection" (Rothstein 1984a, p. 17) may find its projective vehicle in the unattainable love object of the erotomanic person. In certain cases this narcissism may represent masochistic subjugation to an unreachable object (Kernberg 1988), a sense of profound pride that one can endure the greatest rejection and still, like Sisyphus, relentlessly pursue one's impossible dream, the ideal love. In other cases narcissism may be apparent in the aspiration and inherent grandiosity of forming a twinship alliance with the object. Kohut (1971) also referred to this form of transference as an alter-ego transference in which there is the reestablishment of a latency-age need to see and understand, as well as to be seen and understood, by someone like oneself. It is linked to the unconscious fantasy of an imaginary playmate (Wolf 1988). As noted in the case of John Hinckley, Jr., this pursuit may represent a defensive stabilization of the grandiose self-structure through fusion of the ideal self and ideal object concepts in the erotomanic individual's mind. The object concept would, of course, be the idealized love, perhaps implicating a displacement from earlier, but unattainable or lost (Evans et al. 1982), objects of affection. I distinguish this conceptual fusion from *perceptual* fusion between the self and object in the mind of the erotomanic person (Meloy 1985). In the latter case a psychotic decompensation occurs, because no distinction remains between the boundaries of the self and other, either intrapsychically as representation or interpersonally as actual object. The erotomanic individual who is psychotic has merged with the love object in a form of condensation. This most primitive merger transference, in self psychology terms, is normatively present in the archaic infantile phase and is the expansion of the experience of self to include surrounding objects (Wolf 1988). In erotomanic pathology it is a regression from more developed narcissistic transferences, such as mirroring, idealizing, and twinship perceptions of the love object.

Merger transference may be verbally expressed by the erotomanic patient in a religious or teleological manner. Arthur Jackson, a paranoid schizophrenic man who erotomanically pursued the actress Theresa Saldana and then stabbed her ten times during an attack outside her West Hollywood apartment on March 15, 1982, expressed it this way:

> Q. Why did you stab her?
> A. It was divine inspiration . . . but the forces of darkness intervened. . . . I went by instinct and I have a benevolent trust in God, a blind trust . . . it was spiritual lovesickness and divine inspiration . . . it's always been aesthetic and Platonic . . . what if it was the other way around? She was the victim and I was the assailant? [Dietz 1988b][4]

---

4. Note Jackson's confusion. It *was* the other way around. Saldana was the victim and he was the assailant. This reversal could be interpreted as a parapraxis that

The narcissism of the erotomanic individual is most apparent in the sense of entitlement and gross disregard for the suffering of the victim. As narcissistic self-absorption increases, empathic regard for others lessens, increasing the likelihood of public acting out—perhaps in the form of violence.

HYSTERICAL TRAITS

De Clerambault's syndrome is the psychopathology of romance. Imbued with a sense of idyllic union and platonic love for the object, erotomanic persons often exhibit clear hysterical traits in their emotional lability, overinvolvement, dependent and exhibitionistic needs, pseudohypersexuality and sexual inhibition, competitiveness with the same sex, and masochism (Kernberg 1975).

Emotional lability is circumscribed by the pursuit of the object of affection. It may suggest a borderline level of personality organization in its rapidly shifting and polarized expression of boundless affection or unbridled rage, affective correlates of defensive splitting.

Overinvolvement may be manifest in efforts to achieve proximity to the love object in the face of strong aversive consequences, such as temporary restraining orders or threats from those protecting the object. Other adaptive areas of psychosocial functioning may suffer owing to the concentrated pursuit, yet erotomanic individuals demonstrate a quality of *la belle indifférence* to the problems they create. Intrapsychically, the overinvolvement may be expressed in overidentification with the emotional implications of the fantasy of blissful and romantic union with the unrequited love. Such phenomena may signal

---

reveals Jackson's continued delusional belief that Saldana was the assailant and he was the victim. Perhaps this reversal is further indication of projective identification as the actress continues to carry and contain for Jackson his own aggressive and malevolent objects that he must control. Jackson is currently in the California Department of Corrections. On December 5, 1990, he told a Los Angeles County Superior Court jury, "I would have much preferred a handgun. In addition to being more efficient, it would have been more humane . . . I regret very much the extent of the wounds" (*San Diego Union*, December 6, 1990, p. 1). Jackson was being prosecuted again for sending the actress a series of threatening letters in 1988.

regression as the erotomanic person becomes unable, or unwilling, to test these fantasies against reality. An infantile personality, in contrast to the hysterical personality, may express erotomanic desires in a more oral-aggressive, demanding, desperate, and inappropriate manner (Kernberg 1975, Sugarman 1979).

Dependent and exhibitionistic needs of erotomanic persons may blend with narcissistic traits but center around the demand to be the focus of the unrequited love's attention. Affectional coldness in the pursuit of such attention suggests a more narcissistic psychopathology.

Pseudohypersexuality and sexual inhibition will be most apparent in the contradictory behavior of the erotomanic person toward the love object. Overt behavior may suggest a desire for sexual union, but expressed fantasy may reveal a much more inhibited and split-off sexuality; the union with the object may be portrayed in a religious or aesthetic manner. More primitive borderline-level defenses may be apparent in erotomanic patients' gross denial and projection of sexual aggressiveness onto other individuals, and these patients may fantasize rescuing the object of love from such primitive sexual behavior, thus placing third parties at risk of violence.

The erotomanic individual's competitiveness with another person of the same sex suggests oedipal rivalry for the affections of the unattainable maternal or paternal object. In the case of the erotomanic woman, competitiveness with the male may be evidenced in masculine striving, such as more aggressive pursuit of the object than is warranted by a woman in her particular sociocultural milieu, or possession of, and practice with, weapons if the actual or imagined rejection of the erotomanic person has led to predatory and retaliatory fantasies.

Masochism is inherent in erotomania because of the pleasurable suffering of unrequited love. As Hamlet said in his soliloquy, "For who would bear . . . the pangs of despis'd love?" This pathological infatuation with an unattainable love object would be appropriate unconscious punishment for the hysterical character's devalued oedipal meanings of all sexual interest (Kernberg 1988). The "dirty and disgusting" scatological nature of sexuality in the mind of the hysterical person may be at least partially denied by the long-distance touching of the unavailable object: looking, viewing, calling, or perhaps other scopophilic or paraphilic pursuits within which the sexual arousal pattern toward the erotomanic object is consciously denied.

PARANOID TRAITS

Recent theorizing continues to suggest an association between erotomania and the paranoid disorders (Goldstein 1987b). The obvious basis for the erotomanic delusion–that another is in love with oneself–is projection, the defensive operation central to paranoia. Erotomania also finds a psychodynamic linkage to paranoia through a more socially acceptable form of aggressive competition for the exclusivity of the object of attachment, that is, jealousy (S. McGreevy, personal communication, February 13, 1988; see also Freeman 1990). Meissner (1978) noted the jealous individual's sense of wounded narcissistic expectation and injustice toward the object. Berke (1988) noted that jealousy, unlike envy, is not present at birth and only arises when the infant recognizes the parents as a couple in their own right. Unlike envy, jealousy is triangulated, contains both love and hate, and is the exaggeration or imagination of loss of the love to a third object. In certain cases jealousy may function as a defense against the affect of envy. Damaged aspects of the self are projected and displaced onto a third object, the perceived threat to one's love, and affectively mask feelings of envy felt about the love object's qualities when compared to the self.

In forensic settings envy is usually considered a more primitive and culpable emotion. *Malice aforethought,* a legal term which has been legally interpreted to mean an "abandoned and malignant heart," may be motivated by envy and is an element necessary in proving first- or second-degree murder in most states. On the other hand, crimes of passion often find an emotional basis in jealousy and are viewed as less culpable acts of voluntary manslaughter by the criminal law. As Irma Kurtz wrote, "Jealousy fights duels. Envy poisons the soup" (*The New York Times Magazine,* February 22, 1987, p. 42).

In erotomania the intensity of the attachment and the reality basis of the fantasy may be colored by paranoid ideation if the relationship to the object becomes triangulated. Sullivan (1953) was the first clinician to note this distinction between envy and jealousy; the latter necessitating a third party and suggesting an oedipal conflict. In erotomania the risk of violence may increase when third parties, such as the court or friends, attempt to dissuade erotomanic persons from their pursuit of the object. Or a third party – such as a same-sex celebrity or national political figure – may represent an idealized source of oedipal rivalry whose devaluation, perhaps through assault, will usher in the conquest of the erotomanic object. Spielman (1971) distinguished jealousy from envy by noting that the former included a partial component of envy in the wish to possess the object, but that with jealousy, anger was more consistent and intense, suspicion and mistrust were heightened, and greater tension existed owing to unconscious homosexuality when the heterosexual striving was frustrated. The affective confusion of both adoration and hatred toward the object may also heighten tension through ideational rumination and affective constraint. Rorschach indices of Shading blends, Color-shading blends, Vista responses, and Achromatic color responses (Exner 1986a) are important sources of data to ferret out this affective process in the cautious, perhaps paranoid erotomanic patient.

PSYCHOPATHIC TRAITS

Severely psychopathic individuals will not develop erotomania because their attachment disorder is the opposite of borderline erotomania: they are profoundly detached and seek interpersonal relations only to devalue others and to shore up their grandiose self-structure (Gacono et al. 1990, Gacono and Meloy 1991, Meloy 1988a, Meloy and Gacono, in press). However, erotomanic individuals may display psychopathic traits, giving cause for clinical alarm because they signal an increased likelihood of aggressive activity, predation, and acts of sadism to hurt and control the object (Hare and McPherson 1984).

Aggression and criminality are usually present in the history of erotomanic individuals with psychopathic traits. Purposeful devaluation of heterosexual objects through emotional or physical injury conveys the necessity for psychopathically disturbed erotomanic individuals to relate on the basis of dominance and intimidation rather than affection. For example, a 26-year-old male, diagnosed with Bipolar Mood Disorder and Antisocial Personality Disorder, developed an erotomanic attachment toward the attractive female superior court judge who had tried his criminal case. Some of his correspondence conveys his aggressiveness and identification with evil as he relentlessly pursued her:

> Red blood out and black blood in,
> My Nannie says I'm a child of sin.
> How did I choose me my witchcraft kin?
> Know I as soon as dark's dreams begin.
> Shared is my heart in a nightmare's gin.
> Never from terror I but may win.
> [Meloy 1988a, p. 281]

As this man's fantasies of attachment increased during the next several weeks, he sent the judge some notes that implied his narcissistic aspiration for attachment and his derision: "I love you because you've got the balls to wear black" (Meloy 1988a, p. 282). Subsequently, his striving turned to more blatant devaluation, as the judicial system punitively responded to his erotomanic quest: "You're so prim and proper I'll bet you have lilacs for pubic hairs, you whore" (Meloy 1988a, p. 285). This misogynistic and sarcastic phrase is also striking in its split between idealization and devaluation of the seductive (maternal object as virgin/whore), yet unreachable object. After being found incompetent to stand trial, this patient was finally hospitalized for 90 days and restabilized on lithium carbonate. He stated that his erotomanic fixation had diminished. There has been no known approach behavior by this individual toward the judge in the past 7 years.

Predation is a purposeful, planned, and emotionless mode of

violence, in contrast to the more common mode of emotional, or affective, violence (Meloy 1988a). Its presence in erotomanic persons with psychopathic traits suggests a higher risk of unexpected assault against the love object. Predation generally does not appear in pure form in these people because they do experience the narcissistic wounding and retaliatory rage that accompany erotomanic violence. But predatory violence does facilitate stalking the victim over extended periods of time, rehearsal fantasies prior to the violence, a fueling of narcissistic characteristics to steel themselves for the task, and the use of transitional objects in fantasy as preparation for the violence itself (Fintzy 1971, Meloy 1988a). Transitional objects not only help maintain the illusion of omnipotent control over the erotomanic object, but they also function as a Janus-faced object that supports both distancing and disidentification with reality (Meloy 1988a).

Sadism is the derivation of pleasure from inflicting physical or emotional pain on the erotomanic object. It is the wish to hurt and control the object in the face of unrequited affection. The young man who developed an erotomanic attachment to the female judge sent her an audiotape in which he politely introduced himself, screamed obscenities at her, and then sang her a love song, accompanying himself with a guitar. As Shapiro (1981) noted, sadomasochistic sexuality is a highly ideational matter. Ideas and symbols of erotic sexuality are most exciting in a concentrated, extreme, and detached form. Sadism is purposive, willful behavior in which the idea of subjugating the erotomanic object is so stimulating because the actuality of sexual abandonment is unfathomable. John Hinckley, Jr., expressed this dynamic quite well:

I seem to have a need to hurt those people that I love the most. This is true in relation to my family and to Jodie Foster. I love them so much but I have this compulsion to destroy them. On March 30, 1981, I was asking my family to take me back and I was asking Jodie Foster to hold me in her heart. My assassination attempt was an act of love. I'm sorry love has to be so painful. [Caplan 1987, pp. 129–130]

Clarke (1990) researched the available developmental and historical data concerning John Hinckley, Jr., and concluded that his behavior and personality were concordant with Clarke's Type III sociopathic (psychopathic) assassin category. He noted Hinckley's submissive personality, social isolation, indifferent academic performance despite above-average intelligence, family conflict, early preoccupation with suicide, menial jobs and wandering existence, eventual family estrangement, a failed first romance, an interest in handguns and violence, sexual initiation with prostitutes, a captivation with film violence, the consideration of mass murder before choosing assassination (Hinckley had considered a multiple shooting on the Yale campus or the U.S. Senate), his intense interest in previous assassins, the selection of a victim based upon popularity, his predatory violence, and the diaries he kept (Clarke 1990).

Although a clinical determination of Hinckley's psychopathy has yet to be publicly made, Clarke's hypothesis is highly suggestive and somewhat consistent with the known characteristics and development of psychopathic individuals (Meloy 1988a). As Clarke wrote, "John Hinckley grew up never having learned to love, and to be loved, as a man" (1990, p. 85). His alienation from the social world and identification with both strangeness and perversity is captured in his own words:

> I remain the mortal enemy of Man
> I can't escape this torture chamber
> I can't begin to be happy
> I plot revenge in the dark
> I plot escape from this asylum
> I follow the example of perverts.
> [Hinckley 1985, p. 195]

CONCLUSIONS

The delusional (paranoid) disorder of erotomania and other forms of nondelusional, or borderline, erotomania are extreme disorders of attachment. Erotomania is likely to occur in individuals with a co-morbid diagnosis of schizophrenia or mood disorder. It exists in a pure, isolated form in only one of four cases in which the erotomanic delusion is present. Nondelusional, or borderline, erotomania is distinguished by an enduring, intense attachment to a love object that no longer reciprocates the feeling, but there is no clear delusion of love. It is likely to be found in individuals with borderline personality organization with narcissistic, hysterical, paranoid, or psychopathic traits. Each of these character pathologies shapes the expression of the erotomanic behaviors in certain ways.

The erotomanic individual will generally not be violent. Although no data are available, it is a reasonable assumption that most individuals with erotomania do not approach their love object; and of those who do, most will not be physically violent. The best estimate is that less than 5 percent of individuals with the erotomanic subtype of Delusional (Paranoid) Disorder will be violent.

If violence occurs, it will be directed toward the love object or a third party that is perceived as interfering with the pursuit. It will be committed by a male who has a history of violence and probably abuses substances such as alcohol or stimulants. Likely character pathology includes narcissistic, paranoid, or psychopathic traits. The conscious rationalization is to win the love of the object of affection or to prevent her from having other loves. The unconscious psychodynamics usually involve a retaliatory response to narcissistic wounding, and a wish to destroy the envied goodness in the victim. Richard Farley captured the conscious sentiments and unconscious adversity between the erotomanic and his unrequited love when he wrote to Laura Black, "All I ever wanted was to be your friend. . . . When I go to the gas chamber, I'll smile for the cameras and you'll know that you won in the end" (*Los Angeles Daily Journal*, July 10, 1991, p. 3).

Mr. Farley was sentenced to death by a Santa Clara County jury. His case is on appeal.

3

Catathymic Homicide

> Between the acting of a dreadful thing
> And the first motion, all the interim is
> Like a phantasma, or a hideous dream.
> —Shakespeare, *Julius Caesar*, act 2, scene 1

To learn of the sudden, inexplicable murder of someone by an intimate, without apparent motive, momentarily shatters the veneer of safety we feel with our loved ones. The act makes no sense, the perpetrator usually has no prior history of violence, and most remarkably, he or she appears *relieved* that the entire episode is over.

The psychodynamic process that best captures this unusual form of violent attachment is called *catathymia*, first introduced into the psychiatric literature by Maier (1912, 1923). The term is derived from the Greek, *kata* and *thymos*, and can be defined as "in accordance with emotions" (Revitch and Schlesinger 1981). Maier's (1912) paper conceptualized catathymia as a psychological process in which an intense affect–idea complex temporarily overwhelmed internal equilibrium and disrupted secondary process thought. He believed that paranoid delusions were catathymically based, because they were generated by a fixed complex of ideas.

The term catathymia was first applied to criminal psychiatry and psychology by Wertham (1937). His brief but seminal paper deserves special scrutiny. He drew from Maier's definition and wrote, "It consists in a rutlike fixation on one topic and is always accompanied by marked egocentricity" (p. 976). He thought that patients were predisposed to this whenever there was an imbalance between logic and affectivity. He applied it, moreover, to violent acts:

> The patient acquires the idea that he must carry out a violent act against others or against himself. This idea does not arise in an obsessive form. It appears as a definite plan, accompanied by a tremendous urge to carry it out. The plan itself meets such resistance in the mind of the patient that he is likely to hesitate and delay. The violent act usually has some symbolic significance over and above its obvious meaning. There are no definite projections, although the thinking of the patient may have an almost delusional character in its rigidity and inaccessibility to logical reasoning. [p. 976]

Wertham conceptualized the clinical course of violent catathymia in eight stages:

1. A traumatic psychological experience creates a seemingly unsolvable internal psychic state that leads to chronic emotional tension.

2. The patient completely projects responsibility for the internal tension state onto the external situation.

3. Thinking becomes increasingly egocentric.

4. The idea that a violent act toward self or another is the only way out of the situation is suddenly conceived.

5. After a prolonged period of internal conflict the violent act is carried out or attempted.

6. A complete removal of the internal tension occurs immediately following the violence, with no insight.

7. Superficial normalcy is apparent for several months.

8. Internal psychic equilibrium is reestablished with some development of insight.

Wertham concluded with a cogent statement: ". . . the violent act seems to constitute a benign feature. It is an expression of the fight on the part of the patient for the safeguarding of his personality" (p. 978).

The essential feature of catathymic homicide hinted at in Wertham's paper is the "psychological deep structure" (Ogden 1986) that is involved. This term, derived from Chomsky's (1957) notion of linguistic deep structure, refers to the inborn modes of organizing experience that provide the templates for representations of self and others. The actual representations, and their respective affects, are the product of early learning and subsequent development. Necessary correlates of this endogenous form of homicide include an understanding of the *transference* dimension of the violence: What is the deeply felt and historically based significance of the act for the perpetrator? What is the symbolic or emotional significance of the relationship or the victim's behavior that triggered such inexplicable violence? Why has the violence occurred at this time, if one assumes a predisposed transference basis for it?

A number of authors used the term *catathymic crisis* to explain unprovoked violence in the absence of any organic cause. Sedman (1966), in his study of hallucinations, linked early infantile trauma and psychic vulnerability in his understanding of catathymia. He thus implied a transference basis for the incongruity of certain insignificant events and the "powerful affects" (p. 15) that they produced. Gayral and colleagues (1956) labeled nonepileptic emotional outbursts with secondary neurovegetative reactions as *crises catathymiques.*

Others addressed the sudden murderous act that appears to be without motive and sometimes without organic etiology. Menninger and Mayman (1956) coined the term *episodic dyscontrol* to describe a "third order" of stress adaptation that eluded all ego control, was episodic or explosive in nature, and transgressed the strictures of reality. (The other "orders" of stress adaptation included anxiety [first], neurotic symptoms [second], and psychosis [fourth]). They mentioned catathymic crisis and noted that the rationalizations for the deed often had little to do with the underlying motivation.

Menninger and Mayman categorized dyscontrol into organized and disorganized types, and offered the following schematic outline for these regulatory devices, which "forestall more extensive personality disintegration" (p. 163):

Table 3-1.

Episodic Dyscontrol Schema.

A. Organized patterns of aggressive behavior
    1. Sociopathic type
    2. Psychopathic type
B. Disorganized patterns of aggressive behavior
    1. Convulsions
    2. Attacks of assaultive violence, e.g., catathymic crises
    3. Panic and demoralization attacks
    4. Schizoid attacks
    5. Manic attacks

Menninger and Mayman (1956) were describing a psychiatric phenomenon from an economic standpoint and were not interested in the organic basis for some of these dyscontrol categories. They did, however, cite an early paper by Epstein and Ervin (1956), which addressed the psychodynamic significance of seizure content in psychomotor epilepsy. Monroe (1981) would later study episodic dyscontrol as a neurological impairment. In a recent study Monroe (1989) found empirical evidence for his hypothesis that a significant number of patients with episodic disorder involving dyscontrol or psychotic symptoms have a complex partial seizure in the limbic system. I have commented (Meloy 1988a), however, on the gross clinical error of assuming a neurological basis for violence in the absence of objective neurological or neuropsychological findings *and* of data that link the violence and the brain damage.

Menninger and Mayman's (1956) distinction between sociopathy and psychopathy refers to antisocial identifications in the former and the complete absence of value and identification in the latter: roughly the same difference between moderate and severe psychopathy or secondary and primary psychopathy. Episodic dyscontrol in psychopathy can be described as affective, rather than predatory, violence (Meloy 1988a) and will be distinguished by rationalization and the absence of any remorse. Episodic dyscontrol is noted in *DSM-III-R* (1987) as one of the impulse control disorders, Intermittent Explosive Disorder (312.34). Other disorders that may cause such violence, however, must be ruled out, such as psychosis, organic personality syndrome, borderline or antisocial personality disorder, conduct disorder, or intoxication. The exclusion of antisocial personality disorder implies that intermittent explosive disorder should not be diagnosed in the presence of psychopathy, in contrast to the schema of Menninger and Mayman (1956). Regret or self-reproach may follow, but this is not one of the diagnostic criteria.

Felthous and colleagues (1991) found in a sample of 443 men who complained of violence a prevalence rate of 3.4 percent for Intermittent Explosive Disorder (IED). These predominantly Caucasian males ($N = 15$) were generally employed, had average IQ measures, and showed virtually no evidence of significant organic pathology. Only two subjects had somewhat abnormal electroencephalograms (EEGs). The typical victim of their violence was a spouse, lover, or boyfriend/girlfriend. Rage reactions were immediate and without a prodromal period. Most remained oriented during the outburst of violence and reported various degrees of behavioral dyscontrol. Four subjects reported a complete loss of control. Only one subject had no memory of the act, and most attempted to help or comfort the victim after the violence.

They concluded with three plausible explanations for IED: first, it may be symptomatic of borderline personality disorder or other personality disorder that is overlooked by focusing on the patient's antisocial or impulsive history; second, subtle brain dysfunction findings would strengthen the neurological validity of the disorder but were not investigated through neuropsychological testing in their study; and third, the disorder may be socially learned behavior in response to stress.

A research group from the "Social Maladjustment Study Unit" of Malcolm Bliss Mental Health Center, Washington University, St. Louis, published a series of three papers on the sudden murderer (Blackman et al. 1963, Lamberti et al. 1958, Weiss et al. 1960). A "sudden murder" was a "single, isolated, unexpected episode of violent, impulsive acting-out behavior—behavior which is never well thought out, behavior which has no obvious purpose or hope for personal advantage or profit foreseeable as a result" (Weiss et al. 1960,

p. 669). They compared thirteen habitual criminals, thirteen sex offenders, and thirteen sudden murderers on a variety of clinical and demographic variables. Although they did not use any inferential statistics, rendering their conclusions only suggestive, they did note some dramatic differences between the sudden murderers and the other two control groups.

The sudden murderers came from large families where the mother dominated and emphasized conformity to social rules. Father was consistently a negative figure, either hostile or rejecting. Attachment between mother and child was ambivalent, and was characterized by an underlying hostility that had to be repressed or split off during affectional moments by both parties. Controlled anger and unmet dependency needs dominated their emotional development.

As adults they remained tied to their families, but were geographically mobile, looking for opportunity, yet failing when the task was at hand. These failures increased feelings of both insecurity and anger. Clinical presentations included introversion, general insecurity, and the blaming of others for their failures. Unlike the habitual criminals, the sudden murderers did not use projection successfully, because they were too aware of their own inadequacies. Although projective identification is not mentioned as a defense in these studies, the findings are consistent with such an intrapsychic operation and the eventual, absolute control of the devalued victim through homicide. The sudden murderers showed the strongest dependency needs, both clinically and on psychological tests.

A notable finding in all the murderers was a period of overtly adequate adjustment, lasting from a month to a year, prior to the homicide. The authors (Weiss et al. 1960) thought that this period incubated the homicide through increased pressures to conform, the absence of others to blame, and an increasing sense of isolation and intrapsychic tension.

In all thirteen cases there was a precipitating insult, such as belittling rejection, the withholding of a paycheck, criticism of alcohol intake, or ejection from a building. Eight persons shot their victims, the others used blunt instruments or a knife. Five victims were heterosexual partners, two victims were employers, four victims were in other roles, and two victims were strangers.

Eleven of the perpetrators (85 percent) experienced a definite sense of relief after arrest: "I'm glad I did it . . . I'd do it again" (1960, p. 674). The diagnoses of these sudden murderers ranged from schizoid and passive-aggressive personality disorder to schizophrenia (four cases), although we should note the overdiagnosis of schizophrenia at this time in the history of psychiatry *(DSM-I)*. The authors commented on the absence of any physical abuse in the perpetrators' histories and the cohesive nature of the families of origin.

In a subsequent validation study (Blackman et al. 1963), the sample of sudden murderers was increased to forty-three. Confirmation was found for the inadequate and dependent personality patterns, characterized by emotional confusion and a drive to conform, identified in the earlier sample. The authors also clarified the dynamics operative prior to the homicide:

> The very effort to maintain a facade of competence and independence saps some of the strengths and weakens some of the defenses with which the patient wards off his more basic feelings of insecurity and inadequacy . . . the patient's struggle against dependent needs becomes exaggerated, the effort toward denial becomes accentuated, and the precariousness of the "good" adjustment is maintained only to build up to the explosion of violence. [p. 293]

The fundamental psychodynamics in conflict appeared to be feelings of inadequacy vs. need to succeed and isolation vs. drive to conform.

Ruotolo (1968) clinically examined five sudden murderers from a psychoanalytic perspective. He found that one or both of two psychodynamically significant events had taken place. First, a "blow was dealt to the individual's pride system triggering off enormously intense self-hate" (p. 173). This anger was projected onto the victim, which allowed for a "temporary shoring up of the unstable pride system" (p. 173). Second, "a radical move was precipitated away from a formerly held major neurotic solution into a repressed solution, such as from expansiveness to self-effacement" (p. 173). Notwithstanding the ambiguity of this second factor, Ruotolo (1968) also thought it was quite a tentative formulation, insofar as neurotic personality was not well established in his cases. In fact, he noted that ego boundaries were "rather fragile as demonstrated by the onset of psychosis in at least four cases" (p. 173). I think the difficulty with this second psychodynamic formulation is the assumption of a neurotic level of personality, when the likelihood is a preoedipal or borderline personality organization that is at imminent risk of psychotic disintegration. As Ruotolo wrote, "some personalized value was found to take precedence over the 'ultimate' crime of murder. This *sine qua non*, this unique image of oneself, *had* to be maintained by the murderer at any price" (p. 162). He also referenced a paper by Satten and colleagues (1960), which emphasized the prolonged tension and disorganization in the murderer long before actual contact with the victim, whose own behavior unwittingly fit into the unconscious conflicts of the murderer and thus triggered the killing.

Wertham (1966) subsequently defined the catathymic crisis as "delusional thinking with the patient being driven to a violent deed without a rational motive, with the act having a symbolic meaning and the victim not counting as a person, but as a part of an overwhelming image" (p. 229). This redefinition of catathymia as a *psychotic* process suggests that Wertham observed a marked absence of reality testing, at least for a brief period, in most catathymic episodes of violence. Moreover, as the literature of this period shows, borderline personality disorders and these patients' vulnerability to transient psychotic episodes were just beginning to be understood.

Recent advances in our understanding of catathymia began with the work of Revitch and Schlesinger (1978, 1981). They proposed that the catathymic crisis manifests within an ego-threatening relationship and may activate (1) unresolved and conflicted sexual feelings, (2) displacement of emotion onto the victim from another subject with certain symbolic significance, and (3) helpless and confused feelings.

They considered catathymic crisis a psychodynamic process, rather than a diagnosis, and divided it into acute and chronic types.

ACUTE CATATHYMIC VIOLENCE

This form of catathymia is triggered by a sudden, overwhelming affect having certain ideational and symbolic significance that is unconscious at the time of the violence. The incubation period lasts for seconds or minutes, there is usually a flattening of emotions following the event, the victim may be a stranger, and there may be psychogenic amnesia for the violence. Such a form of catathymia may account for those sudden, inexplicable murders in the absence of gross organic or mental disorder, in which the victim has little, if any, actual relationship to the perpetrator.

The mode of violence is clearly affective (Meloy 1988a), delineated by intense autonomic arousal, overwhelming anger during the violence, the perception of the victim as an imminent threat to the ego structure of the perpetrator, a time-limited behavioral sequence, and a goal of threat reduction and a return to intrapsychic homeostasis. What differentiates acute catathymia from other forms of affective violence is the unconscious motivation for the act and the symbolic significance of the victim. An understanding of the *transference distortions* that catapulted the person to violence is critical, and can usually be identified through a careful attachment history taking, a structured diagnostic interview (Kernberg 1984), and psychological testing. Two tests I would recommend include the Rorschach Inkblot Test, to identify structural vulnerabilities in the personality to reality distortion and loss of control (e.g., $X-\% > 15$, $FC < CF + C$, AdjD < 0), and the Thematic Apperception Test (TAT), to identify more conscious self and object representations and predictable interpersonal motivations. Westen (1991) has developed a multidimensional measure for assessing object relations with the TAT, including complexity of representations of people, affect tone of relationship paradigms, capacity for emotional investment in relationships and moral standards, and understanding of social causality. His University of Michigan research group (Westen et al. 1990), for example, found empirical support for the critical role of preoedipal experience in shaping object relations, and the central role of the mother and disrupted attachments in the genesis of object relational pathology in a sample of adolescent girls.

The presence of psychoactive drugs at the time of the violence should not exclude consideration of an acute catathymic crisis, although it does complicate the psychodynamic picture. Alcohol and/or psychostimulants may disinhibit the catathymic tension buildup and function as chemical releasing mechanisms for the violence. The flattening of emotions, and presence of relief following detoxification and awareness of the act, together constitute a clinical clue that the violence may have had an underlying catathymic dimension that warrants further exploration.

The presence or absence of psychosis at the time of the acute catathymic episode also needs to be carefully assessed due to its legal relevance. The presence of psychosis excludes the diagnosis of Intermittent Explosive Disorder *(DSM-III-R)* and was apparent in 3.2 percent of the self-referred violent males in the study by Felthous and colleagues (1991). In the absence of a major mental disorder, such as schizophrenia or mood disorder, organic factors, or schizotypal personality disorder, the appropriate diagnosis would be Brief Reactive Psychosis (298.80). There must, however, be a gross disturbance of sensory perception (formal thought disorder, delusions, hallucinations, or catatonia) and emotional turmoil.

A catathymic crisis may explain the psychodynamic and motivational *reason* for the violence. The assessment of psychosis at the time of the violence is a *present mental state* issue that will only address diagnostic questions. Both motivation and present mental state are necessary foundations of knowledge to answer legal questions, such as responsibility at the time of the crime. These two areas of investigation need to be carefully delineated and not confused; each may shed light on the other.

The most reliable data for the determination of psychosis at the time of the catathymic crisis are witnessing of the violence and the behavior of the perpetrator. Notwithstanding concerns regarding eyewitness testimony (Loftus 1979), a thorough review of the criminal investigation reports, including interviews of witnesses, can reveal behavioral details that suggest the presence or absence of psychosis. Was the perpetrator oriented? Confused? Responding to stimuli not apparent to the observer? Or disorganized? If the only witnesses to the violence were the victim, who may be deceased, and the perpetrator, then the task is more inferential and difficult: investigation should focus on people who observed or interacted with the individual immediately before or after the crime. The closer the temporal proximity, the more reliable the data when inferring state of mind at the time of the offense. I would suggest three other sources of data, all of which may be applied to other forensic psychological investigations of violence:

Systematic Self-Report of Violence (SSRV)

The completion of an SSRV provides a valuable source of data for determining mental state at the time of the violence. Presented in Figure 3–1, it is a three-by-three matrix that has two axes: a temporal one and a psychological one. The temporal axis organizes the patient's recall of the event before, during, and after the actual violence. The psychological axis organizes the patient's recall of his thoughts, emotions, and behavior. The clinician's task is to fill in the complete matrix over the course of an interview or a series of interviews, in any order he chooses. The result will be a microanalysis of the violence through self-report. The value of the SSRV is manifold: it organizes the clinical investigator's thinking so that no area is forgotten; it compels the patient or defendant to recall in detail the offense, which gives the clinician further information concerning recall ability or willingness, and accompanying affects; it provides a data base which can be compared with other eyewitness accounts of the violence, or subsequent recall by the defendant; it can be repeatedly used to ferret out discrepancies or substantiate the reliability of the defendant's memory; and it provides data for answering both diagnostic and motivational questions.

Time

	Before	During	After

		Before	During	After
	Thoughts			
Psychological Operation	Emotions			
	Acts			

Figure 3-1. The Systematic Self-Report of Violence (SSRV) Matrix.

An individual involved in an acute catathymic crisis, for instance, might report on the emotional vector a sudden, inexplicable buildup of tension and feelings of rage just before the violence, feelings of being overwhelmed and out of control during the violence, and a sense of flattening of feeling immediately after the violence. The corollary behavioral vector might include benign or ordinary talking with a friend, a sudden reach for a knife and stabbing of the friend, and subsequent desperate attempts to help the friend, who is now the wounded victim.

The SSRV applied to a psychopath who has committed sexual homicide would be quite different. He might report a period of rehearsal fantasy (Prentky et al. 1989) on the thinking vector before the violence, no memory of thoughts during the violence (which could be malingered amnesia), and planning and preparation after the violence to move the corpse to another "dump site" to avoid capture. The corollary emotional vector might include excitement and antici-pation before the violence, no feeling during the violence, and con-temptuous delight following the violence. The contrast between such sexual predation and acute catathymia should underscore the importance and usefulness of the SSRV.

Gathering data to complete the SSRV is easier if the clinician employs certain techniques borrowed from cognitive therapy: ask the defendant to speak in the present tense when recalling the time before, during, and after the offense; let the person free-associate to his thoughts, feelings, and behavior, without any initial direct questioning; have him visually imagine the crime as he describes it; alternately move him, through suggestive questioning, from external to internal experience and then back; have him adopt alternative visual perspectives on the crime (e.g., How would you have looked to the victim? What would you be doing? If there had been a camera in the wall, what would it have seen? What would the police see when they first arrived at the scene of the crime?); start the recall process several hours, or perhaps even days, before the crime itself, to reduce his anxiety to the questioning; only begin the SSRV when sufficient rapport has been established, usually after the history taking; and leave the SSRV, to continue later, if rapport is lost or affects are too painful and unpleasant.

Psychological Testing

The use of tests to determine state of mind at the time of the crime is at best highly inferential, and at worst grossly misleading. The closer the testing is to the violent offense, the more valid the inference. Test data prior to the violence may exist and should be vigorously pursued through *subpoena duces tecum* if suspected. These data will establish a longitudinal frame of reference when juxtaposed with current test results, and make inferences stronger.

Most psychological tests are measuring present mental state and should be used for that purpose. Some test variables, however, have significant temporal reliability, and if the research literature is available to support this, inferences can be made to the time of the violence. Characterological profiles on the Minnesota Multiphasic Personality Inventory (MMPI) are usually trait, rather than state, indicators and are usually more reliable over time than neurotic or psychotic sloped profiles. The two-point 43/34 MMPI profile, for example, is sometimes apparent in persons who have committed catathymic homicide, and may suggest a propensity to explosive outbursts in an otherwise rigid character prone to deny or repress unpleasant affect. This profile may also be consistent with dissociative pathology. The difficulty with most temporal reliability studies of psychological tests is the brevity of the time frames, usually days or weeks rather than months or years.

For the psychological assessment of suspected catathymic homicide cases, I would suggest, at minimum, the Wechsler Adult Intelligence Scale–Revised (WAIS-R), the Rorschach, the MMPI-2, and the Millon Clinical Multiaxial Inventory-II (MCMI-II). Such data should give the psychologist ample information to determine the presence or absence of a psychotic disorder and any structural vulnerabilities in the personality that could decompensate under stress. Again, the unconscious denial of affect, and the use of preoedipal defenses in a rigid and controlled personality disorder with dependent and narcissistic features, are pathognomonic of catathymia; on the other hand, an impulse-ridden and habitually acting out personality-disordered individual, with or without psychosis, is contraindicated in catathymia.

Previous Psychiatric and Psychological Records

It is extremely rare for an individual to manifest severe psychiatric disturbance for the first time during a violent episode. In fact, in the absence of a psychiatric history, any claims of psychiatric symptoms, such as hallucinations or delusions, during the violence are highly suspect and should be considered malingering unless this hypothesis is vigorously disproved. The most common exception to this rule is a drug-induced psychosis, which in most states would not meet the threshold for legal insanity.[1]

---

1. In California voluntary intoxication can lead to a state of legal insanity if it is "settled insanity": the substance has caused a *fixed and stable* mental disorder that

Aggressive attempts should be made to secure all known and suspected psychiatric and psychological records. In cases where an insanity defense has been entered, a waiver of privilege has also occurred. In cases where counsel is seeking a psychiatric or psychological opinion to determine whether an insanity plea is appropriate, no evaluation should be done until the attorney has provided the clinician with all such records, if available.

The presence of a major mental disorder according to the patient's history will probably rule out an Intermittent Explosive Disorder diagnosis, but may substantiate a history of psychosis that *may* have been present at the time of the catathymic homicide. The activation of the psychosis at the time of the violence, however, should not be assumed unless other data at the time of the crime are consistent with a loss of reality testing. Dissociative experiences, for example, which are common in acute catathymic violence and many homicides, should not be confused with psychotic symptoms: illusions or distortions of reality "sense" (depersonalization, derealization) are not losses of reality "testing" (delusions, hallucinations) and generally exclude one another. Command hallucinations, moreover, should be suspect, because most individuals who hear voices do not hear commands, and of those who do, most successfully resist them (Rogers 1988).

A common misconception among mental health professionals is the assumption of psychotic causality if the offense has been committed in a psychiatric hospital by a mentally disordered patient. This is not necessarily the case.

F. R. was a 27-year-old Caucasian male with a lengthy history of bipolar disorder and intermittent violence. When in remission, his interactions

---

lasts for a reasonable period of time and is dependent on other factors besides the ingestion and duration of the drug (*People* v. *Skinner*, 185 Cal. App. 3d 1050 [1986]). If this is the case, then the McNaghten criteria must also be met: the individual did not understand the nature and quality of his act, or he did not know the difference between right and wrong at the time of the crime. The proliferation of psychostimulants has resulted in a number of insanity findings based upon such *DSM-III-R* diagnoses as cocaine and amphetamine delusional disorders.

were consistent with narcissistic personality disorder. During a brief psychiatric hospitalization while living in the community, F. R. was placed in seclusion for verbal threats and disruption of the milieu. Upon release several hours later, he threw chairs against the wall of the day room, and before he could be contained, he dragged a female patient out of her bed, struck her in the face, and fled the hospital ward. He was subsequently caught and prosecuted, and found not guilty by reason of insanity.

When he filed his first writ to be released from the state hospital several years later, a careful SSRV analysis of the crime revealed no basis for an insanity defense. F. R. reported thinking about taking someone hostage when he was removed from seclusion so he could escape from the hospital. He had witnessed the successful use of a hostage at a Massachusetts hospital several years earlier. He remembered that two female patients slept in a room near the seclusion room. When he pulled the victim from her bed and was holding her by the neck on the floor, a male orderly accosted him. F. R. said, "Get the fuck away from me or I'll kill her." The orderly backed out of the room, and F. R. escaped through one of the fire door exits. After our clinical investigation, F. R. asked me if he could withdraw his insanity acquittal, since he realized he would "do more time" if he remained in the hospital than if he had been sentenced to prison. I advised him to talk to his attorney.

The most troubling aspect of this case was that the court-appointed psychiatrists *never asked the patient about his self-report of the crime*. Their opinion of legal insanity was solely based on a mental status exam, a review of the patient's prior psychiatric history, and the *location* of the instant offense. The apparently affective violence turned out to be, in retrospect, predatory violence, which did not meet the McNaghten criteria for insanity in California. Yet the verdict had been rendered by the trier of fact who trusted the opinion of the expert witnesses. In cases such as this, careful thought should be given to criminal prosecution of the patient if evidence confirms that psychosis did not cause the violence (Meloy 1991). Virtually all cases of predatory violence (Meloy 1988a) in hospital settings should be criminally prosecuted, notwithstanding the reality-testing capacity of the person at the time of the offense.

CHRONIC CATATHYMIC VIOLENCE

Revitch and Schlesinger's (1981) chronic form of catathymia is closest to the crisis described by Wertham (1937). They divided it into three stages: incubation, violent act, and relief. The incubation stage lasts for several days to a year, and cognitions are marked by an obsessive preoccupation with the future victim. Affect states include depression, frustration, and helplessness, and a conscious sense of tension buildup. Formal thought disorder may also be apparent in tangential associations. Thought content is pervaded with fantasies of murder, but suicidal wishes and plans are also apparent. The homicidal wish is usually felt as ego-dystonic, and the individual may consciously suppress it, only to be hounded by its incessant return. Most commonly, the victim is known to the perpetrator, and an emotional bond, or attachment, exists between them. Such catathymic homicides are usually reported by the press as jealousy or rejection.

Murder may occur alone, or may be accompanied by suicide. In a related study, Rosenbaum (1990) found that depression was a prominent characteristic in 75 percent of the perpetrators of murder–suicide between couples, and was not prominent in perpetrators of murder between couples. In the murder–suicide group ($N = 12$), none of the women had gross psychopathology, and the depressed male perpetrators were personality disordered, in a long-term relationship, and separated from the victim at the time of the crime. No attempt was made, however, to determine whether any of these cases would fit the motivational dynamics of chronic catathymic homicide.

Murder–suicide is rare and occurs at the rate of 0.22 per 100,000 population in the United States (Palmer and Humphrey 1980). Generally, the higher the rate of homicide in a country, the lower the proportion of murder–suicide. For instance, in the United States, 4 percent of homicides also involve suicide; but in Denmark, which has a very low homicide rate, 42 percent of homicides also involve suicide (Coid 1983). Despite these variations, the *rate* of murder–suicide in the general population for these two countries is about the same. Coid (1983) suggested that this phenomenon may reflect the similar prevalence of mental illness in any two countries.

Revitch and Schlesinger (1981) noted that depression was the

most common affect during the incubation period of chronic catathymic homicide (see also Rosenbaum and Bennett 1986, Woddis
1957). There also may be a period of brooding before the act itself.
Memory for the event seems to be better preserved in chronic, rather
than acute, catathymia.

FURTHER PSYCHODYNAMIC CONTRIBUTIONS

In an earlier work (Meloy 1988a) I noted that chronic catathymic
violence necessitated both a borderline personality organization and
psychopathic traits. I have found further evidence for the former, but
the notion of psychopathy within this motivational framework rested
on my assumption of conscious planning and intent, that is, predation,
and this needs to be further developed.

Affective versus Predatory Violence

The act of catathymic violence is clearly affective, usually manifest in
a dramatic, explosive upsurge of rage that results in death or injury to
another in close physical proximity. The assumption of conscious
planning and preparation, however, should be tested in the form of a
hypothesis: is there evidence that supports an ego-syntonic wish for
violence during the incubation period? Revitch and Schlesinger (1981)
emphasized the ego-alien nature of all catathymic crises. I would
suggest that the affectively charged complex of ideas that forms the
basis of catathymic incubation may be either ego-syntonic or -dystonic
and should be apparent through careful investigation. If the homicidal
or homicidal-suicidal wish was expressed, how could it be characterized? Ego-syntonic wishes for death of the victim would be conveyed
with pleasurable or comfortable affect, without fear or trepidation, in
a threatening or grandiose manner, in the absence of conscience or
superego constraint, and without reference to the unwanted or obsessional quality of the thoughts. Ego-syntonic behaviors would include
conscious planning and preparation for the crime – perhaps practicing

at a shooting range, experimenting to find the most suitable weapon, or attempting to construct alibis or form alliances with others that would help mitigate responsibility after the offense.

Ego-dystonic thoughts to murder the victim would be conveyed with displeasurable or anxious affect, perhaps with fear and trepidation; may be a genuine cry for help to a professional or close friend; would be absent any sense of grandiosity or omnipotence; may empathically be felt as an impending sense of loss of control; would be accompanied by fears of punishment and anticipated remorse; and would refer to the unwanted nature of the thoughts. Ego-dystonic behaviors would include the securing of a weapon for unusual or unexplainable reasons; no practice with the weapon until the act itself; and no attempts to deny or minimize responsibility for the offense, despite a strong sense of disbelief.

Even though predation may appear to be superficially present, the absence of ego-syntonic thoughts and consciously planned and prepared behaviors would rule it out. The obvious forensic risk in determining affective or predatory violence in catathymia is the clinician's sole dependency on retrospective reporting by the perpetrator. Most defendants will attempt to convince evaluators that their act of predatory violence was actually affective violence, because the latter is more easily mitigated during trial. Reconstruction of wishes and behaviors should only be based on observations by others *before* the homicide, although retrospective reports by the perpetrator can be used to determine his or her veracity.

Borderline Personality Organization

Catathymic homicide appears to necessitate a borderline or psychotic level of personality organization (Kernberg 1984). A lack of an integrated identity, reality testing problems, and so-called "primitive" defenses can be inferred and measured in the post-homicide evaluation of the catathymic individual.

The preoedipal nature of borderline personality organization, however, has recently been challenged by Westen (1989) and deserves comment. He compared several assumptions of psychoanalytic object relations theory with empirical findings in the child development literature.

> The developmental research reviewed here documents that the capacity for ambivalence is not firmly established, self- and object-representations are not complex and integrated, and the capacity to invest maturely in people following transcendence of a need-gratifying interpersonal orientation is not accomplished by the end of the oedipal period. These phenomena are all hallmarks of borderline character pathology, assumed to reflect a preoedipal developmental arrest. If they are not actually transcended by the oedipal period in normal development, then the equation of "primitive" or "preoedipal" in the pathological sense, and "primitive" or "preoedipal" in the normative developmental sense, is problematic. Further, the assumption that object relations in borderlines are strictly dyadic, an assumption that emerged from the attempt to model the theory of borderline psychopathology on the psychoanalytic theory of infancy, does justice neither to borderlines nor to preoedipal children and infants. [p. 342]

Westen's work is significant in this context because it empirically shows the propensity of psychoanalytic thought to mistakenly and prematurely set the benchmarks of "successful" psychological development, in this case, at the 4-to-5-year-old oedipal period; and to wrongly equate all psychopathology with a linear, developmental fixation or regression. The additional latency and preadolescent developmental aspects of borderline psychopathology, and the complexity of "primitive" object relations, moreover, *are* consistent with developmental research, and need to be considered when formulating an understanding of borderline pathology in any context.

The lack of an integrated identity in chronic catathymic violence is evident in the degree to which self and object representations are either good or bad across time and are not held constant despite the vicissitudes of reality. This is most dramatically apparent in the homicidal-suicidal wish that emerges as an obsession during the incubation phase. As one patient murmured, "Either he or I must die, something has to give."

This prototypical verbalization conveys the wish to destroy the bad self or the bad object to somehow resolve the problem. At this moment there is no consciousness of the good self or good object and the inherent wish to live, the libidinal aspect of the self–object dyad. What is notable instead is the aggressive aspect of the self–object dyad, presented as an imperative, and the oscillation of the destructive wish: either self or other must be destroyed. This polarization of self and object representation as either all good or all bad is comparable with that of children between the ages of 2 and 7 years. It occurs after the development of the self as an object (Kagan 1981) but before the achievement of "conservation" of the self (Harter 1983), a span of time generally consistent with Piaget's preoperational period. The immutability of the self has not yet been recognized, and internal representations are concrete, transitory, and contradictory.

The oscillation of the destructive wish also suggests the primitivity of the defenses being utilized in the catathymic individual. The origins of the aggression, pain, and dysphoria are either projected into the object or introjected into the self. The aggressive wish follows: if he dies, I destroy the pain; if I die, I destroy the pain. The suicidal or homicidal nature of the aggressive wish depends upon the perceived origin of the emotional distress, which may rapidly oscillate.

This projective-introjective cycling, however, still assumes a distinction between self and object representations. When this is lost, a psychotic level of personality organization has been regressively reached, and demarcation of self and object is irrelevant. Psychotic symptoms emerge, and the primitive borderline defenses give way to a homicidal envelopment of external reality without boundary. As one psychotic patient stated, "I am legion and must die."

This type of thinking has also been referred to as "event centered thought" (Fast 1985) and may hint at the alloplastic nature of catathymic violence: the remedy is found in the action, not through a more internal, modulated process of change.

Other defenses that are pathognomonic of borderline personality organization are also evident during chronic catathymic violence. The genotypic defense of *splitting* is apparent in the verbalization, "either he or I must die." The imperative is extreme (death), and it is conceived as a dichotomy without any other, more moderate choices worth considering. Options such as leaving the relationship, altering the closeness within the relationship, active problem solving through psychotherapeutic work as an individual or a couple, are never consciously weighed.

Splitting may also occur during the experience of intense, polarized, and alternating affect states. Rage may be felt toward the self and then toward the object. This oscillation of affect could determine, at any moment, the nature of the violence as either homicidal or suicidal, or both in close temporal sequence. The intensity of the rage at the moment of violence also implicates splitting, since there is no blocking or neutralization of discharge that is seen in higher level repressive operations (Kernberg 1976). The absence of synthesis of identifications of opposite valence means that aggressive drives remain raw, unmodulated, and "split off" from conscious expression during the incubation period of catathymia. This is the clinical reason why the actual violence is often experienced as "out of character" (in a sense, it is) and "overwhelming" by the perpetrator. The momentary cathexis of the split-off, rageful affect is a sudden, torrential burst of feeling with little ego control.

Splitting is also inherent in the phenotypic borderline defenses of *primitive idealization* and *devaluation* that are often apparent in catathymia. These are opposite conceptions that may shift between self and object representations, or more subtly, between memory and hope: the devaluation of what once was, and the idealization of what might have been or could be. The unique human capacity to project into the future, to wish and to dream, may paradoxically provide the catalyst for destroying what is real, evident, and conceived as obstructive in the present. The threat of the destruction of hope may unconsciously precipitate the catathymic violence. The violence may also be used to protect the "hypercathected, blown-up, omnipotent ego ideal" (Kernberg 1976, p. 49) which has subsequently developed to protect the borderline-organized individual from the persecutory, malevolent objects that populate his projective field. All of these polarized introjects (if related to the self) or identifications (if felt as part of the self), of course, carry their own affective "charge" that will only be experienced when the mental representation is cathected.

The phenotypic borderline defense most central to understanding catathymic violence is *projective identification*. Although controversy surrounds the nuances of this defensive operation (Goldstein 1991, Grotstein 1981, Kernberg 1976, Klein 1946, Meloy 1991, Ogden 1982, Rosenfeld 1963), for our purposes it can be understood as having two components, *attribution* and *control:* "What is projected outside is still, in part, felt inside, with the additional need to exert control over external objects onto whom aggression has been projected" (Kernberg 1976, p. 49).

In catathymic violence, projective identification serves a defensive purpose. During the incubation period the self will experience feelings of confusion, devitalization (depression), and vulnerability to ideas of influence and control by the object (Grotstein 1981). At this time there is an intrapsychic invasion of the object so as to control it, or be controlled by it, thus eliminating feelings of helplessness. Projective identification, in this sense, is functioning within a borderline level of personality wherein demarcation between self and objects is retained, but *con*fusion is apparent around the origin of psychological content and motivation: Who is doing what to whom? Am I feeling a certain way or is he? This state of mind is often apparent to others during the incubation period, when the patient becomes more intrusive, overt, and confused in her behavior toward the object but perceives this behavior only in the object who will eventually be victimized. Grotstein (1981) has referred to projective identification as an unconscious fantasy, in effect, imagination, and calls what I am describing *symbiotic projective identification* (p. 124).

It is particularly difficult during this time to clinically separate the intrapsychic life of the patient from the increasingly disturbed behavior; the latter will tend to overshadow clinical judgment. The clinician's own projective identification can be used in its most sublimated empathic form to understand the patient's growing sense of being controlled by the object, and the accompanying anger and fear that at first glance seem unfathomable.

The explosive violence of catathymic homicide is propelled by the use of projective identification as a form of magical omnipotent control. The tension buildup, usually lasting months to a year, is finally cathected, and the intolerable feeling of being controlled by the malevolent object is reversed. Absolute control of the object as the source of persecutory distress is acted out through violence.

The relief experienced after catathymic violence has both a physiological and a psychodynamic basis. Intense affect that has been split off, at the cost of depressive and anxious symptoms and muscular tension, is abreacted and "released." There would be a parasympathetic return to baseline autonomic functioning, and a subjective feeling of relief because the perceived threat has been removed. Psychodynamically, the actual object that contained the projective identifications has been destroyed, and the defense, at least for a time, is no longer necessary. Paradoxically, the catathymic individual may return to a wishful, idealized fantasy relationship with the victim, which, in the absence of a capacity to recognize as only imagination, would be considered psychotic. A subtle clinical indicator of such imaginings is the post-homicidal reference to the victim in the present tense, as if he or she were still alive.

Projective identification, moreover, can also be used as a psychotic defense. In this case, the patient's ego boundaries are lost, the location of psychological content is irrelevant (because there are no boundaries), and the object is experienced and controlled as an aspect of the self. Goldstein (1991) theorized that the projection of self representations would mark the psychotic use of projective identifications; and the projection of object representations would mark the borderline or neurotic use of projective identification. The two clinical cases in Chapter 7 illustrate chronic catathymia in a borderline and a psychotic individual, respectively, and also support the distinction that Goldstein made concerning projective identification.

Ruotolo (1968) mentioned the "pride systems" that are affected in sudden murder, but formulated them at a neurotic level of personality. These "systems" are more usefully understood as narcissistic defenses at a borderline level of personality, which are vulnerable to fragmentation when the self is wounded and which may stimulate rage reactions. The catathymic individual is typically both dependent and entitled, an inherently conflictual set of traits that is common in narcissistic disorder. (This dialectic between entitlement and neediness is a pathological and extreme variant of a normal sense of the self as both unique and vulnerable to certain needs. Such pathology is clinically observed in alternating feelings of grandiosity and sensitivity to humiliation.) Wishes to be both admired and taken care of are vulnerable to slight criticism, especially from an actual person to whom the individual is symbiotically bound as a container of his own alternately aggressive or libidinal (good or bad) intrapsychic representations (both introjects and identifications).

A third aspect of borderline personality organization is reality-testing problems, and in catathymic cases one would expect either borderline or psychotic measures of reality testing. Impairments in the patient's ability to distinguish between internal and external reality are expectable when defenses are utilized that distort, negate, deny, split off, and grossly alter whole sectors of experience. The most useful quantitative measure of reality testing is the cognitive mediation group of indices for the Rorschach (Exner 1986a). An intriguing, highly applicable, and relatively new index is the S−%, which is the proportion of minus form level responses that include space. Preliminary validation data link this index to reality testing in the midst of intense anger (J. Exner, personal communication, April, 1992).

Symbiotic Attachment

The psychobiological substrate of chronic catathymic violence is the likelihood of a disorder of attachment to the victim, which probably has genetic roots in early attachment pathology. There exists a psychological *bondage*, rather than a secure bond to the object. This metaphor of being bound or controlled against one's will finds its defensive corollary in the perceived control exerted by the victim during projective identification. Paradoxically, this is also a defense against feelings of helplessness: being controlled and abused by an object (both introjected and actual) defines an oppositional identification against which one measures the self and projects a future course. In this case, the motivational goal becomes destruction of the controlling object. This "object of destiny" (Grotstein 1990, p. 141), no longer an ego ideal, becomes a desired destiny without an object.

The incubation period of catathymic violence appears similar to the "anxious resistant" attachment pathology noted by Bowlby (1960), and characterized by the presence of both depression and anxiety. Bowlby (1988b) also noted that this pattern is promoted by inconsistent availability and threats of abandonment used to control the child. In catathymic violence the latter belief may originate intrapsychically, and once again, through the process of projective identification, the victim is *perceived* as abandoning, and therefore controlling, the perpetrator.

Chronic catathymic violence also spells the end of a disruptive symbiotic attachment. At the beginning of the catathymic course, what had been a mutually dependent relationship suffers internal or external disruption, and separation anxiety is felt that cannot be attenuated by soothing internal objects. Grotstein (1990) noted that stranger anxiety, although discontinuous from separation anxiety, is coeval with it, and in this setting could impose on the "loved one" certain omnipotent and malevolent characteristics whereby the strange is commingled with the familiar. In other words, the victim of catathymia, during the incubation phase, is perceived as a threat, and in extreme cases a predator, who in a magnified and mad sense is doing irreparable harm to the individual. Such stranger anxiety may be engendered by early experiences of abandonment and neglect that are rekindled by the adult experience. During the incubation phase, a pathological identification, which Grotstein calls an "oppositional type" (1990, p. 142), then develops with the targeted victim of the catathymic violence, an identification in which intrapsychic combat is fought, unbeknownst to the future victim until the actual, explosive violence erupts. Grotstein (1990) also urged the use of *folie à deux* not only to describe shared psychoses, but also to explain pathological varieties of collusive attachments, of which catathymic violence may signal both alloplastic destruction of the object and, paradoxically, intrapsychic salvation of the primitive self.

CONCLUSIONS

Catathymic violence has a distinguished history in the forensic psychiatric literature but is a term generally unknown to most contemporary clinicians. It occurs in an acute and chronic form. The latter form is most germane to violent disorders of attachment, and is marked by three characteristics: an incubation period in which anxiety and depression are intermingled with homicidal-suicidal thoughts concerning an intimate; a sudden, explosive, and homicidal act; and emotional relief.

The mode of violence is clearly affective, but there may be an extended period of planning and preparation, usually months to a year, that has certain ego-syntonic or ego-dystonic aspects. The former may qualify for a predatory mode of violence. Catathymic homicide necessitates a borderline or psychotic personality organization. The central defense for understanding this form of violence is projective identification, in which the perpetrator attributes increasingly malevolent and controlling characteristics to the symbiotic partner. The relief following the violence has both a physiological and psychodynamic basis. It marks the end of a disruptive symbiotic attachment, which probably had its roots in early attachment pathology.

4

The Psychopath as Love Object

Cruelty might be very human, and it might be very cultural, but it is not acceptable.

—Jodie Foster

We just get along really good. I don't really know anything about his crimes. I don't need to.

—Christine Lee, faithful prison visitor to Richard Ramirez, the "Nightstalker," convicted of thirteen serial murders in California in 1985

One of the cornerstones of psychopathic personality is the lack of a capacity to form affectional attachments to other living objects (Gacono and Meloy 1991). This does not, however, preclude other individuals from forming attachments to him. Popularized accounts of such relationships will occasionally appear in trade publications, such as Caril Fugate's killing spree with Charles Starkweather (Allen 1976), and Ann Rule's friendship with Theodore Bundy (Rule 1980). These affectional bonds are remarkable for the simple reasons that they are not reciprocated, and the love object is generally known to be exceedingly dangerous.

Oddly and, it seems, inexplicably, there is no published scientific literature concerning this phenomenon. I will attempt in this chapter to understand this disorder of attachment, primarily drawing from psychoanalytic object relations theory and the specific work of Racker (1968) concerning complementary and concordant identifications. The clinical management and treatment of such relationship disorders will be found in Chapter 8, which focuses on three women who were intimately involved, over time, with three primary psychopaths. Two of these women are now serving life in prison, and the third was murdered by her husband. Such relationships do not predict a positive outcome.

PSYCHOPATHIC PERSONALITY

In an earlier work (Meloy 1988a) I defined psychopathy as "a deviant developmental disturbance characterized by an inordinate amount of instinctual aggression and the absence of an object relational capacity to bond" (p. 5). Since the book was published, and regretfully not just because of it, there has been a substantial increase in the research concerning psychopathy in the scientific literature. Most findings have supported this definition, and it appears to still be a useful psychodynamic formulation that acknowledges developmental pathways, constitutional factors, and attachment pathology wedded to intrapsychic representations.

The most important reason for the dramatic upsurge in research concerning psychopathy was the publication of the Psychopathy Checklist (PCL) (Hare 1980) and the subsequent Psychopathy Checklist Revised (PCL-R) (Hare 1985, 1991). This 20-item, 40-point scale, completed after a structured interview and review of all available independent data, provided for the first time a reliable and valid *independent* measure of psychopathic disturbance from which other *dependent* measures could then be made. Prior to the development of this instrument based upon the clinical work of Cleckley (1941), group studies of psychopathy were highly suspect owing to the lack of a reliable and valid measure to select subjects for comparison. Vaillant (1975), for example, wrote a paper that argued that sociopathy was a "mythical beast" (p. 178), based on his study of a small clinical sample of patients he considered sociopaths. Unfortunately, a careful reading of his case data indicates that probably none of his four illustrative patients (two male and two female narcotic addicts) were ever primary psychopaths. His frequently referenced paper becomes a circular argument that sociopathy (psychopathy) doesn't exist when it is not there to begin with. Clinical theory concerning psychopathy prior to the availability of the PCL and PCL-R was paradoxically more accurate than some of the empirical studies (McCord and McCord 1964, Millon 1981, Reid 1978).

Understanding those individuals who form intense attachments to psychopaths is premised on an understanding of psychopathy. The twenty criteria that comprise the Psychopathy Checklist Revised (Hare 1991) are listed in Table 4–1. (Ten of these items are being used as a criteria set for field trials for *DSM-IV* [Widiger et al. 1991].)

The PCL-R consists of two stable, oblique factors that correlate (on average .56) in prison inmates (Hare et al. 1991). Factor 1 includes items 1, 2, 4, 5, 6, 7, 8, and 16, and describes clinical traits of remorselessness, callousness, and egocentricity. It also correlates with prototypicality ratings of narcissistic and histrionic personality disorder and with self-report measures of Machiavellianism and narcissism (Harpur et al. 1989, Hart and Hare 1989). I call this factor *aggressive narcissism*. Factor 2 includes items 3, 9, 10, 12, 13, 14, 15, 18, and 19, and describes a chronically antisocial and unstable lifestyle. It positively correlates with *DSM-III-R* diagnoses of Antisocial Personality Disorder, criminal behaviors, socioeconomic background, and self-report measures of antisocial behavior (Hare 1991, Harpur et al. 1989). I call this factor *antisocial behavior*.

Individuals receive a score of 0, 1, or 2 for each item on the PCL-R. Zero means that the item does not apply, 1 means that it applies somewhat or only in a limited sense, and 2 means that it definitely does apply. Scores can range from 0 to 40, with a mean score of 23.37 (SD = 7.96) in prison inmates (N = 1,065 from six samples) and 20.56 (SD = 7.79) in forensic patients (N = 440 from four samples) (Hare 1991). The distribution of scores is approximately normal, with a slightly negative skew. A cutoff score of 30 is now the research convention to differentiate between psychopathic and nonpsychopathic subjects. The clinical labeling of an individual as psychopathic for

Table 4–1.

The Psychopathy Checklist Revised.

1.	Glibness/superficial charm
2.	Grandiose sense of self-worth
3.	Need for stimulation/proneness to boredom
4.	Pathological lying
5.	Conning/manipulative
6.	Lack of remorse or guilt
7.	Shallow affect
8.	Callous/lack of empathy
9.	Parasitic lifestyle
10.	Poor behavioral controls
11.	Promiscuous sexual behavior
12.	Early behavior problems
13.	Lack of realistic, long-term goals
14.	Impulsivity
15.	Irresponsibility
16.	Failure to accept responsibility for own actions
17.	Many short-term relationships
18.	Juvenile delinquency
19.	Revocation of conditional release
20.	Criminal versatility

treatment or dispositional purposes, however, should always take into account other information besides the PCL-R score, and should consider the standard error of measure (3.25).

Interrater reliability is quite good, with correlations ranging from alphas of 0.87 to intraclass correlations of 0.92 (average of two ratings). Item-total correlations range from 0.30 (many short-term marital relationships) to 0.61 (callous/lack of empathy). The test-retest reliability of the PCL-R is about 0.90 (standard error of prediction is 4.25) (Hare 1991).

The validation literature concerning the PCL and PCL-R, which are psychometrically equivalent, is substantial, and has generally focused on differences between psychopathic (PCL-R > 30) and nonpsychopathic (PCL-R < 30) male criminals (for a comprehensive review, see Hare 1991). Forth and colleagues (1990) also found the instrument, in a modified form, useful in a sample of 13–20-year-old incarcerated adolescents. It correlated with conduct disorder symptoms, previous violent offenses, violent behavior in the institution, and violent recidivism.

Hart and Hare (1989) investigated the validity of the PCL-R in a forensic psychiatric population to address the question of confounding Axis I disorders. They found that psychopathy was significantly related only to antisocial and histrionic personality disorders (Axis II) and nonalcohol substance abuse disorders (Axis I). The PCL-R scores were also positively correlated with prototypicality ratings of antisocial, histrionic, and narcissistic personality disorders, and negatively correlated with ratings of avoidant personality disorder. There was no significant association between schizophrenia, mental retardation, organic disorders, or bipolar disorders and psychopathic personality. Smith and Newman (1990) did find that psychopaths were more likely than nonpsychopaths to have lifetime diagnoses of alcoholism, any drug disorder, and multiple drug disorders. They found substance abuse to be significantly related to Factor 2 (antisocial behavior), but not to Factor 1 (aggressive narcissism).

Psychopathy in women is just beginning to be explored. Preliminary findings indicate that there are gender differences in the manifestation of psychopathy (Hare 1991, Peaslee 1992). Raine and Dunkin (1990) theorized that women must possess stronger biological predispositions toward psychopathy to overcome the greater socialization pressures against the expression of criminality by women. The application of the PCL-R to nonwhite populations appears warranted (Kosson et al. 1990), but race should be included as a factor in all analyses to identify possible racial differences in personality dynamics.

Violence, Sadism, and Psychopathy

Most salient to the psychopath as love object is the validation literature concerning his interpersonal and intrapsychic life. Several studies indicate that psychopaths are more violent than nonpsychopathic criminals. Hare and McPherson (1984) found in three studies that psychopaths committed more violent crimes, were more likely to use a weapon, and were more aggressive in prison than nonpsychopathic criminals. There was no significant difference, however, in attempted suicides or self-mutilations. Intelligence did not mediate the relationship between psychopathy and violence, other than the finding that psychopaths with above-average IQ were more likely to use a weapon. Harris and colleagues (1990) found that significantly more psychopaths than nonpsychopaths committed a violent crime over a 10-year period following release from an intensive therapeutic community program in prison. Rice and associates (1990) also found that the PCL-R and a phallometric index of sexual arousal correctly classified 76.9 percent of rapists released from prison who subsequently reoffended. Hare and colleagues (1988) authored the first study concerning male psychopaths and their criminal careers, and discovered that psychopaths spend more time in prison than other criminals until the age of 40, and then their nonviolent criminal activity dramatically decreases to the level of other nonpsychopathic criminals. This decline, however, appears to plateau beyond the age of 50. Violent behavior, moreover, does not seem to decrease with age and may remain more stable than nonviolent criminality. Data concerning psychopaths beyond the age of 50 are unavailable at present. The aging process seems to decrease Factor 2 (antisocial behavior) of the PCL-R, but not Factor 1 (aggressive narcissism). Arboleda-Florez and Holley (1991) validated some of these findings in a study of "burnout" in a small sample of Antisocial Personality Disordered males ($N = 39$). They found that one third of their cohort, probably psychopaths, did not remit their criminal activity as they aged. Although the authors did not use the Hare measure of psychopathy, about 30 percent of incarcerated APD males would be expected to be primary psychopaths.

The nature of the psychopath's violent behavior is also consistent with his callous, remorseless, and unempathic attitude toward his victims. I theorized (Meloy 1988a) that the psychopath was psychobiologically predisposed to predatory violence, a mode of aggression which is planned, purposeful, and emotionless. My formulations were based upon clinical experience and a model of aggression–predatory versus affective–developed by Flynn and his colleagues (Flynn 1967, Flynn and Bandler 1975). Other research has empirically supported these hypotheses. Williamson and colleagues (1987) compared the criminal histories of fifty-five psychopaths and forty-six nonpsychopaths. They found that psychopaths committed more serious violent assaults and property crimes, although the nonpsychopaths committed more murders. The psychopaths' actions were significantly more often motivated by material gain, whereas the nonpsychopaths' acts were significantly more often due to strong emotional arousal. The psychopaths' victims were generally stranger males, the nonpsychopaths' victims were mostly female family members or friends. Williamson and colleagues (1987) concluded, ". . . [the psychopathic group] violence was callous and coldblooded or part of an aggressive display, without the affective colouring or understandable motives that accompanied [the nonpsychopathic group] violence. These results are consistent with the view that the psychopath's violent and aggressive behavior is frequently associated with proto-emotions and relatively weak inhibitory restraints" (p. 460).

Our Rorschach findings (Gacono and Meloy 1991) lend further understanding to the planned and purposeful use of violence by psychopaths. Despite the unmodulated nature of their affects (FC: CF + C = 1:2.5), their stress tolerance and controls are normal (D = 0, AdjD = 0). These findings are consistent with the psychopath's inclination to *intentionally* use his affects in a raw, unmodulated manner to control the objects in his environment. Impulse control is rarely the clinical and forensic issue in primary psychopathy. The more relevant question is the motivation of the psychopath to engage in predatory violence, or to use his affects in a proto-emotional display.

The omnipotent control of others through the intentional use of affects may also gratify the psychopath's sadism. In one study (Meloy and Gacono 1992a) we found that psychopaths produced significantly more Sadomasochism (SM) responses to the Rorschach than nonpsychopaths. In fact, 41 percent of the psychopathic subjects produced at least one SM response in their record, defined as "any response in which devalued, aggressive, or morbid content is accompanied by pleasurable affect expressed by the subject" (p. 107). Although psychological measures of sadism are extremely limited (R. Prentky, personal communication, August 18, 1991), the SM response may be a specific indicator of this deeply endogenous character trait. Its sensitivity and reliability, however, remain open to further research.

Subtle intrapsychic measures of sadism, such as the SM response, may or may not be expressed in generally cruel or sexually sadistic behavior toward others. Such behavior, however, does appear to be consistent with antisocial behavior and psychopathy (DSM-III-R 1987, Meloy 1988a, Shapiro 1981). Dietz and colleagues (1990) studied a small sample (N = 30) of sexually sadistic criminals and found they all had histories of other antisocial behavior in adulthood. Nearly half their sample (43.3%) were either physically or sexually abused as children. Other notable behaviors included incestuous involvement with their children (30%); known homosexual experience (43.3%); cross-dressing (20%); shared sexual partners (20%); known history of peeping, obscene telephoning, or exhibitionism (20%); nonalcoholic drug abuse (50%); a history of suicide attempt (13.3%); unnecessary automobile driving (40%); and fascination with police (30%). They were also avid collectors of pornography (53%), guns (37%), bondage paraphernalia (27%), and detective magazines (23%).

The offense characteristics of this sample of sexually sadistic criminals included use of an assistant (36.7%), careful planning (93.3%), impersonation of police (23.3%), abduction of the victim to a preselected location (76.7%), captivity for more than 24 hours (60%), and binding of the victim (86.7%). The most frequent assaults were anal rape (73.3%), coerced fellatio (70%), and vaginal rape (56.7%). During the offense, 86.6 percent of the offenders were unemotional and detached and 43.3 percent experienced sexual dysfunction at that time. The majority murdered their victims (73.3%), concealed the corpse (66.6%), and recorded the offense (53.3%) through the use of writings, drawings, photographs, audiotapes, or videotapes. Most of the victims died of strangulation (58.4%).

The most likely victims of these sexually sadistic criminals were stranger adult females[1] of the same race as the offender. In only 17 percent of the cases did the victims appear to have a psychological resemblance to someone in the offender's personal life. This does not preclude, however, the existence of an idealized object in fantasy that may be used to establish a "goodness of fit" (Meloy 1988a) with a potential victim. In virtually all cases of sexual sadism, including sexual homicide, rehearsal fantasy is a prerequisite (Dietz et al. 1990, Meloy 1988a, Prentky et al. 1989, Ressler et al. 1988). This is a method of mentally practicing the act itself, usually with some grandiose elaboration, that psychodynamically fuels the pathological narcissism of the offender and disinhibits the actual predatory behavior. Rehearsal fantasy may be identified on the Rorschach through the use of the $Ma < Mp$ ratio in the Comprehensive System (Exner 1986, Meloy and Gacono 1992b).

One of the most striking findings within the study by Dietz and colleagues (1990) was the failure of mental health clinicians to identify the sexual sadism prior to the first offense, and the ineffectiveness of subsequent clinical contact. It appears that clinicians will often make one of two fundamental mistakes when sexual sadism is clinically encountered: they will minimize or deny this socially dangerous behavior, or they will use psychotherapeutic techniques that inadvertently *stimulate* the sexual sadism.[2] In both cases the motivation may

---

1. Note that the selection of females as victims is the opposite of what is generally predicted among psychopaths in general. This may distinguish the psychopathic character who is sexually sadistic from the psychopathic character whose aggression is nonsexual and generalized. The channeling of sexual sadism may also be enhanced by certain misogynistic beliefs. One sexual murderer that I evaluated resolutely believed that women preferred forced sex, a particularly grievous version of the endemic male attitude that "no means yes" when it comes to female sexual behavior.

2. Dietz and colleagues (1990) noted the psychologist who asked the offender to write out his most bizarre fantasies as part of psychotherapy. The offender wrote detailed accounts of his actual crimes, but the psychologist did not recognize these as memories, only fantasies. We studied the case of a psychotic and sexually sadistic criminal (Meloy and Gacono 1992b) whose psychiatrist was aware that he was stabbing a pillow with a carving knife and having homicidal and sadistic fantasies several months prior to an actual attempted rape and murder. The psychiatrist

be the known absence of any effective mental health treatment for sexual sadism and the clinician's desire to minimize his own anxiety concerning this fact.

The quality, intensity, and directionality of intrapsychic aggression in psychopaths has been idiographically studied through the use of the Rorschach (Meloy and Gacono 1992a). Psychopaths relate to others on the basis of power rather than affection. These power gradients are often expressed in Rorschach responses that minimize affectional relating, and maximize the prey–predator dynamic. This is a Rorschach response of a 32-year-old Caucasian male incarcerated for the rape and murder of a stranger adult female 5 years earlier:

> *Card X:* "I have a busy one here. Ever hear of Frank Stella? I think he did this. Two little alien creatures who have caught a larger creature for game. Who are being threatened to have their catch taken away from them by crablike creatures, real predators. On the hunting trip. I feel like a voyeur. Crab creatures offed them, not knowing their buddy had ate it. They don't know these crab creatures are going to lop their heads off [subject laughs]. That's a Rorschach original." [Meloy and Gacono 1992a, p. 110]

This response is consistent with an intrapsychic world in which relationships are defined by threat and counterthreat, prey–predator pursuit, and power gradients. His identifications shift between "little creatures" and "real predators," and there is both a detached ("voyeur") and grandiose ("a Rorschach original") quality to the response process. There is also a paranoid dimension to this response, as aggression happens to those who don't expect it, the innocents who were once predators: the victimizers as victims. The primary psychopath will often perceive the world as populated with malevolent objects, a product of his own projections and projective identifications. This individual had a sexual assault history before his crime, and rehearsed in fantasy the rape homicide for 2 weeks prior to finding an appropriate victim.

---

recalled that he thought it was a positive therapeutic behavior: a sort of gestalt "unavailable victim" technique.

Psychopathic subjects will often transpose benign and common percepts on the Rorschach into predatory objects. For example, "a butterfly with claws" (Card V), or "a whale with a shark fin" (Card IV). Both of these responses (scored Incongruous Combinations because they do not exist in reality, Exner 1986a) are consistent with the propensity of the psychopathic individual to identify with the aggressor, perhaps an actual parent who was sadistic or neglectful. They also evoke the primary identification of the psychopath with the "stranger selfobject" (Grotstein 1982), a preconceived fantasy that helps anticipate the presence of the predator in the external world, or the prey the psychopath will eventually attack (Meloy 1988a). In either case, these unusual Rorschach objects are detached and isolated from other percepts by virtue of their potential aggression, an interpersonal stance quite familiar to the psychopath.

Anxiety, Attachment, and Psychopathy

Laboratory evidence has generally supported the view that psychopaths do not experience anxiety or worry to the degree that nonpsychopaths do (Hare and Schalling 1978, Ogloff and Wong 1990). Self-report measures of anxiety, such as the State Trait Anxiety Inventory and the Eysenck Personality Questionnaire, indicate a robust negative correlation between Factor 1 (aggressive narcissism) and anxiety (Hare 1991). There is no significant relationship between PCL-R ratings and the Minnesota Multiphasic Personality Inventory (MMPI) Pt scale (−.08) and the Millon Clinical Multiaxial Inventory (MCMI-II) Anxiety scale (−.16) (Hare 1991).

Projective measures of anxiety indicate that psychopathic criminals are significantly less anxious than nonpsychopathic criminals, even when stress tolerance and controls are the same (Gacono and Meloy 1991). This finding appears to be one product of the defensive grandiosity that is maintained by the psychopath through the devaluation of others (Gacono and Meloy 1992). When compared with male Borderline Personality Disordered *(DSM-III-R)* outpatients, psychopaths are also significantly less anxious, and whereas narcissistic

mirroring can serve as a defense against anxiety in both these populations, it is more likely to be used by psychopaths (Gacono et al. 1992).
Narcissistic Personality Disordered *(DSM-III-R)* outpatient males
also appear to be significantly more anxious than psychopaths, despite
the shared pathological narcissism between these two personality
disorders (Gacono et al. 1992).

Psychopathic criminals are significantly more detached than
nonpsychopathic criminals, and appear to have little capacity to form
affectional bonds with others (Gacono and Meloy 1991). When compared with both narcissistic (NPD) and borderline (BPD) outpatient
males, psychopaths are significantly less able to form attachments, a
regulatory function of the grandiose self structure which demands "a
scornful and detached devaluation of others" (Gacono et al. 1992, p. 46).
When attachment capacities are apparent, they are usually suffused
with ambivalence and aggression, perhaps the result of early experiences with an aggressive or sadistic parental object that have been
internalized.[3] Attachments may also occur to nonhuman, hard objects,
such as weapons, from which there is no threat of rejection and into
which grandiose self representations can be projected. The detachment of the psychopath appears to be chronic, and is apparent by
midadolescence (Weber et al. 1992) in Conduct-Disordered *(DSM-III-
R)* inpatients.

Recent research concerning the neurohypophyseal peptide *oxytocin* may eventually contribute to further understanding of the
psychopath's inability to form emotional attachments. This hormone,
produced by the posterior pituitary gland, has been associated with
the induction of maternal behavior, grooming, male reproductive
behavior, female sexual receptivity, alterations in the separation calls

---

3. We have found Rorschach indices that suggest an affectional *hunger* and an
inordinate desire to bond in a few individuals who have committed sexual homicide.
This finding, although unexpected, is combined with indices of anger, dysphoria, and
pathological narcissism. Such inherent conflict may explain the psychodynamics
during the actual sexual homicide itself: the commingling of affectional hunger, rage,
entitlement, and eroticism, resulting in death of the victim and the affective restora-
tion of a defensive grandiosity.

of infants, and species-typical patterns of social affiliation (Insel et al. 1991). In one study, central administration of oxytocin increased the sexual and aggressive behavior of dominant male squirrel monkeys, and increased the associative and marking behavior in subordinate monkeys (Winslow and Insel 1991). It also appears to mimic social contact in infant rats (Insel and Winslow 1991). The attachment disorders of psychopathy, including both chronic detachment and the affectional hunger and rage of sexual aggression, may be mediated by the receptor distribution of this peptide.[4]

If there is a biological basis for this absence of anxiety and attachment, it is probably rooted in the chronic cortical underarousal or, specifically, the peripheral autonomic hyporeactivity to aversive stimuli, apparent in psychopathy (for a review of this literature, see Meloy 1988a). Attachment behavior in the infant is reinforced when anxiety is felt in the absence of the object, and anxiety dissipates when the object is in close proximity. A defect or dysfunction in the limbic portion of the central nervous system, however, could eliminate anxiety as a motivational factor in proximity seeking toward the object, thus negating the possibility of attachment patterns being established throughout childhood. Autonomic hyporeactivity, a lack of anxiety, and emotional detachment form a useful biopsychosocial construct that deserves further research; it may be a major pathogenic basis for psychopathy.

Foreman (1988) used the Interpersonal Adjective Scales (Wiggins 1979) to measure the characteristic mode of interpersonal behavior in a sample of incarcerated prisoners. The dimension of Love (Warmhearted–Coldhearted) was found to correlate negatively with ratings of psychopathy, and the dimension of Dominance (Dominant–Submissive) correlated positively with ratings of psychopathy. His study lends further construct validity to the hypothesis that psychopaths are emotionally detached from others and prefer to relate on the basis of power rather than affection.

---

4. I would like to thank Mark T. Erickson, M.D., for introducing me to this literature.

Narcissism, Hysteria, and Psychopathy

Factor 1 of the PCL-R, aggressive narcissism, has also been called a "selfish, callous, and remorseless use of others" (Harpur et al. 1988, p. 745). It is distinguished from the pathological narcissism of other disorders, such as narcissistic personality disorder, by the *actual* devaluation of others to maintain the grandiose self structure; this contrasts with the *fantasized* devaluation of others that maintains the grandiose equilibrium in other narcissistic pathologies. The psychopath uses a malignant, rather than a benign, mode of narcissistic repair (Kernberg 1975, 1984) to manage the vulnerable aspects of his pseudo-autonomous self-concept; this is observed in rage reactions when he does not get what he believes he is entitled to receive (Gacono and Meloy 1988).

Psychopathic criminals are significantly more narcissistic and self-absorbed than nonpsychopathic criminals (Gacono et al. 1990). This is often clinically expressed through self-aggrandizement and the omnipotent control of others. This latter mechanism is not only an intrapsychic defense against persecutory introjects, but also an interpersonal maneuver, based upon fantasy, that both denigrates others and renders them available as prey.[5] Omnipotent control also serves the more rudimentary defense of projective identification, wherein the psychopath will split off a bad or good aspect of the self (the psychopath may more readily identify with badness), project it into the object, and then render it helpless through control. The narcissism of the psychopath also appears to be quite primitive, suffused with both merging and mirroring wishes that are inherently contradictory (Gacono 1990): a metaphorical mirror shattered by the symbiotic wish to be one with it.

When compared with NPD males, psychopathic males are just as

---

5. The visual stare of the psychopath has been elaborated elsewhere (Meloy 1988a). The unconscious fantasy of the psychopath during the stare is to freeze the prey with his omnipotence as a prelude to his attack and incorporation, or eating. One female psychotherapy patient, married to a psychopath, described the necessity of letting her husband "eat a chunk of me" every now and then to maintain calm in the marriage.

pathologically narcissistic and self-absorbed (Gacono et al. 1992). The NPDs, as noted earlier, have significantly greater capacities for attachment and anxiety, and also use the adaptive defense of idealization more readily. In psychopaths, "entitlement may negate the possibility of idealization, as it inherently suggests an expectation to be served by, rather than idealize, the object" (Gacono et al. 1992, p. 45). The grandiose self-structure of psychopaths and NPDs is not apparent in male BPD outpatients, rendering them more anxious and dependent, but also more amenable to treatment (Gacono et al. 1992).

Hysteria has been linked to psychopathy for a century in the scientific literature (Meloy 1988a). The PCL-R identifies several traits that are consistent with hysterical character: glibness/superficial charm (1), need for stimulation/proneness to boredom (3), shallow affect (7), and promiscuous sexual behavior (11). Horowitz (1991) delineated eight core descriptors of the hysteric: aggressive behavior, emotionality, sexual problems, obstinacy, exhibitionism, egocentricity, sexual provocativeness, and dependency.

Projective data consistent with hysterical traits in psychopathic subjects are found in linkages between affect and cognition. A notable characteristic seems to be the use of rapid and diffuse symbolization to manage affect (Gacono et al. 1990), but this finding is more frequent in BPDs (Gacono et al. 1992) than in psychopaths. It is clearly not specific to psychopathy, but may be characteristic of borderline personality organization, a level of personality shared by both psychopaths and BPDs (Kernberg 1984). Other intrapsychic aspects of antisocial personality that are consistent with hysterical traits (Horowitz 1991) are unmodulated affect, sexual preoccupation, self-absorption, and aggressive expectations of others (Gacono and Meloy 1992).

Shapiro (1965) termed the hysterical cognitive style *impressionistic:* "global, relatively diffuse, and lacking in sharpness, particularly in sharp detail" (p. 111). He also noted three other aspects of hysterical cognition: an incapacity for intellectual concentration, distractibility, and a nonfactual world of thought. Although research concerning psychopathic cognition related to these variables has yet to be done, there is evidence that psychopaths are inclined toward tangential and circumstantial thought, usually in the service of self-aggrandizement

(Gacono and Meloy 1992). In other words, they are distracted and impressed by their own grandiose self-representations, a dynamic pattern of thought disorder that may be consistent with hysterical cognition.

Psychological Defenses and Psychopathy

Hare (1991) noted the defenses of projection and rationalization as ubiquitous in psychopathy, and used them to define the characteristics of PCL-R Item 16, failure to accept responsibility for actions. Our research indicates that the most frequently used defenses in psychopathy are devaluation and massive denial, followed in descending order by projective identification, omnipotence, and splitting (Gacono and Meloy 1992). These defenses are corollaries of both borderline personality organization (Kernberg 1984) and the paranoid-schizoid position (Klein 1946) and suggest the use of manic controls to ward off persecutory anxieties that threaten the self. Such research validates the premise that psychopaths are preoedipally organized and have not, by definition, moved to the depressive position whereby feelings and fantasies are organized around anxiety at the loss of the love object.

Idealization and other higher level defenses, such as rationalization, intellectualization, isolation, and repression, are virtually absent in psychopathy. When idealization is used, it often suggests self-idealization or the enhancement of "hard objects," often the accouterments of power: weapons, money, material goods, or other individuals that have been deanimated into possessions. When borderline and narcissistic males are compared with psychopathic males, the defensive operations are similar, suggesting a common borderline personality organization with associated defenses (Gacono et al. 1992, Kernberg 1984). Psychopaths, however, produce significantly fewer idealization responses than the other groups, suggesting the adaptive nature of this defense as a stimulus for the nonpsychopathic patient's hope and a positive treatment indicator. Psychopaths will manipulate and destroy hope to ward off their own feelings of envy toward the goodness perceived in others. Envy is a primary constitutional feeling and central to the affective regulation of the psychopath, suggestive of oral sadistic and anal sadistic destructive impulses (Klein 1957). It is the feeling that goodness lies outside the self, and is only mitigated by love and gratitude. The latter is dependent upon trust of the object, and is an emotional prelude to generosity, the sense of internal value, and the wish to share (Stein 1990). Psychopathic character, however, precludes the use of love and gratitude to ameliorate envy because object constancy has not been attained, the depressive position is developmentally unavailable, and the paranoid-schizoid position generally defines his internal world. He wards off envy through the destruction of goodness in others.

Primitive Object Relations and Psychopathy

The hypothesis that psychopaths were organized at a borderline level of personality (Meloy 1988a) was empirically tested in a series of studies (Gacono 1990, Gacono et al. 1992, Gacono and Meloy 1992). We used the Rorschach object relations categories of Kwawer (1980).

Gacono (1990) found that psychopaths had a significantly greater number ($p < .01$) of total primitive (borderline) object relations (ten Rorschach categories) than nonpsychopathic criminals. Every subject in the psychopathic criminal group ($N = 14$) produced at least one primitive object relation; this was not the case in the nonpsychopathic group ($N = 19$). In a study with additional subjects, these findings were further validated, with psychopaths producing significantly more narcissistic mirroring, boundary disturbance, and total primitive object relations than nonpsychopaths (Gacono and Meloy 1992).

When psychopaths were compared with samples of nonpsychopathic criminals, NPD outpatients, and BPD outpatients, the psychopathic and borderline subjects produced virtually the same total primitive (borderline) object relations categories, and significantly more than the nonpsychopathic criminals and NPD patients ($p = .0001$) (Gacono et al. 1992):

[Psychopaths] present a malevolent, destructive internalized object world characterized by intense and violent intrapsychic conflict surrounding attachment and separation. . . . The presence of both symbiotic merging and narcissistic mirroring in [psychopaths] suggests an inherently conflicted need to both join, and be perfectly reflected by, the primary object: a logical impossibility, but an apparent psychological desire. [p. 46]

These empirically based findings shed light on a contradiction that I will formulate as a question: If psychopaths are so emotionally detached, why must they continually aggress against other people in such hurtful and destructive ways? The inherently contradictory merging and mirroring wishes within their primitive object relations, consistent with their boundary difficulties (and marginal reality testing; see Gacono and Meloy 1991) may drive their typical interpersonal behavior: narcissistic pseudo-autonomy and indifference toward others punctuated by violent forays into society.[6]

The BPD patients presented object relations similar to the psychopaths, but with a greater amount of unsublimated aggression and libidinal drive material bound by relationship dependencies. The borderline patients appeared to experience their aggressive impulses/introjects as ego-dystonic, whereas the psychopaths experienced their aggressive impulses/identifications as ego-syntonic (Gacono et al. 1992). The psychopaths did not *relate to* the internalized object (introject) created by their aggression as separate from "I," but experienced the internalized object (identification) created by their aggression as a part of "I" (Meloy 1985, 1988a). Borderline patients do not have the benefit of a regulating grandiose self-structure in which real self, ideal self, and ideal objects are conceptually fused in an identification with the aggressor (Meloy 1988a, A. Freud 1936).

Narcissistic personality disordered patients evidenced mirroring

---

6. The childhood and adolescent behavior of the sexual murderer sample of Ressler and colleagues (1988) is an extreme example: isolative immersion into sexually violent fantasy most of the time, and various antisocial and aggressive acts toward peers, animals, and property at other times. The Jeffrey Dahmer case in Milwaukee in 1991 was consistent with these findings.

object relations almost identical to psychopaths, which is consistent with their grandiose self structure as theorized by Kernberg (1984). Unlike the psychopaths, the NPD sample did not evidence the intrapsychic residue of being aggressed against, seen in their significantly less total primitive object relations and less frequent symbiotic merging, violent symbiosis and reunion, and boundary disturbance responses.

Antisocial personality disordered (APD) males *(DSM-III-R)*, of whom roughly one third will be psychopaths according to the PCL-R, also perceive less whole human, and more part human, objects on the Rorschach than do normal males (Exner 1991, Gacono and Meloy 1991). This may be clinically significant in understanding the inner representational world of this character pathology, if it is assumed that such Rorschach perceptions are analogous to the regressive structuralization of part objects rather than whole objects (Lerner and Lerner 1988).

Affect and Psychopathy

The emotionality of the psychopath, and its expression through affects, lacks the subtlety, depth, and relatedness to others that one would expect in normals. Most of the time, his behavior will convey a profound emotional detachment from others, interspersed with displays of affect that are "dramatic, shallow, and short-lived" (see Item 7 of the PCL-R). I hypothesized (Meloy 1988a) that these emotional traits were due to the "intensely narcissistic hues" (p. 113) that developmentally color psychopathic character. In other words, the psychopath lives in a *presocialized* emotional world, where feelings are experienced not in relation to others, but only in relation to the self. It is an emotional stage that is consistent, to some degree, with the toddler prior to reciprocal interaction with his peers, and is dominated by feelings of anger, exhilaration and contempt, and boredom.

The etiology of this emotional abnormality is unknown, but certainly involves the limbic portion of the brain, the biological seat of emotional relatedness, through early conditioning paradigms, genetic dysfunction, or their interaction. Autonomic and central nervous system underarousal as a causal factor in criminality may provide the biological substrate for the paucity of development of socialized emotions. Raine and colleagues (1990) conducted a prospective study of 101 15-year-old male schoolchildren to see if resting heart rate levels (HRL), skin conductance activity (SC), and electroencephalographic (EEG) profiles would be related to criminality 10 years later. They found that the children who engaged in criminal behavior had significantly lower HRLs, lower nonspecific SC responses, and a more underaroused EEG than did the noncriminal children who had grown up. Differences were not mediated by social, demographic, and academic factors. This is the first prospective study to find evidence for underarousal in all three response systems, which appears to be one cause in the development of criminal behavior (Raine and Dunkin 1990). Their study, moreover, is further validation of an extensive body of research that confirms the chronic cortical underarousal and peripheral autonomic hyporeactivity in psychopathy (Meloy 1988a).

Affective dysfunction has also been supported by several studies that found that the emotional meaning of words was not understood by psychopaths (Hare et al. 1988, Williamson et al. 1990). Psychopaths make less use of connotation (affective meaning) in grouping words than do nonpsychopaths. They also fail to show normal behavioral differentiation, measured by reaction time; and electrocortical differentiation, measured by event-related brain potentials (ERPs), when presented with emotional and neutral words (Williamson et al. 1990).

Patrick and Lang (1989) also found that psychopathic sex offenders were different from nonpsychopathic sex offenders in three related areas: the psychopaths had smaller autonomic responses when fearful visual imagery was presented; they failed to show a normal reduction in the eye blink reflex to a sudden noise when viewing affectively charged slides; and they also showed less appropriate facial muscle responses to slides with negative content.

Although we have not yet studied differences between psychopaths and nonpsychopaths on Rorschach measures of affect, certain findings in our Antisocial Personality Disordered sample ($N = 60$) of incarcerated males (about one third of whom are psychopaths) are instructive. When compared with nonpatient adult males (Exner 1991), APD males, as noted earlier, do not modulate affect well. In fact, their modulation of emotion is developmentally comparable to that of a 7-year-old (Exner 1991, Gacono and Meloy 1991), and they are prone to the unrestrained ventilation of feelings. They also tend to be highly defended against their own conscious experience of emotion and avoid emotionality in others.

APD males' emotions play an inconsistent role in thinking, decision making, and problem solving. At times thinking may be strongly influenced by feeling; at other times emotions play a very peripheral role. The early developmental nature of the antisocial individual's affective life finds further support in the frequent confusion about the nature and quality of emotions. An unconscious sense of being emotionally damaged or injured and a chronic anger toward others, present in the majority of APD males, are developmentally abnormal at any age.

Intelligence and Psychopathy

There is a pervasive public belief that psychopaths are more intelligent than average. This is not true. In fact, there appears to be no correlation between standardized measures of intelligence and psychopathy.

Hare (1991) reported that one study found a noncorrelation of $-.05$ when PCL total scores were compared with full-scale IQs on the Wechsler Adult Intelligence Scale–Revised (WAIS-R) or Revised Beta Examination, two widely used measures of intelligence. Kosson and colleagues (1990) also found no correlation in both black and white male inmates between Shipley-Hartford IQ scores and PCL scores, and Hare (1991) reported that a dozen or so studies have found the same lack of relationship.

It appears that intelligence is independent of psychopathy and probably is normally distributed among psychopathic individuals. This would mean that most psychopaths have average intelligence, and that some are either below average or above average. If the distribution is normal, the estimate would be that 2 to 3 percent of psychopaths would be either mentally retarded (IQ < 70) or very superior (IQ > 130) on standardized measures of intelligence. I noted (Meloy 1988a) extremely high or low IQ in psychopathy as one of five factors that would contraindicate treatment efforts.

THOSE WHO LOVE THE PSYCHOPATH

Although there are probably many social and economic reasons why certain people will maintain relationships with psychopaths, my primary interest is to understand those that voluntarily form an intense *attachment* to this detached and aggressive individual. On the face of it, such a relationship is *unreasonable*, yet it may endure despite attempts by others to dissuade the individual from his or her dangerous liaison.

The voluntariness of such a relationship is important and complex. I am purposefully excluding from my discussion those individuals who consciously wish to leave or end a relationship but are being coerced to stay through overt threat. Such threats may involve violence, and the continued unpredictability of violence, toward self or children; sudden loss of familial support; or catastrophic loss of economic support. Much of the research literature in this area has focused on spousal battering and, on occasion, the female's homicidal response to such behavior (Browne 1987, Ewing 1987). Social psychological factors that promote battered woman syndrome continue to be investigated, although not, to my knowledge, in the specific context of psychopathy.

For those that freely stay in such relationships, and perhaps seek them out, the voluntariness may also be an illusion. Choice may be consciously argued and rationalized, but for those observers with a modicum of psychological training, there seem to be certain *unconscious* motivations, wishes, feelings, or defenses that compel the relationship; or, at least, raise questions concerning the actual free will being exercised.

The second quote at the beginning of this chapter is instructive. Ms. Lee, a 23-year-old unemployed mother of two, has visited Richard Ramirez regularly, and they have recently been discussing marriage. She also reportedly said, "What counts for me is that he's really nice to me."[7] An obvious inference from her direct quotes is that Ms. Lee either consciously suppresses, or unconsciously denies, the fact that Richard Ramirez was convicted in Los Angeles in 1989 of thirteen murders and thirty other felonies, including attempted murder, rape, and sodomy, and was sentenced to death; at the time of her visitations he was beginning trial in San Francisco on another killing and injury of a couple. In her mind, his criminality and violence may only be imaginative, because she has never experienced it. Yet there is no concern, perhaps a *la belle indifférence*, that she ever would.

On the other hand, she may have lied to the reporter and actually be titillated by Ramirez's potential for murder, his extreme forms of violent sexual perversion (Ramirez raped and mutilated several of his victims), and his infamy, with which she can narcissistically identify. I think it is highly unlikely she would visit Ramirez if he were a publicly unknown murderer.

The first inference suggests histrionic pathology, the second inference suggests narcissistic pathology, and both are shadowed by a certain sadomasochism that, as yet, remains inchoate. Ms. Lee's visits to the San Francisco jail may be voluntary in the sense that she can choose to go or stay home on any given day; but her psychodynamics, probably unconscious, may compel her to embrace the psychopath as love object. This is the focus of my investigation.

One final note: I am well aware of the controversy surrounding the causative factors of battered woman syndrome. Whether it is predominantly character pathology on the part of the woman (and more importantly, the man), or whether it is mostly situational, social, and economic (Walus-Wigle and Meloy 1988), probably depends on the particular case, with multiple causes likely. This appears to be an ideological debate between feminist social psychologists and psycho-

---

7. Information and quotes concerning Ms. Lee are taken from *USA Today*, July 31, 1991, p. 2A.

analysts, with few empirical studies designed to answer some of the more provocative questions. For instance, there has yet to be a study comparing the psychometric characteristics of a sample of battered women and nonbattered women *prior to* the history of battering, and then *subsequent to* the battering episodes. This would provide the data to ferret out trait versus state aspects of the evident psychopathology of the victim, although it still would not address the traumagenic aspects of the woman's childhood, if any. This is important prospective research that is difficult but possible.

Nevertheless, it is my opinion that personality or character traits should never be excluded from such investigations, even those that focus on social and situational variables. This is sacrificing behavioral science for ideological purity. Battered woman syndrome, as one form of violent relationship (not necessarily attachment), is most likely a product of both psychological and social factors, with perhaps certain biologically rooted personality predispositions. In this chapter the gender focus on females is for two simple reasons: first, most psychopaths are males; and second, most intimate, enduring, and sexualized attachments are between males and females.

COMPLEMENTARY AND CONCORDANT IDENTIFICATIONS

The model that I have found most useful in my study of the psychopath as love object is one derived from Heinrich Racker, head of the Institute of Psychoanalysis in Argentina, who died an untimely death at the age of 50. Racker (1968) delineated two kinds of identifications in his understanding of countertransference in the analytic situation. On the one hand, *concordant identifications* (or homologous identifications) were formed when the analyst empathized and identified with each corresponding part of his patient's personality, "accepting these identifications in his consciousness" (Racker 1968, p. 134). This was the result of the analyst's predisposition "to identify oneself with the analysand, which is the basis of comprehension" (p. 134). Such identifications would be considered ego-syntonic, and the same as the patient's conscious experience of self.

On the other hand, *complementary identifications*—what Deutsch (1926) called complementary attitudes—were formed when the analyst identified with the patient's internal objects. These identifications are often the opposite of what is consciously felt to be a part of the self by the patient (that is, ego-dystonic), but nevertheless may recapitulate a relationship to an early actual object that has now been internalized. For instance, the analyst might portray a characteristic of the biological parent, such as passive and submissive, and the patient might consciously behave in an active and dominant manner. Intrapsychically, the analyst has identified with the passive parental introject of the patient that has been projected onto the analyst.

Racker noted (1968) that these two forms of identifications can coexist, and their destiny is closely connected. The degree to which the analyst fails in the concordant identifications will intensify certain complementary identifications.

> It is clear that rejection of a part or tendency in the analyst himself—his aggressiveness, for instance—may lead to a rejection of the patient's aggressiveness (whereby this concordant identification fails) and that such a situation leads to a greater complementary identification with the patient's rejecting object, towards which this aggressive impulse is directed. [p. 135]

Both identifications are carried by way of introjection and projection, "the resonance of the exterior in the interior" (p. 134). Racker did not address the role of projective identification in this process, despite other references to Melanie Klein, even though the defense seems applicable, if not necessary. Hamilton (1990) persuasively argued for an understanding of the analyst's projective identification as a therapeutic vehicle that conveys to the patient "both the transformed, original projection from the patient and an aspect of the analyst's self—the containing aspect of the analyst, the analyzing function itself—which he wishes, however benignly and gently, to insinuate into the patient so as to influence him" (p. 446).

Hamilton went on to conclude that all interpretations have an element of containing, and therefore of projective identification. In the Racker model, such interventions would transform, modulate, give meaning to, and return to the patient aspects of himself that were experienced by the analyst as complementary or concordant counter-transference reactions, depending on their origin in the mind of the patient. Racker also noted that countertransference understanding at the time of his writing was generally limited to only complementary identifications.

If this model is taken out of the therapeutic context and applied to the subject at hand, a certain symmetry of characterological inter-action emerges. Table 4-2 lists the complementary and concordant identifications that would be expected in the individual who forms an enduring attachment to the psychopath. The complementary identifications are generally opposite in nature to the psychopath's conscious experience of himself, yet they *complete* his interpersonal pathology. For example, the conscious and overt sadism of the psychopath necessitates the masochistic submission of the object, and the actual search for a person who will suffer at his hands. Likewise, the masochistic individual may find in the psychopath a person who will act out her own unconscious sadism, allowing this aspect of herself to remain out of awareness, yet gratified.

The concordant identifications are similar in nature to the psychopath's conscious experience of himself, and generally shore up his grandiosity. Instead of being a *reflection* of the psychopathic character, as the complementary identifications are, the concordant identifications are an *extension* of his character. In the person who forms the attachment to the psychopath, however, these concordant identi-

Table 4-2.

Complementary and Concordant Identifications with the Psychopathic Character as Love Object.

Complementary	Concordant
Masochistic	Sadistic
Hysterical	Psychopathic

fications will usually be unconscious and not recognized as an aspect of the self.

I have chosen four words – masochistic, hysterical, sadistic, and psychopathic – to describe these identifications. I am using these terms, which unfortunately are pregnant with a variety of meanings, to describe both interpersonal behavior and intrapsychic structure and function. "Identifications" in this sense may be manifest in certain observable activity, or used to infer a predictable self–object dyad with associated affective components. I will attempt, moreover, to abide by my earlier understanding of the term: "the nascent self representation becoming like the perceived object" (Meloy 1988a, p. 45). This is similar to Schafer's (1968) definition of identification as the modification of the self or behavior to increase resemblance to the object.

MASOCHISTIC IDENTIFICATION

The first, and probably most common, complementary identification with the psychopath is masochistic. It is apparent in the behavior of the individual who appears to seek and derive pleasure from suffering at the behest of the psychopath. This pleasure is usually sexualized, and is more than just a "self-defeating" attitude (Schafer 1988). The masochistic attitude fits the characterological sadism of the primary psychopath the way a glove fits the hand. It gratifies his continual wish to devalue, control, and injure objects that are perceived as good, and consequently a threat to the bad (in some cases, evil) identifications that are conscious for the psychopath. Masochism demonstrates the primacy of object seeking, or attachment, over pleasure seeking.

The term *masochism* was coined by Krafft-Ebing (1906) after he studied the novels of Leopold von Sacher-Masoch, most notably *Venus in Furs* (1870). He defined it as "the wish to suffer pain and be subjected to force, the idea of being completely and unconditionally subject to the will of a person of the opposite sex; of being treated by this person, as by a master, humiliated and abused" (1906, p. 131). Interestingly, he believed that the development of a masochistic perversion was biologically predisposed, the result of a psychopathic constitution, which drew upon the more general formulations of *psychopathic inferiority* popular in the German psychiatric community at the time (Koch 1891).

The major Freudian papers on masochism (Freud 1905, 1919, 1924) document his evolution of thought from the primacy of sadism in masochism to a *primary* masochism that accounts for the physiology of pleasure in pain. In his early work Freud postulated that sadism was a primary drive of the active self to master the object, and secondarily, masochism was aggression directed toward the passive self. In his seminal paper "A Child is Being Beaten" (1919), Freud elaborated upon a fantasy that he believed was central to masochism. Gleaned from a small sample of patients ($N = 6$), these beating fantasies crystallized during the oedipal period and had three phases: the fantasy of a rival being beaten by the father ("My father is beating the child whom I hate," p. 185); the unconscious fantasy of self being beaten by the father ("I am being beaten by my father," p. 185);[8] and the fantasy of others, usually unknown boys, being beaten by a teacher ("I am probably looking on," p. 186), which was highly sexually arousing.

This three-phase fantasy in female patients traces the guilt induced by the forbidden genital relation with the father, and the regressive substitute of a masochistic beating fantasy to assuage the guilt through punishment by the father. The fantasied act, moreover, is condensed with sexual love, which is anally expressed (beating of the buttocks).

In his final paper on masochism, Freud (1924) introduced the term *moral masochism* and placed it alongside feminine and erotogenic masochism, the latter being the genotypic "pleasure in pain" of all masochism. This moral type is distinguished because "the suffering itself is what matters; whether it is decreed by someone who is loved or by someone who is indifferent is of no importance" (p. 165). It is still

---

8. Freud noted that this was the most "momentous" of all phases, although it was never consciously remembered, and could only be reconstructed in analysis. It was, however, "accompanied by a high degree of pleasure" (1919, p. 185).

sexualized, but is more broadly construed as the ego's seeking of punishment by the superego. Masochism for Freud originated during the oedipal period and was primarily defensive, framed by his tripartite structural theory of the mind as superego against ego. He did no further theoretical exploring of its preoedipal aspects and the relation between overtly masochistic sexual behavior and masochistic character pathology.

Historically, writings since Freud have focused on the multidetermined and complex nature of masochistic phenomena, and the degree to which the term should remain closely allied to sexual arousal. Reich (1933) emphasized masochism as characterological armoring against early aggression stimulated by frustration and hurt in childhood, whereas Horney (1937) focused on the passive-to-active reversal of the child to repair his narcissistic wounds and injured omnipotence. Brenman (1952) emphasized the defenses of projection, denial, and reaction formation in masochism, and noted that his "giving becomes an aggressive, smothering attempt to control experienced by the object not as a gift but as an enslavement" (p. 273).

Menaker (1953) focused on the mother's earliest responses to the child and their effect upon his ego development. If hatred of the child predominated in the mother, later feelings of worthlessness would stimulate masochistic behavior by the child to defend against the fear of abandonment and preserve an idealized fantasy of being loved.

Bergler's (1961) main contribution to the masochism literature was his delineation of its relation to narcissism as an attempt to maintain infantile megalomania; he also probably went too far in believing that "psychic masochism" (p. 18) was the one basic neurosis acquired during infancy. Eidelberg's (1959) contribution to the dynamic relation between narcissism and masochism is also noteworthy.

Approaching the subject of masochism from an object relations perspective, Berliner (1940, 1942, 1947, 1958) shifted the origins of masochism onto the parents who treated the child in a cruel and sadistic manner. He viewed it as an adaptive mechanism to preserve the preoedipal oral object attachment, a defensive denial and erotization of suffering at the hands of the primary care-givers: "masochism means loving a person who gives hate and ill treatment" (1958, p. 40).

It was an object-seeking compromise formation that implied an identification with the aggressor. Rothstein (1984b) drew upon this notion
to discuss the overdetermined nature of fear in the masochistic
patient as a result of humiliation by the sadistic parent.

Loewenstein (1957) underscored Berliner's perspective and introduced the term *protomasochism* to describe preoedipal attempts
to seduce the aggressive parent to defend against loss of the love
object. He saw masochism as the "weapon of the weak" (p. 230), a
magical attempt to reverse hostile aggression into loving passivity
that would protect the child's security and sexuality. Valenstein's
(1973) contribution to an object relations theory of masochism addressed the preverbal attachment to pain as an affect that derived
from the early experience with the primary object. His important
formulations noted the equivalency of self and object representations
during infancy, and the degree to which the incipient self-concept is
dependent upon the object relation and its accompanying affects. If
attachment seeking requires the enduring of pain, then pain may
become an affective parameter that defines the notion of self. Valenstein's theorizing underscores a crucial point in our discussion: *Masochism indicates the dominance of attachment (object) seeking over
the pleasure principle.* This notion is consistent with Fairbairn's
(1963) belief that instincts were fundamentally object related rather
than pleasure related.

Contemporary theory and research concerning masochism per se
has been marked by its identification as a personality disorder de-
serving of further research in *DSM-III-R* (so-called Self Defeating
Personality Disorder); psychoanalytic studies of large samples of
masochistic children (Novick and Novick 1972, 1987, 1991); and the
publication of several edited volumes devoted to masochism in clinical
practice (Blum 1991, Glick and Meyers 1988, Montgomery and Greif
1989).

Novick and Novick's work is the largest and most detailed
psychoanalytic study of a sample of masochistic patients to date ($N =$
111 children in the 1972 study; an additional 11 children in the 1987
study; 41 children, adolescents, and adults in the 1991 study, 19 of
whom were new subjects). Their developmental theory of masochism

has focused on the elucidation of two types of beating fantasies, transitory and fixed; the development of masochism during toddlerhood, the phallic-oedipal stage, latency, and adolescence; and, most recently, the centrality of a delusion of omnipotence in masochism, resulting from the failure to achieve competent interactions with others.

In this delusion of omnipotence, safety, attachment, and omnipotent control are magically linked to pain. The content of the delusion is that "only they themselves [are] powerful enough to inhibit their omnipotent impulses, and then only by resorting to severe masochistic measures such as killing their feelings, provoking attack, or attempting to kill themselves" (1991, p. 311). Denial of pain is maintained through these omnipotent fantasies by turning pain into a sign of specialness and power. Yet this delusion as defense also becomes a source of pathological devaluation of real achievement later in life: success is due to omnipotence rather than real effort. Achievement also means destruction of others and thus compels the provocation of hurt. Novick and Novick's (1991) psychodynamic sequencing of this process has five phases: (1) the external source of pain is denied; (2) pain is transformed into a sign of attachment (how this occurs is a matter of speculation, but may be the result of classical conditioning and the biological shaping of certain neuronal pathways through repetitive learning); (3) pain is further transformed into a sign of specialness and power to destroy; (4) then into a sign of equality with the parents; (5) then into an omnipotent capacity to coerce others to gratify all wishes. This delusion functions as both a defense against rage and helplessness and a source of self-esteem.

Novick and Novick also wrote one of the clearest definitions of masochism in the literature: "Masochism is the active pursuit of psychic or physical pain, suffering, or humiliation in the service of adaptation, defense, and instinctual gratification at oral, anal, and phallic levels" (1987, p. 381).

Other contemporary contributions are also useful. Kernberg (1988) proposed a general classification of masochistic pathology and included self-defeating behaviors, depressive-masochistic personality disorder, sadomasochistic personality disorder, pathological infatuation, and masochistic sexual perversion. He emphasized that ego organization, object relations, superego development, narcissistic organization, and polymorphous infantile sexuality are codeterminants of masochistic pathology. Cooper (1988) attempted an integration of narcissistic and masochistic character as one and the same (see also Cooper 1981, Glenn 1981, Rosenfeld 1988). Gedo (1988) delineated the preverbal patterns of affects and the need of the masochistic patient to use the analyst as a source of symbiotic masochistic self-regulation. And Galenson (1988) discussed the advent of protomasochistic phenomena between 8 and 24 months when aggression was excessively stimulated by the environment (parents, physical illness, or noxious nonhuman stimuli).

Other authors have discussed sadomasochism (SM) in the context of sexual excitement (Coen 1988, Kernberg 1991), as a compromise formation involving narcissistic fantasies and depressive affect in neurosis (Rothstein 1991), as a perversion which attempts to destroy the reality of the paternal universe (Chasseguet-Smirgel 1991), and as a defense against the recall of painful affect (Blos 1991).

Katz (1990) analyzed masochism from an unusual angle and identified five masochistic paradoxes. These are listed in Table 4–3. Katz believed these five paradoxes represented both compromise formations and failures to compromise.

In summary, the contemporary psychoanalytic literature concerning masochism is extensive, although clinical studies are limited to single or multiple cases, with Novick and Novick's work being the laudable exception. Comparative, large-group studies of masochism

Table 4–3.

The Paradoxes of Masochism.

1.	Pleasure and success are a crime.
2.	Painful self-deprivation, alienation, and despair are noble and powerful.
3.	Pain is inherent in the quest for perfection.
4.	Submission, the bridge to attachment, leads to pain and hatred of the object.
5.	Pleasure evokes traumatic physical pain.

are generally found in the nonanalytic sadomasochism literature and will be reviewed in the next section.

Sugarman (1991) identified three shared beliefs in the psychoanalytic literature concerning masochism, to which I would add a fourth. First, specific masochistic phenomena should be differentiated from general, self-defeating behavior. Second, the phenomenon of masochism is highly complex. Third, masochism emerges from the oedipal stage as a resolution of certain conflicts, but protomasochistic forerunners at preoedipal stages of development are important and involve drives, defenses, superego elements, self and object representations, and early interpersonal relations. Fourth, sadism and masochism are inextricably bound and should be considered so in any clinical endeavor. Sugarman (1991) elegantly illustrated this last belief of mine in his psychoanalysis of a 3-year-old girl.

The complementary masochistic identification with the psych path includes a number of psychodynamics that have been tou upon in my brief review of the literature.

The Triumph of Omnipotence

By allowing herself to enter the primitive object relational orbit of the psychopath, the woman must submit to his omnipotent control. This is a defense of the psychopath that enhances his grandiosity (a pathological self-esteem formation) and wards off his persecutory objects. Submission to his omnipotent control, however, is transformed into the experience of *being* in control with him, and is the delusional triumph that turns passive into active, and helpless rage into grandiose exhilaration (Novick and Novick 1991).[9] When other objects are devalued by him, the couple's dyadic sadomasochistic bond is triangulated and becomes a repetitive oedipal triumph that is developmen-

---

9. Sadomasochistic sexual activity always includes the identification of a "top" (the sadist) and a "bottom" (the masochist). Paradoxically, the "bottom" is always in final control of the SM activity and orchestrates it with certain predetermined signals.

tally progressive, although quite pathological. Helpless rage is transformed into an oedipal (Electra) triumph that destroys the maternal object in fantasy. The price paid, however, is complete submission when third parties are unavailable as targets for devaluation.

The Acting Out of the Beating Fantasy

She who loves the psychopath may find his sexual aggression a source of unconscious gratification through the acting out of the beating fantasy. Ubiquitous in masochistic children (Novick and Novick 1987), the beating fantasy in this context is fixed, and is derived from disturbances in infancy. There was probably a reciprocal lack of pleasure between mother and child, and the pain seeking may represent a "substitute of withdrawal of cathexis from the mother" (1987, p. 359). There will usually be a layer of "unfused, primitive omnipotent aggression" (p. 364) that will eventually emerge in the analytic transference. Mothers of these women were probably both psychologically (through projection of blame) and physically intrusive, and the women as children felt as if their mothers completely controlled their bodies: subsequent rage was turned against the self.

One 42-year-old female patient, married to an economically successful psychopath, had a nonverbal "feeling" memory of her mother "grabbing" at her vagina when she was 6 to 8 months old. She would also masochistically submit to her husband's wishes, believing that she was controlling him through her acts, despite his oral aggression. He completely controlled her economically and assaulted her several times during the marriage. She lost the battle of autonomy for years, a recapitulation of her experience with mother, and only began to regain it through her divorce, an extremely painful mourning process because it meant the loss of a sadomasochistic internal object that was ambivalently cathected.

She no longer needed to be a helpless object to both her mother and ex-husband, but struggled with her own omnipotent fantasies and rage. These became projectively identified into the therapist once her masochistic defenses of denial and reaction formation began to change.

She also experienced her husband as metaphorically "biting" chunks out of her, a primitive, hypercathected mode of receptivity to the oral rage of her husband in his attempts to incorporate her–and perhaps stimulating in her an earlier oral fear of being [b]eaten by the predator.

Her affectional hunger, suffused with the expectation of aggression from the object of her attachment, was reflected in her abnormal number of tactile (T = 2) responses to the Rorschach, a somatosensory analog of early skin contact with the mother (Meloy 1988a). Her response to Card VI, for example, was "a furry bearskin that's been nailed to the wall." This response infers her pairing of tactile stimuli with aggression and masochistic submission, what we call an "aggressive past" response (Meloy and Gacono 1992a).

Painful Attachment as an Affect of Self-identification

Katz's (1990) fourth paradox captures another aspect of the woman's complementary masochistic identification with the psychopath: attachment to the psychopath is emotionally painful, and painful affect is an identifying quality of the concept of self. Kernberg (1976) noted the affect complexes that will surround object relations, and considered them "the basic organizing element bringing together into a common memory trace . . . the primitive perception of bodily states" (p. 63). Affects differentiate along with the various self–object representations and define the emotional quality of the perception, and later conception, of the self and others (Meloy 1985). If pain is a prerequisite of attachment to the primary object, which is the likely preverbal experience of the masochistic patient, then pain becomes a familiar affect that bathes the self and helps conceive it. The same patient I mentioned above said in one of her psychotherapy sessions, "Pain is so familiar to me. It's the emotion I've known. Other feelings frighten me, I don't know what they mean and what to expect."

The psychopath provides a relationship in which unpleasant,

painful emotion can be restimulated and experienced. His cruel behavior paradoxically reassures the woman that a bonded relationship
exists, and provides a real-world correlate of the self–object representational unit in which painful affect partially defines the self.

Devaluation as a Source of Continual Punishment

The woman in relationship with a psychopathic man will be the
continuous target of his devaluation. As one colleague said, "the
psychopath tarnishes his object world" (Don Viglione, PhD, personal
communication, March 3, 1991). Devaluation is a prominent defense in
psychopathic character, and unconsciously provides the psychological
support for the grandiose self structure (Gacono 1990, Meloy 1988a). It
also wards off feelings of envy by rendering objects unworthy of
regard. For the person who seeks continual punishment, the Freudian
notion of "moral masochism" (Freud 1924), the psychopath is the
perfect (in her eyes) source of gratification. The motivational aspects
for this behavior may vary from a neurotic sense of oedipal guilt to
more crude and primitive gratification of sadistic superego precursors
in the woman, directed against herself.

In one case, that of a 48-year-old woman divorcing a very successful corporate executive who was also psychopathic, this moral
masochism had two dimensions: first, she experienced profound guilt
that she had failed him as a wife; and for a number of years, until her
rage got the better of her, she blamed herself in a pattern consistent
with introjective depression for the failures of the marriage. Second,
her striving to fix the marriage despite his psychopathology was
imbued with her own grandiosity that she could. This narcissistic
quality, attached to her own masochism, helped maintain the idealized
fantasy that if enough suffering was endured, things would be perfect.
This, of course, never happened, and as the years went by, the
narcissistic fantasy took on a more desperate feature: she was the only
one that could endure his abuse, love him, and stay with him. Eventually he would recognize how wonderful she was.

Her husband was never physically cruel to her or to their

children, but over the course of a 15-year marriage, his psychopathy was evident in his psychological cruelty, open philandering with other women, and emotional detachment from the family. She also deluded herself into thinking that his profound indifference to her and her children's feelings was due to "men not being in touch with their emotions." This rationalization became more apparent to her when she delineated in psychotherapy the times when his deep rage and contempt for others was visible. What was missing for him was empathic relatedness toward others, not emotion in general.

This woman's psychological testing was instructive. Her MMPI was within normal limits, with a two-point codetype of 46 (T = 67). She showed a compulsive personality disorder on the MCMI-II. Her Rorschach was constricted (R = 14), and suggested a rigid individual who was affectively "shut down" and exhibited impaired reality testing (X-% = 21). She had the expectation of positive and cooperative relations (COP = 4), and a predominance of whole human objects in her inner representational world. These objects, however, were fantasy-based rather than reality-based (H = 2, [H] = 4). This woman's father, an alcoholic, deserted her mother when she was 8 years old. Although she had a normative amount of tactile response (T = 1) to the Rorschach, the response itself, to Card IV, captured her fear and ambivalence concerning affectional bonding to the male figure: "A monster, in a science fiction movie, grotesque with huge feet and tentacles. [Inquiry] A beady head, one eye, slimy, yucky hands, because he looks awful, lumbering, too big for his arms and hands, ominous and ugly, that's scary."

A Source of Danger for Sexual Masochism

For those women who are more regressed in their personality organization, the psychopath may represent a source of real danger that is exciting. This aspect of the complementary identification of masochism is most often evident in women who are organized at a borderline or psychotic level of personality, and are prone to engage in overt sadomasochistic sexual behavior with the psychopath. The excitement is usually erotically tinged and may be linked with the witnessing of violence. Often the predatory nature of the psychopathic character, clinically observed in his instinctual, threatening stare, will be experienced by this woman as bewitching and mesmerizing. She may feel caught by his look, and instead of reeling from it, is drawn to him in a magnetic manner. She may feel as if he represents her "object of destiny" (Grotstein 1980), a philosophical disavowal of personal choice that may gratify the masochistic wish to submit totally to the "dominatrix," and a negative image of the ego ideal. One sadomasochistic, and sometimes psychotic, woman who established a 4-month relationship with a serial murderer, described him as "her perfect partner." For a brief period of time she helped him murder and sexually assault prostitutes after death (this case is detailed in Chapter 8).

Kernberg (1988) noted that these forms of masochism are way beyond the "as if" or play-acting quality of sadomasochistic rituals at a neurotic level. Often this sadomasochism involves polymorphous, aggressive sexual activity in which multiple orifices are assaulted and perhaps even injured. There is a pregenital quality to this activity, and a background threat that the actual self may be annihilated through accidental death. Kernberg (1988) wrote that this regressed sexual masochism has five characteristics: strong and primitive aggressive impulses, severe object relations pathology, a predominance of preoedipal conflicts and aims that are sexually masochistic, a lack of integrated superego, and sexual identity confusion. There is a joint deterioration of differentiation between sexes and object relations (Chasseguet-Smirgel 1984) in these cases.

SADISTIC IDENTIFICATION

The second, concordant identification with the psychopath is sadistic. It is apparent in the behavior of the individual who attaches to the psychopath and seems to vicariously enjoy his sadism toward others. Yet there is no conscious recognition of this identification, and generally no overtly sadistic behavior is displayed by the loving object. The concordant identification is an extension of the character pathology of the psychopath, and the bond serves as both a source of gratification and a defense against the awareness of sadistic fantasy.

The sadistic concordant identification is the hidden polarity of the masochistic complementary identification. It provides the psychopath with an ally in cruelty who positively reinforces his sadistic acts through acquiescence or, in more obvious situations, openly contemptuous delight. She is a field of dreams for him, and her complementary and concordant identifications (masochism and sadism) may oscillate throughout the duration of their relationship. These intrapsychic shifts will be marked by her willingness, at times, to masochistically submit to his cruelty, and at other times to actively participate in, and enjoy, his pleasurable devaluation of others.

The term *sadism* has its etymological roots in the French word *sadisme*, which refers to the fictions of Donatien-Alphonse-François, Marquis de Sade (1740–1814). Krafft-Ebing (1906) popularized the term, and medically linked sexual arousal to the infliction of physical pain or suffering on the victim: "The association of lust and cruelty, which is indicated in the physiological consciousness, becomes strongly marked on a psychically degenerated basis" (p. 65). Schrenk-Notzing (1895) was the first to view sadism and masochism as paired opposites, and Eulenberg (1911) broadened the term to include emotional pain in the form of humiliation and degradation.

Early psychoanalytic papers concerning sadism explored its erotic aggression (Freud 1905); anal (Abraham 1923) and oral roots (Abraham 1925, Fairbairn 1936); biopsychical aspects (Bonaparte 1952); role in symptom formation (Gero 1962); presence in the projective tests of delinquent girls (Jackson 1949); relation to sexual violence (Bromberg 1951, Ophnijsen 1929); role in the psychology of hatred and cruelty (Stekel 1929); link to symbol formation and the ego (Klein 1930); relation to sadistic fantasy and early anxiety (Klein 1945); role in the evolution of culture (Roheim 1934); and presence in the delinquent behavior of very young children (Reiser 1963).

These historical papers document an evolution of the term from a purely sexual connotation to a more broadly construed usage that defined sadism as the experience of pleasure, whether erotic or not, through inflicting or witnessing another's physical or emotional pain. Shapiro (1981) categorized sexual sadism as a subtype of sadism: the former involving explicit sexual arousal, the latter only necessitating pleasure. Arndt (1991) cautioned that cruelty should not be equated with sadism, although sadism always involves cruelty. A clinical example would be the important distinction between the child who is cruel to his pet and experiences anger as he hurts it, in contrast to the child who is cruel to his pet and feels pleasure as he inflicts pain. Only the latter child would be considered sadistic, and would present a much poorer prognosis.

History has also marked an increased emphasis in the literature upon the controlling and dominating aspects of sadism (Karpman 1954, Shapiro 1981, Weinberg 1987). Perhaps the clearest contemporary definition of sexual sadism is found in a seminal paper on sexual homicide: "the repeated practice of behavior and fantasy which is characterized by a wish to control another person by domination, denigration, or inflicting pain, for the purpose of producing mental pleasure and sexual arousal (whether or not accompanied by orgasm) in the sadist" (MacCulloch et al. 1983, p. 20).

A computer search of the world's English-language scientific papers concerning sadism or sadomasochism during the past 25 years yielded seventy citations. Twenty-nine percent were theoretical psychoanalytic papers, 33 percent were empirical studies of groups, 24 percent were empirical case studies, 10 percent were nonanalytic reviews, and 4 percent were unclassifiable. These quantitative data are striking for two reasons: the impressive growth of empirical research, and the virtual absence of any measurable *treatment* studies. Only three papers (4 percent) reported measurable treatment results, and although they were uncontrolled case studies, they did report positive outcomes.

Bradford and Pawlak (1987) treated a 23-year-old sadistic homosexual pedophile with cyproterone acetate (50–100 mg per day). This anti-androgen reduced deviant pedophilic arousal and increased the patient's ability to suppress his arousal. Laws and colleagues (1978) treated a 29-year-old male sexual sadist by an olfactory aversion procedure for 8 weeks, using the odoriferous gas of valeric acid. The classical pairing of the gas and sadistic stimuli immediately and permanently suppressed the patient's sadistic sexual arousal and did not generalize to his nonsadistic sexual arousal patterns. Treatment effects remained 8 months after treatment. Hayes and associates (1978) treated an exhibitionistic and sadistic 25-year-old male with self-administered covert sensitization in a multiple baseline design. At the end of treatment the patient displayed low levels of arousal to the two deviant stimuli while maintaining appropriate heterosexual arousal. These three studies cast some doubt upon the conventional wisdom that sexual sadism is untreatable (Freund 1976), but do not address the immutability of characterological sadism.

The empirical studies of groups of sadists and sadomasochists are generally nonanalytic and descriptive. Gosselin and colleagues (1991) found that sadomasochistic women were more extraverted, stable, lower in neuroticism, higher in psychoticism, and more sexually active than controls. (The term *psychoticism* in this study is a misnomer; one of the measures used, the Eysenck Personality Questionnaire, defines psychoticism in a manner that is similar to *psychopathy*, and not in a manner that equates with loss of reality testing.) Several studies have found significant right-sided temporal horn dilation in computerized tomographic (CT) scans of sadists when compared to nonsadistic sexual aggressors and controls (Hucker et al. 1988, Langevin et al. 1988). Moser and Levitt (1987) found in a questionnaire sampling ($N = 225$) of self-defined sadomasochists that they were predominately heterosexual, well educated, relatively affluent, interested in both domination and submission, and engaged in a wide range of SM activities, although 16 percent had sought psychological help. Breslow and colleagues (1985) were also able to document through questionnaires a meaningful presence of females in the subculture of sadomasochism, although when it came to such mutilating behavior as erotic piercing of the genitals, males advertised in publications twenty-five times more frequently than females (Buhrich 1983).

Case studies have explored the significantly increased bilateral activation of the brain in sadists during experimental arousal (Garnett et al. 1988); a sadomasochistic fantasy of phallic intrusion in a female who made compulsive telephone calls to her mother (Richards 1989);

the "blame" transference in borderline patients (Pekowsky 1988); sadomasochistic fantasy in two adolescent boys suffering from congenital illness (Dubinsky 1986); sadomasochism in patient–therapist sexual abuse (Smith 1984); addiction to near-death (Joseph 1982); the role of sadomasochistic fantasy in asthma (Karol 1980–1981, Mintz 1980–1981, Wilson 1980–1981); the relation between Adolf Eichmann and the Marquis de Sade (Kulcsar 1976); and the use of voyeurism as a defense against sexual sadism (Socarides 1974).

The concordant sadistic identification with the psychopath includes several psychodynamics that link pleasure and cruelty in the mind of his partner.

Identification with the Aggressor

The relationship with the psychopath may facilitate the transformation of persecutory introjects into predatory identifications. Instead of being hounded by internal objects that stimulate thoughts and fantasies that are self-critical and condemning, and are not experienced as part of the self, these objects are projected onto others outside the dyad of the psychopath and his love. The partner sees herself as the aggressive twin of the psychopath, and intrapsychically she may consolidate her own grandiose self-structure, identifying with her own sadistic superego precursors to wreak havoc on the world through the omnipotent control and devaluation of others. She becomes like the predator. One woman responded to Card I of the Rorschach with the response, "It's two carnivorous wolves . . . I wish I could see doves mating."

Such identifications are likely to have their roots in early experiences with a neglectful or abusive parent, in which aggression and sexuality may have been fused in a primitive and horrible manner. The same woman noted above who participated in prostitute killings with a serial murderer was sexually molested for the first time by her father on the eve of her mother's funeral. He entered her room and told her during his sexual assault, "Now that your mother's dead, you will be my sexual love." This traumagenic experience was central to her pairing of eroticism with death, and formed the basis for her sexual excitement when her psychopathic mate murdered a prostitute during an act of fellatio, which she observed and assisted. Identification with the aggressor is easiest when the relationship is triangulated, and a third object, such as a prostitute, becomes a literal disposal for their mutually hated and devalued internal objects. Kernberg (1991) noted that "the unconscious identification with the aggressor linked with the erotization of pain facilitates a sexualization of primitive omnipotence, a primitive condensation of love and hatred that may proceed in several directions" (p. 342). In this context the direction is highly pathological, insofar as sexual excitement between partners is linked to cruel punishment of a third object for being weak and inferior, and omnipotence is only momentarily experienced through destruction (murder) of the third object. This identification with the aggressor in a triangulated form also implicates an oedipal (Electra) triumph over the maternal object, an opportunity in unconscious fantasy to destroy the mother and mate with the father.

Voyeurism as a Defense against Sadism

The sadistic concordant identification will further insulate the person who bonds to the psychopath from consciously experiencing her own sadism through the opportunity to look. This use of voyeurism as a defense against sadism, illustrated in a case of sexual sadism (Socarides 1974), is a form of visual reassurance without the fear of engulfment or merging with the object. It is usually sexually exciting, but at a primitive level in which the object which is looked at is a part-object, rather than a whole object of erotic desire.[10] Voyeurism keeps the

---

10. Kernberg (1991) drew the distinction between the part objects of sexual excitement and the whole objects of erotic desire, the latter being more object related and developmentally progressive. This is also illustrated by the differences in photographs between nude magazines, such as *Playboy*, and the more pornographic magazines. In the former, women are photographed as whole objects with accompanying biographical stories that attempt an "in depth" look at their interests and pursuits. In the latter, woman's *parts* are photographed, namely primary and sec-

sadistic impulse split off, or dissociated, from consciousness, but gratifies it through the opportunity to observe the psychopath being sadistic toward others. It also parallels the degree to which sadism necessitates detachment, and furthers sadomasochistic sexuality as a "highly ideational matter, far more a product of the imagination than of the senses" (Shapiro 1981, pp. 128–129). Voyeurism is long-distance touching.

The voyeurism may also unconsciously gratify the beating fantasy (Freud 1919), in which the third stage *is* a sadistic-voyeuristic experience in which the child imagines other children being beaten, usually by a teacher, and is highly sexually aroused. Objects in this unconscious fantasy are usually unknown boys, a striking parallel to the usual victim pool of the psychopath who is habitually violent: stranger males (Williamson et al. 1987). Such a sadistic-voyeuristic dynamic may be orchestrated in settings in which the psychopathic male may encounter other males whom he perceives as competing for *his* woman. Flirtation by the woman may stimulate other male advances, sparking jealousy and violence in her psychopathic boyfriend, which subsequently can be viewed by her with great, but perhaps concealed, pleasure. His violence is often characterized as a proto-emotional "display."

Sexual Excitement through Cruelty

The third concordant sadistic identification is the experience of sexual excitement through cruelty. Although actual sadomasochistic activity is more common in men (Arndt 1991), Kernberg noted (1991) that sadomasochistic masturbation fantasies are probably more frequent in women. Sexual excitement is considered a basic affect (Kernberg

---

ondary genitals, with an attempt to photograph internal as well as external anatomy, and no interest is paid to other aspects of the person's life. This form of voyeurism is more regressive, primitive, and only part-object related, and in more hard-core pornographic material, will be accompanied by coercive and degrading portrayals of the female as victim.

1991) and serves to neutralize aggression, overcome primitive splitting of love and hatred, and support the toleration of ambivalence in
normal development. In early abusive situations, however, it may
foster sadomasochistic fantasy and intense sexual inhibition.

> A 43-year-old woman was sexually molested by a minister when she was
> 6 years old, in a ritualized manner with other children. She was forced
> to perform various sex acts with the other children and the minister, all
> the while being told that she was a special religious person and had a
> special relationship with the minister. She reported feelings of confu-
> sion and excitement at the time, although her conscious memories and
> emotions concerning this episode did not surface until she was in
> psychoanalysis. She recounted having "bonded to his penis" and felt
> devastated when he moved from the neighborhood. Her sexual inhibi-
> tion as an adult was accompanied by sadomasochistic fantasies in which
> she was punished, and also punished others.

In this case, the trauma during the oedipal period suffused her
budding genital sexuality with themes of cruelty and aggression, and
subsequent guilt, and led to a general sexual inhibition that defended
against the conscious experience of sadomasochistic fantasy; the unconscious fantasy, in turn, provided a means by which the sexual
excitement of cruelty (toward self and others) could be sustained, as it
had been experienced as a child.

In sexual excitement through sadism, the action facilitates the
fantasy, rather than the reverse as seen in normal sexuality (Shapiro
1981). The central role of fantasy as a primary drive mechanism in
sadism and sadistic excitement should not be underestimated. It is
also consonant with fantasy as the primary drive mechanism in
extreme forms of sexual aggression, such as sexual homicide (MacCulloch et al. 1983, Meloy 1988a, Prentky et al. 1989, Ressler et al. 1988).
The genesis and pervasiveness of such fantasy may be the result of its
failure to master impulses stimulated by child abuse and trauma
(Grossman 1991); hence the repetitive and compulsive nature of both
the fantasy and the sexual violence. The erotic value of distressed
females in bondage and its association with antisociality in males has

been measured (Heilbrun and Seif 1988) and also implicates the centrality of visual stimulation and fantasy in antisocial character.

The fantasy also serves to maintain the control and detachment that are prerequisites of sadistic interest. This wish for control of others, however, must also contain a contempt for others, and an attitude of superiority over the inferior wills of others. "This contemptuous punishment of weakness or inferiority, especially unrepentant inferiority, of the undisciplined, the disrespectful, is what we call sadism" (Shapiro 1981, p. 107). In the person who bonds to the psychopath, such control and detachment may serve to defend against a deeply felt neediness that also threatens merger and fusion with the love object. Through sadistic identification, a cold and detached attitude can be maintained that transforms the seeking of relations based upon *affectional need* into relations based upon *power gradients* of dominance and submission. The actuality of abandonment to feelings of affectional and sexual need may be so foreboding that the idea of subjugating another to one's will takes on an intense sexual excitement. Object relations in such a context are devoid of any depth, dimensionality, or feeling, and are mechanized into a part-object sexual excitement that is intensely *sensual:* circumscribed to the realm of touching, seeing, hearing, tasting, and smelling that, because of its limitations, is highly erotically charged and maybe even dangerous. The felt pleasure of sadism, both sexual and nonsexual, is *not* based upon reciprocity and empathy. It is the result of feelings and fantasies of omnipotent control of the devalued object.

The Conversion of Passive into Active

Sadistic identification is a means by which passive attitude and behavior can be converted into activity. The psychopath is an extrovert who generally leads an exciting, stimulating life. Such a life is inherently dangerous because he lives with impunity, and social rules are not made for him. The sadistic identification is an opportunity to do something to an object, rather than being done to. It is a developmental progression from an oral receptive position to an oral aggres-

sive and anal expulsive position. It is a shift from an object-dependent role, to at least a pseudo-autonomous role that is marked by the capability, if not the actuality, of destroying the object. One woman, married to an aggressive, paranoid, and sometimes delusional religious leader, only took on the role of the sadist during sex. Her husband preferred her to be the dominatrix, and much of the forced sexual activity focused on her penetration of his anus with various paraphernalia. This active penetration of forbidden orifices and the violation through pain and cruelty of the husband's skin boundary have been explored in depth by Chasseguet-Smirgel (1991) and have been noted to overlap with an organized perversion in the malignant narcissistic character (Kernberg 1991). In her case, such sadistic sexual activity was the only time her sadism was allowed to be expressed by her controlling, sadistic husband. At other times she assumed the role of a dependent and masochistic wife, and suffered through his other philandering and cruel behavior. The sadistic scenarios, orchestrated by him, also provided her with an opportunity to vent her rage toward him in a controlled and approved manner; each wound that she inflicted upon him bore his imprimatur.

HYSTERICAL IDENTIFICATION

The third complementary identification is hysterical. It is apparent in the woman who forms an intense attachment to the psychopath and displays the various characteristics that are used to describe the hysterical personality: aggressive behavior, emotionality, sexual problems, obstinacy, exhibitionism, egocentricity, sexual provocativeness, and dependency (Blacker and Tupin 1991). These behaviors are generally consonant with histrionic personality disorder in *DSM-III-R*, but describe hysteria from a broader psychoanalytic perspective of character pathology, rather than a discrete subtype method of classification.

I have selected this approach because my clinical experience and the research of others (Gabbard 1990, Horowitz 1991) substantiate a wide array of hysterical behavior, in both men and women. It ranges from the so-called "good hysteric," organized at a higher level of neurotic personality with genital conflicts, to the "bad hysteric," organized at a borderline or psychotic level of personality with more primitive and preoedipal defenses (Zetzel 1968). The genitally fixated hysteric is less oral and narcissistically vulnerable, and may have a good social adaptation. Under stress one would clinically expect depressive or psychosomatic complaints, such as those noted under the somatoform disorders of *DSM-III-R*. Higher levels of denial (rationalization, minimization, and negation), conversion symptoms, and repression are the operable defenses.

The preoedipal hysteric is characterized by identity diffusion, poor reality testing, and the use of borderline defenses. When stressed, the patient is likely to regress to a more passive, depressed, or psychotic state with a serious suicide risk. Social adaptation is unstable, unpredictable, and lonely. Relationships are intense and chaotic, and may be highly sexualized and aggressive, as the individual vacillates between the caricatures of a feminine and a masculine identity. Although relationships are confused, they are eagerly sought, and sexual acting out may be a compulsive source of nurturance and affection (Blacker and Tupin 1991). Predominant defenses are lower levels of denial, splitting, and idealization through projective identification. Severe and uncomfortable dissociative experiences, ranging from depersonalization to multiple personality disorder, are more likely in the preoedipal hysterical personality and are the result of splitting and fragmentation of the ego, rather than repression.

The cognitive style of the hysteric, more obvious at the preoedipal level, is, in a word, impressionistic (Shapiro 1965). Thinking is global, diffuse, and pervaded with a "flood plain" of emotionality, much of which may defend against the experience of deeper, more meaningful affective experiences (Metcalf 1991). The thinking of the hysteric strikes the clinician as muddled, unclear, divorced from reality, although usually not delusional, and marked by subtle formal thought disorder. Tangential and circumstantial words that are colorfully elaborated with affective hues may present an entertaining, yet distressing clinical picture. Often this thinking style is buttressed by the defense of denial, and is most apparent in times of crisis. One colleague noted the quintessential hysterical response: "My house is on fire, but oh, the colors are beautiful!" (Phil Erdberg, Ph.D., personal communication, December 13, 1991).

Although the literature concerning hysteria is extensive, several recent texts offer the clinician a readily available guide to the genetic, developmental, and psychodynamic understanding and treatment of hysterical pathology. Gabbard (1990) offered a clear and concise differentiation of the higher level hysterical personality disorder from the lower level histrionic personality disorder, noting that the latter "is more florid than the hysteric in virtually every way" (p. 426). His most important and original contribution to the hysteria literature is the management of the erotic transference. Horowitz (1991) and his research group from the University of California, San Francisco, provided an updated compendium on hysterical personality style and histrionic personality disorder, ranging from an analysis of the core traits to the process of structural change through treatment of this "dramatic state of mind" (p. 5), perhaps the most concise definition of hysteria in the literature. Slavney (1990) produced a clear and comprehensive historical review of the term "hysteria" and framed it according to disease, dimension, behavior, and life story. He found empirical support for the dimensional (trait) and behavioral manifestations of hysteria, and noted that the term, despite its popular pejorative use, describes clinical realities and will probably not go away.

As I have previously noted (Meloy 1988a), the link between psychopathy and hysteria has been apparent for a century. Moravesik (1894) reported a high prevalence of criminal histories among hysterical subjects, and Kraepelin (1915) observed a frequent commingling of antisocial and hysterical traits in his patients. Psychodynamic theories underscoring the two disorders have been developed (Chodoff 1982, Meloy 1988a), and the core determinants of the hysterical personality—early maternal deprivation, a distorted resolution of the oedipal situation, and emergent sex role identification problems (Blacker and Tupin 1991)—are not unusual in the pathogenesis of psychopathy. Hysterical conversion reactions and somatization disorders, discrete symptom patterns associated with *DSM-III-R* histrionic personality disorder (Pfohl 1990), have also been empirically linked to psychopathy (Spalt 1980).

One of the most interesting parallels is found in what Blacker and Tupin (1991) referred to as the "pseudosociopathic" male. This is the Don Juan individual who is a caricature of masculinity and will exaggerate the traditionally accepted male role behavior. He will be prone to engage in daredevil activities, will be considered an exhibitionist (not in a paraphilic sense, but in a characterological sense) and sensation seeker, and is likely to be a womanizer or philanderer, seducing in the sense of "conquest" the women who fall prey to his wiles, not unlike his seventeenth-century namesake. I would label this individual a *pseudopsychopath*, and although his aggressiveness and antisociality might mislead the clinician into thinking about genuine psychopathy, some of the characteristics listed in Table 4–4 would distinguish him from the psychopathic character. Many of these traits were noted in a study by Luisada et al. (1974) concerning hysterical personality and men. The hypochondriacal complaints, suicidal threats and gestures, anxiety, depression, and attachment hunger are not consistent with psychopathic character (Hare 1991). The misdiagnosis of psychopathy in the pseudopsychopathic hysterical male may be one of the reasons for the convergence in the literature between hysteria and psychopathy. Further research is needed, perhaps care-

Table 4–4.

Clinical Characteristics of the Pseudopsychopathic (Hysterical) Male.

1. History of antisocial and criminal behavior
2. Hypermasculine traits and behaviors that are displayed in an exhibitionistic manner
3. Hypochondriacal complaints and psychosomatic symptoms
4. Absent or passive father by history
5. Suicidal gestures, threats, or attempts with periods of intense anxiety and depression
6. Promiscuous, unstable heterosexual relations; if married, probably to an older woman
7. Fleeting but intense attachments

fully looking at the relationship between primary psychopathy as operationalized by Hare (1991) and the *DSM-IV* diagnosis of histrionic personality disorder. I would hypothesize that the pseudopsychopathic (hysteric) male would generally not meet the 30-point threshold for psychopathy on the Hare Psychopathy Checklist–Revised (1991), and would more likely be in the 20–29 range. This is suggested by some of our Rorschach data (Meloy and Gacono, in press).

The complementary hysterical identification with the psychopath by his female object has several dynamic and structural components.

Idealization of the Psychopath

The hysterical character will idealize her psychopathic partner owing to her early maternal deprivation during infancy and childhood. Both nurturant and identificatory needs have not been met by the mother, so the little girl turns to her father to seek his attention through coy, seductive, and flirtatious behavior that sustains his approval. This idealization is the most overt manifestation of the "breast–penis equation" (Gabbard 1990, p. 432), as the phallus becomes the longed-for breast. One male patient who was attracted to, and actively sexual with, a variety of hysterical females, described the curious phenomenon of waking up and finding these women asleep, but holding on to his penis; he also described their inordinate desire to perform fellatio on him when compared with sexual partners who did not evidence hysterical traits. (Carl Gacono, Ph.D., labeled this pattern "to strike while the idealization is hot," personal communication, April 18, 1992.) The act of fellatio may be a condensation of the unconscious oral (genital) wish to suck milk (semen) from the breast (penis) which was not gratified as an infant: a merging of libidinal zones, psychosexual stages, and individual–species survival (food–reproduction). Another female patient with hysterical and dependent traits described this act as "eating" her boyfriend, and consciously equated the protein content of semen with milk as a source of nurturance. This patient also found scatologia very sexually arousing, a passive oral form of sexuality. She continued in her fourth decade of life to have weekly telephone contact with her father for him "to know how I'm doing," and displayed marked ambivalence in her adult heterosexual relations.

In the higher level, neurotic hysterical individual, this idealization of the psychopath is more subtle but may be apparent in fierce defense of his activities, continual verbal praise that to others seems misplaced, and initially a sudden, romantic "falling in love" that is immune to the insults of his actual behavior. Idealization at a preoedipal level is sustained through the defenses of projection and projective identification. Both defenses in this context implicate the projection of *good* aspects of the self, a dimension of this defense that is often overlooked (Ramchandani 1989).

The psychopath responds to the idealization very positively, because it enhances his own grandiosity and consciously felt quality of perfection. The complementary hysterical identification, however, exacts a severe toll from the woman, because she is identifying with what the psychopath unconsciously thinks of her as an object: a dependent, submissive, and devalued extension of himself that may, at times, serve a useful purpose.[11] Conflicts between the psychopath and his object in this context will usually result in her submitting to his devaluation, idealizing him, and vowing to "change for the better." Her submission and internalization of "badness" also facilitates his omnipotent control in both fantasy and partial reality. This sense of omnipotence further supports his grandiosity, one aspect of his aggressive narcissism.

A Source of Intense Stimulus Gratification

Millon (1981) defined the histrionic personality disorder as an "active dependent" type, in which attention and nurturance are aggressively

---

11. Sometimes the psychopath will idealize his female object, but this is usually limited to surface aspects, such as her physical beauty, and is a reflection of his own narcissistic investment in appearances. McGinnis (1989) reported the case of a psychopathic insurance salesman who had his wife murdered by contract. During the solicitation and planning of the murder, he told the perpetrator, "I don't want (you) to mar the beauty of my wife, Maria" (p. 227).

sought in an inappropriate and incessant manner. He also speculated that the biological and experiential roots of the disorder may be found in a hyperreactive autonomic nervous system that is exposed in childhood to "brief, highly charged, and irregular stimulus reinforcements" (p. 151) that define the hysteric's early attachments.

If his hypotheses are correct, these traits would nicely mesh with those of the psychopath. He is autonomically underaroused (Meloy 1988a), and the pairing with a person who has a low threshold for autonomic reactivity may provide a complementary biological fit that, in a genetic sense, "completes" his central nervous system. On the other hand, his sensation-seeking behavior, well documented in the literature (Hare 1991), provides the hysterical character with an adult source of intense stimulus that is irregular, unpredictable, and often sexualized: an experience that fills her unconscious transference wishes. He is the explosive flame that she, mothlike, wants to be near.

Her exhibitionism is also stimulated by his voyeurism. He is looking, and she yearns to be looked upon, or even within. It is usually an erotically tinged act that, for the psychopath, is also the prelude to aggression. This may be felt by her as an overture to sexualized aggression that is both frightening and titillating, but nevertheless, quite autonomically arousing.

These feelings, of course, have no conscious thought. The hysterical identification means that one responds, and then forgets. Bowlby (1988b) noted that the seduced child learns to respond to intensely stimulating sexualized attention, but to forget the adult's invitation to gain pleasure through these avenues of forbidden impulse.

The sexual innocence of the hysterical character may also arouse the psychopath and stimulate his own sadomasochistic fantasy, if she appears to engage on a nonverbal, erotic, and physical level without "knowing" what she is doing. This is the appeal of the "dumb blonde" in popular culture, a caricature of hysteria who is voluptuous and enticing but does not consciously recognize the impact on men of her highly charged, erotic behavior. She is intensely stimulating for the psychopath whose sexual pleasures are defined by parameters of dominance and submission, knowing and unknowing, and omnipotent control and object surrender.

A Container of Hope

The hysterical character's complementary identification with the psychopath is also expressed in her containment of his hopefulness. Hope is an anticipatory feeling that implies the presence of idealization, the sense that things are better than they seem, or will become better. It is the optimistic sense that goodness will prevail. It is Annie singing, "Tomorrow, tomorrow, tomorrow."

Hope is consciously intolerable for the psychopath and is therefore projectively identified into others. The hysterical character is the prototypical container because of her receptivity to the idealization of others, including her psychopathic mate, and her Pollyannish sense that there is a silver lining in every cloud. Sometimes there isn't.

Once this hope is projected, however, it is subjected to devaluation by the psychopath to ward off other feelings of envy. He wishes to destroy goodness so he does not consciously envy in others what he does not see in himself. His capricious attention, and then disgust, is the manner in which he will also manipulate her hope. One moment of kindness, as a positive intermittent reinforcer in behavioral terms, is a powerful stimulant to the hysteric's hope: the belief that he will change, things will get better, the pain will stop. Perhaps there is enough hope to sustain the emotional pain and suffering that occupy most of her time in relationship to the psychopath. His manipulation of hope is also a means to ensure her dependence by encouraging her wish to please him.

Encouragement of Passivity and Dependency

One of the cornerstones of hysterical pathology is the suppression of anger and assertiveness (Sperling 1973). Metcalf (1991) noted the degree to which the child, already in an insecure relation with mother, will not openly express anger and frustration. But instead, passive-aggression and dependency are taught as a means to gain the attention of the adult caretaker.

This pattern of behavior is also consonant with the hysterical complementary identification with the psychopath. He discourages her direct expression of anger and aggression, oftentimes by threatening her with his own. Yet she can voyeuristically participate in aggression by watching his violence toward others. Her attempts to triangulate their relationship to displace his aggression onto someone else may also serve as a point of affective relief in her own struggle to manage his violence. Such interpersonal maneuvers will solidify the use of primitive defenses such as splitting in the lower level hysteric, and in the higher level hysteric, repression. One of the case studies in Chapter 8 illustrates how the threat of being killed herself motivated a woman to confess to the police that she and her boyfriend had murdered several prostitutes. He would keep a loaded weapon on his side of their bed and warn her before they went to sleep that she might not wake up in the morning.

Cognitive Barriers to the Reality of the Psychopath

Perhaps the most striking example of the complementary hysterical identification is the nature of the hysteric's thinking and its relation to that of the psychopath. Shapiro's (1965) excellent portrayal of the hysteric's impressionistic cognitive style has already been mentioned, particularly the degree to which it lacks a capacity for intense intellectual concentration, leading to a remarkably nonfactual existence.

The cognitive vulnerability, yet complementary fit, is manifest in two ways (Meloy 1988a). First, she will be quite susceptible to believing the psychopath's rationalizations for his behavior, and unwilling to pay attention to the contradictions in his self-reported activities. These are cognitive tasks demanding concentration, persistence, and attention to detail that are not within the hysteric's repertoire. She will have no desire to study such historical facts – and if she is forced to do so by others, the signal anxiety that may be aroused will quickly motivate her to do something else and to attend to something different. When other witnesses do not corroborate her psychopathic partner's recall of events, she will forget or distort their versions and fall back on her feelings toward her mate.

Second, her defensive operations will ensure that her fantasied relationship with the psychopath is intact, despite its discordant relationship to reality. At higher levels of hysteria, repression will prompt a certain amount of forgetting so that only the residue of emotion is left and life remains to be lived in the present. One of the hallmarks of the nonviolent psychopathic "con man," for instance, is the absence of any verifiable history, or the presence of several personal "histories," each designed to fit the "con." These individuals will prey upon people and develop intimate relationships with those who are disinterested in personal history or naively believe that a person's history is irrelevant to his current behavior. Massive repression, marked by a singular lack of factual knowledge about oneself or one's partner, will strike the clinician as remarkably naive, and is typical of the "good hysteric."

At borderline and psychotic levels of personality, the hysterical character will use denial as a prominent defense to ward off her awareness of the psychopath's reality. This defense may be an impenetrable barrier against the conscious realization that there is evil, pain, malevolence, badness, or injustice in the world, let alone in her mate. A common and illustrative example is the woman who will defend her criminal and psychopathic husband in the face of overwhelming evidence that he committed a particular offense. Usually her response combines the defense of denial, followed in close sequence by a pleasurable feeling state: "I know he is innocent, and I love him." It is as if her capacity to love negates the existence of his hate and the acts that flow from it.

PSYCHOPATHIC IDENTIFICATION

The fourth, concordant identification with the psychopath is thinking, feeling, and behaving as he does—psychopathically. Clinical observation of this identification is highly unusual, just as the prevalence rate for severe psychopathy in women is three times less than it is for men. (If one assumes that the *DSM-III-R* prevalence rates are accurate for Antisocial Personality Disorder, 3 percent of American males and less than 1 percent of American females, then the rates for psychopathic personality, which are no more than one third of any APD sample, would be 1 percent for males and *at most* 0.33 percent for females.)

The woman who identifies with her psychopathic mate and fully expresses his character pathology would behaviorally meet many of the criteria in Table 4–1. Her affects, defenses, and object relations would likewise be similar to the psychopathic male as outlined at the beginning of this chapter and in my textbook (Meloy 1988a).

I would like to elaborate upon four aspects of this concordant identification that capture the essence of this transference behavior.

The Compensatory Feeling of Grandiosity

It is highly probable that the woman who evidences a psychopathic concordant identification is the product of a mean and abusive up-bringing, biologically predisposed to psychopathy, or both. Forming an alliance with a psychopath means that she can experience a narcissistic twinship identification (Kohut 1971) in which her own grandiosity can compensate for feelings of being disregarded and unworthy. She may be able to solidify her own grandiose self-structure (Kernberg 1975) through the transference use of her psychopathic mate as an idealized object image which is condensed with her self-concept. In this manner, she can dissociate or split off unacceptable aspects of her real self through the devastating devaluation of actual objects in her previous life.

A wealthy, middle-aged couple sought consultation because their 20-year-old daughter was involved with a 24-year-old male who had convinced her she should have no contact with her parents. During the young couple's brief courtship the parents believed that he had stolen a large coin collection from their home. The young man subsequently threatened them with phone calls over the course of 3 years, during which the daughter refused to see them. One transcribed message went as follows: "You will never, underscore never, see your daughter again. I mean it. She doesn't want to see you, and I am going to go out of my way to run interference so you will never find her again . . . I hope you're enjoying your evening." Other calls threatened their son, their reputation, their marriage, and complete control of their daughter. A subsequent private investigation, paid for by the parents, revealed that their daughter was living with this young man in another part of the city, and was coming and going of her own free will. There was no criminal liability for kidnap or false imprisonment, and the daughter was legally an adult. She later confirmed to the parents, by letter and telephone, that she completely agreed with her boyfriend and had no further wish to see them because they were liars.

Although the complexity of this case is beyond the scope of this chapter, this brief vignette illustrates the potentially devastating impact of such a concordant identification. The young man's history and behavior, through information gathered by the private investigator, was consistent with psychopathy. The parents' reaction to their daughter's telephone and letter responses found her to be "cold and aloof," an interpersonal style they saw as completely distressing and inexplicable.

A Pseudomasculine Identity and Hard-Object Cathexis

Blacker and Tupin (1991) wrote about the pseudomasculine adjustment in hysteria that may occur in both biological males and females. They noted that the pseudomasculine adjustment in females is less well recognized and would likely represent the "butch" adaptation of the lesbian. A similar process occurs in the cathexis of, or attachment to, hard objects and pseudomasculine identity in the female mate of the psychopath. This is another facet of an identification with the aggressor and is the female expression of Reich's (1933) phallic-narcissistic character. I have modified Blacker and Tupin's (1991) list of pseudomasculine expressions to capture these behaviors: threatens others with verbal or physical fights and resists any overt signs of dependency; denies feelings, especially those perceived as vulnerable or sentimental; sexually exploits other men, and prefers the role of the dominatrix in her sexual liaisons; is stubborn around issues that others perceive as trivial; exhibits strength, bravery, and tolerance for pain, and dresses in ways that suggest such body armor; flaunts her self-absorption and self-interest, and may express this through traditionally masculine tattoos; and willingly engages in criminal behavior.

The hard-object identification is manifest in an attraction to, and idealization of, weapons. The weapon itself may function as a regressive transitional object that defines the boundary between internal fantasy and external reality. Its precision tooling may be conceived as a perfect extension of the self, and may provide a source of "feeding" for the grandiose hunger of omnipotence. The weapon as a hard object negates the soft, tactile nature of normal transitional objects, and instead of being a safe repository for undigested feelings and fantasies, it becomes a narcissistic reflection of, and projective container for, the absolute cold and impenetrable exterior of the character armor. It is also a sign of aggressive potential that can ward off threats from persecutory objects, and remains in the complete control of the possessor (Meloy and Gacono 1992a).

Abandonment of Attachments and Values

The concordant psychopathic identification also signals the abandonment of affectional attachments, and with them, larger prosocial values. The relationship to the psychopath is willingly defined on the basis of power gradients, and a dominance–submission struggle, perhaps characterized through sadomasochistic interactions, may chiefly shape the relationship. Ego ideals are lost, having been fused within the grandiose self-structure, and no longer provide any demarcation between the superego and ego. The value of truth is foregone, and pathological lying and deception become an obvious pattern of interaction. This facet of psychopathic identification is unlikely in the oedipally organized female, and is more often seen in borderline and psychotic personality organization where the depressive position has not been attained. Although self and object representations have been differentiated, good and bad aspects of both have not been integrated, so phenotypic expressions of splitting, such as idealization and devaluation, predominate the defensive picture. Antisocial behavior becomes the ideal, and prosocial behavior is devalued. This is a psychology of reversal, and may be concordant with the woman's developmental history, or strikingly opposite, as in the case vignette noted above.

A Defense against Loss and Mourning

The woman who forms a concordant psychopathic identification may use it as a defense against innumerable losses and the overwhelming emotional pain of mourning those losses. It is a fixation at, or regression to, a level of personality that precedes the depressive position, and by definition precludes the experience of guilt and remorse for the loss of the loved object. This is most likely in women who have experienced physical or sexual abuse at the hands of the parent, and have not had the developmental opportunity to autonomously separate from a loving presence; and then subsequently, to experience the socialized feelings of remorse at the way they have treated the parents and gratitude toward their constancy. It is an emotional stance that manages the schizoid fear of annihilation through the vigilance of paranoia (Klein 1946, 1957).

CONCLUSIONS

The psychopath as love object is an oxymoron. It is inconceivable to the reasonable observer unless the unconscious identifications that cement the relationship are explored. In this chapter I have delineated four such identifications—masochistic, sadistic, hysteric, and psychopathic—two of which are concordant (what the psychopath thinks of himself) and two of which are complementary (what the psychopath thinks of the object). Racker's (1968) insightful formulations shed light on the person, usually a woman, who stays in such a relationship for no apparent coercive reason. It is a tale of woe that usually resists change until the long-term self-destruction of the psychopathic character tears apart the emotional fabric of this bond.

5

Assassination and Pathological Attachment

There is no borderline between one's personal world and the world in general.

— Lee Harvey Oswald

I have never forgotten the words I once heard in a foreign film, although I have not be able to remember, despite intense effort, the title of the film itself. So with advance apologies to both the screen-writer and director, I will paraphrase the impression they left on my mind: "There are three kinds of people in the world: leaders, followers, and assassins."

Although this is an obviously simplistic typology of human behavior, I was struck by the degree to which these words captured the enduring patterns of public behavior that I have observed in people: the wish to care for and direct, the wish to be cared for and directed, or the wish to destroy the caretaker. This latter wish may be motivated by a variety of factors, including envy of the goodness of the leader, jealousy toward those for whom the leader cares, or a paranoid and delusional condensation of beliefs concerning the malevolent role of the leader in the personal life of the assassin. The leader may be first idealized as a transference paternal object through whom the pleasant early memories of childhood can be magnified and embellished, or from whom the painful memories of childhood can be repressed or split off. The constancy and trust of parental holding can be rekindled through the spirit of the leader's promises, or imaginatively constructed in the absence of an early trust that was never actually felt. The political leader's words and appearance may become mirrors for what is transferentially seen, and objects with whom concordant or complementary (Racker 1968) identifications are made.

He may, on the other hand, become a devalued object, a depository for the earliest demons, the persecutory objects of one's desires. This phenomenon is exacerbated by real disappointments in the political leader, collective empathic failures, and may be carried to a violent outcome, on occasion, if his shortcomings are perceptually distorted and conceptually magnified through the psychological lens of preoedipal personality organization. As one political pundit said, "politics is knowing who to hate." For those who perceive reality in polarized opposites, with realistic shades of gray meaning having succumbed to the opposing colors of black evil and white goodness, hatred is deeply felt. It becomes an emotional wellspring for righteous violence.

Although psychiatric diagnoses have often been used to explain the behavior of assassins, particularly American assassins (Clarke 1982), object relations and attachment theories have never been applied to this rare form of violence that, when it occurs, has monumental social and psychological sequelae.

The usefulness of this method is twofold. Although psychiatric disorder is not ruled out, diagnostic categorization is secondary to understanding the nature of the assassin's internal world: the way in which self and others, particularly the political object of hatred, is represented, and the respective affective complexes that surround these representations. Defensive operations are also elaborated (Kernberg 1976), and other metapsychological and structural inferences can then be made from this object relations perspective. Second, attachment theory provides a negative template for understanding assassination: an analysis of the motivation to seek proximity to an object of hatred, the experience of negative affect in the presence of the object, distress at the loss of such proximity, and the predatory nature of such activity whose purpose is to destroy the object of attachment. Attachment theory, rooted in the early experience of the child, may also aid in understanding the developmental link between the adult as assassin and interpersonal experience with the parental object as a child.

The word assassin is derived from the Arabic *hashashin,* meaning a user of hashish. This mild hallucinogen and intoxicant was smoked by the Fida'is, or devoted ones, the actual first assassins, members of the Ismailites, a sect of the Shi'ite Muslims. Founded by Hassan-i-Sabbah in the eleventh century, the sect trained young peasant males to obediently kill certain political rivals in the southern region of the Caspian Sea, in what is now Iran. The sect thrived for several hundred years. Those who became Ismailites were protected, those who refused were killed. The Middle Ages brought an end to their rule, however, and the few Ismaili merchants and farmers who survived are now ruled by a hereditary leader with the title of His Highness the Aga Khan (McConnell 1970).

EMPIRICAL RESEARCH

The extant scientific research concerning assassination is rather limited. Investigators have used two approaches that seem to yield disparate results: they either study those individuals who appear to be *at risk* for assassinating a public figure, or those individuals who have *actually attempted* to assassinate a public figure.

David Shore and his colleagues (Shore et al. 1985, 1988, 1989) from the National Institute of Mental Health and St. Elizabeth's Hospital completed a series of papers concerning those ostensibly at risk for violence to public figures. In the first paper (Shore et al. 1985), 328 delusional visitors to the White House between 1971 and 1974 were studied. These so-called "White House Cases" were those individuals designated by the United States Secret Service as being mentally disordered and a potential danger to a public official, and subsequently civilly committed.

Results indicated that a majority of the visitors were Caucasian males in their late thirties without a current heterosexual pair bond. The modal diagnosis at discharge from their civil commitment was paranoid schizophrenia (66 percent). Ninety-one percent of the subjects had some form of schizophrenia or paranoid condition. Twenty-two percent threatened some prominent political figure before or after this index hospitalization. The threateners, when compared to the nonthreateners, were more likely to be unattached and Caucasian.

When compared with White House cases from the past (Hoffman 1943, Keller et al. 1965, Sebastiani and Foy 1965), there was a significant decrease in those who were foreign born and Caucasian, and a significant increase in those with no religious affiliation (although a plurality remained Protestant). Despite the change in racial characteristics, nonwhite males are still underrepresented in this violence risk group. This is exactly the opposite finding when compared to other, more common, forms of violence. In fact, there has never been an assassination attempt by a black male in the United States, despite the historical espousal of political violence by certain black leaders.[1]

Shore and colleagues (1988, 1989) did a follow-up study of 217 of their White House cases 9 to 12 years after discharge, to generate hypotheses concerning violence prediction. Thirty-one (14 percent) had one or more subsequent arrests for murder or assault. Seventy-one (33 percent) had subsequent arrests for nonviolent crimes. None of the subjects attempted to harm a prominent political figure, but one shot and killed a Secret Service agent in 1980.

Those arrested for subsequent violent crimes were more likely to

---

1. During the 1960s, Malcolm X, the leader of the Black Muslims, and various leaders of the Black Panthers such as Eldridge Cleaver and Huey Newton, advocated the use of violence in response to the oppression of the urban black community. H. Rap Brown was often quoted as saying, "violence is American as apple pie." None of their oratory, or subsequent violence, was specifically directed at the president, although both Malcolm X and Huey Newton were subsequently murdered, the latter in a drug deal in Oakland 25 years later. Tyrone Robinson, 27 years old, was found guilty of first-degree murder in the death of Newton, who was shot in the head three times near a West Oakland crack house on Aug. 22, 1989. The motivation appeared to be to gain standing with the Black Guerilla Family prison gang.

have been arrested for violent crimes before their White House visit. This was the most useful predictor of future violence, along with male gender and nonwhite race. Threats against prominent political figures were also associated with arrests for violent crime but did not predict the imminency of the violence nor the choice of eventual victim. A weapons history and hospital incidents requiring seclusion were the strongest correlates of subsequent violence in those with prior arrests for violence ($N = 31$). Persecutory delusions were the only clinical variable associated with subsequent violence in those subjects with prior arrests for nonviolent crimes ($N = 74$).

The Shore studies, despite the diagnostic homogeneity of their sample, emphasize the primacy of heterogeneous demographic factors in assessing violence risk (past history of violence, gender, race, weapons possession). And, most importantly, the actual victims of these subjects were not prominent political figures and no assassinations were attempted. The definition of these subjects as "White House cases" may be misleading, since such approach behavior and subsequent hospitalization by the Secret Service may be an anomaly in an otherwise plebeian history of mental disorder and violence. Only 11 percent of the subjects actually threatened a prominent political figure at admission, and 38 percent were attempting to have the prominent political figure help them. As Shore and colleagues noted (1988), they came to the White House for several reasons: to provide special information or advice, to request relief from imagined persecution, to warn of impending danger, or to obtain money or another reward. Their delusional grandiosity and willingness to travel to Washington, D.C., may have been the only factors that distinguished them from other paranoid and schizophrenic individuals at risk for violence. A comparison of the Shore subjects with other samples of paranoid schizophrenics, with and without histories of violence, would be quite useful.

A related study (Dietz et al. 1991b) examined the characteristics of threatening and otherwise inappropriate communications sent to members of the United States Congress by eighty-six subjects, twenty of whom threatened assassination. The most remarkable finding in this study was that threateners were significantly *less* likely to pursue an encounter with the congressmen than were inappropriate letter writers who did not threaten, regardless of the type of threat or the harm threatened. Although this study did not directly investigate the subjects, only their communications, the empirical finding concerning threats is completely opposite the usual clinical assumption that written threats increase the risk of actual attack.

The second approach to assassination is to study the small number of individuals who have actually attempted to kill a prominent political figure in the United States. Between 1835, when Richard Lawrence failed to kill President Andew Jackson, and 1981, when John Hinckley, Jr., wounded President Ronald Reagan, there have been sixteen actual attempts by seventeen individuals. Seven of the victims died of their wounds, a 44 percent mortality risk. And seven, or 44 percent, of the attempts have occurred since 1963.

The most comprehensive and systematic attempt to study American assassins was conducted by James Clarke (1982, 1990), a professor of political science at the University of Arizona. His major criticism of prior analyses of assassins was the reductive attempt to explain the behavior only in terms of psychopathology. He took a much broader perspective, studying the cultural, political, and social contexts of the assassination event, in addition to the personality characteristics and emotional life of the assassin.

His comprehensive and detailed study (1982), which mostly relied on primary source material, yielded a typology of four categories. It successfully classified 89 percent of the assassins in American history.

Type I assassins view their acts as a "sacrifice of self for a political ideal" (p. 14). Personal interest and evident psychopathology are secondary to a primary political motivation. Subsequent arrest or death is an acceptable, if not sought-after, risk to further their political agenda. Their violence is rationally based if understood from their social-political perspective.

American assassins who fit this first type include John Wilkes Booth, an actor who loved the South and hated President Abraham Lincoln enough to kill him on April 14, 1865, in Ford's Theater; Leon Czolgosz, a Czechoslovakian anarchist who shot and fatally wounded

President William McKinley on September 6, 1901, in Buffalo, New York; Oscar Collazo and Griselio Torresola, two Puerto Rican Nationalists who failed to assassinate President Harry Truman on November 7, 1950, when they staged an assault on Blair House in Washington; and Sirhan Sirhan, the Palestinian immigrant who shot and killed presidential aspirant Robert F. Kennedy on June 5, 1968, in the pantry of the Ambassador Hotel in Los Angeles (see Chapter 9).

Type II assassins are persons with "overwhelming and aggressive egocentric needs for acceptance, recognition, and status" (p. 14). They are highly anxious and dysphoric individuals who have experienced much affectional deprivation in their personal lives. The assassination is a displacement of hatred toward those who have narcissistically wounded them, and the act is fundamentally a rageful seeking of attention that is politically rationalized. Although Clarke (1982) used the word "neurotic" (p. 15) to describe this type, it seems more likely that borderline psychopathology would dominate the clinical picture of these individuals, and a significant degree of reality impairment would be present, without psychosis, that would be dynamically associated with affect-complexes concerning actual objects of attachment and loss.

American assassins who fit this second type include Lee Harvey Oswald, an anxious young man who was rejected by his wife and allegedly killed President John F. Kennedy in Dallas on November 22, 1963; Samuel Byck, also unloved by his wife and children, who committed suicide following an abortive attempt to kill President Richard Nixon by hijacking a commercial airliner and crashing it into the White House on February 22, 1974; Lynette "Squeaky" Fromme, the follower of Charles Manson who pointed a .45-caliber pistol at President Gerald Ford's genitals on September 5, 1975, in Sacramento; and Sara Jane Moore, a middle-aged FBI informant estranged from her radical friends, who fired one shot from a .38-caliber revolver at President Gerald Ford 2½ weeks later in San Francisco.

Type III assassins are psychopaths. They experience life as meaningless, and their motivation for assassination is the nonpolitical expression of rage. They are usually devoid of human attachments and do not experience the more socialized emotions of guilt, shame, remorse, or depression. As Clarke wrote, "they are belligerently contemptuous of morality and social convention" (p. 15). Although sharing with the Type II assassin a drive for attention and control, they are not searching for a scapegoat for their own personal wounds, but a public figure, either politician or celebrity, with whom they can narcissistically identify, and contemptuously waste. The act is an outrageous, yet emotionless display against a society from which they feel completely alienated (Meloy 1988a).

American assassins who fit this third type include Giuseppe Zangara, an Italian immigrant who failed to kill President Franklin Roosevelt but did mortally wound Chicago Mayor Anton Cermak on February 13, 1933, in Miami; Arthur Bremer, who crippled Alabama Governor George Wallace with four shots from a .38-caliber revolver on May 15, 1972, in Laurel, Maryland; and John Hinckley, Jr., the son of a Colorado industrialist who wounded President Ronald Reagan with one "devastator" exploding .22-caliber bullet on March 30, 1981, outside the Washington Hilton Hotel.

Type IV assassins are those with diagnosable major mental disorders manifest in hallucinations and delusions. The latter symptoms are either persecutory or grandiose, and the psychosis is evident at the time of the assassination. Approximately one half of the individuals who come to the attention of the Secret Service as threats to the president have a history of mental illness (Clarke 1990).

American assassins who fit this fourth category include Richard Lawrence, a paranoid schizophrenic man who failed in his attempt to kill President Andrew Jackson on January 30, 1835, in the east portico of the Capitol; Charles Guiteau, a grandiose and delusional self-described "lawyer, theologian, and politician" (Clarke 1982, p. 204), who mortally wounded President James Garfield on July 2, 1881, at the Baltimore and Potomac Railroad station; and John Schrank, a mild-mannered, yet delusional Bavarian who wounded presidential candidate Theodore Roosevelt on October 14, 1912, at the Hotel Gilpatrick in Milwaukee. The shock of his .38-caliber bullet was absorbed by a fifty-page folded speech and spectacle case in Roosevelt's left breast pocket.

Clarke was unable to categorize the two remaining American

assassins: Carl Weiss and James Earl Ray. Weiss was a happily married, apolitical physician who killed Senator Huey P. Long on September 8, 1935, in Baton Rouge, Louisiana. Ray, a habitual criminal, contracted for and killed Martin Luther King, Jr., on April 4, 1968, as King stood on the balcony of the Lorraine Motel in Memphis.

A second level of inference concerning this typology is the disorder of attachment expressed in a grandiose and politicized manner in each one of these categories. The Type I assassins, consciously motivated by political cause, seek proximity to the object felt to omnipotently control their people's destiny. The Type II assassins, experiencing the abandonment rage of the borderline individual, repair their wounds through aggression and hatred displaced upon a collectively "loved" object of affection. The Type III assassins, psychopathically detached and devoid of developmentally mature modes of relatedness, express the meaninglessness in their lives by attempting to destroy all goodness. This violent devaluation of the actual object shores up their own grandiosity and wards off intolerable feelings of envy for those who belong. The psychopathic assassin is a stranger outside the political and cultural family. The Type IV assassins, caught in the throes of psychosis, have forsaken any attachment struggles in the real world. Their proximity seeking is primarily intrapsychic, a cathecting of internal objects that are delusionally embellished and privately idiosyncratic. The inner world of the psychotic assassin is unpredictable, because it is only known through verbal utterances and violent behavior, secondary to the psychosis, which may seem inexplicable. The grandiosity of the psychotic assassin, however, is always present and shared with the other three types. He often finds confirmation in the real world for his persecutory and expansive delusions:

> Patient K. S. had paranoid schizophrenia. He believed that all men were evil, and women should stay away from them. He began to write Nancy Reagan in 1983, warning her that she should divorce Ronald Reagan because of the evil inherent in his maleness. One day as he was sitting in his room and composing another letter to her, someone knocked on the door. It was an agent from the U.S. Secret Service wanting to

interview him. K. S. was elated that his mission and beliefs were finally receiving the national attention they deserved.

My interest and study of the psychopathology of assassination has focused upon one individual, Sirhan Bishara Sirhan, the assassin of Robert F. Kennedy. As of this writing, Sirhan continues to be imprisoned in San Quentin and is considered for parole every several years by the California Board of Prison Terms. His death sentence was commuted to life with the possibility of parole following the United States Supreme Court's decision in 1972 (*Furman* v. *Georgia*, 408 U.S. 238). The Court held that the unlimited discretion given juries to do what they pleased in deciding who received the death penalty was unconstitutional. (In subsequent cases, the Court upheld certain guided discretion death penalty statutes, as long as they required examination of factors that argued both for and against execution–so called aggravating and mitigating circumstances. This minimized the risk of "arbitrary, capricious, or unpredictable" executions. See, for example, *Gregg* v. *Georgia*, 428 U.S. 153 [1976] and *California* v. *Brown*, 479 U.S. 538 [1987].)

The investigation of Sirhan Sirhan led me to the work of Kaiser (1970), and his remarkably detailed study of the Robert Kennedy assassination. Within his book I also discovered the first Rorschach of Sirhan, taken several months after the killing. Chapter 9 is an archival study of this psychological evidence through the use of technology unavailable in 1968. This study was originally presented at the Society for Personality Assessment in New Orleans, March 8, 1991. Although it contains technical and statistical data that may not be understood by nonpsychologist mental health clinicians, it is an intriguing case study of political hatred, psychopathology and disordered attachment that I think has important historical implications.

THE CLINICIAN'S RESPONSE TO THREATS AGAINST THE PRESIDENT

The Clarke (1982) typology and the psychometric investigation of one assassin's personality structure (Chapter 9) are instructive of the complex psychological, social, political, and cultural dynamics that usually contribute to assassination threats. The inpatient or outpatient mental health clinician, however, still needs some practical guidelines to manage such a threat that provide a counterpoint to my theoretical and research perspective.

The Legal Framework

The United States Code (18 U.S.C. § 871) states that

> whoever knowingly and willfully deposits for conveyance in the mail ... any letter, paper, writing, print, missive, or document containing any threat to take the life of, to kidnap, or to inflict bodily harm upon the President of the United States ... or knowingly or willfully otherwise makes any such threat against the President ... shall be fined not more than $1,000 or imprisoned not more than five years, or both.

In other words, it is a federal crime to threaten the President, even if there is no intent to injure.

All threatening utterances, however, may not be criminal. In *Watts* v. *United States* (394 U.S. 705 [1976]), the United States Supreme Court ruled that a Vietnam War protester's statements were political hyperbole and were protected by the First Amendment. The court has further ruled that statements need to be serious, deliberate, not in jest, and not in response to provocation to be interpreted as real and threatening (See *United States* v. *Carrier*, 708 F2d 77 [1983]; *United States* v. *Frederickson*, 601 F2d 1358 [1979]).

Debates have also centered around an objective or subjective definition of "knowingly and willfully." The objective standard is based upon the perceptions of those who hear the threat (*Roy* v. *United States*, 416 F2d 874 [1969]). The subjective standard is based upon the mental status of the person uttering the threat (*United States* v. *Howell*, 719 F2d 1258 [1984]).

Griffith and colleagues (1988) argued, moreover, that Section 871 does not impose a legal obligation to report a threat to the President, and this would not constitute misprision of a felony (failure to report a crime), because no positive action has occurred. Courts have generally upheld this latter interpretation. (See *United States* v. *Ciambrone*, 750 F2d 1416 [1984]; *United States* v. *Baez*, 732 F2d 780 [1984]; *United States* v. *Davila*, 698 F2d 715 [1983]; *United States* v. *Sampol*, 636 F2d 621 [1980].)

Mental health clinicians should respond to a threat against the President by considering these basic legal parameters, and any relevant state statutes or case law that address threats toward third parties. Most of these laws find their roots in the second *Tarasoff* v. *Regents of the University of California* decision (17 Cal 3D 425 [1976]). Interestingly, the opinion in this case mentioned assassination threats despite the facts of the case, which centered on an erotomanic Indian male and his female victim at the University of California, Berkeley. The California Supreme Court wrote, "We would hesitate to hold that the therapist who is aware that his patient expects to attempt to assassinate the President of the United States would not be obligated to warn the authorities because the therapist cannot predict with accuracy that his patient will commit the crime. . . . The protective privilege ends where the public peril begins" (pp. 346–347).

I think the court was also cognizant of clinicians' tendencies to overstep their clinical boundaries and attempt to influence social policy or legal matters. Griffith and colleagues (1988) were soundly criticized for such an approach (Letters to the Editor, *Hospital and Community Psychiatry*, 1989, 40:647–650), although their concern for patient rights and privacy is commendable. I would advise that whenever the treating or evaluating clinician determines that the patient has made a serious threat of physical harm to the President of the United States, the Secret Service should be immediately contacted by telephone. The patient should be advised that the Secret Service is being notified and given an opportunity to consult with counsel before the arrival of the agent. Complete documentation of the threat, in verbatim form, should be recorded in the medical record, as well as the time of notification of the Secret Service.

My professional experience with this law enforcement agency

has been very positive. They will generally send an agent within several hours to the clinical site who will interview the patient, request a photograph, and attempt to get the patient to sign a release of information to review his medical records. Issues of competency to consent to the interview and to release information should not be a concern of the clinician, because a psychiatric interview is not being conducted and the proper setting for determining competency is a judicial and not a clinical one. Although prosecutions are sought in less than 5 percent of cases investigated by the Secret Service, clinicians may have an opportunity to testify to the patient's competency in subsequent criminal proceedings. Moreover, it is critical that clinicians involved in such a referral remind themselves of the limits of their own competencies. Most mental health clinicians have no training or experience in law enforcement, criminal investigation, or federal law. Characterization of a threat to the President as a criminal act is *not* the province of the clinician. This is a prosecutorial decision. Determination that the words of the patient constitute a knowing (to convey the impression of a serious threat) and willful (voluntary, intelligent, intentional) threat is a clinical decision.

The Clinical Framework

It has been my clinical experience that most threats directed toward the President in mental health settings are attention-seeking behaviors by patients who are angry, narcissistic, and grandiose. This implicates some of the more acting-out personality disorders, namely the paranoid, narcissistic, antisocial, histrionic, and borderline types. Determination of the presence of these character pathologies can be useful when consulting, with the patient's permission, with the United States Secret Service, and the Millon Clinical Multiaxial Inventory II is an especially helpful psychometric measure of these disorders.

Rorschach data can also be very useful, with a particular focus upon the individual's reality testing $(X - \%)$, affect modulation $(FC:CF + C)$, and stress tolerance and control (D, Adjusted D). In our sample of antisocial personality disorders (Gacono and Meloy 1991), the mean FC:CF + C ratio is 1:2.5, yet the AdjD mean is 0. This does not suggest a lack of impulse control, but the deliberate use of unmodulated affect to control objects in the environment. This may be a critical group of indices on the Rorschach when offering an opinion about impulse control, or lack thereof, in a patient who has threatened the President. Elevated Lambda, Egocentricity Ratio, and the presence of at least one reflection response would also be suggestive of narcissistic character pathology in an individual threatener oblivious to the long-term consequences of his actions. Clinicians, however, must keep in mind the limited value of psychological tests in assessing violence risk, and the heavy loading of situational factors in any violence risk equation. Such proximity-seeking variables, and Secret Service actions to attenuate their impact, are not the expertise of the clinician.[2]

Threats to the President that are solely motivated by delusional thinking appear to be clinically unique. As noted in the research above, a minority of psychotic visitors to the White House (11 percent) actually threatened a public figure upon hospital admission, and most were seeking help. Only three (19 percent) of sixteen American assassins (Clarke 1982) were overtly delusional. The clinical determination as to whether the threat is delusionally based is important in assessing risk but should not be the determining factor in referring to the Secret Service. A statement can be both knowing and willful, and still be based upon delusion. Acts of violence that are delusionally based may also be carried out in a predatory fashion (Meloy 1988b), a mode of violence that accounts for virtually all assassination attempts. The actual risk inherent in threats that are motivated by delusion, rather than by personality disorder, are the domain of the Secret Service.

---

2. I have found my own sense of self-importance inflated when I have consulted with the Secret Service. My narcissistic wish to protect the father and be identified with him (the office of the President rather than the actual person in office) could just as easily find its opposite in the clinician who identifies with the potentially persecuted (prosecuted) patient (son) and refuses to inform the Secret Service. In both cases, the depth of emotion stirred by a threat to the President is remarkable, given the absence of an actual relationship or bond and the always present transference implications.

When the President of the United States travels, the Secret Service will attempt to locate those individuals who are considered a threat to his safety, before his arrival in their geographic area. This facilitates their surveillance and potential control of these individuals should they attempt to approach the President. Positive identification of these people through such a "lookout" strategy in close physical proximity to the President will usually result in immediate detainment by agents until the President has left the area. Within certain geographical perimeters of the President, individual rights are suspended, an unknowing agreement when one chooses to go hear him speak and crosses this "floating" boundary of protection.

The mental health clinician may be drawn into this surveillance of threateners of the President through a request by the Secret Service to further detain an individual in a hospital setting until the President has left the area, or to keep them informed of the outpatient's whereabouts during the President's visit. Such accommodations should not be made unless they are clinically based, and in the latter case, unless the patient's explicit written permission is received.

Psychotherapy and pharmacotherapy approaches to such patients would be determined by the primary psychodiagnosis and the motivation to threaten the President. In 10 to 20 percent of the cases, the threat will probably be delusionally based and may dissipate in the course of neuroleptic treatment. In the remaining 80 percent of cases, the threat will probably be grounded in characterological disorder and will not be affected by pharmacological intervention. Attention from the Secret Service, although unavoidable, may also positively reinforce the angry grandiosity and stimulate further acting out. In certain cases, federal prosecution and containment in a correctional setting may be the only alternative to control the threatening person and alter behavior through aversive conditioning, or punishment (Meloy 1991a).

CONCLUSIONS

Pathological attachment finds its most grandiose expression in the assassination of public figures. Although the motivations and typologies vary, proximity seeking toward the object of hatred is a negative template of attachment that deepens our understanding of this most public form of violence. As John Hinckley, Jr., said, "I was desperate in some bold way to get . . . attention" (Clarke 1990, p. 97). His fictional mentor, Travis Bickle in the movie *Taxi Driver*, uttered similar words in his notoriously angry and guarded line, "You talkin' to me?" Of course, in his heart of hearts, he hoped somebody was.

Part II

CLINICAL DIAGNOSIS AND TREATMENT

6

Erotomanic and Other Nondelusional Attachments

> Is not this something more than fantasy?
> *—Hamlet*

I have selected six case studies, five that resulted in violence, which illustrate both the diagnosis and treatment of delusional and borderline erotomania. Two of these cases resulted in the homicide of the love object. The other four cases resulted in injury, or the threat of injury, to the love object or other individuals. Although my sample is quite small, it isolates a subgroup of erotomanic individuals who killed their love object or intended to kill someone. The sample also includes three males from Hispanic, North African, and Middle Eastern cultures, which introduces an important, additional cultural variable. Psychological test data have been included when available, and all identifying information has been altered to adequately disguise the subjects.

CASE 1: FATAL ATTRACTION IN AN ANTISOCIAL FEMALE

An 18-year-old Caucasian female moved in with her new boyfriend very soon after meeting him. After a short time he wanted her to move out. A tumultuous course of intermittent contact followed for the next

145

several years, during which the couple lived together for brief periods. The male's attempts to end the relationship were met with intense depression and hostility on the part of the female. In her mid-twenties, she purchased a handgun, practiced shooting, and eventually murdered her ex-boyfriend in front of his apartment.

Psychological testing prior to trial indicated a woman of average intelligence. One response during the completion of the Wechsler Adult Intelligence Scale–Revised (WAIS-R) Comprehension subtest, a measure of social judgment, is particularly revealing: When asked, "What should you do if while in the movies you are the first person to see smoke and fire?" (*WAIS-R Manual*, p. 83) she responded, "I would get up and leave and not think of the welfare of others, but I was brought up to think of others, tell the management, but I wouldn't do it for the same reason I wouldn't mail the letter [previous response]. I believe in survival of the fittest. I'm selfish. I don't like people very much, I'm a loner. I believe so many people don't deserve to be here." This response suggests both narcissistic and psychopathic character traits and would increase the risk of violence in this erotomanic context.

The Minnesota Multiphasic Personality Inventory (MMPI) indicated a valid, but highly elevated profile, commonly associated with borderline personality disorder in females. Highest elevations occurred on Scale 8 (T = 98), Scale 2 (T = 94), and Scale 4 (T = 93). Scales 3, 6, and 7 had T scores greater than 80. Scale 5 was scored T = 45. This "gullwing"-shaped profile suggests an individual who experiences multiple and pervasive psychiatric problems. Although adhering to traditional feminine attitudes and behaviors, she is severely depressed, alienated from herself and others, intolerant of authority, and likely to be experiencing bizarre sensory and perceptual stimuli. She is anxious and ruminative, and habitually, although ineffectively, uses denial to ward off intense hostility and manage aggressive impulses. She is suspicious and guarded, perhaps to a delusional degree. Her current depressive state is dampening a usually energetic and impulsive pattern of behavior (Scale 9, T = 68).

Although the Rorschach was invalid due to a constricted response pattern (R = 13), content and sequence analysis of two responses is instructive:

Card I: It looks like dancers. [Inquiry] In flight, on their toes, their hands. Four dancers coming at each other.

Card II: Looks like a bullet wound. [Inquiry] The red, looks like blood, the opening, looks like a woman, the black looks like skin. He had on a gray shirt that night.

The first response hints at aggression among the dancers, in a rather peculiar characterization of movement. The cathexis of aggression becomes blatantly obvious in the next response, a direct reference to the murder and the victim. Analysis of the aggression in these two responses indicates potential aggression *(AgPot)* (Gacono 1990) followed by past aggression *(AgPast)* (Gacono 1990), a temporal sequencing that has been linked to sadistic and masochistic relations to objects (Meloy and Gacono 1992a). The second response, when scored according to the Comprehensive System (Exner 1986a), infers the experience of insufficiently modulated affect (CF) in an oppositional, or negativistic context (Ws), immediately followed by constraint of the affect (C'F), felt as both painful and confusing (Color-shading blend). This unpleasant affective experience is embedded in the sense of self and others as defective, or damaged (Morbid), but is managed by shoring up the self-image through a reference to a personal experience (Personal) (Exner 1986a). We have found Personals to be significantly more frequent in psychopathic Rorschach protocols, and have seen them as indications of both defensive grandiosity and identification with the aggressor (Gacono et al. 1990).

Primitive, regressed imagery is noted in this response with the use of blood, sex, and human detail. From an instinctual perspective, there is a fusion of aggressive and sexual drives. She associates the female genitalia and the condensed meaning of blood to both wounding and menstruation. Oscillation occurs between male and female sexuality, with references to both penetration and reception. A prototypical borderline personality organization (Kernberg 1984) response is apparent in her confusion regarding the origin of her aggressive and sexual drives and their demarcation, confusion between male and female, and the suggestion of both projective identification (Cooper and Arnow 1986) and malignant internal processes (Kwawer 1980). Part-object references also suggest a developmentally earlier representational world than would be found in oedipal personality. Despite the primitive nature of this response (part objects suffused with both aggressive and sexual drives), form level is adequate, although unusual. This is a common finding in borderline personality organization, wherein reality testing will be adequate, although unconventional, but projective data indicate a plethora of part-object representations, unmodulated affect, and highly ambivalent modes of relating (Kwawer 1980).

The most personalized nature of this response suggests her attempt to defensively consolidate her self-image, but it is also a clear evocation of the memory of the homicide. We have found this to occur with some frequency in post-homicide evaluations when using the Rorschach (Meloy and Gacono 1992a). The reference to black skin may be an actual memory trace of the Caucasian victim's skin surrounding the wound. Powder soot from near-contact wounds and powder tattooing from intermediate range gunshot wounds will leave characteristic black markings on the skin (Di Maio 1985).

The psychologist who conducted this evaluation concluded that the individual had a borderline personality disorder with antisocial features. A psychiatrist, who is also a psychoanalyst, concurred with the diagnosis. The patient was considered extremely vulnerable to abandonment, could not bear the depression of loss, and her hostility, at times, would reach psychotic proportions. She also reported to the examiner experiences consistent with depersonalization during the homicide.

CASE 2: ASSAULT WITH INJURY BY AN EROTOMANIC HISPANIC MALE

A 34-year-old unemployed Hispanic male developed an erotomanic attachment to a 27-year-old Hispanic female over the course of 8 years. The man, whom I will call Juan, had never been married, had no children, and reportedly sold illicit drugs for income. His parents were divorced, and his mother was viewed by others as "crazy." During the escalation in the pursuit of the love object, Juan was using hallucinogens, cocaine, and marijuana.

I was asked to consult on the case by the woman's attorney, who was both concerned for her safety and her psychological stability. I interviewed her for 3 hours on three different occasions, and also read the correspondence that he sent her. I did not interview, nor test, Juan. Psychodiagnostic inferences from such a data base are highly suspect, but motivations, defenses, and behavioral patterns can be inferred from such sources.

The final product of this consultation was a letter that I sent to the referring attorney. The legal proceeding in which my expertise was relevant was a misdemeanor criminal trial against Juan. He was charged with two counts of California Penal Code § 242/243 (a), the willful and unlawful use of force against a person; one count of Penal Code § 602.5, the entering or remaining in a noncommercial dwelling without the consent of the owner; and one count of Penal Code § 602(n), trespassing.

The chronological sequence of events that I outlined in my letter reveal the insidious nature of some erotomanic attachments, and the ways in which the victim becomes an unwitting accomplice by doing things that are intermittently positively reinforcing:

February, first year – Lorena meets Juan through her boyfriend. Lorena and her boyfriend are married in July. During the next 2 years, Juan remains friends with the couple and visits them two or three times a month.

July, second year – Lorena becomes pregnant with her first and only child, and Juan joins the couple for dinner weekly.

February, third year – A daughter is born. Juan continues to have daily contact with Lorena's husband and other friends.

April, third year – Lorena's husband returns to work, and Lorena begins "going to the beach" weekly with Juan.

May, third year – Lorena receives a phone call from Juan in which he states he is suicidal. She talks to him for 3 hours.

September, third year – Juan tells Lorena that if she was his wife, her newborn would be his daughter.

October, third year – Lorena and her family move. Juan is now visiting the home every other day and calling her daily.

February, fourth year – Lorena celebrates her birthday and allows Juan to take her out to buy gifts for her. He begins visiting her without calling, and she decides to distance herself from him.

March, fourth year – Juan increases his telephone calls, and begins to aggressively question her. Lorena refuses any further contact, but Juan keeps visiting her husband twice weekly.

January, sixth year – Juan begins to tell Lorena that she is in love with him. He states that she won't talk to him because she is being manipulated by her husband and is afraid of him. She tells Juan that she hates him, but he responds that she doesn't need to pretend.

September, sixth year – Lorena begins working in a florist supply store. Juan calls her repeatedly at work and visits her work location.

January, seventh year – Juan continues telephoning and visiting. He tells her husband that she is having an affair with her brother.

May, eighth year – Juan paints two white crosses on the pavement on either side of her car, with arrows pointing toward the car. He also paints a face with black tears and a broken heart in red. He begins to speed by her house and accuses her of multiple affairs.

June, eighth year – Lorena goes to a beach house in Mexico. Juan attempts to visit her there on two occasions. She informs Juan that she will get a Temporary Restraining Order. Juan destroys property in his father's business office in Mexico, stops her car with his car, and verbally threatens to kill her.

September, eighth year – Lorena returns to the United States. Juan threatens to kidnap her daughter if she seeks a Temporary Restraining Order. She changes her telephone number four times this year.

October, eighth year – He continues to phone her, sends her letters, and writes *puta* on her sidewalk in red in front of her home. The three letters contain useful material for understanding the psychological state of Juan prior to the instant offense:

Letter 1:

"I am not attacking you, I am simply being an instrument of God, and the bad which you believe to perceive in me is in reality a good, if you can see the bigger lesson. 'There is no wrong that by good does not come.' You now have before you a *great test* and it is yet to be seen *how you choose to respond*. We shall see if you choose the path of evil or the path of good" (writer's emphasis).

Letter 2:

"The more you accused me of doing so-called bad things, the more I discovered you doing things truly inappropriate. And as long as this cold and uncommunicative sentiment exists in you, a cold part will exist in me that does not forgive nor give second opportunities, and is also prepared to without mercy expose to the whole world things that I have come to know and that I can prove about you. . . . If this tension created by lack of communication and understanding, combined with other factors and persons, continues, I hope it does not result in disagreeable and sudden results in the future."

Letter 3:

"You've barely begun to open your eyes to what has happened and to what is coming. Just as I knew this would happen, I also promise you that things will not be as rosy and beautiful as you believe. *This is a promise from the heart*. Remember it when it is occurring" (writer's emphasis).

These three letters capture the emotional dependency that Juan experiences with Lorena. What she feels determines what he feels. The nature of the pathological attachment also suggests a projective-introjective cycling of affective states, typical of the processing of emotion between the borderline organized individual and actual objects. Projective identification is most apparent in Letter 2: the way in which the "cold and uncommunicative sentiment" perceived in her (projection) is felt by Juan to exist in him (identification) as long as the projection is maintained. The perception of "attacking" in Letter 1 is undone through Juan's narcissistic identification as an "instrument of God." The ruminative concern with goodness and badness is also indicative of the defense of splitting and Juan's inability to tolerate ambivalence in himself or the object (Grotstein 1981). Yet there is no loss of boundary in this case between the self and other, which would be pathognomonic of a psychotic identification with the love object. The most ominous theme in these letters is the tension of a future event that is inextricably bound to, perhaps predestined to occur within, the relationship. It is not a positive event and is independent of the personal motivations of either Juan or Lorena. It is also imbued with a certain eschatology, as if a divine intervention will be needed to resolve this painful split, both within Juan and between them. It also suggests the subsequent use of denial if anything untoward should happen to Lorena.

On December 10 of the eighth year, Lorena took her dog for a walk around a nearby lake. Juan drove by, parked his car, and began jogging around the lake, hiding next to someone else who was also jogging. Juan approached Lorena and began accusing her of having other affairs. Lorena was talking to another male, and as they returned to their cars, Juan followed them, accusing the male of thinking he was God.

Lorena returned home with her daughter. At 1:30 P.M. she looked out her living room window and noticed Juan holding her daughter in the front yard. Immediately scared and angry, she screamed at him, "Don't touch her!" He hugged the daughter and smiled. He kissed her. Lorena ran to Juan, pulling her 5-year-old daughter from his arms. "I just want to talk to you," he said. Lorena said, "He grabbed me by the arms, we're now in the street. He got red, I got scared. I pulled his shirt. I scratched his face. He held my shoulders, twisted me, and I fell down."

Lorena had the anterior crucial ligaments torn from her left knee. On January 25, she spent 6 hours in surgery. Juan called the day after the assault and accused Lorena of lying about her injury. He continued to telephone daily for another month. Generally the calls consisted of silence, noises, and clicks. At the time of my evaluation of Lorena, she evidenced symptoms and signs of major depression and post-traumatic stress disorder.

Although there was no clinical interview of the erotomanic in this case, the behaviors of Juan toward Lorena, and his written products, suggest an erotomanic disorder that was predisposed in a socially isolated male and precipitated by the affections of a young married woman. The long course of the disorder followed a typical progression: first, initial affectional contact resulted in idealization of the love object; second, explicit approaches to the love object triggered rejection by the love object. In normative attachment this would result in narcissistic insult, experienced as "hurt," reciprocated rejection, perhaps devaluation of the pursued object, mourning of the loss, and a search for another object of affection. In this case, however, the pathological attachment of Juan, and Lorena's subsequent attempt to reject him, led to the third stage, a defensive use of projection and displacement to ward off the narcissistic insult. *She* actually loves *him*, and *others* are interfering with the consummation of their relationship. The natural course of the disorder then led to devaluation of the love object, the attitudinal opposite of idealization; the wish for a teleological, or purposive event to correct the perceived abandonment, which is actually an unconscious talionic wish for private retribution (Jacoby 1983); and an orchestrated act of aggression against the love object's daughter with behavioral hints of sadism: "He hugged her and smiled." This "attack on linking," to borrow a phrase from Bion (1959), was Juan's use of Lorena's daughter, her primary object of attachment, to stimulate her maternal fear and rage, and thus provide a projective vehicle for his own aggression, an act that can then be easily rationalized, as he did. Once again, triangulation of the erotomanic relationship becomes a prelude to actual violence. The triangulation with Lorena's daughter is also a form of narcissistic twinship (Kohut 1971), in self psychology terms, in which Juan momentarily identifies with the primary object of Lorena's affection: as she looks through her living room window at her daughter with both love and fear, she also looks at Juan. He is doubly gratified by also fulfilling his desire to sadistically taunt Lorena by threatening her maternal shield.

CASE 3: BORDERLINE EROTOMANIA
IN A BIPOLAR FEMALE

This 54-year-old Caucasian female was evaluated to determine whether she could safely return to the community following a 3-year commitment to a state hospital as Not Guilty by Reason of Insanity. The following data are excerpts from a formal report that was prepared for the Superior Court recommending that she be released to an involuntary outpatient treatment program (Meloy et al. 1990):

On March 30, 1985, Thomas Smith, the patient's ex-husband, was awakened by his dogs barking at his home. He saw his ex-wife, Jane Smith, on the patio deck, outside glass French doors, and heard her yelling, "You're the Devil. You killed our children." She threw a large rock through the door, reached in, and unlocked the doors. As she came in, he saw that she was carrying a long silver object that he thought was a knife. She was holding this metal object above her head in a striking position. Mr. Smith grabbed a wooden chair and hit her with it; she fell to the ground and he held her there. His wife, Mary Smith, telephoned the police. When they arrived, they observed the patient rolling and flailing her arms and Thomas Smith holding her down. She had lacerations on her scalp and hands. The police held her until paramedics arrived. While waiting for the paramedics, the patient yelled, "I've got to kill him, he is the Devil."

Mr. Smith informed the investigating detective that he and the patient had been divorced for 8 years because of her mental problems, and her belief that she was "Christ's Crusader." He stated that she had been in a mental hospital several times and had tried to kill him one time before with a barbecue fork. Officers had taken her to the local mental hospital, but the husband did not prosecute her because of her mental problems. Prior to the instant offense, he had not seen her for several years, but she had called several days before. Jane Smith told the police officers that God spoke to her and told her that her husband was the "evil Devil" and that she should kill him. He had refused to come to her house, so she had gone to his. She had picked up some rocks to break his windows, so she could get in. She also said, "No matter what happens to me, someday I will kill him because I am on God's mission. I have tried to kill him before and someday I will be successful."

The patient's criminal history consists only of the instant offense, when she was charged with assault with a deadly weapon, Penal Code

§ 245(a) (1), and burglary, Penal Code § 459. Prior psychiatric history is extensive. At the age of 14, Jane was diagnosed with schizophrenia and hypothyroidism and was psychiatrically hospitalized. She was considered a hyperactive child in school. During the first month of Jane's life, her mother was hospitalized for unknown reasons. The patient reports electroshock treatment during her first hospitalization; she was subsequently hospitalized on six different occasions for medication noncompliance. She received intermittent outpatient treatment, and eventually was treated with thioridazine and desipramine.

The patient has one older sister and four grown children. There is no indication of psychiatric disability in any of the children. Her marriage to Thomas Smith ended after 24 years, following a first attempt by the patient to kill her husband. A second attempt occurred several months later; the third attempt is the instant offense.

The patient's diagnosis at the state hospital is Bipolar Disorder, not otherwise specified (NOS); Dependent Personality Disorder; and mild obesity. When asked about her homicidal or assaultive history, she reported three different events. The first occurred in 1978 when she "grabbed a fork and tried to kill my husband." When asked why, she said, "I felt like he dominated me too much." The second event was a threat and an approach. "I told him, 'I came here to kill you.' I had a knife, but didn't take it out. I hated him, he was too domineering. I thought he was the Devil." Regarding the instant offense, she stated that at 3 A.M. she had experienced racing thoughts to kill her husband. She went to her husband's home and, during her travel in the car, the car ran out of gas. She got out and began walking along the highway. She picked up a chrome strip along the road and some rocks. When she got to the house, she broke a window and told her husband, "I'm here to kill you and I think you're the Devil." She said the chrome strip was 2 feet long, and she scraped him with it across the stomach. He picked up a wooden chair and hit her. When asked how she felt during this violent encounter, she said, "I hated him. I felt upset, nervous, fearful, angry." When asked how she felt immediately after the violence, she stated, "He really hurt me bad," and reported she was depressed and crying.

We then explored with her why she stayed in the 24-year marriage when she had such negative feelings about being dominated. She said, "I was afraid I couldn't work and support myself. That is also my fear now. I'm still afraid of him." We asked if she knew where her ex-husband lived. She gave us his current address. We asked if she ever called him. She telephoned him while in jail: "I told him I was sorry." We then asked her if she still felt attached to him or in love. She said, "Sometimes I think I still am. Love and hate are so close. I let him assume all the responsibility." When we pressed further for her current feelings, she said she does not feel attached to him but sometimes does want to see him. She smiled and said, "He can be nice." She also knew Mr. Smith's current wife's name.

Insight into her early relationships and their transference implications for current relations was limited, but she was able to say, "I was dependent upon my mother a lot, and I let my husband deal with all the problems." When asked if she could identify symptoms within herself if she began to decompensate, she said, "not taking my medications, not sleeping, and getting high. I'd get panicky, I'd be going fast speed, I couldn't relax." She also reported that she'd have feelings "to destroy myself." When asked what she thought her husband's response would be to her return to the community, she said, "I think he'd like it."

Results of the patient's psychological testing indicated a subclinical 72 MMPI profile. The Rorschach test was quite revealing as a means to understand the personality traits of Ms. Smith despite the full remission of her bipolar disorder. Several individual responses are notable:

Card V: A bat with a lady and a man on either side of the bat. [Inquiry] The lady and man are merged with the bat; they're black and standing like a man and a woman.

Card VI: A cat made into a rug (laughs). [Inquiry] The fur, feet, skin (rubs the card), the cat's head and whiskers.

Card VII: Two dogs at the bottom. [Inquiry] Furry (rubs card), like dogs are.

Card IX: Devils, birds, and women. [Inquiry] Shooting fire, orange color like a dragon, the shape of birds, pink color for women.

Content analysis of Card V indicates a primitive (borderline) object relation (Kwawer 1980) categorized as "symbiotic merging." This is pathognomonic of a borderline organized personality, and here conveys the patient's wishful, infantile yearning for attachment. It is curiously linked to a popular, conventional response ("bat"), creating the structural basis for a fabulized combination, indicative of the patient's formal thought disorder. Card VI begins with a sadomasochistic response (SM) (Meloy 1988a), that is, felt pleasure at something damaged or destroyed, and then is remarkably transposed into a tactile response when she rubs the card. This is extraordinary for an adult and is generally seen only in children (Exner 1986a). Virtually all adults, if responding to texture on the Rorschach, will verbalize it rather than use a somatosensory form of communication such as touching the card. This conveys the patient's infantile attachment needs, despite her chronological age, and perhaps telescopes back to the temporary loss of her mother at 1 month of age. Yet the yearning is expressed in the context of willful hurting or being hurt through control. Card VII repeats the process, but instead of a sadomasochistic prelude there is a minus form level, indicating a momentary loss of reality testing in the midst of her primitive affectional needs. The presence of two tactile (T) responses is also abnormal in any one protocol and indicates an attachment hunger (only 14 percent of nonpatient adult females produce T > 1; Exner 1990a).

Card IX is notable for the unrealistic juxtaposition of content ("devils, birds, and women"), indicating her serious thought disorder, the veiled reference to males as devils in relation to women, and the aggression expressed through unmodulated affect ("shooting fire").

Structural Rorschach variables (Exner 1986a) that are important in the diagnosis and prognosis of erotomania included Ms. Smith's Ma:Mp (2:3) ratio, indicating a propensity to abuse imagination by using passive fantasy to ameliorate problems, rather than an active form of engaged problem solving; her FC:CF + C (0:3) ratio, indicating very poor modulation of affect, normative for a child under 5 years old; an Egocentricity ratio (0.64) that suggests a high degree of self-absorption; a Food response (1) indicating abnormal dependency; and an X - % of 21, suggesting impaired reality testing.

Despite these rather ominous characteristics, she also evidences realistic aspirations (W:M, 8:5); representations of self and others as whole, real, and meaningful (Pure H = 3); normative psychological resources (EA = 8.5); and a good capacity for control and stress tolerance (both D and AdjD = 0).

Integration of the psychological testing resulted in the following findings: Ms. Smith is a flexible thinker. She does take excessive flight into fantasy and will depend on others to problem-solve for her. She shows a serious amount of loose associations, and her formal thought disorder indicates inconsistent, disorganized, and primitive ideational patterns. Despite confusion in her thinking, there is no evidence of any delusions. She does perceive reality in a rather unconventional and idiosyncratic way, and works excessively hard to take in as many stimuli as possible. She shows an adequate ability to tolerate stress and satisfactory psychological controls. She is not experiencing personal distress and has enough psychological resources to cope with the demands of the environment.

Ms. Smith consciously constrains her emotions. She expends much energy holding back her feelings, and this problem is magnified by indicators that she is extremely needy and hungry for affectional contact with others. She copes with this by avoiding externally emotionally provoking stimuli. She has poor modulation of her affects and controls them by "biting her tongue." She shows little ability to problem-solve in an affect-free manner within herself. Her feelings are generally pleasant and not negativistic, sullen, or angry. A typical intrapsychic pattern is to experience helpless thoughts, which trigger unmodulated emotion, which she then consciously constrains.

Ms. Smith has a sense of herself as quite emotionally needy, and this self-concept tends to overwhelm other reality demands of the environment. She is constantly striving for closeness to others, and this will be manifested in rather unrealistic and childlike ways. Other people are perceived as cooperative and willing to have emotional contact with her, but male figures are largely seen as negativistic, threatening, and devalued. These latter perceptions are generally unconscious, and a reaction formation is apparent through her pursuit of intimacy with males.

Following the completion of this report, I received a note from

Ms. Smith that said, "I love you." I had a moment of consternation, but then placed this behavior within the context of the overall evaluation. Ms. Smith had a very positive transference response to me during our one encounter, and this was an important vehicle for the soliciting of the clinical data partially noted above. The note also confirmed for me Ms. Smith's rather infantile, unrealistic, and dependent approach to males, and may also have been a transparent manipulation to elicit a positive recommendation from me for her release.

It worked. We recommended Ms. Smith's placement in the community, and the California Superior Court concurred. Her previous victim pool (Meloy 1988b) consisted only of her husband, and she showed no evidence of a continuing erotomanic fixation upon him. Motivational analysis also suggested that if Ms. Smith's psychosis was kept in remission with medications, she would not develop a further erotomanic delusion despite her predisposing dependent personality traits. In this case it was abundantly clear that the patient's tenacious attachment to her ex-husband was motivated by infantile dependency needs, but her *violence* toward her husband was fueled by the delusion that he was the Devil. Psychiatric treatment with medications and supportive psychotherapy were the treatment modalities to ensure her safety in the community. The lack of a history of weapons skill and versatility, or of substance abuse, also contraindicated future violence. Her mood disorder diagnosis underscored the importance of considering this form of psychosis in cases of erotomania (Rudden et al. 1990), and the degree to which manic energy can literally fuel violent approaches toward the love object. Since Ms. Smith's release she has been a stable, resilient, and optimistic outpatient.

CASE 4: ACUTE EROTOMANIA IN A PARANOID SCHIZOPHRENIC MALE

Samuel Jones was the second oldest in a family of four siblings, born and raised in an intact, Caucasian, middle-class family. Social and developmental records do not indicate any attachment disruptions in childhood, although an extensive history of polydrug abuse began at age 16. Until the time of the instant offense, when Samuel was 30 years old, substance use included alcohol, nicotine, sedative-hypnotics, barbiturates, amphetamine, cannabis, hallucinogens, inhalants, and phencyclidine.

Samuel graduated from high school despite a chronic record of truancy and attended college for 1 month. He then joined the Air Force, from which he was discharged 20 months later for psychiatric reasons. Clinical reports at this time are ambiguous, referring to "heavy use of drugs and alcohol," "exhibiting bizarre behavior," and "hearing voices and paranoid thinking." He subsequently returned to live with his parents, his sister, or by himself in close proximity to his family. Sam also completed an associate arts degree in real estate and became licensed as a real estate salesman. His psychiatric treatment continued on an outpatient basis, and twice on an inpatient basis, through the local Veterans Administration hospital. Alcohol use continued until age 27, although the polydrug experimentation had ended when Sam was discharged from the service. He also sustained employment during this time as an offset pressman and a salesman. Sam never married and had no constant heterosexual pair bond during this time. In the several years prior to the instant offense, he regularly sought out prostitutes for sexual liaisons.

Samuel Jones's clinical diagnosis was Schizophrenia, Paranoid Type, Chronic, and Mixed Substance Abuse *(DSM-III)*. This has been consistent throughout his history except for one psychiatrist who thought that Organic Personality Syndrome, Explosive Type, should be considered. Although no antisocial diagnosis was given, his history also indicates a pattern of adult antisocial behavior beginning at age 18. He was once charged with possession of a dangerous weapon. Four years later he was twice charged with drunk driving on a highway. He received 36 months' probation but was subsequently charged with drunk driving on a highway, hit and run, and property damage. At age 26 he was charged with two counts of battery on a police officer, two counts of assault on a person, obstructing and resisting a public officer, and vandalism. The latter case was plea bargained, and he was convicted and sentenced on the vandalism offense.

Samuel's weapons history is also significant for the instant offense and his risk of dangerousness. He had an abiding interest in weapons and had purchased his first shotgun at age 14. In the interim he owned two other shotguns and had been trained in the use of the M-16, a small-caliber, high-velocity automatic rifle, in the Air Force. He also owned a Hi-Standard .22-caliber, 9-shot revolver, and a Brazilian made .38-caliber revolver.

In August, 1984, after 2 years of sobriety, Samuel Jones began drinking alcohol again. His pattern was to frequent bars by himself, usually starting at 1 P.M., and continue drinking into the evening once or twice a week. A year earlier, he had moved out of his parents' home and rented an apartment. He also ceased taking his neuroleptic medications.

One week before Christmas, 1984, Samuel frequented a nude dancing bar and saw a dancer that looked like a girlfriend he'd had when he was 13.[1] He returned twice to see her and was sexually aroused by her dancing. He waited until she left the bar, thinking that she would be going to her second job. As he drove to the restaurant he thought she was in, he remembers thinking, "She'll be inside and we'll have a relationship." She was not there, and he began a search of three different restaurants, returning to his car and "playing with my gun," which was loaded at the time. Samuel, in retrospect, also reported thinking, "I was imagining I could rob a store, I was angry and paranoid. I'd load the gun and put it away over the course of three days."

Samuel continued this behavior for a week. "I thought I knew her car. I chased all over town. I found a car that I was sure was hers, but

---

1. I consider nude dancing an invitation to erotomanic delusion, particularly when the dancer will have direct eye contact with the male watcher and affectionally relate to him with pleasurable affect and even touching. The invitation to the male is to suspend disbelief and revel in the fantasy of an erotic-affectional relationship for the moment—and at an economic price. This illusory marriage of exhibitionism and voyeurism works well if the male's reality testing is adequate. If not, a delusional pursuit may occur. A small sampling of women who erotically dance indicates that delusional following is not unusual, and is directed toward the dancers with the largest breasts—perhaps a condensing of affectional-maternal neediness and unfulfilled sexual desire.

she didn't come out. I was frustrated and angry. I drove all over town looking for her. I went back to the nude parlor three times and didn't find her. I also was having paranoid delusions of being poisoned. *All we had to do was meet and a relation would happen. Once she saw me she would know we were supposed to have a relationship* [author's emphasis]."

On Christmas Day, 1984, Samuel Jones stopped looking for her. He drove through his community and randomly fired his weapons at two occupied motor vehicles, both containing families with children; several parked cars and houses; a Thrifty Store; and a savings bank. At one point he held his gun out the window, aimed it directly at three people who were standing in the front yard of their home, did not shoot, and drove on. When Samuel was apprehended, he had seventy-seven expended .22- and .38-caliber cartridges in his auto, and eighteen live rounds. The police also found his .22-caliber Hi-Standard revolver and his .38-caliber Brazilian revolver. A Model 120 buck knife in a sheath and a battle-ax were also confiscated. Remarkably, no one had been injured.

Samuel's recall of the instant offense 6 years later was succinct and nonchalant. "I did some random drive-by shootings. I made a conscious decision *not* to go to the park and shoot children. I didn't take aim, I took pot shots."

Samuel Jones was found Guilty, but Not Guilty By Reason of Insanity, of three counts of assault with a firearm and one count of vandalism. He was committed to a regional state hospital and remained there for 4 years.

Inpatient psychiatric and psychological evaluations following the offense indicate that the crime was precipitated by anger toward his family for their "meddlesome" attitude; they wanted him to spend time with them on the holiday, and he wanted to be alone. He claimed that he was looking for an open target range to practice shooting, but because they were all closed he suddenly decided to practice out the window of his car. "I pretty much shot up the whole town. I said 'screw it,' I just wanted to let off a little steam." Records also indicate profound ambivalence toward his family, both a wish for continued dependency and anger at their intrusiveness. His clearest memory of his father is an angry episode at the dinner table when Dad threw his plate at the ceiling "and it stuck." This early memory may provide a characterological template for the patient's impulsiveness when angry, in that the memory finishes with a silly and harmless outcome, a rationalization for sudden violence.

What is striking for its absence from the hospital records is the erotomanic delusion of this patient as a precipitant of the violence. It is mentioned in passing, but only after 2 years of hospitalization. The patient concealed this information from clinicians, both at the time of the determination of his sanity, and for the first several years of his commitment. Nevertheless, it is also discounted as a specific precipitant even after it became known to the hospital treatment team.

If this case is analyzed from an attachment and object relations perspective, both the predisposing and precipitating factors consistent with violence become clearer. Samuel Jones's attachment disruptions appear to have begun in early adolescence with polysubstance abuse. Although the impact of the chronic ingestion of psychoactive substances on the biochemistry of self-regulation and proximity seeking to an object is unknown, I think it is reasonable to assume that such an interference exists. This would seem particularly damaging at two stages in a person's life: neonatal and postnatal development of the central nervous system—a time of biological vulnerability; and adolescent development, when sensitivity to the object is necessary for the genesis of heterosexual (or homosexual) pair bonding, the relinquishing of parental dependencies, and the integration of a cohesive identity—a time of psychological vulnerability.

In a sense, Samuel's chronic polydrug abuse since early adolescence may have psychobiologically frozen his developmental clock, anesthetizing both his capacity for heterosexual pair bonding experimentation and the eventual maturation of his attachment behaviors as an adult. At the time of the offense, he was a 30-year-old man with the object relational fantasies and attachment behaviors of an early adolescent, both in relation to family and an erotic stranger female.

Another predisposing factor in his risk of violence is his weapons history. This factor cannot be overemphasized, and in retrospect contributes to *lethality* risk in all assessments of dangerousness.

Where there is proximity to a weapon, especially a handgun, the risk of serious injury or homicide if aggression occurs dramatically increases. Appendix II is the complete Weapons History Assessment Method (WHAM) that I have developed for addressing this individual factor with patients. It is a structured interview that will yield voluminous information when completed with a cooperative and honest patient. An abbreviated form of this instrument consists of the questions listed in Table 6-1.

These questions should be asked in sequence. Any one positive response should prompt further inquiry with reference to specifically relevant questions from the structured interview in Appendix II. The last question delves into weapons approach behaviors and includes such activities as gun magazine reading (e.g., *Soldier of Fortune, Guns and Ammo*), repetitive viewing of violent movies with an enhanced weaponry focus (*Lethal Weapon* showcased the 9-mm Barretta semi-automatic pistol; *Quigley Down Under* showcased the Sharps .50-caliber long rifle; *Taxi Driver* showcased the personalized concealment of multiple weapons), visits to gun shops, visits to gun conventions, or purchasing of military equipment and clothing. All these approach behaviors suggest hedonic fantasy or ideation positively reinforced by the behavior, and therefore likely to be repeated.

In the case of Samuel Jones, the interest in weapons, skill, possession, criminal use, and unconscious link to sexual-aggressive fantasy ("playing with my gun" as he searched for the nude dancer), were all readily apparent in his history and just prior to the offense.[2]

The paranoid dynamic, clinically documented in this patient 8 years prior to the instant offense, and diagnosed as paranoid schizophrenia, also predisposed the violence. This perception of persecutory objects outside the self is the quintessential mental prelude to acts of

---

2. Weapons assessment for mental health professionals, unlike criminal investigators, is a foreign concept. It contradicts therapeutic optimism and may be philosophically abhorrent if the clinician is very much pro–gun control. Unfortunately, the ubiquity of lethal weapons in American society in the late twentieth century is a reality. It is thus a major risk factor in violence assessment and should be done with both knowledge and neutrality. One recent study (Anderson et al. 1989) found that 8.4 percent of individuals entering a psychiatric emergency room were in possession of a weapon, usually a cutting instrument.

Table 6–1.

Weapons History Assessment Method Screen.

1. Have you ever owned or possessed a weapon?
2. Have you been trained in the use of weapons?
3. Do you continue to practice your skill with weapons?
4. Do you own or possess a weapon now?
5. If not, do you like to do things associated with weapons?

homicide. MacDonald (1968) found that 35 percent of 100 patients admitted to the Colorado State Hospital for homicidal threats evidenced paranoid delusions. Lewis and colleagues (1985) identified paranoid ideation in eight individuals in her prospective sample ($N = 9$) of children who later murdered. Meissner (1978) expounded on the high levels of persecutory and homosexual anxiety expected in paranoid individuals. Paranoia also tends to be associated with affective, rather than predatory, violence because intense autonomic arousal usually results from the perception of a threat and may lead to a preemptive, reactive strike (Meloy 1988a). In the case of Samuel, aggressive penetration of the object (the search for the nude dancer to consummate a relationship, and the substituted discharge of weapons) was accompanied by the oral incorporative fear of the object (being poisoned), consciously raged against as a "meddlesome" family whose phone invitations on Christmas day became intrusive, auditory invasions.

Samuel's criminal history also predisposed him to further violence. As his frequency of offenses increased, the likelihood of further offenses increased. And his prior offenses involved automobiles, alcohol, weapons, impulsivity, and aggression toward objects. Ironically, all these elements were condensed in the instant offense that resulted in his insanity acquittal.

The precipitating, or trigger, factors in this patient's instant offense began with his leaving his parents' home in April, 1983. Even though Samuel felt great ambivalence toward his family, the severance of this attached, holding relationship increased his violence risk. Klassen and O'Connor (1988) found in their prospective study of 239 males admitted to an acute inpatient setting that certain situational variables emerged in their stepwise discriminant analysis to predict violence (6-month follow-up after discharge): dissatisfaction with extended family, lessened contact with mother, increased length of time since last sexual intercourse, dissatisfaction with siblings, and not living with parents. Their study underscores the importance of the disrupted attachment paradigm in Samuel's history. He was also very angry at his sexual impotence caused by the neuroleptics.

Samuel's return to alcohol after a 2-year hiatus also precipitated his violence. Its disinhibiting characteristics are well known and appear to be biochemically associated with a decrease in circulating levels of serotonin. Recent studies, however, have urged the simultaneous measurement of individual differences and situational variables in exploring the alcohol–aggression equation (Lang and Sibrel 1989).

Most central to the hypothesis of this chapter is the role of Samuel's erotomanic delusion as a precipitant of his violence. There is no diagnostic question that Delusional (Paranoid) Disorder, Erotomanic Subtype, was present in Samuel's clinical state the week prior to his offense. It appears, moreover, to have defended against the actual loss of familial attachments and the chronic absence of a sexual pair bond. The nude dancer evoked memories of a girlfriend he'd had at age 13, the same time his developing attachment capacities were disrupted by chemical abuse. The magical wish of the early adolescent became the regressive sanctuary of the adult erotomanic lost in time. His growing anger at the persecutory objects in the world, magnified by his psychosis, could for a time be sexualized in an attachment fantasy. Erotomania in this sense forestalled violence until the blunt trauma of reality obliterated his delusional belief. Unlike the previous three cases, Samuel Jones is an example of acute, or situational, erotomania, which defended against a chronic pattern of paranoid rage for a short time.

Psychological test data on Samuel Jones indicate an MMPI and MMPI-2 single scale 4 elevation (T = 80) when his paranoid schizophrenia is in full remission. Rorschach data suggest an individual with limited psychological resources (EA = 3.5), although adequate stress tolerance and controls (AdjD = 0). Although lacking a normative capacity to form attachments (T = 0), the patient does show an interest in others as whole, real, and meaningful objects (Pure H = 3). Although able to process affect as readily as most (Afr = 0.50), his modulation of affect is inordinately constricted (FC:CF + C = 3:0). He is highly defended against affect (L = 1.57), and is unlikely to foresee long-term consequences of his actions. Although evidencing some signs of formal thought disorder (WSum6 = 13), his reality testing is adequate (X − % = 11). He remains highly self-absorbed (EgoC = 0.61), but not pathologically narcissistic (Fr + rF = 0).

CASE 5: DELUSIONAL FOLLOWING BY A PSYCHOTIC LIBYAN MALE

Mr. Ahmed was a 37-year-old Libyan male evaluated to determine whether he was suffering from a mental disorder that would predispose him to violence toward his victim. The defendant was sent to our evaluation unit because he had violated a temporary restraining order five times in three months. Review of the available records revealed the allegations of violation of the restraining order and an envelope containing a bird feather stained in blood, on which was written, "I would appreciate it if you write me a receipt, and send it to me in the enclosed envelope. Ahmed." Another letter was reviewed which was addressed to the female victim: "Racist . . . a very dirty one . . . let us see how your stupid mind will get you out of this one. More public money to protect a racist who knows no limits! Well, kid, to your advantage, I am obliged to tell you that I am inside you and not out there." Another letter written by the female victim indicates a 4-year history of harassment by Mr. Ahmed. She reports that she is nervous, fearful, and anxious. She claims Mr. Ahmed would make silent phone calls to her home, to her mother's home, and to her place of employment. The defendant would also find her car in various parking lots and place flowers on the windshield. She writes that she never had a relationship with this man, and "He was setting me up and I thought he might rape me . . . he has caused me to lose 4 years of my life, and the life of my family to be in fear." The female victim spent six hundred dollars in counseling for her anxious state.

Mr. Ahmed was born in Libya, North Africa. His father died at the age of 65 with hypertension. His mother is alive and well, and he has two brothers, 40 and 39 years old. He also has eight sisters, all younger than he, living in Tripoli. He has no relatives in the United States.

The defendant finished high school at age 17, and worked in the family clothing store. He did various jobs for the next decade in Libya, but then felt "there was too much political pressure and uncertainty," and decided to emigrate. He arrived in Tulsa, Oklahoma, where he knew some compatriots from Libya. He realized he had to learn English, so he attended a junior college and received an associate degree in science. He supported himself with family money and a scholarship from the Libyan Minister of Education. He then moved to California and completed both his bachelor's and master's degrees in international relations at a private regional university.

Mr. Ahmed has continued to work at minor jobs that are not commensurate with his education. He has been a maintenance man, a travel agency courier, a mail clerk, a parking attendant, a business college recruiter, and a taxi driver. He reports, "the best thing for me is to keep with my education."

His heterosexual history is extremely limited by Western European and American standards. He was engaged for 2 years to a first cousin. She was 10 years younger, and eventually this ended because "she chose somebody else."

Mr. Ahmed denied the current offenses. He stated that he was a classmate of the female victim while at the university. He never spoke with her, and when he would address her, she would not respond. He mentioned some "nonverbal communication" between them, and this encouraged him to continue the relationship: "The way she looked at me, the way she did her hair, she gave a smile from a distance, like she wanted to engage in a puzzle . . . the challenge is what kept me going."

When asked to explain the meaning of her nonverbal communication, he said there were three possibilities. "The first one could be some sort of politics, she could have been a young, Jewish-American girl who was trying to put me in a weak position, to put me in a laughable position. The second possibility would be that maybe she was interested in me, and the third one was that she was trying to communicate something to me, but because of social customs she couldn't, that she was suffering, that she was not normal." When asked to elaborate on her lack of normality, he reported her ignoring his verbal overtures.

When asked if he had fallen in love with the victim, he said guardedly, "I liked her sometimes." When asked how Arab women show their interest and love, he responded that they are only seen in family situations. Mr. Ahmed denied any personal mental or emotional problems. He denied any delusions. When queried as to the victim's need for a restraining order, he said, "Because she thought I am a dangerous man."

Mr. Ahmed lost contact with the victim for 2 years after his graduation. He eventually relocated her through the university alumni book. He began appearing at her bus stop on the route to her bank employment, and would stare at her. He said, "I wanted the truth. I started putting flowers on her car." He denied sending her the bloody feather but did say he sent her fifty dollars and a request for a receipt. During this period of time, he also received a threatening phone call from the victim's husband. Mr. Ahmed did not think this was her husband. He also reported receiving "silent phone calls" while still attending the university, and believed the female victim was calling him. At one time he heard a "sigh" on the telephone. The next day at school he was reading a notice on the bulletin board and heard the exact same sigh. He looked behind him and saw the victim. He knew she had called him the night before. His silent phone calls have continued to the victim. In response to being asked why he never spoke to her, he said, "I don't know. I felt I was responding to something. I thought she was there." He called the victim's mother once to explain his behavior toward her daughter.

Mental status exam of the defendant revealed a middle-aged Libyan male who appeared in good contact with the environment. He was neatly attired and groomed. His motor activity was normal, and his speech was rational, coherent, and relevant. Hallucinations were not suggested. Ideas of reference were evident, in that he believed that the victim had some special interest in him. His affect was within normal limits, and his mood was anxious and depressed. His attention was unimpaired, and his recent and remote memory were intact. His judgment regarding the offense was grossly impaired, but his activities of daily living were normal.

Psychological testing included the Shipley Institute of Living Scale, the MMPI, and the Rorschach. The Shipley indicated a bright normal IQ (WAIS-R equivalent 111). The MMPI was a subclinical 872 profile and a "fake good" validity configuration ($F - K = -22$). Supplemental scales of interest included the Megargee OH Scale ($T = 77$), Harris and Lingoes HY2 Need for Affection ($T = 71$) and HY5 Inhibition of Aggression ($T = 68$), Dependency ($T = 39$) and Dominance ($T = 62$) indicating autonomous, self-initiating traits, Harris and Lingoes PA3 Naivete ($T = 68$) indicating a moral righteousness and unwillingness to forgive, and Harris and Lingoes MA3 Imperturbability ($T = 65$). The Weiner-Harmon Subtle–Obvious subscales suggested dissembling, or concealment of depression, use of denial, unconventional attitudes, and paranoia. Subtle scores exceeded obvious scores across the five subscales by 110 T.

The Rorschach was valid but highly constricted ($R = 14$). Results indicated an individual organized at a psychotic level of personality (Kernberg 1984) who would experience difficulties with reality testing, interpersonal relatedness, and modulation of affect.

Mr. Ahmed's self-concept was one of damage and inadequacy ($MOR = 3$, Egocentricity $= 0.14$). He had very few organized psychological resources available to him ($EA = 3.5$), although his stress tolerance was adequate ($D = 0$, $AdjD = 0$). His aspirations were grandiose ($W{:}M = 9{:}1$) and far outstripped his abilities. He approached reality in a simplistic manner without foresight (Lambda $= 1.80$) and did not have a well-developed method of problem solving (EB = ambitent).

Most salient to his erotomanic delusion were his cognitive impairments. Mr. Ahmed organized percepts as frequently as most ($R = 14$, $Zf = 6$), but did it poorly and would miss obvious aspects of his perceptual field ($Zd = -3.5$). His cognitive mediation was severely impaired, with idiosyncratic and unconventional attribution of meaning ($X + \% = 36$, $F + \% = 33$), and serious impairments in reality testing (X – % = 21). Ideational problems, or formal thought disorders, were notable (WSum6 = 29), with marked tendencies to think in peculiar and circumstantial ways, and to draw illogical conclusions (ALOG = 3).

Affect processing and modulation were also problematic. Mr. Ahmed was highly defended against his own internal emotions (L = 1.80) and would avoid emotionally provoking stimuli in the environment (Afr = 0.27). His experience of affect, although quite constricted, would be unmodulated and prone to emotional outbursts (FC:CF + C = 0:2, C = 1). He was experiencing some confusing and painful affect at the time of the examination (CF.FC'). He chronically defended against emotion through the use of denial, projection, and intellectualization (AB + ART = 9).

Interpersonal relations were also quite impaired. Although Mr. Ahmed had a normative amount of attachment seeking (T = 1), others were not perceived as whole, real, and meaningful objects (Pure H = 0). In fact, object relations were primarily fantasy-based and part-object constructed (H[H]:Hd[Hd] = 1:3) and would be considered preoedipal in a developmental context. He was not, however, prone to only passively fantasize (a:p = 2:0, Ma:Mp = 1:0), which increased the risk of continued acting out toward the object of love. There was a yearning for a symbiotic at best, autistic at worst, relationship to the object, with the risk of loss of boundaries and psychotic decompensation when in the presence of the love object.

Content analysis of this patient's Rorschach revealed a plethora of responses related to symbiotic merging (Kwawer 1980). These are responses that "symbolize processes of attachment, merger, fusion, reuniting, and the denial of separateness, as symbiotic attachments are attempted or resisted" (Kwawer 1980, p. 92). Such characteristics of the Rorschach are based on psychoanalytic developmental theory that early encoding of patterns of relatedness does occur, and can later be symbolized. Ahmed's final response to the Rorschach, Card X: "Again balances. Two things at work. I can't see anything in particular. Lungs, two things that are connected. Connection all the time. Something that brings them together. Two parts together. Cultural problem. [Inquiry] Lungs. Lungs are connected with airpipe, close to idea of lungs. Everything is connected. This part has no connection with overall structure. These two parts are connected."

This is a primitive, regressive response that contains several structural and psychodynamic themes: part-objects *within* the body provide the content for the response; symbiotic attachment, that is, a linkage that must be maintained for the survival of each object, is emphasized; biological integrity of the organism developmentally supersedes psychological integrity through the implied act of breathing; and there is a tangential reference to culture. This is a response pathognomonic of borderline or psychotic personality organization, but is culture relevant to both the diagnosis and behavior?

Cross-cultural analysis of the Rorschach has been pioneered by the work of De Vos and his colleagues (De Vos and Boyer 1989) and their scoring of affective inferences. Flesh or visceral anatomy responses, such as this one by Ahmed, generally imply a turning inward of destructive affects. Although there are no published studies available of Rorschach data with Libyan males, Miner and De Vos (1960) reported Rorschach data collected in 1950 from sixty-four Algerian Arab males, aged 20 to 50. They divided the group into "oasis" and "urban" samples, and their findings speak directly to the case of Ahmed. Through a symbolic analysis of their Rorschachs, the proportion of unpleasant content was significantly higher among the urban Arabs, most notable in content indicative of body preoccupation and hostility. Two patterns of adjustment were frequent in the urbanized Arabs: greater rigidity and internalization of aggression, as suggested by anatomical responses; or a more complex, flexible ego that perceived the external environment as hostile and dangerous. Interpersonal attitudes expressed through Rorschach content were striking. Rarely were human figures moving or engaged in positive activity. When movement was perceived, it was attributed to a foreign or supernatural figure. Often humans were incomplete or mutilated, and the latter usually involved a reference to the genitals. The Arab men were also loath to see women: only twelve of the entire eighty-two human percepts in all the Rorschachs were female. They did not move and attention was focused on their sexual organs. Another characteristic, evident in Ahmed's protocol, was the attachment of human figures to each other in a rather passive and immobile manner.

Studies concerning North African or Middle Eastern males and erotomania are also absent from the world psychiatric literature. El-Assra (1989) did report a case of erotomania in a Saudi Arabian woman. I have included two cases of delusional or borderline erotomania in males from these cultures to emphasize the importance of cultural factors in behavior. The most salient information to be gathered is the male's perception of female behavior in the culture of origin, and the meanings attached to it. In traditional Islamic countries, such as Libya, direct male observation of female behavior is usually limited to the mother and sisters, and heterosexual experimentation, whether "dating" or actual sexual activity, is prohibited prior to marriage. Strict containment of the erotic impulse in adolescence and young adulthood is possible if customs are rigid and pervasive, but immigration to a more sexually open and permissive culture may lead to gross misperception of female behavior. As noted in the case of Ahmed, the most prevalent psychiatric symptoms are ideas of reference, whereupon behaviors by the female are personalized and made heterosexually meaningful. The acculturation of the traditional Islamic male into American and Western European society appears to provide fertile ground for the pathogenesis of erotomania.

Although we did not think that Ahmed posed a significant risk of physical violence toward the victim, we did suggest to the court that his approaches, and psychological intimidation, would continue. We recommended that Ahmed be sentenced to custody or deported from the country.

CASE 6: IMMOLATION OF THE LOVE OBJECT BY A DEPRESSED IRANIAN MALE

(The entire court-ordered evaluation of this case is contained in Appendix I for those readers interested in the relation of erotomania to the insanity defense.) Hossein is a 35-year-old Iranian male, born and raised in the city of Mshad, east of Tehran. He was the middle child of nine siblings, his mother was a housewife, and his father was an employee of the government. His childhood was unremarkable, with no reported injuries or illnesses. He attended college in Tehran and lived with his brother. Hossein served in the military from 1977 until 1979, just prior to the Iranian revolution that overthrew Muhammed Reza Shah and saw the ascension of Khomeini as the ayatollah. He eventually immigrated to Germany at the age of 28. Although he had no criminal history as a young adult, he did see a psychiatrist twice, on the advice of his brother, because he "was angry a lot."

While living in Germany, Hossein investigated the possibility of marrying to obtain a "green card" to enter the United States. He received several names of Iranian females in the United States, and his second telephone call was with Menija. He remembers, "The minute I talked to her I had a different feeling . . . never before. Her voice was the type, I knew she could make me happy in life, grow in life. Nobody ever made me to get this type of feeling before." Menija visited Hossein in Germany 3 months later after he deposited five thousand dollars to her account. His memory of their first meeting: "I found someone I'd been looking for . . . an ideal person that has always been in my head, my heart, I knew she was the one." The goodness of fit with Hossein's idealized representation of a woman was complete. What is commonly referred to as romantic love usually begins with this intense idealizing transference, and the anticipation of boundless love and absolute safety.

She suddenly left after several weeks of visiting, telling Hossein she didn't want to marry. There had been no sexual intimacies. He began sending her gifts, and money when requested. He knew that she loved him, although these words were never spoken. Telephone conversations resumed, and Hossein contented himself with working and occasional drinking, nurturing the fantasy of coming to the United States to be with Menija.

One year later he succeeded in obtaining a false passport to Canada and began living in Calgary. Several months passed, and Menija visited him, again at his urging: "The same feelings . . . all came back." She returned to the United States after 5 days, saying her brother was in a hospital. They had slept in separate rooms. "She wasn't ready . . . there was a lot on her mind."

After two attempts Hossein succeeded in illegally crossing the border into the United States and flying to Los Angeles. He was elated, and moved in with his cousin and brother. Menija, however, was ambivalent. She was angry that he hadn't told her he was coming to the United States. Despite her mixed feelings, they began to see each other. Hossein and Menija would walk through various malls, and he would buy her gifts. On one occasion he lent her his car for 2 months. Menija was the same age as Hossein, although she had been married before. She lived in Los Angeles with her mother and nephew, and worked as a nurse.

During this year it is estimated that Hossein spent another five thousand dollars on gifts for Menija. In the fall of 1989, however, Menija's acquiescence dissipated. She began to refuse to see him or talk to him. She continued to accept his gifts but would ask why he gave things to her. "I'd tell her not to worry about it."

Hossein quit his valet parking job and attempted, without success, to start his own cabinet business so that she would introduce him to her family. He began drinking whiskey and beer each day, experiencing periods of amnesia. In January 1990, he telephoned her mother and told her that he would give his life for Menija, and not even death could separate them. She agreed not to tell Menija about this telephone call.

Menija did consent to see him once more. On January 22, 1990, he bought her flowers and took her out to dinner. He was shocked when she asked, "Are you still bringing me flowers?" Several days later, he visited her at school and saw her with another man. She refused to talk to Hossein. When he confronted her by telephone later that night, she told him that the man was a family friend, but Hossein thought, "I'm going to lose her, something's happening." She told Hossein, "He wants to marry me," but in his words, "She didn't sound happy. Her family was pushing her to marry him. Her family wasn't letting her talk to me. I told her she was making a mistake. She told me not to talk to anyone about this. I told her we were meant to be together and no other alternatives. I knew she wanted to be with me but her family was pushing her." When Hossein was asked how he knew these things, he said, "I could recognize the way she talked, her tone of voice."

Hossein's psychopathology now begins to manifest as his idealizing attachment to Menija is threatened. Clinical aspects of his erotomania are suggested by three characteristics: first, he cannot attribute the attachment threat to Menija's ambivalence or, at worst, her outright rejection. Instead, the relationship is *triangulated* through the involvement of third parties (her family), onto whom he displaces the nefarious, malevolent motivations that threaten their relationship. It cannot be Menija's fault; it is the influence of badness from her family. Second, the basis for Hossein's logic is not grounded in reality, but only in fantasy. When pressed about the empirical verification of his thinking, he can only attribute it to her *tone* of voice. Her voice was also the singular stimulus for his initial idealizing transference. This erotic and emotional auditory massage is felt as deeply pleasurable, despite the rejecting content of her conversation. And third, there is a polarizing and narrowing of behavioral choices, suggested by Hossein's conversation with the mother in which the "stakes" of the relationship are elevated to life and death decisions. This is pathognomonic of the genotypic defense of splitting in borderline pathology, and in this case, it is the elimination of other, less drastic choices, such as finding another Persian woman to date. Menija equals life; the loss of Menija equals death. This is the stuff of preoedipal drama but does not reflect the adequately tuned exteroception of good reality testing.

Hossein began to call Menija every day, four to five times. His alcohol consumption increased. His brother and cousin reported that during these weeks his sleeping and eating decreased, and his personal hygiene deteriorated. On January 30, 1990, he purchased a bottle of sulfuric acid in Los Angeles. When asked why, Hossein responded, "I'll buy acid and throw it on her face and when she becomes ugly she'll realize that guy doesn't love her and I still do; but I didn't want to hurt her."

On Thursday evening Hossein drank so much that he lost consciousness. He awoke in the early morning hours of February 1, 1990, and wrote a farewell note to his family. He remembers, "I went to the station and bought some gasoline; I wanted to make a point by burning myself, I'd rather kill myself. I liked her enough to kill myself. I didn't care." He denied being angry or depressed. "I parked my car, other things on my mind. They kept changing, changing. What would be the right thing to do? I had different ideas every minute. Should I talk? No, better to burn myself. Acid on her first, I don't know, I saw her get in her car. I decided to hit her car so we can both die. We'd be together in the other world. I went towards her." Hossein claims amnesia for any further memory until his treatment by the paramedics on the way to the hospital.

Reconstruction of the homicide by witnesses indicates that Hossein drove his own car into the victim's car at approximately 26–30 miles per hour, hitting Menija on the driver's side and forcing both cars onto the lawn outside her home. He then threw sulfuric acid into her face and poured gasoline over her while she was sitting in the driver's seat. He ignited her with a cigarette lighter and she burned to death inside her car, attempting to escape from the car through the passenger door. Autopsy reports indicate that the cause of death was fourth-degree burns over 90 percent of her body and smoke inhalation; there was also evidence of blunt force trauma with laceration of her left lung and intrathoracic hemorrhage.

Hossein ran to the victim's house, banging his head on the front door and yelling, "*Man koshtamesh* [I killed her]" in Farsi. The victim's cousin wrestled with Hossein, ran to the car, and tried unsuccessfully to open the doors. He heard screams from inside the car. Hossein ran and threw himself in front of two trucks, the second one hitting him. Uninjured, he climbed aboard a third truck, but the driver ejected him. He was arrested without resistance by the police.

Comments made by the defendant at the scene of the homicide included, "I want to die. If I escape will you kill me . . . I wanted to hurt her. I got the car up to about 60 and crashed the car . . . I poured acid on her face and then gasoline and torched the car . . . I wanted to kill her, she bothered me . . . if you see the movie *War of the Roses*, it will explain."

Retrospective questioning of Hossein following the homicide

indicates that he did remember mentioning the movie *War of the Roses* to the paramedics. When asked about its story line, he said, "They both decided to die and be together." This was *not* the conscious intent of the characters in this movie, although the result was their mutual deaths. The movie was actually about abandonment rage and the obsessive wish to retaliate, perhaps consistent with Hossein's unconscious motivation. He denied thinking of *her* death until he was accelerating his car toward hers. He also consistently denied taking direct responsibility for her death: In response to the question, Did you kill her? he said, "She died, but the decision I made was to be together." When asked the same question again, he responded, "Her death was the cause of my action, but I thought it would be good. If I was dead it would be better." When asked if he would be judged by Allah, he said, "It depends on how you look. I did it for her and me. God knows how much I love her, it was not happy for her. We had to be together." When asked if the fallen angel Iblis had a role in the homicide, he smiled and said, "I've never thought about it."[3]

Months after the homicide, Hossein mourned the death of Menija. Grief reactions to the loss of the victim by the person committing the homicide are not unusual, although rarely discussed (Hambridge 1990). Such emotional reactions appear contradictory, unless one considers the attachment that exists between most victims and perpetrators of homicide, and the abrupt severing of the bond naturally leading to a mourning process, regardless of the cause of the loss. In homicide perpetrators it is complicated by the feelings of guilt and remorse if conscience, or superego, is present, which was the case with Hossein. He evidenced both signs and symptoms of major depression (Jablensky et al. 1981), and both suicidal ideation and intent were intermittently expressed (Gharagozlu-Hamadani 1970). He experienced recurrent dreams of her and talked of them with a mixture of sadness and pleasure.

---

3. Iblis is a heavenly figure in the Islamic religion who leads the *jinn*, creatures from fire who are both angels and demons. Iblis acts like Satan, and is the tempter of mankind. He was responsible for the fall of Adam. It is thought that the word is the Arabic version of the Greek word for devil, *diabolos* (Hopfe 1987).

"We're talking and walking around the street. When I dream, I'm happy. Then I wake up and she's not here. How come she's by herself, alone, and I'm here? I can't see her; I can feel that she's with me. I still see her, I dream about her every week. I don't believe she's dead. I don't know, maybe she's not. We still communicate, a little bit . . . I remember her face, but not her voice . . . if I'm sadder, it's better, I dream about her more. When she's not around, I don't want to be happy at all . . . I just want to die and go to her."

The nature of projective identification is fundamental to understanding the primitive dynamics operative in this erotomanic homicide. Although it is difficult to substantiate a delusional (paranoid) disorder, erotomanic subtype, owing to the actual approach behavior and reciprocity of the love object, Menija, it is clear that Hossein, from his first contact with her, projectively identified with her. Initially, it was a part object, her voice. When she visited him, the "unconscious phantasy of translocating" the self (Grotstein 1981, p. 123) intensified into an active romantic experience, which in this case was primarily a defense against feelings of helplessness, probably toward the maternal object. This is a form of projective identification that Grotstein (1981) has termed *symbiotic projective identification* (p. 124), in contrast to autistic, evacuative, inchoate perceptions and thinking, exploratory, and interpersonal forms of this mechanism. As an instinctual process, projective identification is later unconsciously used by Hossein as a vehicle of omnipotent control, culminating in the homicide.

The idealization of her as a maternal object (their relationship was asexual) continued for almost 2 years, and with it the disorienting euphoria of being controlled by her. There is a trancelike quality to this period in the memory of Hossein, marked by his fainting in the airport in Germany when she first left him: "I fainted for a moment, fell to the ground. I couldn't see. A couple of people picked me up. I went home after an hour. I couldn't see anything, so I fell." This was probably a hysterical conversion reaction, a brief, dissociative, trancelike state that was characterologically predisposed. Later psychological testing would support this hypothesis.

When she no longer wished to see him, however, he became filled with abandonment rage. Clinically he became depressed and began abusing alcohol. Psychosis did not follow, because the link was not an autistic state of dedifferentiation; what did transpire, and maintained the projective identification as a primary borderline mechanism, was a defensive maneuver to intra-psychically protect the idealized object. Hossein displaced his abandonment rage onto the family. The family became the malevolent object, the triangulation was complete. They were the persecutors, she was the victim, and he was the rescuer. In a sense, this is a negation or reversal of *khastegari*, an Islamic courtship ritual in which the male and his family visit the home of the female and a marriage interest is expressed to her family. Hossein's request for such a meeting had been denied by Menija's mother.

He now experienced her abandonment as a loss of control by her (of him and her family), and another reversal took place. He must control her through the only means available to him, physical force. This also signaled a regressive shift to a form of omnipotent control, the belief that he did have the capacity to influence events that negated the autonomous striving of the object. The first conscious thought was disfigurement of her, rationalized as a means of demon-strating his love, but unconsciously warding off feelings of jealousy toward the family and the other suitor, and gratifying his impulse to strike back deeply, to hurt as he had been hurt, the *lex talionis*.

His second conscious thought was self-immolation, an act of martyrdom, which finds sustenance in his culture and religion (Swenson 1985). Hossein is a Shi'ite Muslim, and the martyrdom of Hussein in the seventh century provides a mythological template for his plan of action.

> The events leading to Hussein's martyrdom began with the divi-
> sion of Islam into Sunni and Shi'ite branches upon the death of the
> Prophet in the seventh century c.e. (the first century of the
> Muslim era). When Muhammed died in 632, c.e., his religious
> community, which was also the first Islamic state, faced a consti-
> tutional crisis: How was his successor to be chosen? One faction,
> the Sunnites, who derived their name from the Arabic word
> meaning "tradition," argued that a caliph should be chosen the way
> Arab chiefs customarily are, through election. The Shi'ites argued

that Muhammed had been so extraordinary that his successors should come from his bloodlines, and they thought 'Ali was a perfect man, immune from sin and error in both spiritual and temporal matters.

For a while, the dispute seemed to have been settled in favor of the Sunnites, but when 'Ali himself was assassinated after becoming the fourth caliph, trouble broke out anew. Hassan, one of 'Ali's two sons, was poisoned, and the other, Hussein, was invited by the Shi'ites of Kufa (near present-day Baghdad in Iraq) to become their leader. Hussein set out for Kufa, but spies informed his political and religious opponent, the Sunni caliph Yazid, who sent a large military force to intercept him on the sun-scorched plain of Kerbala.

Hussein's small band was encircled before it could reach the Euphrates to get needed water. Yazid's military commander tried to force Hussein to pay homage to the caliph, which he refused to do since, according to Shi'a doctrine, the caliphate should have been in his own hands.

After 10 days of siege, on the 10th of Muharram, Hussein, all his male next of kin, and their supporters were shot with arrows and cut to bits by the swords of the enemy army. Their dismembered bodies were trampled into the desert under the hooves of horses, and their severed heads brought to Yazid in Damascus, together with Hussein's chained female relatives.

Over the intervening centuries, Hussein's martyrdom has come to be regarded by the Shi'a community as the supreme self-sacrifice, and his suffering is relived in the annual mourning for him. [Chelkowski 1980, p. 32]

Swenson (1985) noted that the annual reenactment of this historical event, *ta'ziyeh*, sanctifies suffering. It is also a dimensional shift from passive to active, reflecting Freud's principle of self-initiated active reversal of passive experience (Freud 1931). Martyrdom is the ultimate act of freedom and redemption, "the assertion of the omnipotent archaic self premised on the exercise of personal judgment" (Swenson 1985, p. 139). It is a conversion of passivity, depression, and suffering into an aggressive act that fulfills the wish for omnipotent control of the self. It is victory through defeat. This increase in one's own suffering also gives license to offend others. It is imbued with the narcissistic wish to hate others as much as one likes, since they will still love because they see how much one suffers (Hart 1952). Hidden within this wish is the sadistic gratification that martyrdom, as a masochistic act, fulfills. Martyrdom for the Iranian male, moreover, stimulates a twinship narcissistic transference with the historical figure Hussein (Kohut 1972, Swenson 1985), as both real time and mythic time are merged: I am (like) Hussein.

But in our case, Hossein did not martyr himself. In fact, the planned act of suicide became an act of homicide. This is clinically quite common in forensic cases when there is retrospective evidence that a suicide was intended, yet only a homicide occurred. It is a testament to the biological instinct to survive through destruction of the tormenting object, despite the conscious psychological plan to end one's suffering through destruction of the tormented self. In the case of Hossein, it may also evidence the severe misogyny that is pervasive in Persian culture (Omidsalar 1984). Usually such homicidal-suicidal dynamics are wished, or expressed, within an attachment paradigm where abandonment rage is split off or dissociated until actual contact with the victim. Affective violence (Meloy 1988a) then explosively manifests, and the planned act of self-destruction in front of the object, the suicidal exhibition, is lost in a moment of homicidal rage. Suicidal intent, however, should never be assumed without physical evidence, such as a suicide note, or witnesses. It is an easily feigned motivation to mitigate homicidal responsibility.

The three imagined acts of Hossein—disfigurement, suicide, and suicide-homicide—all entailed destruction of himself or the love object. But he consciously rationalized them as a means to maintain a symbiotic tie to her. They would be together in death (suicide-homicide) or life (disfigurement), inasmuch as no other man would want her. Yet all these acts suggested the unconscious, envious wish to destroy Menija's goodness; and to take from her or damage her so that she could no longer possess what Hossein wanted but could not have.

Following her death, she is reconstituted as an idealized object in Hossein's mind, now congruent with his fantasy of union with her. He dreams of her continually. They are pleasant, asexual dreams of being together, and upon awakening he experiences reality as intrusive and depressing. This is a remarkable example of the projective identification coming full circle: the idealization of Menija and symbiotic sense of being controlled by her; the threatened loss of her through her own actual misgivings and withdrawal; the homicidal expression of abandonment rage, which destroys the tormenting object in real life; and the re-presentation of Menija as an idealized intrapsychic object with which he can maintain an erotomanic relationship, but only in states of dreaming and reverie.

The psychological testing of Hossein was limited to the MMPI and the Rorschach owing to the lack of normative test data of Iranian males and the paucity of research concerning Iranian psychology (a search of Psychological Abstracts from 1967–1990 yielded only 126 citations in the world literature. The most extensively used psychological instrument was the Eysenck Personality Inventory). The Rorschach produced only ten responses and was therefore invalid. Hossein gave one human response to Card III: "Looks like two human beings, but not real human beings. Not a normal picture, it doesn't make sense to me."

The MMPI was valid, and was a 28 (T > 100) high-point profile. The test was computer scored and interpreted by the Caldwell Report. I would like to quote directly from this computer-based test interpretation (CBTI). The reader should keep in mind that the CBTI had no other input beyond the MMPI profile, age, and sex of the patient.

> The profile shows a moderate to severe depressive disorder. This may prove to be a psychotic depression or a schizoaffective schizophrenic decompensation. He tests as markedly fearful of emotional closeness, with severe frustrations in his close relationships. He is apt to have many ways of keeping others at a distance. Multiple anxieties, ambivalences, and obsessive self-criticisms are suggested, along with such possible symptoms as compulsive habits and phobic fearfulness. Others would see him as disengaged and as very slow to involve himself in changing his current circumstances. Disturbances of sleep are common with this pattern. He would be threatened by a loss of control, unable to let go

even when appropriate. Severely shy, introverted, and socially panicky, he could become grossly withdrawn. His current functioning appears severely decompensated.

The profile has often been associated with physical symptoms that are secondary to the patient's anxiety and are displaced expressions of current conflicts. Conversionlike symbolizations of unreleased resentments, tensions, and aggressive impulses are particularly common. In similar cases such symptoms have included odd muscular symptoms, dizziness, fainting, anorexia, weakness, and paralyses. In addition, the numerous somatic preoccupations that he expressed on the test suggest a wide variety of chronic physical complaints lacking a sufficient organic basis. Gastrointestinal distress, headache, and fatigue would be typical, as would be concern about poor or declining health and overreactions to minor physical dysfunctions. He is likely to attribute many of his current difficulties to his health problems.

He may have been repeatedly hurt in his past close relationships and, as a result, [is] quick to be distrustful and resentful. His considerable underlying anger could be expressed through negativistic, ill-judged and inappropriate behaviors. [Because he is] lacking in stable, solid, long-term goals, his tolerance of frustrations and ability to handle pressures and demands on him appear poor. Underneath his self-blame or when less depressed, he appears prone to rationalize resentments and to feel that his difficulties cannot really be relieved unless other people or circumstances change.

He obtained the so-called "burnt child" pattern type for which the phrase "the burnt child fears the fire" has aptly characterized the chronic fears of emotional closeness and involvement. Many men with this pattern enter suddenly and impulsively into marriages or other man–woman relationships. This then reactivates their mother–son dependency struggles, especially as they want and invite maternalistic behavior from the women in their lives. Typical histories associated with this pattern have included uneven past achievements that were poor relative to the patient's intelligence and general potentials. Lacking in acceptance of his self-centered impulses, he tests as having many sexual fears and inhibitions.

Hossein was convicted of first-degree murder with special circumstances. He was sentenced to life without the possibility of parole. The district attorney did not seek the death penalty.

SUMMARY FINDINGS

Table 6–2 summarizes the clinical and demographic findings of these six case studies. There are several distinguishing features of this small sample of violent borderline or delusional erotomanic individuals. First, the perpetrators were not young adults and had lived long enough to have been exposed to the vagaries of romantic and sexual attachments as observers or participants. Second, the racial characteristics of this sample are less important than the immigration experiences of three of the subjects. Although I have mentioned the importance of sociocultural attitudes toward the female, particularly misogyny, the stressors inherent in immigration and loss of cultural familiarity also appear to be precipitants in the development of erotomania in immigrating males predisposed to such mental disorder. Third, all of the erotomanic objects were heterosexually linked to the erotomanic individual. There are still no published cases of a homosexual erotomanic.[4] Fourth, if there was an actual victim, it was the erotomanic object. This sample does not support an inordinate risk toward third parties and suggests that victims of erotomanic violence will most likely be the initial object of affection. Fifth, the nature of the weapon was closely associated with lethality risk. When no weapon or

---

4. As a practicing clinician, I have had one case of a schizophrenic patient who was pursued by a homosexual male. The male appeared to be aggressive, hysterical, and paranoid in his behaviors, and unfortunately resisted all attempts to be evaluated or treated. He would approach the patient on numerous occasions and scream, "Why won't you see me? You love me!" His pursuit of this patient persisted for several months, and he was finally dissuaded by threats of criminal trespass if he continued to enter the clinic to see the patient. Too little was clinically known about this man to present him as a case of homosexual erotomania, but clearly, for a period of time, he was obsessed and driven to be with another man who wanted nothing to do with him.

Table 6-2.

Six Cases of Delusional or Borderline Erotomania Resulting in Violence or Threats of Violence.

Case No.	Age	Gender	Race (Country)	Diagnosis	Actual Relation to Love Object	Violence	Weapon	Onset Time*
1	27	F	White	Borderline personality disorder with antisocial traits	Previous girlfriend	Murder	.357 magnum revolver	8 years
2	34	M	Hispanic (Mexico)	Unknown	Friend of husband	Assault with injury	None	8 years
3	54	F	White	Bipolar disorder, dependent personality disorder	Ex-wife	Minor injury	Metal rod	8 years
4	30	M	White	Paranoid schizophrenia, adult antisocial behavior, mixed substance abuse	None	Random shooting	.22-caliber revolver .38-caliber revolver	1 week
5	37	M	White (Libya)	Delusional disorder	None	None	None	4 years
6	35	M	White (Iran)	Delusional disorder, major depression, alcohol abuse, schizoid personality disorder with dependent traits	Friend	Murder	Acid and gasoline	3 years

*This is the time between the beginning of the erotomanic belief and the actual violence. In only one case (No. 4) was violence directed against people other than the "love" object. This case was also distinguished by its acute onset.

an object not meant to be used as a weapon was involved, no homicide resulted. When the weapon was a handgun or a flammable solvent, death resulted in two out of three cases. This should underscore the importance of investigating the erotomanic's possession of weapons or dangerous substances as a measure of both lethality risk and, perhaps, imminency of violence. Sixth, the psychodiagnosis of these cases is consistent with other research (Rudden et al. 1990) that documents the comorbidity of erotomania with other mental disorders, particularly the affective and schizophrenic disorders. It does not often appear to exist by itself. Personality traits and disorders, particularly borderline, antisocial, and dependent types, are also notable in this small sample. And sixth, if one is an erotomanic purist, only two cases would meet the threshold for paranoid (delusional) disorder in the absence of any actual relationship with the love object. I think this exclusiveness unduly constricts our understanding of this disorder of attachment and the few individuals who will become violent as a result of its acute or chronic onset.

TREATMENT

In evaluating erotomanic patients, clinicians should be aware that once these individuals are coerced into treatment by friends or the judicial system, they may quickly recognize the social desirability of *not* expressing erotomanic beliefs. Therefore they are likely to dissemble, or conceal their beliefs from the clinician, even if they continue to harbor such thoughts. One should clinically assume the continued presence of erotomanic beliefs, even if patients deny them during treatment. A patient may have successfully assaulted the erotomanic object or third party and accomplished certain narcissistic goals (such as talionic revenge, union with the object, or notable publicity) yet still be erotomanically attached. Again, Dietz's testimony during the Hinckley trial is instructive: "I asked . . . whether he thought he had accomplished that goal, and he said, 'You know, actually, I accomplished everything I was going for there. Actually I

should feel good that I accomplished everything on a grand scale' "
(Low et al. 1986, p. 44).

Several guidelines should be followed in the evaluation, treatment, and management of the erotomanic individual:

First, both Axis I and Axis II *DSM-III-R* descriptive diagnoses should be considered. A delusional (paranoid) disorder, erotomanic subtype, will often mask the personality structure. The clinician should carefully rule out the schizophrenias, mood disorders, and organic disorders, because erotomanic symptoms may accompany each of these diagnoses. As noted earlier, Rudden and co-workers (1990) found that nearly half of their small erotomanic sample were schizophrenic, and another one third were mood disordered. Only one fourth were diagnosed with pure delusional disorder. Two cases of erotomania in senile dementia have been reported (Carrier 1990, Drevets and Rubin 1987).

Second, the individual's personality structure and functioning should be assessed using both objective and projective psychological tests. Specific attention should be given to the degree of narcissism, hysteria, paranoia, and psychopathy in the character organization, because these factors will contribute to the assessment of violence risk. Dependent and schizoid personality characteristics may also be common, and although they do not contribute to violence risk, such traits are inherently conflictual and may lead to internal states of constrained dysphoria. The Rorschach is particularly useful in understanding the structure and dynamics of the erotomanic individual. From a structural perspective (Exner 1986a), careful attention should be paid to the following indices, which may indicate a higher risk of violence: $FC < CF + C$, Pure C, Egocentricity Index > 0.45 or < 0.30, Affective Ratio > 0.80, $T > 1$ or < 1, Personals > 3, Reflections > 0, and D and AdjD < 0. Content analysis should look for indications of borderline defenses (Cooper and Arnow 1986) and primitive modes of relating (Kwawer 1980). Responses that refer to predation or aggression (Meloy and Gacono 1992a) with morbid or devalued content are quite revealing and may be indicative of sadistic, masochistic, or psychopathic traits.

Generally, the more obvious the presence of paranoid and psychopathic traits, the greater the risk of violence, especially if the erotomanic individual meets other criteria. Particular caution should be paid to the use of alcohol or psychostimulants and a history of past violence, both of which correlate with future violence (Meloy 1987, 1988b).

Third, although psychotherapeutic treatment is difficult if not impossible, neuroleptic medications may provide symptomatic relief (Goldstein 1987a), especially with the Axis I schizophrenic erotomanic. Patients who present borderline erotomanic symptoms in the absence of delusion may respond to low doses of neuroleptics and intensive psychotherapy, depending upon their capacity to form an attachment, motivation to change, and internalization of prosocial values (Kernberg 1984, Meloy 1988a, Searles 1986). Other pharmacotherapy may be useful with certain varieties of pathology. Three cases reporting the successful use of pimozide, an antipsychotic medication, in the treatment of pathological jealousy have been reported (Dorian 1979, Munro 1984, Pollock 1982). Although morbid jealousy is not erotomania, it is another subtype of delusional (paranoid) disorder with similar psychodynamics. Valproic acid, an antiepileptic agent, was successful in the treatment of a 34-year-old bipolar-disordered erotomanic male (Wood and Poe 1990). In the study by Rudden and associates (1990), three fourths of the patients were treated with neuroleptics, one third were treated with lithium carbonate, and one third were treated with antidepressants, with obvious overlap. The schizophrenic erotomanic patients did least well in terms of chronicity and rehospitalization. The mood-disordered erotomanic patients (mostly schizoaffective diagnoses) had an intermediate course. And the pure erotomanic delusional-disordered patients had the highest level of functioning and best treatment outcome. It appears from this study that the presence and type of the comorbid disorder is more predictive of clinical outcome than is the erotomanic delusion itself.

Fourth, legal interventions to protect the erotomanic person's love object must be carefully weighed. In some cases they will work, but in other cases judicial sanction may only enrage the erotomanically disturbed patient, spurring the person on to more intrusive and violent behavior. Individual and situational correlates of violence risk

(Meloy 1987) must be thoughtfully considered, with particular attention to the individual's history of violence, the recency and frequency of approach behavior, threatening aspects of this behavior, escalation of this behavior over time, the procurement of a weapon, and the overall intensity and irrationality of attachment to the object.

It may be useful for the clinician who attempts to treat an erotomanic patient to secure written, informed consent from the patient to release treatment information to the love object. Thus the clinician can play an active role, with the patient's full knowledge, in advising the love object of the progress, or lack thereof, of treatment. Such preliminary measures can also diminish the impact of a *Tarasoff* warning to the love object if the erotomanic patient begins to devalue, and perhaps overtly threaten, the love object during treatment. (In California there must be a serious threat of physical harm to a reasonably identifiable victim before the psychotherapist is obligated to inform the third party and contact law enforcement [California Civil Code § 43.92]. Jumping the gun, so to speak, could result in a malpractice suit; failure to warn, when such criteria are met, could likewise result in civil liability. Of course, the definitions of "serious threat," "physical harm," and a "reasonably identifiable victim" are subject to wide interpretation in the persuasive and adversarial climate of the courtroom.)

Clinicians should also urge officers of the court to act judiciously when managing such an individual. Often clinicians can directly influence court decisions if they will risk initiating contact with the various attorneys and the judge involved in a particular case. Mental health professionals, however, must understand their role in any single case (e.g., court appointed examiner versus psychotherapist), avoid dual roles, and be cognizant of local statutory and case law concerning privileged communication.

Although most individuals with erotomania – whether it is the diagnosable delusional (paranoid) disorder or the nondelusional borderline type I have introduced – are not violent, a small percentage will be. Empirical knowledge of this psychopathology has not caught up with psychodynamic theorizing, but the paths appear to clinically converge. It is a profound disorder of attachment, and one which most clinicians will encounter at least once during their professional careers. Perhaps Kathy Bates, in her Academy Award–winning portrayal of Annie Wilkes in the film adaptation of Stephen King's *Misery,* captured it best: "You'll never know how scary it is to lose someone like you if you're someone like me." After all, Annie was her love object's number one fan.

7

Borderline and Psychotic Catathymia

The inward and the outward play into each other.
—Thomas Mann

Dreadful is my thought,
Dreadful will be my deed.
—Orestes, in Euripides' *Electra*

I have selected two cases that illustrate chronic catathymic violence. The first case involves a 42-year-old woman who murdered her ex-husband and his new spouse. Her psychopathology is consistent with personality organized at a borderline level. The second case involves a 56-year-old man who murdered his spouse. His psychopathology is consistent with psychotic personality organization. Both homicides, despite diagnostic differences between the perpetrators, took place within a highly conflicted and symbiotic relationship, unfolded over the course of several years, resulted in sudden killing(s), and were retrospectively experienced as profoundly relieving by the perpetrators.

CASE 1: CHRONIC CATATHYMIC HOMICIDE IN A BORDERLINE FEMALE

In the early morning hours of November 5, 1989, Betty Booth, 2 days away from her forty-second birthday, awakened from sleep and drove the 12-minute drive to her ex-husband's home. They had been separated for 5 years, but the divorce had only been finalized 9 months earlier.

She parked in front of his house, and entered through a rear door, avoiding the front door, for which she had a key. Betty was dressed in flat, rubber-soled shoes, a pink jogging suit, and had her shoulder-length blonde hair pulled back in a bun. She quietly climbed the stairs, her right hand gripping a .38-caliber Smith and Wesson revolver loaded with five 180-grain hollow-point bullets. She bypassed the large front entrance to the bedroom and entered through a side door. Looking to her right, she saw a lamp and a table, and next to that were the sleeping figures of Dan and his new bride of several months. The dawn sunlight was beginning to illuminate the room from windows facing the east. It was 5:30 A.M. "I went into the room to talk to them or to wake them up or something. . . . I just stood there and it looked like Linda moved and she went toward Dan and Dan went toward the phone. . . . They moved, I moved and it was over."[1] Betty rapidly fired five rounds, emptying the handgun. The first bullet probably struck Linda, hitting her in the upper left chest and exiting into the mattress. The second bullet struck Dan in the lower back, fracturing a rib and tearing his right lung. He fell or lunged to the floor on the other side of the bed from Betty. Two other bullets lodged in the bedroom furniture and wall. Linda had rolled onto her right side, and a fifth bullet entered her brainstem and instantly killed her. Betty walked around the bed, pulled the telephone out, and threw it against the wall. Later she would testify, "I wanted to kill myself right in front of him and splash my brains all over his goddam house so everyone would know that that's why, that I just wasn't crazy. He wanted me to kill myself so that he could go on living and say, 'See, I told you all she was just a nut.'" She recalled taking her gun, "as a show of force, a way to make him listen to me." She never remembered pulling the trigger, only hearing "five fast explosions . . . I went to get out of the room, to flee." She had purchased the gun for self-protection 8 months earlier. There was some evidence that she had practiced at a shooting range,

---

1. All quotations in this case study are taken from testimony at trial.

but she denied this. Before she left the house Dan reportedly said to her, "O.K., you shot me, I am dead."

Betty quickly left the house and made several phone calls to a daughter and a friend. She went to her daughter's home, was crying, and reportedly vomited some tea her daughter made for her. Later that day she located an attorney and, with him accompanying her, turned herself into the police.

Betty and Dan had met in 1965, just before her eighteenth birthday. She had travelled with a friend from New York for a football game at Notre Dame, where Dan was a senior. He introduced himself to her as an MDA, "medical doctor almost." When she returned to school at Mount Saint Vincent in the Bronx, she remembered thinking he was a nerd.

He courted her with letters and telegrams, however, and they began dating a year later. Dan was a first-year medical student at Cornell University's New York campus, and Betty was living with her parents in Bronxville while attending college. They married in 1969.

Dan was the first-born child of nine from a Roman Catholic family in Pittsburgh. His father was the grandson of an Irish immigrant and had graduated from Notre Dame, entering the Navy and eventually the wholesale lumber trade. Betty was the third of six children of a New York City building contractor. They both reportedly wanted the same things: wealth, social status, and a large family. Soon after the marriage, however, Betty felt things went from "bliss to disaster." She was living with Dan in his medical school dormitory room and was pregnant. She taught third grade until Kimberley was born in January 1970. Early in the relationship, she remembered, "He pulled the car over, turned off the key and said 'Let's just get this straight, you don't tell me what we're going to do.'" She partially consented. "I halfway let him take over all the decisions."

Dan sensed opportunity in the medical malpractice field, and after receiving his MD, was accepted into Harvard Law School. They moved to the blue-collar community of Somerville, Massachusetts, and Betty became pregnant a second time. Lee was born, Dan graduated from law school, and the family moved west. Two years later, Betty would abort a third pregnancy. She testified that Dan was away skiing with friends during this medical emergency and the subsequent death of the baby, after which she attempted to overdose with pills. She later wrote in an unpublished account of her marriage, "I went from being accomplished, well connected and free to being isolated from family and friends . . . and trapped with two children for whom I was 100 percent responsible. . . . Dan went from being a student on his own, with no possessions, no savings, no connections or contacts, to being an MD/JD who had many, many contacts." Dan specialized in personal injury and insurance law, and built a reputation as a prominent medical malpractice attorney.

By the time the third child, Dan IV, was born in 1976, their financial concerns lessened and they bought their first house, a five-bedroom tract home in a wealthy California coastal community. A fourth child, Rhett, named after Dan's favorite movie character, Rhett Butler, was born in 1979; Dan had begun his private practice one year earlier. Although the family began living an upper-class lifestyle with a boat, several sports cars, a ski condominium in Colorado, private schools for the children, and European vacations, the family was not peaceful. Betty would often be angry at Dan, locking him out of their home. Once she wedged his favorite skis in the door so he couldn't open it. The daughters also report that she would throw frozen food at them. Betty would continually threaten to leave Dan. She threw a catsup bottle at him in 1972, and told him to leave. There was no evidence, however, of any physical or sexual abuse between the couple or toward the children. By 1982, Betty had all the money she needed and Dan was busy with his practice, remaining aloof from the marital strife and the parenting. She testified that they once attended a Catholic marriage encounter during which Dan said, "If I only had five or ten minutes with you, I really would. You would be the first person I would spend it with, but I just really don't have the time."

In September 1983, Dan hired an assistant named Linda. Betty noted that time as the beginning of the dissolution of their marriage, and referred to previous time as "pre-cunt." Twenty-two-year-old Linda was a former stewardess and paralegal from Salt Lake City. She was intelligent, energetic, and very well organized. Several months later, while on vacation in New York City, Dan told Betty that he no longer loved her. He denied any sexual involvement with Linda and told Betty that she was "hallucinating." Betty claimed that she attempted suicide around this time, "using a man's razor with my right hand." Her scars were later scrutinized at trial by the district attorney, who didn't see anything. A plastic surgeon, however, testified to the presence of lateral scar tissue. When she was directed to show her scar to the jurors, she had to be admonished not to talk to them. Betty wrote in her unpublished account, "This was just a phase, a bad time – too stupid to be true. That girl had nothing on me. I am prettier, smarter, classier; she is a dumb, uneducated tramp with no background or education or talent. He'll definitely get over it."

He didn't. Betty attempted to surprise Dan in his office for his thirty-ninth birthday and found the leftovers of a party. The receptionist told Betty they had been gone most of the day. Betty returned home, piled Dan's clothes in the back yard, and set them on fire. When Dan came home, she handed him his checkbook and bid him farewell.

Dan refused to leave. Betty relented. "I felt like an idiot. I believed him." His brother attributed this to his Catholic upbringing. In September 1984, the entire family moved to a rented house so that repairs could be done to the foundation of their coastal home. Dan moved out in February 1985, and returned to the damaged home by himself; he reasoned that he "just needed some space sometime." Two months later, Betty deposited the four children on Dan's doorstep, recalling later that she did this to show him how difficult parenting was, and to keep the family intact. In June, however, she returned to the home, broke bedroom mirrors, and spray-painted the walls, curtains, and brick fireplace black. She returned two more times, smearing cream pie over the master bedroom and smashing windows and a sliding glass door with several bottles of wine. She would deny portions of this behavior at trial.

Dan got a temporary restraining order, which did not deter her. It is alleged that she threw an umbrella through a large picture window and smashed a toaster, but she denied these outbursts. Dan sent Betty a summons for a dissolution proceeding on October 28, 1985. Betty testified, "I was very nervous, very scared. I didn't feel like I had much control over anything." In November 1985, he filed criminal contempt charges against her. Several months later, he sold their home through a legal maneuver, a "4-hour notice," that avoided Betty's signature. That same day she drove her car through the front door of his new home, and an 8-inch kitchen knife was found in the car. That evening she was taken to a local community hospital and committed for a 72-hour detention.

Hospital records indicate that Betty listed Dan as a "physician," although he was not licensed to practice medicine. The provisional diagnosis was Bipolar Affective Disorder, Mixed Type, Hypomanic Phase, and Borderline Personality Disorder. The treating psychiatrist noted evidence of denial and projection, as well as a lack of reality testing. He saw her personality disorder as histrionic, antisocial, and borderline. Betty also refused to cooperate with the first psychiatrist because she believed her husband controlled him.

Excerpts from the computerized interpretation of the Millon Clinical Multiaxial Inventory (MCMI) were quite consistent with professional observations.

> This woman has been typified by a social undependability and a tendency to exploitation, capriciousness and irresponsible behavior, a glib social style, the persistent seeking of excitement, and frequent seductive and self-dramatizing behavior. Interpersonal relationships are characteristically shallow or tense, and she appears indifferent to the welfare of others.
>
> Notable also is that her energies may be devoted to clever deceptions designed to seduce others into supporting her immature or irresponsible excesses. She will typically offer only fleeting and superficial displays of affection in return for meeting her demands. Her inability to sustain meaningful and trustworthy relationships with others may have recently disrupted her characteristically unruffled composure. Current difficulties may stem from family problems or legal entanglements resulting from impulsive and immature behavior.

This MCMI was completed almost four years before Betty committed the double homicide, and is prescient of her subsequent behavior.

Dan received sole physical and legal custody of the four children in July 1986. Betty had lost her husband and children but was to receive $9,000 a month, tax free. Betty began leaving obscene telephone messages on Dan's answering machine. "I'm so glad you put the machine on, fuckhead. I like talking to the machine and I'm sure you're just recording every little word for the future . . . She's [Linda] ruined six lives, and her life was never anything that counted to anyone anyway, so she had nothing to lose, has nothing to lose. Once a cunt, always a cunt." Betty later testified that she had never heard this word before, and picked it up from a friend. She also testified that in late 1986, she began getting anonymous advertisements in the mail for wrinkle cream and weight loss clinics. One picture of Dan and Linda sent to her had an attached note, "Eat your heart out, bitch." She testified that Dan used his legal influence to harass her through contempt proceedings and to delay their divorce proceedings. She said she called them vulgar names out of frustration. Dan had made her feel like "I was operating under the most outrageous stress levels that any human being could be under. I don't remember things. I was a crazy person. He was telling people that I was crazy. I went crazy. I was like this (she rolls her eyes, grimaces, and sticks out her tongue). You see pictures of me like this, you know, like I am some kind of electrified crazy person."

She testified that Dan had instituted "twenty-ish" contempt proceedings against her. She was actually held in contempt four times. Dan began punishing her for the obscene messages and trespassing – $100 for every obscene word, $250 for trespass on his property, $500 for entry into his house, and $1,000 for taking their children without his permission. In one month, Betty testified that she was fined so much she owed Dan $1,300. A judge later ordered the settlement increased to $12,500 a month, and later this was increased to $16,000 a month. Linda, however, would not return Betty's wedding china, even after receiving her own.

Dan and Linda were engaged to be married in June 1988, a year and a half before they were killed. The legal custody battles continued. The youngest daughter, Lee, dropped out of high school and Dan disowned her. Betty attempted to maintain close contact with the two young boys. Dan would turn off the ringer on his phone and forward calls to his answering machine, which often carried Linda's voice. At one point, he wrote her a letter, "I know your first impulse upon reading this letter will be a violent one. You have told the kids that if I withhold any money this month . . . you will kill me and see that not a brick is left standing in my house. You better think twice about that. If you make any attack on me or my property, you will never again get a red cent out of me without a court order."

During this period, 1988–1989, Betty testified that she was "in a state of escalating stress and depression about everything." She also believed that "Linda hated me, I never knew why." It appears that Linda had a very strong alliance with Dan and began to participate in the devaluation of Betty, probably to defend against the anxiety she experienced from Betty's impulsive and sudden threats. Linda's contempt was returned in kind through Betty's condensing of hatred onto, and perhaps into, Linda as a projective vehicle, a third party, who *caused* the destruction of her life. She testified, "It was as though Linda stepped into my life. My life kept going with my husband, my traditions, my friends and children. The only difference in what's wrong with this picture, Linda was there instead of me."

Betty returned to her marital vows and the diaries from their marriage encounter to anchor her reality testing in these soothing, inanimate objects, which could be controlled by her. In a sense, these mementos of pleasure in the attachment to Dan functioned as transitional objects, a dreamlike possession of distraction, consolation, and comfort (Grolnick et al. 1978). "I would read it from time to time to assure myself that I was not crazy . . . I would read to convince myself that I was not delusionary, insane, a maniac, that in fact, that Dan did love me, we were a couple, we had these children, we had a definite plan for our future."

But Betty was increasingly caught in the throes of her own projective identification: the attribution to Dan of her hateful feelings and malevolent impulses, and perception that these impulses and feelings, now emanating from him, were controlling her. Excerpts from her testimony capture her growing disquietude and fear. "I felt that I was being attacked, outnumbered, and assaulted . . . and I was totally defenseless to stave off these attacks. . . . The whole thing was a very scary, harassing, overpowering situation . . . I was always scared of Dan . . . I was just basically scared of him . . . things were all ultimately in Dan's control . . . I was definitely afraid, I was afraid of him attacking me, maligning me. . . . He didn't want me alive, right. He didn't want me anywhere."

Betty's use of projective identification does not absolve Dan of the legal maneuvers and other behaviors that stripped Betty *in actuality* of her identity as a wife and mother. This borderline defense, and its role in the catathymic homicide, does predict, however, the continuous magnification and exaggeration of Dan's behavior in Betty's perception as an *omnipotent and malevolent force* in her life; a life still symbiotically bound to Dan through the affective adhesion of abandonment fear and rage.

On January 30, 1989, a final settlement was reached. Betty won custody of the two girls, and Dan won custody of the boys. She also received $16,000 per month, a pension plan, and a community property split. Her feelings "were beyond my capabilities to put into words." Dan and Linda began planning their wedding in earnest. On March 12, 1989, Betty stole the wedding list from Dan's home after her perception of a humiliating experience in court. There was also evidence that Linda entered her home to recover the list. On March 14, Betty bought a .38-caliber Smith and Wesson revolver. The incubation period of the catathymic homicide had begun.

When Dan and Linda were married, he hired undercover security guards. Linda wanted him to wear a bulletproof vest, but he declined. Linda remained nervous. The wish to kill and the fear of it were palpable. She attempted to file a temporary restraining order against Betty, but Dan refused to let her. Friends of Dan felt his limit setting was too weak and intermittent.

During the summer of 1989, Betty saw several therapists and began planning another legal foray to gain custody of her sons. Linda's voice, moreover, returned to the answering machine. Betty testified, "I felt that it was going back to the beginning, starting all over again . . . she was the wife now . . . I wasn't able to get out of the assault, I felt that everything was totally out of my control, that life was just over." She did develop another relationship with a man six years her junior. He was a businessman and sailor, and they had dined and slept together since 1986. Betty denied that she was ever sexually intimate with him. A week before the homicides they spent the weekend in Acapulco.

Testimony at the preliminary hearing also revealed that Betty's cruelty was often channeled through her children. One account was that Betty told her son Rhett that if he loved his mother he would stab Linda in the stomach. Betty would tell her children she hated them. She testified that the frequent obscenities directed at Dan and Linda were viewed by her young boys as "water off a duck's back." She turned down an appearance on the Oprah Winfrey show, which was to be called "Messiest Divorces in America." She denied ever telling her children to kill their father, or telling them that she would kill him. She said her youngest child "would always ask me, 'Would you kill Daddy?' I'd say no. He kept asking me, 'Are you going to kill Daddy?' I said, 'What are you talking about? Will you cut it out?'"

Evidence indicates that Betty's verbal threats toward Dan were frequent and demonstrative. Any one threat, however, was a false positive; yet in retrospect, and as a totality, they provided a wishful and brazen attitude that, coupled with her hysterical denial ("I have this habit of pretending that things are fine"), rehearsed in fantasy the eventual deed itself. She demanded that others ignore the meaning of her words, and through their incessant use desensitized others to their importance. She didn't *remember* these verbal threats and later claimed they had no *meaning*, yet she did actually kill the object of her desire and rage. In the absence of hysterical cognition (Shapiro 1965), the denial of whole sectors of unpleasant reality, her statements are inexplicable.

Although the evidence that she practiced with the handgun prior to the homicides is unclear, the proximity of the gun to Betty is instructive. She first kept it in a plastic case in the closet, then it moved to the nightstand or top drawer of a built-in unit at the foot of the bed, and then finally into her purse. Such movement usually has psychological significance, and in this case marked Betty's increased sense of being out of control, at risk of imminent assault by Dan, and in need of *life or death* protection. This is the splitting, or polarization of choice, during the incubation period, the narrowing of the field of perception to only the extremes, and a conscious fear of death masking an unconscious wish to kill.

On the weekend of the homicides Betty received legal papers that further exacerbated her anxious and depressed affective state. "I was sick of it. It was just more of the same threats and manipulations. I could not get out of the hole that I had been dug into, I was slumped over, I was depressed, I was sad." Her rage probably mobilized her chronic depression at times, giving her periods of respite, but in this testimony, the sense of being attacked as the cause of her depression is clear. She holds no responsibility for her pain. "It was two days away from my birthdate, I was standing in the kitchen saying Jesus Christ, I am turning 42 years old, I have been put through this bullshit since I was 35, seven years of my life wasted. I haven't been able to get a job or make a decision about where I am living or help my kids or do anything [note the exaggeration through the use of dichotomy]. *I keep hearing him saying it will never be over* [this is probably a persecutory introject rather than a hallucination]. I would rather be dead. I have no life left."

The legal papers offered Betty custody of Danny and Rhett, and also threatened criminal contempt charges unless she stopped leaving obscene messages on his answering machine. The offer of custody of their two boys had stipulations. She would have them on a trial basis, with an "automatic revert" clause so Dan wouldn't have to return to court if the arrangement didn't work. Betty wrote across the papers the morning of the killings, "This has got to end." In her testimony they were the trigger for her intended suicide in front of Dan, what actually became a double homicide.

"I didn't have a plan, I gave up on life, I didn't want to live anymore . . . I just wanted to die, just die, that is it. That is the end of the story." She denied taking the handgun with her into the car, only remembering that it was in the purse, which was already in her car.

As Betty drove to Dan's home, she testified that her motivation was "just to talk to him like I had before, just tell him that if he doesn't cut this out, I'm just going to kill myself." She said that she took the gun as a "show of force, a way to make him listen to me." As she entered his home, she thought, "I just, I can't, I can't do this anymore, I just can't go to court, I can't go to jail, I've just got to make this stop, I just have got to put an end to it. I just saw no reason for this to continue. I just had to make it stop or I was going to kill myself, no problem. I couldn't live like this anymore . . . I was scared and nervous because whenever I confronted Dan, he scared me, every time I went to see Dan it was a confrontation."

The homicidal-suicidal dynamic is conspicuous in this testimony: the conscious thought is her own death, yet she is behaviorally moving toward Dan and Linda in a predatory manner with the lethal means to kill them. The resolve to end the rageful, frightening, and tumultuous attachment is immense. The prominent affect is fear, yet her ex-husband is a most vulnerable object at the moment, sleeping and unaware of her approach. Betty is awash in her own projective identifications as she enters their bedroom and in the dim morning light actually *sees* her husband lying quietly and peacefully next to another woman, the final narcissistic wound of abandonment and exclusion. After all, Linda now occupies the envious position of Betty's memory of herself. Envy in a Kleinian sense, the wish to destroy goodness, pulls the trigger.

"I remember the real loud noise, five times, but I didn't clearly remember it then, I mean, I just remember the noise . . . real fast." She testified that she grabbed the phone because "I didn't want him to call the police and have me arrested." She recounted that she thought about suicide in the room, "but I didn't have any ammunition or any other bullets for the gun." This testimony is typical in homicides involving intense affect and the perception of an imminent threat, regardless of its objective presence: emptying of all the weapon's rounds, no tactile memory of pulling the trigger multiple times, and a clear auditory memory for the multiple discharge of the weapon.[2]

---

2. Most self-defense law is built on the principle that an individual is reacting to a perceived imminent threat to his life that a "reasonable person" would also perceive, given the same circumstances. A purely subjective measure of imminent threat would open the door to acquittals based upon all kinds of psychopathological conditions:

When Betty fled the home, she called a close friend from a telephone booth and said, "I shot the fucker, I finally did it." When questioned, however, Betty wasn't sure if she had shot him and didn't know if Linda was shot. The witness later changed her testimony to hearing Betty say, "I shot Dan, I finally did it."

She went to her daughter Cathy's house, woke her and her boyfriend up, and told them that she had shot Dan. Betty was variously described as being hysterical, vomiting, and incoherent. She recalled her own behavior as "shaking and totally upset, throwing up and talking real fast and no, I was, I was very much in shock." Betty was in enough behavioral control, however, to have multiple telephone conversations with friends during those several post-homicide hours, and eventually made arrangements to turn herself in to the police with an attorney later that day.

What is most compelling about the post-homicide period, and what confirms the catathymic homicide pattern, is her sense of *relief* once she was arrested and booked into custody. She called a friend from the jail and said to her, "I have never been happier in my whole life, it had to end, there was so much unhappiness before, I couldn't feel better." Psychiatric records the first several days in custody indicate that she, when asked about suicide ideation or intent, reported no plans because the situation was resolved. The psychiatrist noted that Betty referred to her husband in the present tense, as if he were still alive and hurting her. He also noted a quality of *la belle indifférence*, and massive denial concerning the actual double homicide. She testified, "When I was first in jail, I don't remember being there. I don't remember being checked in, I don't remember the first week or two at all. And then I started coming out of it a little, and then I, I slept. I was able to sleep for the first in what seemed like interminable years to me. I was happy to be locked in a dark, safe little

---

imagine the paranoid individual who killed on the basis of his paranoid belief at the moment and did feel imminently threatened. His perception is subjectively genuine, but objectively not reasonable. See Ewing (1990) and Morse (1990) for a thoughtful debate on the merits of psychological, rather than physical, self-defense as a justification for homicide; and Fletcher (1988) for a comprehensive discussion of self-defense law in the context of the Bernhard Goetz case.

world where nobody could get me." When asked if she felt relief, she said yes. She also wrote many letters on arrival in jail, including instructions on how to take care of her bills, her condominium, and changing her magazine subscription addresses to the women's jail.

This constellation of behaviors also support the hysterical features of her personality: the use of massive denial, the confusion of past memory with current reality, and the continued focus on the object of her own persecution, despite a pervasive sense of relief and ability to carry out rather mundane and frivolous tasks from her new home in jail.

Throughout her entire testimony and trial she showed no indication, through word or deed, of regret or remorse. She testified, in fact, "Dan and Linda never suffered for a minute during the 7 years me and my kids suffered terribly." Again, the use of splitting as a defense to deny Dan and Linda's suffering, *despite the fact that she killed them*, and the exaggeration of her own pain, are evident.

Psychological and psychiatric evaluations for both the defense and prosecution were similar, with different emphases. The defense psychologist diagnosed Major Depressive Episode and a Borderline Personality Disorder with some narcissistic and histrionic features. The prosecution psychiatrist diagnosed a Mixed Personality Disorder with narcissistic and histrionic traits. Curiously, neither doctor emphasized the strong dependency features of Betty's personality and their role in the violence, nor discussed the psychological motivation for the killing. Such testimony begs the false positive question: How do we understand this particular individual and her motivation for homicide, since most women who suffer the emotional and physical pain of divorce *don't* kill their ex-husbands?

The complete absence of guilt and remorse in Betty is a striking clinical example of her preoedipal personality organization. The capacity to mourn lost self or object representations necessitates their perception as whole, real, and meaningful images with both good and bad characteristics. This perception, moreover, is dependent upon the combining of opposite valences through the renunciation of splitting as a defense. Such developmental maturity is heralded by the defense of repression and the experience of ambivalence toward the self and object world; and also the capacity for concern, guilt, mourning, and gratitude. Betty never achieved this level of emotional maturity and did not experience these *socialized* emotions. Her preoedipal and, in a sense, *presocial* emotional life, once she was abandoned, was marked by rage, fear, and envy, structured by her narcissistic (e.g., omnipotent control) and histrionic (e.g., denial) defensive operations (Jacobson 1971, Meloy 1988a).

Betty was charged with two counts of first-degree murder, special circumstances, in the deaths of Dan and Linda. The prosecution sought a punishment of life in prison without the possibility of parole and did not seek the death penalty. The trial lasted for several weeks, the jury could not reach a verdict, and a mistrial was declared by the judge. Betty was retried on all charges a year later, but maintained her sense of humor. On April Fool's Day, she called her attorney and said, "I escaped. I'm at the 7-11. Come get me" (La Jolla *Light,* April 25, 1991, p. A8).

She was convicted of two counts of second-degree murder at her second trial, and sentenced to 32 years to life in prison. Betty's case is a clinical example of chronic catathymic homicide marked by the three stages of incubation, explosive violence, and relief. Her case also illustrates the ways in which certain aspects of borderline personality organization – defenses, identifications, and reality testing – converge to foster such a motivational sequence of violence. The use of splitting and projective identification are defensive cornerstones of this form of violence, narrowing the choice points and magnifying the perceived threat of the eventual victim. In Betty's case, the groundwork for her abandonment rage and fear was laid during a seventeen-year marriage in which the narcissistic desires for attention, success, and "ideal" love of both husband and wife were gratified, despite a tumultuous bond. As Betty wrote in her diary, "He picked the right girl to marry, but he picked the wrong girl to fuck."

Treatment Suggestions

The clinical management of cases similar to Betty's focus upon two time periods: the incubation phase and the post-homicide phase.

During the former period, clinical management should focus on aggressive psychotherapeutic and pharmacological methods, including individual psychotherapy and the probable use of mood-stabilizing agents, such as the minor tranquilizers, antidepressants, or lithium. Fluoxetine has been found to be an effective treatment for pathological jealousy (Gross 1991, Lane 1990), which may be a readily diagnosable condition during the incubation phase of catathymic homicide. The presence of systematized delusions is unlikely in cases similar to Betty's, but there is a sense of rigidity and obsessional focus that is suggestive of a paranoid process. In such cases, small doses of antipsychotic medications may attenuate some of the grosser aspects of the patient's reality distortions.

The second major focus during the incubation period is an ongoing and realistic assessment of the violence risk the patient presents toward the symbiotic partner. This may necessitate several third-party warnings if *Tarasoff* legal criteria are met, and other, more "containing" interventions, such as hospitalization. It may also disrupt or terminate the treatment. Collateral information on the patient's behavior, moreover, can be *received* from friends and family without violating the patient's confidentiality. When a friend of a patient telephones me and asks to discuss the patient with me, I will do two things if I think the call is genuine and urgent: I will tell him that I cannot reveal anything about the patient, but *I will listen to what he wants to tell me;* I also tell him *before he begins talking* that I will fully inform the patient of his call. This protects the patient's confidentiality, lowers the risk of stimulating paranoid thoughts in the patient, and still allows me to receive information that may be critical to patient care or, in this case, violence risk.

The difficulty with clinical management of a case such as this is the usual focus upon individual psychopathology, rather than the pathology of the couple; family and marital therapy, when possible, is an important, adjunctive treatment and will allow for clinical observation of the potential victim and the interpersonal behaviors of both individuals that may foster the homicidal-suicidal dynamic.

The post-homicide treatment efforts will generally take place in a custody environment. The psychodynamics of Betty's case leave little room for a mental disability defense, and the likelihood of an insanity finding and hospitalization is remote. Certain states, however, allow the use of psychiatric and psychological testimony to diminish responsibility for the crime, thus reducing the degree of the homicide and its consequent punishment.[3] This may reduce the length of sentence, but the treatment limits of a custody environment will remain the same.

Early recognition of an individual being brought into custody as the result of a catathymic homicide begins with two observations: the individual expresses "relief" to the clinician that the victim is dead, with an apparent disregard for the implications of his statement; and the individual appears strikingly composed, given the immediate stressors he is facing. A thorough clinical interview should follow, with appropriate psychological testing to determine the current personality structure and psychodynamics. Post-custody behavior may be consistent with Post-Traumatic Stress Disorder or Major Depression. The clinician should be alert for signs and symptoms of abnormal anxiety and depression, and should not disregard such symptoms of trauma and loss because the patient instigated the act. This is a subtle bias that may wind its way into diagnostic and treatment discussions. Particular vigilance should be paid to suicidal ideation, intent, and behavior during the first several weeks of custody, regardless of what the patient verbalizes. Chronic catathy-

---

3. Diminished capacity was eliminated from the California statutes in 1982, owing primarily to the public's perception that this Wells-Gorshen lineage of case law had reached its height of absurdity in the Dan White double homicide "Twinkie" defense, wherein abnormal blood sugar levels were implicated in the motivation for the killings of Harvey Milk and George Moscone, a supervisor and the mayor, respectively, of San Francisco. Subsequent case and statutory law in California still permits testimony as to "diminished actuality" during the penalty phase of the trial, as long as the expert does not testify to any "ultimate" psycholegal questions. These conclusions are rightfully left to the trier of fact. Dan White committed suicide within a year of his parole release, after serving less than six years in prison for two counts of voluntary manslaughter.

mic homicide implicates an appalling lack of personal insight into the reasons for one's behavior, which will not immediately improve upon arrest.

Over the course of time, however, some insight may develop (Wertham 1937). This will depend upon the intelligence, motivation, and attachment capacity of the patient in custody. Long-term psychotherapeutic work may benefit both the patient and society, since it is highly likely such individuals will reenter the community and establish other intimate, heterosexual relations.

CASE 2: CHRONIC CATATHYMIC HOMICIDE IN A PSYCHOTIC MALE

The criminal case of Donald Swan began on a Sunday morning in December 1984, when he murdered his wife. Preliminary hearing[4] testimony indicated that Donald struck his wife four to six times with the blunt and sharp ends of an ax, hitting her from behind while she was reclining in a blue easy chair in their family room.

These blows resulted in massive trauma, primarily to the frontal portion of her cortex; she was pronounced dead thirty minutes later at a local community hospital. Donald telephoned 911 immediately following the first assault and then returned once to strike his wife several more times during his conversation with the police dispatcher. When police officers arrived at the scene, the patient identified himself as the perpetrator and was placed under arrest without further incident. He told the arresting officer, "I am the one you're looking for," when he opened the sliding glass door to allow the officer into his home. He made two additional statements while being trans-

---

4. This is a hearing before a judge that follows arraignment and precedes the trial. The prosecution must present enough evidence at this hearing for the judge to reasonably believe that the crime has been committed. He then binds the defendant over for trial. In our federal criminal system, the grand jury renders the opinion after hearing evidence. If they believe the evidence calls for a federal criminal trial, they indict the defendant.

ported into custody: "I want my wife's blood tested for venereal disease," and "Make sure my house is locked up."

Mr. Swan pled guilty to second-degree murder with a weapon enhancement, and not guilty by reason of insanity. He was acquitted by reason of insanity five months later and was committed to a regional forensic hospital where he remained in treatment for the next five years.

When Donald murdered his wife, he was 56 years old. His psychiatric history predated this event by at least thirteen years. It included at least two suicide attempts, multiple hospitalizations at the local Veterans Administration (VA) hospital and several local public and private psychiatric hospitals, intermittent treatment through the VA outpatient clinic, and a conservatorship of both his person and estate by his wife. He was consistently diagnosed with a functional psychotic disorder, usually an affective type.

His onset of mental illness preceded by several years his layoff as an engineer from a major military-industrial contractor. During these subsequent years he remained unemployed and stayed at home with his spouse (this is the first data point that suggests the hypothesis of chronic catathymic homicide). Nancy, nine years his senior, married Donald when he was 25. The marriage produced two sons. Records indicate that their relationship was highly conflicted and was notable for Mr. Swan's passivity and anger. Mrs. Swan worked as a real estate agent and was observed by neighbors and friends to be both angry toward, and fearful of, her husband. Psychiatric interventions during this period were generally inadequate, chiefly owing to Mr. Swan's reluctance to consistently take his medications and the limits of civil commitment law. Records state that he physically struck his wife, on occasion, since 1970. His behavior during this fourteen-year period, however, was generally passive. Donald would listen to music, sit at home, and intermittently cycle through manic and depressive mood states. At these times his delusional thoughts of omniscience and omnipotence were most apparent. The most prominent fixed and false beliefs concerned his being the next "pope of the world" and the "secretary general of the United Nations." These delusions functioned as obvious compensatory mechanisms for his actual social and occupational failures following the onset of his major mental disorder, and for his hostile dependency toward his spouse.

Although the intrapsychic and interpersonal world of Donald Swan was fertile ground for alcoholism, he chose, instead, another drug. For a twelve-year period he consumed approximately 50 mg of benzodiazepine a day.

His biological family history was significant for the reported mental illness of both his mother and his youngest sister, Sally, eight years his junior. She had also been committed to the same regional forensic hospital with a diagnosis of manic-depression, and died a year before the homicide.

Donald was born in central California and raised in an intact family on a date farm. Records indicate that he felt quite isolated and had only his sisters with whom to play. He was not fond of them. Although he described his father as "easygoing," he resented his mother and found her to be emotional, flamboyant, domineering, and inconsistent (these data points also suggest a transference basis for the catathymic homicide).

He joined the Army when he was 18, and served for fifteen months immediately after World War II. He rejoined the Air Force after a stint at college and then eventually completed his bachelor of science degree in electrical engineering. He was steadily employed until the late onset of his affective illness.

My clinical investigation of the case of Donald Swan began five years after the homicide, when he was recommended by the state hospital to "not constitute a danger to the health and safety of others" (California Penal Code § 1603) if he was released to the community and placed in an involuntary outpatient program, what is referred to in California as the Mental Health Conditional Release Program.

Statutorily mandated by the California legislature in 1985, the Conditional Release Program provides involuntary outpatient treatment to penally committed patients; most of these individuals were found not guilty by reason of insanity for a violent felony and were initially committed to a regional forensic hospital for a number of years. Upon conditional release by superior court order, they must continue outpatient care through the designated "Conrep" program.

This care *minimally* consists of certain "core standards" of treatment: individual psychotherapy and group psychotherapy each week, random urine toxicology screens four times per month, medication visits once or twice per month, annual psychological testing, collateral contacts, and home visits once per month by the treating "clinician-supervisor." The Conrep program also controls the residence of the patient, and approves all travel by the patient outside his county of residence.

Since the inception of this program in California, 710 individuals have been admitted to it. The rearrest rate was 8.3 percent after one year in the community, 13.2 percent after two years, and 16.7 percent after three years. The rehospitalization rate was 21 percent for the first two years of operation. Less than half of those who reoffended were charged with violent crimes. Most of the patients are clinically and demographically similar to other insanity populations, modally described as a Caucasian male with a diagnosis of schizophrenia who committed a violent felony. In San Diego County, California, the second most populated area of the state (over two million inhabitants) and the sixth largest city in the United States, sixty-four individuals were treated by the local Conditional Release Program from one to five years (1986-1990 inclusive). There were two reoffenses, both nonviolent, for a reoffense rate of 3.1 percent. One patient absconded from the program and was later rearrested in Vermont; another patient was revoked for possession of a controlled substance.

The remarkable success of this program is attributed to the low patient–staff ratio (10:1) and the mandated core standards of treatment. Although annual costs per patient average $14,000-20,000, this is only one fourth of the costs of state hospitalization (Meloy et al. 1990, Weideranders 1991).

Mr. Swan wanted very much to be conditionally released from the hospital and placed in the program. Inpatient records at the hospital, in fact, indicated a compliant, helpful patient who demonstrated no visible signs or symptoms of mental illness. He consistently attended his treatment and assigned work, and showed no assaultive behavior since admission. His progress, as documented, had been slow and steady, with initial remission of acute symptoms, followed by incremental increases in his ability to interact and socialize, although he preferred to be alone. Mr. Swan was taking 100 mg of Mellaril t.i.d., and 150 mg of Sinequan h.s.

The forensic clinical evaluation rests on three anchor points (see Figure 7-1), and Mr. Swan's case was no different: careful scrutiny of historical data independent of the patient's self-report; a clinical examination, including the patient's self-report of personal history, the offense (see SSRV, p. 49–51), and mental status exam; and testing, which in most cases will only be psychological testing but could expand to include other neuropsychological and neurological measures when indicated.

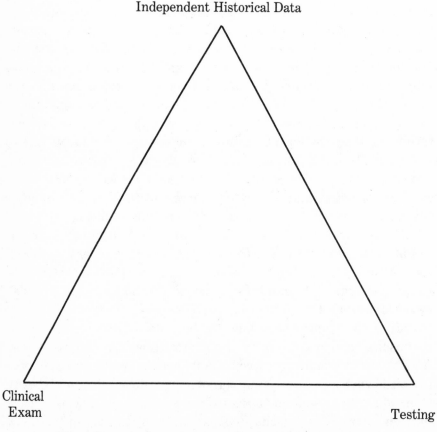

Figure 7-1. Anchor points for a Forensic Clinical Evaluation.

In this particular clinical case, there was no significant medical history that pertained to Mr. Swan's psychiatric diagnosis, and there was no history of central nervous system defect, disease, or trauma, thus eliminating the need for additional testing other than the psychologicals.

Prior to the interview, the history of the patient was reviewed, including all available psychiatric and psychological reports over the patient's lifespan: hospital records and summary reports since the patient's insanity commitment; the district attorney's file, which contained audiotapes, police reports, witness reports, preliminary hearing transcripts, autopsy reports, and crime scene photographs; and letters sent by the defendant's sisters and son, who were fearful of his release. This material provided an extensive historical basis for understanding the patient gathered *independently* of the patient's self-report. This is a critical anchor point that should be done prior to any evaluation, so that areas of inconsistency when the patient is interviewed will not be missed and can be understood through further questioning. (The archaic convention that the clinician should know as *little* as possible about the patient before the first interview to facilitate an open mind and empathic atunement is fine for certain psychotherapeutic enterprises; it is absurd in forensic psychological interviews, and should be considered professional incompetence.)

Mr. Swan's history raised two central questions to be addressed upon interview: first, despite the obvious psychosis at the time of the murder, what were the psychodynamic motivations for Mr. Swan to kill his wife? The presence of delusions may explain the conscious rationalization, albeit a psychotic one, for the criminal act, but it does not explain the drive to murder that culminates in the act itself. Second, has anything changed, other than the remission of the psychosis, for Mr. Swan since he has been hospitalized? This question addresses the more structural, enduring aspects of Mr. Swan's personality that may have motivated him to kill. He would be returning to the same community he had left, beginning other relationships and potentially reestablishing the same object relations that had resulted in the death of his wife. Neuroleptic medications, if taken regularly, might prevent the return of psychosis, but they would have no impact on the emotional and interpersonal expectancies that Mr. Swan seemed to have with women: necessary, but hostile and dominant figures. Fundamental changes in personality structure, perhaps a product of intensive psychotherapy, could alter these patterns and would be measurable through psychological testing.

Mr. Swan presented to the interview team[5] as a 62-year-old male, dressed casually and neatly. He greeted us in a quiet and friendly manner, and remained that way throughout our interview. His affect was generally flat or blunted, regardless of the questions or thought content.

We first advised him of the nature of the interview, and the fact that none of the information he revealed would be privileged. He verbally understood and agreed to continue. We then asked him if he understood the conditional release program. He was able to explain, "I'd live in a board and care and attend groups and doctor's appointments. I'd take my medications and I would be in the program for at least a year."

We then asked him to recall his personal history. He reported the details outlined earlier in this case study, and said that his delusions had finally disappeared one month after being at the hospital. His depression remitted four months later. When we asked him why he had gone into remission, he said, "I don't know. Reality caught up with me. I'd been on meds for fifteen years: lithium, Sinequan, Valium." When we asked him what his diagnosis was, he said, "bipolar with repressed manic phase." He reported that the Mellaril had been added to his medication regimen at the hospital.

When asked what treatment factors had helped, Mr. Swan said, "Medications, the environment, one-to-one treatment with Dr. Kirk. I had a breakthrough with her for a month of treatment, a change in attitude." He felt that treatment was "no special attachment. The time was right for me to cooperate. Any psychologist could have done it." In groups he had "learned better communication, and how to express myself, talking about myself and my problems. But it hinged on my cooperating." He believed that medications also helped. "I sleep better

---

5. Dawn Brown, RN, C, Douglas Smith, LCSW, and myself.

with Mellaril." He accurately reported his medications and their purpose.

We then asked him if he knew what a psychosis was. He said, "a severe mental disorder." He defined his mental disorder as "schizoaffective disorder, bipolar, manic-depression. You go through mood swings and return to normal. You can become psychotic and develop delusions of grandeur." He defined these symptoms as "great things would happen to me, I was all-wise and all-knowing." He denied any history of hallucinations.

When asked what had triggered his psychosis, he said, "I was depressed from my job, the working conditions, for two years. I was laid off, and then worked at another firm for ten months. I then slit my throat with a knife, my only suicide attempt, at age 42. My wife was supporting me with her real estate work. My delusions continued. I was isolated in my room. The only contact was with my wife. The children were grown up."

His current family contacts were limited to his older sister. "I understand they're not happy for what I did. I miss them, but it's not a big miss. My oldest and youngest sons visited once two years ago. The visit went well. I felt quite happy."

We then asked Mr. Swan a series of questions concerning the details of the homicide to begin to complete the SSRV. He answered all these inquiries with a normal rate of speech and blunted affect. "I was having these events in my mind, severe delusions, a feeling of being all-knowing, all-wise, and all-powerful. I could kill my wife and not be responsible." When did you first think this? "One week before I killed her. She was in the way. Great things were happening to me." How did you feel? "Tense. I could go ahead and kill her and nothing will happen to me. I kept all the delusions to myself, always." Were you paranoid? "Some people were for me, some were against me. I thought, 'Are you going to miss this wonderful chance?'"

Did you sleep the night before the murder? "I dozed a little, getting ready to do something. My concentration was gone." Were you on medications? "Lithium, Sinequan, but I wanted to push the situation. At 0630 we ate breakfast and went to church." Are you a Christian? "No. But I liked the music and liked the preacher." What happened when you returned home? "The thought hit me, 'Now's the time to strike.' I felt elated. I went and picked up a hatchet in the garage. I slipped around behind my wife in the family room. She's doing some crocheting. Sitting in the chair, no rocking. She turned to the left and said, 'What is the meaning of this?' I was elated. I'm finally doing something about this. It seemed to be the right way to go about it. I raised both hands and hit her four or five times. I thought, 'Now I'm getting somewhere.' I was tense and elated. I called 911, felt I needed to clear up the situation. There'd be a lot of clerical proceedings to clear up the problem of her dying on me. The police arrived, I opened the door, and held up my hands." Did you hit her during your 911 conversation? "I wanted to try and stop the convulsions, to hit her again. It wasn't a pleasant thing to watch." How did you feel when the police arrived? "Tense and shaking." What were you thinking? "I finally made some progress, arriving on the public scene as the pope of the Roman Catholics and the secretary general of the U.N." Was the Not Guilty by Reason of Insanity plea a good one for you? "A question of time, I'd made a mistake that needed to be rectified."

We then asked Mr. Swan about his marriage. "I was far better off being married than single. We had our disagreements. I didn't talk much, she loved flowers. I ought to have helped, but I didn't have anything to do with it. It made me feel guilty." We then asked him to describe Nancy in full detail so that we could form a picture of her in our own minds.[6] "She was a hard worker, been raised on a farm in Kansas, a good cook, baker, kept a clean house, quite loving and affectionate, but her big trouble, she talked too much. She talked without listening. She did all right in real estate. Made money with duplexes."

Mr. Swan's earliest memory (Bruhn 1990): "As a baby I drank

---

6. This is a technique developed by Kernberg (1984) to measure the capacity of the patient to form whole, real, and meaningful object representations in his mind. It is based upon the premise that as the patient verbalizes his representation, the clinician will be using the patient's words to form a similar representation in *his* mind that he can use to judge the patient's ability, or lack thereof, to represent others as integrated objects. It demands that the clinician use his attentional and visualization abilities in a *tabula rasa* manner, but when successful, gives a potent isomorphic glimpse of the patient's internal object world.

milk out of a bottle. I'd wake up and drink the milk. I'm in a crib, 1 year old. I actually remember being alone, the sensation of tasting milk." His earliest memory of his mother: "She held me up while Dad took a picture of us, I was carried inside. My sister insisted that she be in the picture too." His earliest memory of father: "My grandfather was visiting us. I was sitting on the living room floor. He came and sat down by me. My father told my grandfather to come and eat. My grandfather said, 'What about this young man?' My dad said, 'Oh, yes, we'll feed him later.' " He dismissed questions concerning his childhood with the cryptic response, "I was dominated by my older sister. I accepted it."

Mr. Swan's feelings about women were explored. "I don't have any special feelings about men or women. They're good and bad ones. It's about how they react. A good person is interested, a bad person is threatened."

His weapons history was limited to owning a BB gun as a child, and shooting the M1 carbine in the Army. He denied ever shooting a pistol, and stated he had no interest in possessing a weapon or a firearm.

We asked Mr. Swan what he would do if released. He said, "I'd play bridge, read books. I'd rather be by myself." When asked about sexual activity, he said, "I have no further interest in females. The Mellaril has taken care of that. I have no erections or sexual fantasies."

He reported contact with his sons through letters. If his family wanted no contact with him, he would "be disappointed, but I wouldn't do anything. I'd like to visit my grandchildren. But I'd accept it. Hopefully, they'd change their minds."

He reported to us that he receives approximately $700 through Social Security Disability Income. His estate was approximately $150,000, which the State of California successfully claimed for his treatment. "I don't like it, but it doesn't do me any good to get angry." We then asked about his processing of anger. "I do or say something. I start thinking about the consequences. I see red around the periphery of my eyes. It's happened six times in my life. I did feel anger toward my wife, but I didn't see red." Was there any reality basis for anger toward your wife? "No." Was it just the psychosis? "Yes."

Mr. Swan's mental status exam revealed that he was alert and oriented to person, place, and time. His affect was flat to blunted. He was in a pleasant and cooperative mood. He showed no evidence of formal thought disorder, and his attention and concentration were normal. His fund of information was consistent for an individual with an estimated superior IQ. Concept formation was normal except for one peculiar response to the similarity between a wrench and a hammer: "You can hit with both of them." His immediate, short-term, long-term, and remote memory was normal. He showed no evidence of delusions, auditory or visual hallucinations, paranoid ideation, other ideas of reference, thought insertion, thought withdrawal, or thought broadcasting. There was no evidence of homicidal or suicidal ideation. Mr. Swan's psychosis was in complete remission.

Fortunately, Mr. Swan had been tested using the Minnesota Multiphasic Inventory (MMPI) and the Rorschach within four months of his admission to the regional forensic hospital, which was eight months post-homicide. This allowed us to readminister the same tests and conduct a longitudinal comparison of the results, an objectively measurable approach to change or lack thereof, over time, in Mr. Swan's psychiatric status and personality structure. The clinical evaluation was generally negative for any signs or symptoms of psychosis, the gross pathology evident at the time of the killing, but the more subtle, motivational questions remained partially unanswered.

The MMPI results following five years of treatment at the hospital indicated significant, positive change in the psychiatric condition of Mr. Swan.

The earlier profile, completed three months after admission, suggested a patient who was clinically depressed, sullen, anxious, ruminative, and obsessive (724 high point). Such a patient would also be resistant to authority, experiencing feelings of alienation from himself and others, and would be in the throes of family conflict. He was also isolated, reclusive, and introverted. The profile, however, showed no signs of psychosis, which is consistent with Mr. Swan's self-report (and the hospital record) that his psychosis went into remission within a month of his admission to the hospital.

The profile five years later was within normal range for all clinical scales. It suggested an individual who showed no signs or symptoms of psychiatric disorder. Such an individual, however, has certain personality traits that are notable on the MMPI. He will tend to deny and inhibit aggressive impulses to a significant degree, but prefers to dominate relationships. This is inherently conflictual. He will experience mild problems with authority figures. He is introspective and critical of himself, and despite his efforts to appear somewhat defensively normal, uses denial to ward off unpleasant affect states. He is now much more comfortable with socializing and interpersonal activity.

The Rorschach data were also significant for consistent indications that Mr. Swan's personality structure had become less psychopathological. Although personality changes little over time, enduring traits can be modified through long-term, intensive psychotherapeutic endeavors if the patient has a capacity for insight and the motivation to change (Weiner and Exner 1991).

Table 7–1 compares selected Rorschach indices (Comprehensive System) for Mr. Swan at the time of both testings, separated by almost 5 years. The data demonstrate a dramatic and quantifiable shift in the personality structure of this patient.

The cognitive processing of Mr. Swan indicates that he continues to perceive the world visually, and solve problems, in a simple item-by-item manner, with little capacity to foresee the long-term consequences of his behavior (Lambda = 4.33). He is less energetic in attempting to organize his percepts than he was at the first testing, but the quality of his perceptual organization is within normal range (Zd = -1.0).

The reality testing of this patient indicates a dramatic shift from a psychotic level (X–% = 0.38) to a borderline level (X–% = 0.19) almost five years later. He continues to perceive the world in unconventional ways with little change (X+% = 0.38), but we can be reassured that his reality testing, although distorted at times, is intact. This is referred to as "cognitive mediation" in the Comprehensive System (Exner 1986).

Mr. Swan continues to show virtually no signs of formal thought disorder (WSum6 = 4) and remains ideationally flexible (a:p = 2:1). This is also a positive prognostic indicator, and supports the clinical observation that the patient's thinking remains logical and coherent.

The affective life of Mr. Swan is generally unconscious, with

Table 7-1.

Selected Rorschach Indices of a Psychotic Male Who Committed a Chronic Catathymic Murder, 9 Months and 5.5 Years Post-homicide, Following Intensive Hospital Treatment.

Rorschach Indices	9 Months	5.5 Years
Cognitive Processing		
Zd	3.5	−1.0
X+%	0.34	0.38
X−%	0.38	0.19
M	1	3
a:p	1:2	2:1
WSum6	0	4
FM	2	0
m	0	0
Affective Functions		
Lambda	4.33	4.33
Afr	0.39	0.45
FC:CF + C	0:0	1:1
Pure C	0	0
C'	1	0
V	0	0
Y	2	1
T	0	0
Stress Tolerance		
D	−1	+1
AdjD	−1	+1
Interpersonal Relations		
H	2	5
Hd	11	1
Self-Relations		
Egocentricity Index	0.44	0.34
Morbid	1	0
Miscellaneous		
Suicide Constellation	4	1

marked indicators of defense against his own affect (Lambda = 4.33) and others' (Afr = 0.45). This latter indicator is improved since the first testing (0.39), but remains 1.5 standard deviations below the mean for nonpatient adults (0.69, SD = 0.16). We can clinically infer from this data that about 90 percent of adults are better able to consciously process affect than Mr. Swan. There are indications, moreover, that this patient does experience affect on occasion (FC:CF + C = 1:1) and can modulate it, in contrast to his affective "shutdown" indicated on the first testing (FC:CF + C = 0:0). He also shows a normative amount of anxiety (Y = 1) but, unfortunately, still shows no attachment capacity or interest (T = 0). This psychotherapeutic gain in the experiencing of affect is critical for Mr. Swan. Although still abnormal, the quantitative movement is in the right direction and should contribute to future awareness of emotion, in contrast to the lack of conscious affect at the time of the homicide.[7]

The absence of T does not bode well for psychotherapeutic progress with an outpatient therapist, but does contribute to his lowered future violence risk: without a desire to form subsequent attachments, Mr. Swan will be less inclined to do so, and the probability of another chronic catathymic pattern developing, which might result in homicide, is lessened. In this particular case, the schizoid character formation is a forensically useful defense against his dependent impulses and hostile affects (Deutsch 1942, Klein 1946).

Mr. Swan's stress tolerance and capacity for control show a dramatic change from his first Rorschach (D and AdjD = −1) to his second (+1). The D score on the Rorschach (Exner 1986) is a scaled difference score that measures the relationship between volitional and nonvolitional ideation and affect. Scores below zero, the mean for nonpatient adults (0.04), indicate decreased stress tolerance and main-

---

7. This absence of conscious feeling at the time of the homicide and the first testing is not only a product of his character formation, which the alert reader may have correctly determined to be schizoid; but also a characteristic of predatory violence (Meloy 1988a), a form of planned and purposeful aggression that is emotion*less*. Mr. Swan engaged in predation during the few minutes preceding the killing, with probable concomitant physiological changes. Note that he denied anger as a motivation for the killing, and only referred to being "tense and elated" at the time of the act.

tenance of controls, while scores above zero indicate increased resiliency to stressors and sturdy psychological controls. This structural indicator may correlate with "ego strength" (perhaps the Es supplemental scale on the MMPI) in psychoanalytic terminology. The adjusted D (AdjD) factors out certain situational variables (all but 1 m and 1 Y) that are state specific to determine the trait aspects of stress tolerance and control.

In Mr. Swan's case, the shift toward resiliency in his psychological operations is a quite positive prognostic indicator and parallels his subclinical MMPI (and Es T score of 64). His overall psychological resources (EA = 4.5), however, are significantly below the mean for nonpatient adults (8.82, SD = 2.18) and may be due to the ravages of a biochemical disorder of his brain that remained unchecked for a significant portion of his adult life. In a sense, his psychological "thin shell" has been repaired, but will need continuous psychotherapeutic and pharmacological maintenance.

The object world of Mr. Swan has also changed for the better. His internal representation of others was dominated by part-objects (Hd = 11) during the first testing, with whole and real human objects (H = 2) significantly below the average for nonpatient adults (3.39, SD = 1.80). At the second testing, the ratio has reversed, and we see a plethora of whole, real, and meaningful human objects (H = 5), and only one part-object of a human. The protocol also contains significantly more human movement responses (M = 3) of ordinary form quality, closer to the mean for nonpatients (M = 4.30) than at first testing (M = 1). These Rorschach variables suggest that Mr. Swan has a normative interest in other people and represents them in his mind as integrated objects capable of empathic interaction with each other. He still remains, however, dynamically predisposed to form hostile relations with women and expects females to be the source of his interpersonal conflict (Card III: "Two people arguing over a stool." [Inquiry] "The head, neck, body, legs, the outline here."). Fortunately, he is not motivated to pursue such relationships.

His self representations have also shifted in a positive direction. No longer as self-absorbed (EgoC = 0.34) as he was at the first testing (EgoC = 0.44), he also shows no indications of pathological narcissism

(Reflections = 0) and no indications of feeling damaged or injured (Morbid = 0). His suicide constellation has predictably decreased from 4 to 1. He also continues to have little interest or capacity to develop insight (FD = 0) and experiences no guilt or remorse (V = 0). We would not expect the latter in catathymic homicide.

We rendered a *DSM-III-R* diagnosis of Schizoaffective Disorder, in remission, and Schizoid Personality Disorder. Our report to the court, which would determine whether he was released to the community, noted the following findings:

First, the patient did have a mental disorder, which is currently in full remission. He also has a personality disorder that is likely to remain unchanged and will be chiefly characterized by a desire to be alone and to avoid close relations with others. Both of these findings support a low risk of violence if he is returned to the community.

Second, the instant offense, the murder of his spouse, was consciously motivated by delusions of grandeur wherein she was perceived as standing in the way of his actualizing his grandiose beliefs. The psychodynamic motivations for the homicide, which shaped his delusions and actually fueled the killing, involved deeply felt rage toward his wife that was both the result of their isolative, conflictual living situation, and Mr. Swan's developmental history of hostility toward women for dominating him. The transference basis for these feelings is found in his early perceived experiences with his mother and oldest sister, and his "repetition compulsion" to overcome these feelings by marrying an outspoken, older woman. Nowhere is this psychodynamic more apparent than in his comment to the 911 female dispatcher *during* the hatchet murder of his spouse. He said to her, "She uses her tongue to cut me up." Here we have a primitive and concretized psychotic statement of his own feelings that were acted out in a talionic manner by "cutting up" his own spouse. This created in actuality a cavity in her skull that was, for him, disguised wish fulfillment. His delusional fear just prior to the homicide was that "she had been born without a cerebral cortex. This had left her to go through life acting only on reflex, much like a chicken with its head chopped off." Mr. Swan was able to confirm this psychotic belief when he killed his wife and observed, in the midst of the traumatized tissue, a brainstem without a cortex.[8] In his psychotic state, it verified his delusion; in actuality his homicidal act created the injury that would be perceived to verify his delusion.

There is also a crude parallel between the primitive psychotic defenses utilized by Mr. Swan at the time of the homicide and the act itself. The *splitting* of her skull and cortex, and the actual penetration *into* her brain are the transmutation of the psychotic defenses of splitting and projective identification into measurable, albeit horrible, behaviors. Mr. Swan perceives himself as omnipotent, when in actuality he is impotent: one split that focuses on self-perception. Mr. Swan also perceives himself to be controlled by his wife (mother) *into* whom he projects his own bad parts and attempts to control them. At the time of the homicide, the psychological battle within Mr. Swan has reached the delusional proportionality of life and death, as she stands in the way of his achieving omnipotent, *life-giving* roles: secretary general of the United Nations, and the pope.

Third, the chronic catathymic nature of this homicide is evident in the intensely hostile and dependent relationship between the patient and his spouse, the incubation period which, in this case, was consciously apparent for one week prior to the homicide; and the sense of tension, elation, and relief felt by Mr. Swan as the act was completed. There is also a curiously compulsive[9] and detached attitude immediately following the killing, as he remembers, "There'd be a lot of clerical proceedings to clear up the problem of her dying on me." His clinical approach to the aftermath of her death, and his lack of responsibility for it, support the degree to which his schizoid character dominates the psychopathology. It also raises the intriguing question as to whether a generally isolative schizoid personality is more prone to develop a catathymic pattern of relating by virtue of a single, intense relationship that may foster certain maternal ambivalences (Klein 1946).

Fourth, Mr. Swan's hospital records, clinical interview, and psy-

---

8. Axe wounds not only cut into the skin, but also cause contusions and structural damage. Injuries to the posterior portion of the head however are more likely to be fatal than injuries to the anterior portion of the head (Geberth 1990).

9. Klein (1946) noted that one root of obsessional mechanisms in schizoid personality results from infantile projective processes and the impulse to control other people.

chological testing all consistently substantiate slow and progressive clinical success.

Fifth, there are no indications of antisocial or psychopathic character in this patient.

Sixth, his aspirations and plans for return to the community are limited but realistic, given his extensive history of mental disorder and personality disorder.

Seventh, Mr. Swan shows full compliance with, and understanding of, his need for medications. This is a central treatment focus to ensure that his psychosis stays in remission.

Eighth, although his immediate family have expressed grave concern for their safety if he is released, our evaluation indicates that these concerns are unfounded and are not based upon the current clinical status of this patient. Such family antagonism, however, will continue to be a source of stress for the patient and will need to be monitored.

Ninth, there is no significant history of alcohol, stimulant, or weapons use that would aggravate his violence risk. The dependence upon benzodiazepine did not appear to contribute to the homicide, and the patient appears to be at low risk for returning to this addiction.

Tenth, Mr. Swan's potential future victim pool is an older or same-aged woman with whom he would form a hostile-dependent relationship. She could be at risk if the patient decompensated and a psychotic transference developed (Searles 1961, 1963). The frequent clinical contacts the patient will have with the Conditional Release Program (twice weekly) suggest that such decompensation will not occur without knowledge of the staff, and Mr. Swan could then be hospitalized in a timely manner.

We recommended that Mr. Swan be released to the community and placed in the Mental Health Conditional Release Program. Although the Superior Court Judge was hesitant, over the course of a protracted hearing and testimony from several expert witnesses, she agreed. She noted that the evidentiary standard was a "preponderance of the evidence" (the lowest standard of proof, often quantified as 51 percent), and she would not have found him to be safe if the standard was "clear and convincing" (often quantified as 75 percent).

Mr. Swan, as of this writing, has been living in the community for one year. He continues to take his medications and has been fully compliant with the "core standards" of treatment. He spends most of his time alone, reading and listening to classical music, and appropriately tolerates contact with other residents at his "board and care." His psychotherapy has been characterized by his clinician as friendly but superficial, and she was unsure that he had any emotional feelings toward her until he was recently transferred to another female therapist. He has displayed, to his new clinician's surprise, some anger that he was transferred. This has manifested itself in displaced teasing of the new, and younger, clinician. Mr. Swan shows little desire to explore his past, whether it be his childhood or his marriage, and shows even less interest in his own internal world. He appeared quite pleased that his case would be printed in this book, and gave his written consent. His case is also a matter of public record, and the evaluation data were given as oral testimony at trial.

CONCLUSIONS

These two cases illustrate the chronic catathymic homicide pattern in two rather different diagnostic contexts: borderline personality organization with histrionic, narcissistic, and antisocial character in a 42-year-old female; and psychotic personality organization with schizoid character in a 56-year-old male. The homicidal acts resulted in the deaths of three victims, all intimately associated with the perpetrator.

I have highlighted the three phases of chronic catathymic homicide—incubation, sudden violence, and relief—and have also emphasized the necessity of preoedipal personality organization for such violence to occur. Clinical experience indicates that this hypothesis is quite reasonable; but, of course, it should be tested with the data gathered in any one case. I have also elaborated on the importance of projective identification as a central defense in this motivational pattern, and the degree to which it crystallizes the perception that the symbiotic object is malevolently controlling the individual. The degree to which the actual violence is either affective or predatory will generally depend upon the time frame between the conscious wish to kill and the act itself. In most cases the actual violence will be preceded by a period of predation. In Ms. Booth's case it was approximately 12–15 minutes; in Mr. Swan's case it was a matter of a few minutes.

Treatment depends upon the point at which the clinician enters the case. Prehomicidal pattern identification demands rigorous efforts to intervene, usually both psychotherapeutically and psychopharmacologically, and exercise of any duty to warn that becomes apparent. Such a duty to warn may necessitate a lengthy explanation to the potential victim, as this form of violence is generally inexplicable to the lay person and will not be preceded by a history of violent acts.

Post-homicidal treatment will be much easier in cases where the perpetrator was psychotic at the time, owing to the possibility of an insanity finding and hospitalization. Clinicians, however, must not assume a "cure" in the absence of an Axis I disorder. Careful and comprehensive psychological testing and history taking are necessary to understand the personality and motivational dynamics that contributed to the killing. If this is not done, the clinician may be unwittingly contributing to factors that result in another low-frequency, but highly tragic, violent attachment.

8

The Female Victim
of the Psychopath

So we beat on, boats against the current, borne back ceaselessly
into the past.
                    —F. Scott Fitzgerald, *The Great Gatsby*, 1925

I have selected three case studies that explore the relationship
between the psychopathic character and those who bond to him. Each
of these cases is quite distinctive, and the evident psychopathology in
these three women varies in nature and degree.

Although I did not evaluate the male partners in any of these
cases, their behavior as recorded by independent criminal investigation is quite consistent with severe, or primary, psychopathy. Nevertheless, without a clinical evaluation I cannot be certain that psychopathic character was present, and I am not rendering a diagnosis. The
reader is left to judge the degree of psychopathy in each of these men.

The outcome of all these cases was tragic. In the first two, the
women were convicted with their male companions of multiple murders and are currently in prison for life. In the third case, the woman
was killed by her husband, who was recently convicted of first-degree
murder with a special circumstance, and sentenced to life in prison
without the possibility of parole.

Identifying information in each case study has been changed to attempt to adequately disguise the data. Readers familiar with these people, however, may recognize identities despite my efforts, due to extensive media coverage of the evidence at trial. In Case 1 the woman consented to publication of her case without disguise; in Case 2 no consent was given so I have purposely omitted most information other than the psychological data; in Case 3 the deceased woman's family consented to the publication of her story.

CASE 1: SERIAL SEXUAL HOMICIDE

Karen was born in 1943 in Boston, Massachusetts, the second sibling of three in a French-Catholic intact family. Her father worked in the movie house business as a "troubleshooter" and her mother was a housewife. The family traveled throughout the country.

Karen recalled her earliest memory of her mother: "I was 4 years old and my mother had an old-fashioned wringer washer. I pulled up the sheets and got my arms caught in the wringer. She freed me and they took me to a doctor and x-rayed my arms." Her earliest memory of father: "Sis and I are in the back seat of a car. Dad is outside. He's introducing us–'These are my daughters, Karen and Victoria.' " As young children, she and her sister were extras in a number of movies.

Karen's earliest memory without her parents also contains the theme of sudden, unexpected injury: "I was 20 months old and my brother was bouncing on his bed. I climbed up. He said, 'Don't do it, you'll fall.' I did and broke my collarbone." She generally characterized her parents as "very warm, loving, caring, and giving people" when asked if they had provided for her needs as a child.

Karen's descriptions of her childhood are vague, idealized, and contradictory. In retrospect, little factual information is available concerning her early years. Descriptions of her parents include the word "normal," with her mother perceived as "aloof but loving," and her father "warm and affectionate." Her use of splitting as a primitive defense in adulthood is apparent in her characterization of mother as both the "light of the family" and "an ogre with eyes in the back of her head." There do not appear to have been any significant childhood illnesses or injuries, although she does report an early onset of puberty (age 11).

When Karen was 15 years old, her mother died of cardiac arrest. She described her father's reaction: "He was dependent on my mother. She was the sun and my father rotated around her. After she died, there was nowhere to shine."

The night of her mother's death, Karen's father came into her bedroom and attempted to orally copulate her. "I was the shining star in my father's eyes. . . . I didn't know I had been sexually abused. I was confused and angry. It was wrong. My mother had just died." She rebuffed him, and he went to her sister.

Karen began sexually acting out. On one occasion she danced nude on the roof of her house. At other times she would peek through the bedroom windows of her neighbors. Exhibitionism and voyeurism would remain paraphilic constants in her sexual history.

Her father emotionally abandoned Karen, and she began to lose control of her life. Eighteen months after her mother's death, he remarried and was spurned on his wedding night. He made his first suicide attempt shortly thereafter and killed the house cat, smearing its blood on the walls of their home. The children were placed in foster care and then went to live with their uncle. She remembers, "It was a degrading process."

When Karen was 18, her father committed suicide by hanging and she was raped by her boyfriend's brother. Two days later, the assailant committed suicide. These became the second and third formative events that linked, or paired, sexuality and death in Karen's mind. "I was lonely and unhappy. There was no guidance and control. No affection. I related sexuality with affection. I had frequent sexual intercourse with whomever, whenever. I always had animosity in my feelings for men. In retrospect, I can see that I didn't select well-integrated men. I fostered my own neurosis."

She first married at age 18 to a man she had known for twelve days. It lasted for another six. He pressed her into prostitution, physically assaulted her, and wanted to sodomize her. "He was a street creep, a transient – but charming and good looking." Her second relationship was with an impotent man who wrote pornographic novels. It lasted for eight years, and he sent her to nursing school, where she became a licensed vocational nurse. "There was intense rapport, but no sex." She described him as the "best of friends," but he left her after two years and went to Portland. She followed him, and they remained together for another six years.

During these latter years, when Karen was in her mid-twenties, she met and married her second husband, Jack. She described him as "exclusively homosexual." Their marriage was "uncomfortable and strange." They separated five times, and the union produced two boys. Karen is diabetic, and both pregnancies were medically risky. She had pneumonia following the first child's birth, had a subsequent miscarriage, and the second child was taken by cesarean section at 8 months.

As this marriage deteriorated – not a surprising outcome given her previous object relational patterns and attachment histories with men – she met Daniel on December 28, 1979. Daniel was ten years her junior but befriended her in their apartment complex. Karen, eager for male company now that she was separated from her husband, was captivated. "He had total control over me. I had a lack of will. He had a soft, drowning, sensuous voice." Over the course of their eight-month relationship, however, there was mounting tension. Once living together, their domestic life was chaotic. Daniel would teach her two sons mock knife fighting. On several occasions he came home at night and fell on the floor, exhausted and covered with blood. He also appeared to be an alcoholic.

But the sexual relationship was unusually exciting. "We had fantasies. Incredibly neat sexual fantasies. Part of the fantasies involved capturing young women and subduing them, using them sexually. And from there he branched out to this business of necrophilia and killing people. I was thinking it was just pure fantasy and I didn't think there was any possibility of him delving into it. We fantasied together, sometimes during sex, sometimes having no sex at all – we'd just lay in bed and describe possible sex scenes for different things to do." She eventually sent her two boys to live with their paternal grandmother "for their own safety." Karen was taking 10 mg of Librium, as needed, to manage her anxiety.

On June 20, 1980, she and Daniel picked up a girl named Cathy in

Hollywood. They had not decided who would kill the girl, but if Karen wanted to do it, she would speak a code word and Daniel would let her. While Cathy orally copulated Daniel in the front seat of his car, he signaled Karen to hand him the .25-caliber revolver. She drew it from her purse and gave it to him. He shot Cathy in the head. While Daniel drove, Karen held the dying girl on her lap and removed her clothing and jewelry. She had seven dollars in her pocket. They dumped her body in an isolated area of Los Angeles, and nicknamed her "river rat" because she had been thrown near a stream. On March 3, 1981, sheriff's deputies found the remains of a young woman matching the general description of Cathy.

"Cathy was the only one that I actually . . . because little girls were reluctant to get into the car with another woman. But Cathy did. She was a blonde girl, 17 to 20. Had a nice . . . had a pretty body . . . natural blonde because her pubic hair was blonde. He had me strip her in the car after she was shot. We picked her up on Highland Avenue. The usual line was, 'My wife doesn't like to give blow jobs and I really could use one. Would you mind?' She was reluctant at first, but she got in the car. She was dumb, stupid, little. I was in the back seat. I had the gun in my purse. In fact, we still hadn't made up our mind to do her. She was sweet, gentle, obliging, very polite and dumb. Down-to-earth dumb. First she says, 'My name's Cathy.' And I said 'My name's Barbara,' which it isn't of course. And she said, 'Pleased to meet you.' Just like that. A real dumb little kid. Anyhow she was kind of cute and so Daniel got back in the car. He was checking out the parking lot that we were behind, trying to decide if it was discreet enough. At the very worst he was going to get a blow job out of it. Out of the very best he was going to show off to me, you know, what he was doing.

"This kid was blowing him and I kept trying to signal him did he want the gun or didn't he . . . his gun was over on Cathy, on the driver's side, between the walls of the door and seat. My gun was in my purse. This was the one break in the pattern. We really wanted it all on the one gun so the other gun would be clean. My gun had one under the hammer. It was cocked and ready to go. But I didn't understand his signals. I was the one that was supposed to do the hit.

But he . . . I had the option of stopping if I did not want to make the hit. I was to give him a certain signal. If I wanted to do it, I was supposed to say, 'Boy, am I having a blast.' He had the ultimate decision whether to go ahead and do it one way or the other. So we had this silent argument back and forth. He kept shaking his head no, and she was getting uptight. Finally he reached back his hand, like this. And then he waved his fingers like this. So I took the gun and I slapped it in his hand, but stupid me, inexperienced me, I didn't have it pointing in the direction that it needed to be proper. So he's trying to maneuver this damn gun around so it will be in firing position and she got nervous and she started to sit up. So he . . . you know, he got her. He hit her in the side of the head. I think he hit her with the left hand. I think it was more convenient. Otherwise, if he shot her with the right hand he might have blown away part. I think he did her, yeah, did her lefthanded because I put the gun in his left hand.

"She didn't die right away. She kept breathing hard and I'm sitting in the back and he, see, he's yelling at me. 'All right, I know you're nervous. But, cool, be cool, remember your abc's.' And I sat back there and said I'm fine. This was the first. He shot her once and she collapsed in the front seat. She bled like a stuck pig all over my blouse. Her head was in my lap. And he didn't want to shoot her again. It was obviously a terminal shot, but she was doing a lot of huffing and puffing and I kept checking her pulse rate which was strong and steady and good, and she might have survived. I think there is a possibility she could have been saved. He reached–we always kept what we call the kill bag in the car, which contains paper towels, clean plastic bags, we haven't handled . . . usually rubber gloves of some sort. Lately we've added a knife and things of that sort. He's telling me to strip her, strip her down. So I got all her jewelry off, everything off, underneath a jacket in the front seat. And if you don't think it isn't a bitch to get a dress off of a dead girl who isn't cooperating in the least bit . . . anyway, in the front seat of the damn car with a man freaking out beside me nervous as hell. I wasn't. This astounded me because this . . . because I hadn't been involved with him before. I wasn't the least bit nervous. I was very cool. I wasn't turned on to it. I wasn't turned off with it. I was intellectually interested in the outcome."[1]

Daniel and Karen came to enjoy their ventures. Shortly before they were arrested on August 11, 1980, they went out almost every night looking for someone to kill. They fantasized about capturing young women, subduing them, and sexually using them. The plan was to make the killings look progressively more gruesome. They wanted to kill black prostitutes because of "their smugness." On one occasion Karen assisted in the molestation of an 11-year-old girl. Karen took photographs of her orally copulating and engaging in other sexual acts with Daniel. She also molested her.

They called the girls that were to be killed "bitches, botches, or butches." On June 23, 1980, Daniel murdered a prostitute named Exxie and decapitated her. Karen suggested to him that he dismember the woman so that the murder would look as "psychotic as possible" and the police would look for "some nut" rather than them. Daniel brought the victim's head home to Karen. They put it in the refrigerator and froze it. They had discussed this in fantasy, and when he did it, they "had a lot of fun with her." Karen said, "Where I had my fun with the head was the makeup. I took a lot of cosmetics and would make up the face. I treated her like a Barbie doll. But one of her eyelids kept folding in a strange manner. She was still half frozen. After I painted her face, Daniel would take her head into the shower. He would stuff his penis into her mouth. He would masturbate in her mouth in the shower. We used to pick her up by the hair. Daniel would swing it back and forth by the hair."[2] Karen and Daniel were careful not to touch the box that they bought for the head, which might leave fingerprints. They disposed of it by dumping it in an alley.

---

1. This material is taken from the transcript of the criminal interrogation following Karen's arrest.

2. During the clinical interview, Karen told us that Daniel always wanted her to put makeup on the contusion on the victim's head, "so no one would think that he hurt her." When confronted with the gross illogic of this statement, Karen used it to rationalize that Daniel was not sadistic because he killed the victims *before* he sexually assaulted or mutilated them.

By August 1, 1980, Karen was extremely concerned about her own safety with Daniel. She sought out a man named Jack, a former lover, and found him in a bar with another woman. He told her to wait. After several hours, she finally was able to confess her involvement in the murders. "I had it in my mind for Jack to hide me. It was not specific." She also consumed four mixed drinks and a "handful" of Librium. Jack told Karen he was going to the police, so she decided to kill him.

Karen waited in her car near Jack's van until he left the bar. She put her gun in her waistband, a pair of leather gloves and a cleaning rag in her pocket, and knife in her purse. When Jack returned, she entered the van with him. He told her, "You caused me to lose the other girl. I want you to take care of this." She performed fellatio on him. He slapped her and told her she "was fucking crazy."

She then engaged in oral/anal sex, and while Jack was facing away from her, she drew her gun, put it to the back of his head, and fired. She checked his pulse, which was still steady and regular. Then she shot him a second time in the head, "just to make sure he was dead." Karen sat there and looked at him for a period of time, thinking, "Daniel will sure be mad at me." She then stabbed him in the back about six times. Using a fish deboning knife that she kept in her "kill bag" in her car, she decapitated him for the purpose of getting the bullets out of the van. She did not realize that the pistol ejected the spent cartridges. She reported that she really didn't have any conscious feelings as she was decapitating him. "It wasn't me. But I still had to function. I had to decide what to do. It was nauseating, revolting." She described a state of depersonalization, with no conscious awareness of affect.

Karen then sliced the victim's buttocks "to make the murder more gruesome, like a sexual pervert type thing." She put the victim's head in a plastic bag, which she dropped in the street when she fled the van. She put the head back in the bag and took it home, and Daniel helped her dispose of both the head and the knife she had used. She later told the police, "Now that I've done it, it was really kind of interesting. It sure as hell is not like going to the beach or barbecuing. Does it gross you out to think that a woman could climb in, kill a friend of hers, somebody that she cares about, not in anger, not in passion, not in any normal relation that you would expect, and then behead him? What really surprised me, of course, was my advantage of having been blind for a while so that I could know how to deal in the dark. That van was pitch black. I really am thoroughly amazed that I didn't become messier than hell. When I left that van I was clean. I shouldn't have been. But the way the situation was, I was doing my very best to make it look like it was a psycho killing, rather than somebody who was hitting, a personal thing. . . ."

One week after her murder of Jack, Karen confessed to the police and was arrested. During her first contact with the police in her apartment, she revealed some of her own psychodynamics: "The situation started out as a fantasy that just got badly out of control. . . . Daniel is really a . . . a . . . a real doll and I do love him. So part of me feels like a real shit for telling on him. On the other hand, there is a man out there who is going around killing people who has no sense of or regard for anything.[3] It doesn't matter if the prostitutes are young girls. He is not picking on old ladies. His criteria, believe it or not, for whether or not they die, is whether or not they give a decent blow job. I don't know enough psychology to say whether or not I'm paranoid schizophrenic. I'm obviously not paranoid. Whether or not I'm schizophrenic, I don't know. Sane people don't go around killing people. I don't want to face the gas chamber. I can't stay with Daniel because he will ultimately hurt me. But he hasn't struck me. He's never injured me. I've never seen him strike anybody. In which case that wouldn't be so bad either, if you understand. The way he did it was a nice, quick, clean show. . . ."

Karen pled guilty to two counts of first-degree murder and admitted to a use allegation. The special circumstances (multiple murder and witness killing) that could have condemned her to death, or life without the possibility of parole, were dropped. She was sentenced to 52 years to life in prison.

---

3. This is a striking example of splitting. She alternately conceives of Daniel as both a good and bad man, but not at the same time. Her verbiage sounds like she is talking about two completely different people.

We[4] evaluated Karen eight years after her relationship with Daniel during a day-long visit to the California Institute for Women. Karen presented as a short, slightly obese 45-year-old woman who was remarkable for her lack of distinguishing features. She wore glasses for cataracts. Her cropped, brown hair framed a face that was pleasant, round, and plain. She appeared neither masculine nor particularly feminine.

Karen is an articulate woman and relished the attention we gave her. She described her history with rich detail and was never embarrassed or hesitant when discussing the most sensitive material. She was, however, quite emotionally labile. She would escalate into uncontrollable giggling and, during the Rorschach, slammed one of the cards on the table in a moment of dramatic outburst. When we began the interview, she assertively wanted to know all about our credentials, in turn, to decide if we were worth talking to. She responded, however, to limit setting in a quick, meek fashion. Throughout the course of our time together, which totaled eight hours, she was very sensitive to the amount of attention she was receiving. She even interpreted my withdrawal of attention from her during one of the self-report tests, the Minnesota Multiphasic Personality Inventory (MMPI), as sadistic on my part.

Karen's mental status exam showed no indications of psychotic process. There were no evident delusions, hallucinations, or formal thought disorders on clinical exam, and she had no history of psychotropic medications during her years in prison. The content of our interview focused upon a detailed recounting of her life and criminal history with Daniel, which has been described above. Her telling of her story was generally consistent with other corrobative data from the Los Angeles County District Attorney's Office,[5] although she tended to minimize, and take less responsibility for, the acts of serial violence she performed. This is not unusual and underscores the importance of comparing the recall of the individual's crimes (the

---

4. Carl Gacono, Ph.D., Judith Meyers, Psy.D., and myself.
5. I would especially like to thank David Guthman, J.D., for his help.

Systematic Self-Report of Violence, SSRV; see Chapter 3) with other, independent accounts.

We used the Quick Test, MMPI, Millon, Thematic Apperception Test (TAT), and Rorschach to psychologically test Karen. All of these instruments were completed during the one-day interview. Karen's intelligence was reliably estimated to be in the bright normal range (IQ 110–119). This was consistent with her educational achievement and work history as a nurse.

The Millon Clinical Multiaxial Inventory II showed marked elevations (BR > 85) on the Avoidant, Self-defeating, and Borderline personality scales. Although the profile suggested that Karen was exaggerating her psychopathology (Disclosure BR 93, Debasement BR 94), these elevations may also be associated with an acute episode of emotional turmoil. This latter hypothesis, however, was not supported by the Rorschach. The MCMI-II described a woman who had a history of disappointments in relationships, and a tendency to precipitate self-defeating encounters with others. She was also likely to experience periods of marked emotional, cognitive, and behavioral dysfunction.

She expected others to be rejecting and disparaging, and despite her longing for warmth and affection, she withdraws to maintain a safe distance from others. Her surface apathy conceals an intense sensitivity, which may be expressed in bursts of anger toward those she sees as unsupportive. There is also a likely history of self-damaging acts and suicidal gestures. "Innumerable wrangles and disappointments with others occur as she vacillates among self-denial, sullen passivity, self-destructive activities, and explosive anger."

The expectation of ridicule and derision is seen in Karen's tendency to exaggerate disinterest by others into complete condemnation. She then responds with impulsive hostility. Constraint is followed by outbursts that are, in turn, followed by remorse and regret.

The MCMI-II also identified a major depression and a generalized anxiety disorder, both part of her enduring character structure. Treatment recommendations, according to this instrument, focused upon the rapid implementation of pharmacotherapy or supportive psychotherapy to ameliorate her Axis I symptoms of depression and anxiety. Once she was stabilized, long-term psychotherapeutic work could begin to bolster her low self-esteem, but would likely be responded to with limit testing and withdrawal. Karen would be deterred from psychotherapy because the rekindling of hope would remind her of past failed relations, and the humiliations that resulted. Certainly her history reflects such a plethora of disappointments. She would likely struggle to maintain a safe distance from others to keep a level of adjustment to which she was accustomed.

Karen produced a valid "bad apple" MMPI profile, with clinical elevations on Scale 4 (T = 81), Scale 8 (T = 77), Scale 6 (T = 73), and Scale 9 (T = 70). Validity scales showed no distortion in the direction of malingering (fake bad) or dissembling (fake good). Supplemental scales gave a more complete clinical picture of Karen. There was a wide discrepancy between her Dependency scale (T = 71) and her Dominance scale (T = 45), suggesting an individual who is inclined to subsume her needs to the wishes of others, and who will not take an active, initiating role in her behavior. Although Scale 2 was not clinically elevated (T = 65), the Brooding subscale (D5) was in the clinical range (T = 72), and supported Karen's propensity to ruminate about slights and her melancholic state of mind. Although one would expect elevations on Scale 3, Karen's Hysteria score was normative (T = 52). She did, however, show an elevation on HY5, Inhibition of Aggression (T = 67), suggesting her tendency to deny and inhibit angry or hostile impulses, and perhaps be gratified if others act out these impulses in her presence (Karen's score on the passive-aggressive personality scale of the MCMI-II had been BR 81).

Her Scale 4 elevations were impressive and consistent with her antisocial history prior to incarceration. Familial discord (T = 69), Authority Problems (T = 69), Social Alienation (T = 74), and Self-Alienation (T = 70) all suggest that Karen has psychopathic characteristics that predominate the clinical picture. The one subscale that was not elevated, Social Imperturbability (T = 47), is consistent with Karen's inability to maintain her Faustian bargain with Daniel during the killings, and her subsequent confession. Her psychopathy is also supported by her elevated Narcissism-Hypersensitivity subscale (T = 70, MF1), and Amorality subscale (T = 72, MA1).

Although Karen showed no clinical indications of psychosis, there were elevations on the Persecutory Ideas subscale (T = 75) and the Poignancy subscale (T = 76). These scales are consistent with her hypervigilant search for insult and her feeling that she has been singled out for persecution, respectively. Likewise, several of the Scale 8 (Schizophrenia) subscales were elevated: Emotional Alienation (T = 76) and Lack of Ego Mastery, Conative (T = 74). There were no elevations on the subscales that would suggest psychotic perceptions (hallucinations). Karen's introversive personality, despite her superficial assertiveness, was evidenced by her elevated 0 scale (T = 65), and an extreme elevation on the Inferiority and Personal Discomfort subscale (T = 92, SI1).

The overall impression from the MMPI is that of a character-disordered woman who is antisocial, unconventional and rebellious, mistrustful of others, and extremely alienated from the world around her. She is mildly depressed and anxious, quite introverted, and prone to form impulsive, dependent attachments to individuals who will mistreat her. She is not psychotic, but her perceptions and associations will reflect a certain amount of persecutory expectation.

Karen's TAT, a measure of her self and object relations, captures some of her more conscious attitudes toward herself, others, and the world around her:

Card 15. "A morbid one. This is time realizing its own mortality. That's it, the beginning, middle, and end. [Inquiry] Trapped, desperate. He's running out of his own essence. Time. He doesn't know how to stop it. Every middle-aged man and woman who saw time slipping away and didn't know how to stop it. I could have told you he was a casket saleman (laughter)."

Card 5. "Mother's come upstairs. She's calling her son. Time to go to school. You'll be late. [How does she feel?] Harried and put upon. [How does he feel?] Sleepy. He is a lazy, little asshole, bastard kid. 'Mom, I'm sick.' Another cliché. [What's the ending?] She pulls the bedclothes off, tickles his feet until he wakes up."

Card 3BM. "Total despondency. This woman has been crushed by life and all its enormity. Whatever has been – total devastation. Off in the corner is her friend watching her, hurting for her and with her. Until this one is ready to pull back into life. For a while she's closed out her support. She knows it's there. She takes strength from knowing her friend is there. They'll hold and console each other. They'll share with each other. [What is the item on the floor?] A set of keys. A carrot with a bite out of it."

Card 13MF. "His inflatable doll just sprung a leak. (laughter) Geez. I think he just shot his wife. He did something to her. He's feeling extreme remorse. Why or what got out of control. [What is the ending?] I don't know. It's not over, though."

Card 18GF. "Two spinster sisters spent their lives together. Both are afraid to face the world. Both are reclusive, interdependent with a tremendous amount of mutual hatred and rage. Forty-five years of togetherness. One woman is banging her sister's head against the banister. The sister who lives will become reclusive and miserable in her own self. She will die a lonely old age. Her situation does not improve. She blames her sister and her friends for her problems. They've festered and grown bigger."

Card 12M. "He is sort of a faith healer. She is sick in her bed. She's turned to her religious practitioner in the hope that he can help her. It's her last hope. He's laying on his hands. He orders her to heal. [What is the ending?] He fails. He doesn't get his fee and goes off to live somewhere else. Her faith stays resolute. She still maintains her hope."

The TAT findings, although not to be relied upon in forensic evaluations or testimony because of the lack of normative data, are a rich source of object relational and emotional hypotheses. In these responses, themes of anger toward the self, dependency needs, hopefulness, despair, and the expectation of failure are obvious. There is also the hint of sadism and perversion in her laughter to Cards 15 and 13MF, references to both death and sex that have been immutably linked throughout Karen's history. This test lends further support to the centrality of hostility and dependency in Karen's object relations.

The Rorschach is the final test we administered to Karen, and it marks the last stop on the psychometric journey from conscious self-report (MMPI, MCMI-II) through attachment and object relational themes (TAT) to unconscious personality structure and psychodynamics (Rorschach). These tests provide levels of analysis of a patient's psychology that can then be ordered, and compared, on a continuum from conscious to unconscious.

Karen's Rorschach yielded sixteen responses, a valid but constricted protocol. It was scored using the Comprehensive System (Exner 1986a) and RSP2. A structural analysis of Karen's psychological operations indicates that she has a normal amount of psychological resources (EA = 8.5), but does not have a delineated problem-solving style (EB = 5:3.5). Her stress tolerance and controls are normal (D = 0, AdjD = 0). The only abnormally elevated characteristic on the nonvolitional side of her operations is a heightened physiological need state at the time of testing (FM = 5).

Karen's affects are characterized by grossly unmodulated emotion (FC:CF + C = 0:3) and a tendency toward emotional explosiveness (C = 1), which we observed. Although she avoids emotionally provoking stimuli (Afr = 0.33), she is not defended against internal affect (Lambda = 0.07). There is no indication of a chronically angry character pattern (S = 1), and a surprising absence of confused, remorseful, painful, or dysphoric feeling states (C' = 2, V = 0, T = 0, Y = 1, no Color/Shading blends). She shows no desire or capacity to form an emotional bond with others (T = 0), a characteristic found in only 11 percent of nonpatient females, but ubiquitous in psychopathic males (Gacono and Meloy 1991).

Her interpersonal perceptions are marked by the expectation of cooperativeness (COP = 2) and an inordinate desire to depend on others (Food = 2). She is isolative (Isolate/R = 0.38), and has a general, childlike disinterest in others as whole, real, and meaningful individuals (H:(H)Hd(Hd) = 2:1). Her perception of self is pathologically narcissistic (Fr = 2)[6] and self-absorbed (Egocentricity = 0.63), with a propensity to self-aggrandize and identify with the aggressor (PER = 3, Gacono et al. 1990). There is no capacity to reflect in a

---

6. Only 7 percent of women produce one or more reflection responses (Exner 1991).

balanced and introspective manner (FD = 0), and she is not psycho-somatically preoccupied (An + Xy = 0).

Her cognitive processing is notable for her propensity to scan the environment haphazardly and miss important visual cues (Zd = −6.0). She attempts to visually organize as much as others (Zf = 12) but does a poor job of it, seeking and failing to grasp the entire percept at once. She also tends to unconventionally perceive the world and attach idiosyncratic meaning to its components (X+% = 56), yet her reality testing is unimpaired. In fact, it is normal for nonpatient females (X−% = 6). On the other hand, she shows indications of pervasive but moderate formal thought disorder (WSum6 = 53, no level 2 scores), most of them related to tangential or circumstantial responses (DR = 11). She does have one indicator that is pathognomonic of schizo-phrenic thought (Alog = 1; Meloy and Singer 1991), and is only produced by 4 percent of nonpatient females. Karen did not score positive for any of the constellations.

In summary, Karen's Rorschach indicates a personality struc-ture that is marked by contradiction, yet not in a state of emotional distress: dependency upon others and disinterest in them; patholog-ical narcissism and the expectation of cooperativeness; personal isola-tiveness and normal stress tolerance; unmodulated affects and normal controls. The psychodynamics of her personality are captured in her first response to the Rorschach:

Card I. "A wily coyote in an aggressive mode. Wiley Coyote is the one that chases the roadrunner on the cartoons. My initial impres-sion is a carnivore. Is that an unusual response? He needs eyeballs. [Inquiry] These look like eyes that are hostile, angry. White orbs. These look like pupils, appear to be ears (hostile?). Without going into the details of the cartoons, there is a way of drawing the eyes that look angry. My first impression was aggression. Wiley Coyote about to attack the roadrunner. Yes, there is a large aggressive part of me. He looks like a carnivore ready to strike. All I see is the eyes and a hostile mouth, what else is there to see? *I wish I could see doves mating. Something soft and gentle. Something that's not hostile.*"

This one response is remarkable from a content analytic perspec-tive. Karen first perceives aggression, what has been termed aggressive potential (Gacono 1990), and related to sadism (Meloy and Gacono 1992a). It is also suffused with a paranoid quality of piercing, staring predatory eyes (Meloy 1988a). But all within the context of a childlike, cartoon character, a measure of the degree to which hysterical denial can operate as a defense in psychopathic character. Then the response is personalized in an identification with the aggressor (A. Freud 1936), and oral aggression becomes an explicit focus ("hostile mouth"). Then there is a primitive split-through wish to a benign, yet sexual percept ("doves mating") that is not perceived, only conceived. Once again, the fusion of aggression and sexuality is evident in Karen's psychology, epitomized by her association with a man who linked sexuality and death in a most horrible manner.

Karen is a woman organized at a borderline level of personality with predominantly masochistic, histrionic, and psychopathic character traits. Her psychology is dominated by two psychodynamic themes: the pairing of sexuality and death, and the centrality of dominance and submission. The linking of sexuality and death began with the three traumagenic events in adolescence: the death of her mother and sexual abuse by father, her rape and subsequent suicide of the perpetrator, and her father's suicide. This bizarre pattern was repeated in impulsive bonding with abusive, if not impotent, males (perhaps a reaction formation), and culminated in her intense attachment to a serial sexual murderer whose most delightful necrophilic act was to experience the vaginal contractions of a woman as she died at his hands. As Karen said, "He was the perfect partner for me."

The centrality of dominance and submission is also apparent in Karen's history, clinical interview, and psychological testing. She repeated the cycle of degradation begun by her father in a desperate search to undo it, only finding that mastery of the situation was beyond her grasp. She overtly identified with her masochistic character, and even carried this through in prison. Karen formed a sadomasochistic relationship with a woman in prison *who was terminally ill with cancer.* She would masturbate on the floor in front of her, dance nude for her, and allow herself to be beaten with a fly swatter. "I belonged to her and she could do with me as she pleased."

But Karen also had a sadistic aspect to her character that

remained unconscious. She would seek out males that would act out her sadism, and thus gratify this passive-aggressive aspect of her own personality: the wish to hurt and control the withholding love object. This reached its pinnacle in the atrocities that she would witness Daniel commit, a voyeuristic deed in which she could watch herself as the prostitute, in fantasy, be humiliated and killed by the sadist time and again, and could identify and participate with him in the acts themselves. This is an unusual form of triangulated projective identi- fication in which Karen placed devalued aspects of herself into the young prostitutes, and then could passively enjoy Daniel's dominance and control of them, including their annihilation, by identifying with him as the aggressor. This triangulation also suggests the oedipal theme of actually killing the mother during the act of mating with father so that the daughter can be with the father as a sexual and romantic equal. Karen repeated this act time and again with Daniel, a man whose psychopathy provided a real-world stage for Karen's most primitive impulses, and meant the end of her life as she knew it.

Karen's treatment in prison should focus on the alleviation of any depressive or anxious symptoms, neither of which rose to a clinical threshold at the time of our evaluation. Her character pathology is probably untreatable without an intensive form of psychotherapy or psychoanalysis, both of which would be unavailable to her. Any form of therapeutic alliance is unlikely, given the absence of indices of attachment capacity on the Rorschach and her propensity to form impulsive, sadomasochistic relations that have no enduring, empathic dimension.

Her risk of future dangerousness is probably extremely low, unless she formed a subsequent attachment to a male who could, once again, act out her unconscious sadism. Unfortunately, controlling this possibility if Karen was released to the community would be ex- tremely difficult. Her failure to learn from her experience is also disconcerting. She continues to receive an occasional letter from Daniel, who is now awaiting execution in San Quentin, and corre- sponds in return. Daniel also manages to telephone her sons, now young adults, each time they move, to remind them that he knows where they live – a psychopathic attempt to induce fear and omnipotently control others, even from Death Row.

CASE 2: RELIGION, SEXUAL PERVERSITY, AND MULTIPLE MURDER

Sara is a 38-year-old Caucasian woman who was sentenced to life in prison for the multiple murder of a family, an act that she blamed on her husband of twenty years, a self-proclaimed minister and prophet. Joseph, her husband, has a prototypical psychopathic history and demeanor. Among his more salient characteristics are an unstable work history, violence toward his spouse and others, sexual promiscuity and perversity, a charismatic charm, a grandiose sense of self-worth, proneness to boredom and impulsive travel, rationalization of his behavior and projection of blame, and financial dependence on others through manipulation and exploitation. He would likely score in the primary psychopathy range of the Hare Psychopathy Checklist-Revised (Hare 1991).

Although the factual details of this case must be deliberately sparse to disguise the identity of Sara, her earliest memories begin to paint a picture of her internal world: "I'm at the sink washing her (mother's) blue willow dishes. I smell Ivory soap. The shape and design of the sink. Grandma is in the kitchen baking bread. I felt happy." The earliest memory of her mother also expresses the theme of work, but with a rejecting quality: "Mom helping with the house and I was told to get out of the way. The rose bush in the yard. I felt OK." And with father: "Sitting on Dad's lap, lying in bed, tying red bows on his pajamas. I felt happy. He was always so patient. We'd eat ginger snaps and milk together." Sara describes an almost idyllic visualization.

During the clinical interview after her arrest, Sara, a small person with short brown hair, impressed me as an intelligent, quiet, articulate, but despondent woman who adamantly proclaimed her innocence. She was polite and cooperative and was able to recount aspects of her relation with Joseph that I found difficult to comprehend as I looked at her. She detailed his history of bigamy in which he would rationalize his behavior through religious belief, and force her to watch or participate in sexual activity with his other wife. Sara would cope through explosiveness or subservience, all the while denying the experience by thinking, "No, this can't be." At times her resistance triggered an assault by Joseph, and on at least one occasion he broke her eardrum.

Their own sexual relationship was also unusual. "Joseph is a highly sexual person. His sex preferences are varied. Homosexual fantasies, but only heterosexual activity. He liked to masturbate while I put dildos up his anus. It was seldom mutual sex. It was always to him and for him. He liked me to dress him up in female clothes, makeup, and ribbons. He wanted me to dominate him, but he was always in control. He'd like me to put a catheter in his penis and pull it out just before he ejaculated. I took care of all the objects." Sara had been trained as a nurse.

On one occasion Sara attempted suicide with aspirin and liquor when Joseph threatened to take the children and his second wife and leave. He kept her conscious when he found out, and told her that the other wife and he would take care of her until she died. She was never taken to a hospital. The next day he laid her on the floor of their bathroom, squatted down and defecated on her, smeared the feces on her face and body, and then masturbated and ejaculated onto her face. He then bathed Sara, dressed her, and washed her hair. She was bruised from being assaulted by him the night before. "Feces are his favorite thing. They are tests of my will to submit to him."

Sara's story was a litany of such events, but it differs from Karen's case by the extraordinary stability, at least in time, of a twenty-year marriage and the parenting of four children. The longevity of their relationship would not be predicted by Joseph's psychopathy, and was probably due, in part, to the midwestern values of family, marriage, and religion inculcated into Sara as a child in a large, extended family. These rather plebeian beliefs became negative templates for an uncommon degree of sexual perversity and eventually, multiple murder of another family. Perhaps Sara's complicity in the murders – she was not physically present – was the intrapsychic wish to destroy her own family romance, one that had been degraded by her own husband for years (see Horner and Rosenberg 1991, for a developmental and historical perspective on the family romance).

Sara's psychology was probed through test data that were gathered while she was in custody. Her IQ on the Quick Test was reliably estimated to be in the above-average range (108–110), placing Sara at the 70–75th percentile for Caucasian adults.

She was also administered the MMPI and MMPI-2 within eleven days of each other, and produced a clear, valid, and concordant two-point (46) profile on both tests. This has been described as the "wounded victim" profile (Richard Levak, PhD, personal communication, November 23, 1991), and Sara's scores (Pd = T95, Pa = T91, MMPI) were extremely elevated. Such individuals are grossly alienated from themselves and others, emotionally angry, and very fearful of attack. In the context of Sara's predicament, these test data conveyed a high degree of acute psychological turmoil in the absence of psychosis.

The Harris and Lingoes subscales of Scale 4 (Pd) suggested that most of the loading was attributable to Sara's perceptions of family conflict and discord (Pd1 = T69) and profound alienation from herself (Pd4B = T74). The loading on the subscales for Scale 6 (Pa) suggested that Sara believed she was being plotted against by others (Pa1 = T80) and had been targeted for persecution in an unfair and singularly cruel manner (Pa2 = T69). Both of these perceptions contained a kernel of truth.

Her 46 two-point profile was accompanied by data that suggested Sara was clinically depressed (D = T73) with predominant feelings of subjective dysphoria (D1 = T71), psychomotor retardation (D2 = T66), and a tendency to brood (D5 = T66). There was somatic preoccupation (Hs = T74), and she was worrying about unexpected events in an anxious and ruminative manner (Pt = T69). Her cognitive-perceptual experience, despite an elevation on Scale 8 (Sc = T77), was not impaired to a significant degree, and mostly represented her feelings of alienation from others (Sc1A = T64) and her own emotions (Sc1B = T67). Her energy level remained slightly elevated despite her depression (Ma = T58), and she adhered to a very traditional feminine role (Mf = T41). This was in direct conflict with her inclination to take initiative and make her own decisions (DO = T65), rather than being led by others (DY = T51). This may partially explain her willingness to participate in sadomasochistic activity, with her husband as the submissive and she as the dominatrix.

The MMPI-2 added some information to her psychological profile. Sara was positive for one of the Post Traumatic Stress Disorder scales (PK = T68), but its meaning in this context is unknown. She was also clinically at risk for chemical addiction (MAC−R = T70, raw score 27), but this was strenuously denied during my clinical interview. On the MMPI-2 content scales, she was only positive for Depression (DEP = T78). Just nine items on this scale overlap with Scale 2 (D), so it is measuring a different domain with an emphasis on suicidality and health concerns.

Other Harris-Lingoes subscales were positive on the MMPI-2 and not on the MMPI: Authority Problems (Pd2 = T70), Naivete or "moral righteousness" (Pa3 = T65), and a Lack of Ego Mastery of Impulses (Sc4 = T65). She was also clinically positive for the new Social Avoidance subscale (T = 74) of Scale 0, conveying her desire to avoid public gatherings.

I also administered the Rorschach to Sara. She produced a constricted but valid protocol (R = 14). When scored with the Comprehensive System (Exner 1991), it was extraordinarily similar to Karen's Rorschach. Sara has a normative amount of psychological resources (EA = 7.5), and satisfactory stress tolerance and controls (D = 0, AdjD = 0). She does not have a clearly developed problem-solving style, and her emotions will impact her thinking in an inconsistent manner.

Sara's emotional life is marked by an inability to modulate affect (FC:CF + C = 0:3) and a proneness to sudden, explosive outbursts of feeling (C = 3). She has virtually no defenses against her own affects (Lambda = 0.17), and avoids emotional stimulation in the environment as much as possible (Afr = 0.40). Unlike Karen, however, Sara is feeling anxious and helpless (Y = 2), remorseful (V = 1), and emotionally confused (one Color–Shading blend, C.Y, that suggests the internal experience of unmodulated feeling followed by unbound anxiety). Sara was positive for the Depression Index (6), suggesting a clinical depression, consistent with her MMPI/MMPI-2 data.

Although Karen produced no T responses, an abnormal finding in the direction of emotional detachment, Sara produced two T responses, a likewise abnormal finding suggesting an attachment loss, deprivation, and emotional hunger to bond. Only 14 percent of adult females produce more than one T response (Exner 1991). This finding is further confirmation of the abnormal attachment processes that can be expected in such cases involving the psychopath as love object.

Sara's interpersonal perceptions and relations suggest an individual who expects cooperative interaction (COP = 1, AG = 0) but is dependent on those with whom she engages (Food = 2). Both of her food responses are ambivalent (Gacono and Meloy 1991), which may be analogous to her ambivalence around attachment, despite its intensity. She responds to Card IX, for example, "Looks like Jason's been in the kitchen messing, Koolaid and mustard, a Jason mess." [Inquiry] "Because it's red, yellow and red colors, mustard and ketchup, he makes big messes." She has a consequent tendency to be isolative (Isolate/R = 0.29), but does have a capacity to represent others in her mind as whole, real, and meaningful individuals (Pure H = 2). Sara also has a proclivity to be authoritarian in her relations with others, especially when she perceives challenges to herself (PER = 6). We have found a predominance of personal responses in psychopathic protocols, and view them as identifications with the aggressor in the service of self-aggrandizement (Gacono et al. 1990). These object relational–structural indices on the Rorschach are virtually identical to Karen's Rorschach.

A complementary scoring of Sara's Rorschach using the Kwawer (1980) criteria for primitive (borderline) interpersonal modes of relating yields four responses: one birth and rebirth, one violent symbiosis, separation, and reunion, and two narcissistic mirroring responses. This lends support to the hypothesis that Sara is organized at a borderline level of personality (Kernberg 1984), insofar as 29 percent of her responses meet Kwawer's (1980) criteria. It also suggests a dynamic conflict between her infantile wish for mirroring by the primary object and ongoing difficulties with attachment and separation, associated with conflict, during the separation-individuation stage of development (Mahler et al. 1975). Often psychodynamic analyses of the Rorschach using empirically based scoring will complement a structural analysis.

Sara's self-perception is also akin to Karen's. She is very self-focused and self-absorbed (Egocentricity = 0.71) and pathologically narcissistic (Reflection = 2).[7] Sara has no capacity for balanced insight (FD = 0) at present, yet does not perceive herself as damaged or injured (MOR = 0). These findings underscore a pervasive conflict for both Sara and Karen: a sense of grandiosity and entitlement coupled with a profound dependency on others and naivete about interpersonal relations.

At a cognitive level Sara is motivated to process information (Zf = 10), but in a simple and childlike manner (W:D = 13:0). Her idiosyncratic perception of reality is expected (X+% = 71), yet she shows no impairment in reality testing (X−% = 7), cognitive mediation processes that are virtually the same as for Karen.

Despite her normal reality testing, Sara does show evidence of pervasive formal thought disorder (WSum6 = 20), with the addition of level 2 scores (2 DR, 1 FAB). Both of her Deviant Responses (Exner 1986a), what we would clinically label tangentiality or derailment, are also associated with a personal recollection. She responds, for example, to Card III: "Joseph's philosophies have developed as the result of mirror imaging. They're direct opposites of each other. He would use the human body as an example, the eyes, ears, nostrils, an example of the chiasm, the pattern, a reversal, center line." [Inquiry] "The dividing line here, a mirror image of the other side." This is a process we have also observed in psychopaths wherein the form of thought is disturbed in the service of self-aggrandizement, a dynamic, rather than structural, explanation for such disorders of thinking, and perhaps the distinction between borderline and schizophrenic thought, respectively (Meloy and Singer 1991). This pervasiveness of formal

---

7. Twice as many ambitents produce reflection responses as extratensives or introversives. Sara is an ambitent (Exner 1991).

thought disorder was also apparent in Karen's Rorschach, and presents an unusual combination in these two women: the linkage of normal reality testing with formal thought disorder. The clinical expectation is the presence of abnormality in both areas of perceptual association, rather than just one.

Sara also showed an inclination to abuse fantasy (Ma:Mp = 1:2) which may be associated with her wishful dependency upon others. She also works hard to intellectualize her emotional difficulties (2AB + Art + Ay = 7).

The most compelling response on Sara's Rorschach is to Card IV, the traditional "father" card: "The dust monster under my bed when I was a little girl. Two reoccurring nightmares, the frog and iceberg nightmares, when I was a little girl. My drawers would open and thousands of frogs would come up, but the bed was safe. The iceberg nightmare: my whole family, all on an ice floe, broke apart. I was on a block by myself, we drifted apart, I was always alone." [Inquiry] "The feet, tail, ears, face, dusty. Shaggy, dark, dirty (?) The raggedness on the edges (?) The contrast between the light and the dark."

This response captures the oedipal wishes and fears of Sara as a little girl, but more importantly, the profound sense of loneliness and affectional neediness she felt. This early experience of emotional abandonment, remembered in both her dreams and recollections, coupled with her narcissistic adaptation, suggests an "adhesive identification" (Meltzer 1975) that would keep her tenaciously bound to such a man as Joseph. This response would also be scored as a violent symbiosis, separation, and reunion response with the Kwawer (1980) method.

In summary, Sara presents as a passive and dependent woman who has been victimized by her husband. She is clinically depressed and anxious, and treatment should address her presenting symptoms. Rapid implementation of antidepressant or antianxiety pharmacological agents are indicated. There are no clinical indicators of psychosis, or the risk of a psychotic decompensation. Her character pathology, however, presents additional, and somewhat intractable problems. She is affectionally hungry, and would likely form an intense attachment quite readily to her therapist. Unfortunately, her dependency and narcissism would probably lead to resentments and anger that she is not being properly taken care of by her psychotherapist. This would be experienced by Sara in an unmodulated manner, and she might be explosive in encounters with her treating clinician. Such behaviors would likely be followed by feelings of anxiety and remorse, and subsequent attempts to submit to the perceived "will" or wishes of the psychotherapist. The clinical task, at least initially, would be to stay removed from the dominance–submission transference paradigm that Sara would stimulate, all the while displaying less coping ability than she actually possesses. Countertransference issues would involve helpless feelings on the part of the psychotherapist when change was not as rapid as expected, and perhaps sadistic impulses in the form of spontaneous fantasies or feelings when Sara was most submissive and agreeable to the treatment plan (Meloy 1988a).

When compared with Karen, Sara is much more amenable to treatment. They share histrionic, masochistic, and narcissistic features organized at a borderline level of personality, but Karen's unconscious sadism and psychopathy are much more virulent and dangerous, and would generally rule out psychotherapy for her. Sara's capacity to bond and psychological resources are positive prognostic indicators. She was a complement to her husband, rather than a predominantly concordant twin, as Karen was to Daniel during their sexual killings. Sara captured this contrast in a statement, as she wept following her sentencing: "I am not a cold-blooded murderer. He is. I, too, was numbered on the list of intended victims. I am not the 'Angel of Death.' I am the mother of four."

CASE 3: THE PSYCHOPATH, BANALITY, AND SPOUSAL MURDER

Robert Beech awakened with a start. It was 0400 on February 1, 1987, and he was sleeping in his usual spot – in some heavy brush on the east side of Torrey Pines Road, a beautiful and windy traverse running north from La Jolla, California, along the Pacific coast. Robert was a psychiatrically disabled Vietnam veteran who was homeless. He was diagnosed as a Borderline Personality Disorder and was receiving Social Security Disability Income. He drifted off to sleep again.

District Attorney: And how did it come to pass that you were awakened the second time?

Robert: I heard a loud scream.

DA: And how would you characterize the scream?

Robert: It sounded like a–it was a woman's–a woman screaming, sounded like a–a–somebody's being hurt real bad. It was a horrible scream. It was like–the way I described it before, it was like a woman, somebody going off the top of a roller coaster and going down a real steep grade, and lasted about three seconds.

It was now 0500. Robert heard the last sounds of Pamela Ross, 33, before she was murdered by her husband of four years, Charles, aged 36. Crime scene reconstruction and autopsy reports indicated that Pamela had been assaulted. Her head had been slammed into the left rear wheel of her Mercedes, leaving deep gashes in her forehead. She then wandered off into the pitch black northbound lane of Torrey Pines Road. Her perpetrator got into her car, started the engine, and tracked her with the headlights, looking first on the right shoulder and then into the middle of the deserted road. She walked about 800 feet and then turned to face her own car, driven by her husband, accelerating toward her. The sudden impact sprawled her onto the hood and windshield of her car. She was carried for about 20 feet, and then rolled off the hood after the car stopped. The driver then ran over her, crushing her skull and upper vertebrae. He backed onto the shoulder once again, returned to his gray Mercedes parked nearby, and left the scene of the crime.

Charles Ross said he searched all night to try to find Pamela after she awoke him at 12:30 A.M. and told him she was going to her downtown art studio to get some photo negatives. He was certain something had happened to her when she didn't return by 0230, but couldn't locate her at her art studio in downtown San Diego, nor at friends' homes. He finally called her mother, Ginger, wondering where she was. Ginger called her art studio and left an urgent message on the machine because no one answered, and then called Charles back at his condominium. No one answered there.

Charles was becoming more frantic. He had multiple contacts with the 911 dispatcher beginning at 7:48 A.M., inquiring as to whether they knew anything of her disappearance. The dispatcher, on order from the homicide investigators, gave out no information. Charles would later change his story concerning his phone calls to Pamela's art studio. He first said the phone just kept ringing, and he thought it odd that the answering machine was turned off. He then said the phone was busy. After a homicide detective successfully left a message on her answering machine several hours after the killing, and discovering that there wasn't a message from her husband, Mr. Ross finally said he must have dialed the wrong number.

The outpouring of grief and rage over this murder was overwhelming. Pamela was an accomplished artist and dancer, and was loved by many. She was also a beautiful, blonde woman who took great pride in her California tan and physical health. The murder itself was inexplicable at first. Charles appeared grief-stricken, and subsequently moved in with his sister. An apparently successful businessman, he and Pamela had been together as a couple since she was 16. It had been her first romance, and she completely fell in love with him. Ginger, her mother, however, didn't like him at first. She remembers their first date, when she told him to take care of her baby. He said, "I think too much of myself not to drive carefully." She was dumbfounded and annoyed, but worked hard to like him.

They didn't marry for twelve years. Pamela went on to college, graduating with an arts major from the University of California, Santa Cruz. Charles never graduated from college, but did often manage to live near Pam and carry on their relationship. His work history was transient—he moved a lot, living in New Mexico and Montana, carrying on various business deals that always lost money and created the necessity of leaving the area. Pamela also was suspicious at times of his involvement with other women, but only "caught him in bed" once with another woman. She forgave him.

Pamela idealized Charles and trusted him implicitly. She would defend him against any accusations, even from her family, to whom she was very attached—her two older brothers and her widowed mother. She also left behind a diary of the last three years of her life. Her feelings toward Charles are captured in her own words: "I modeled a new teddy nighty I had bought for special nights. I was going to put it on before we made love, but as soon as we got home Chuck was in the mood. We were all dirty and sweaty from our busy afternoon and somehow it just seemed like more fun to hop in bed right away rather than spending time getting ready to do something we were ready for. But I wanted to show off so I modeled the teddy later . . . It was a very nice day and I'm glad I have such a wonderful husband . . . I think Chuck is a unique, special, and gifted person. I feel lucky to be able to share my life with him." This passage was written nine months before he murdered her.

Their relationship, however, showed signs of strain. Pamela became tired of Charles's other friends and his constant desire to party. Five months before she was killed, she wrote, "Friendship sucks. . . . It is frustrating that this is the only common denominator I have with my friends and husband . . . I want to grow with my free time, not sit around the bars drinking. I want to have respect for life. But because it seems so important to my husband and friends I am trying to learn to like it. It makes me sad. Maybe when I'm grown I'll like to shoot the bull more, but right now I would like to learn (celebrate) nature and love naturally. . . . Chuck is the one person I really like, respect, and love. I want to work this out so I can help him not to be sad. His sadness is making me sad. I don't think being sad all the time is right. When I'm sad I'm sick."

This diary passage reflects an interpersonal dynamic that was consistently documented by Pamela during the last year of her life: disagreement and anger between them, her internalization of blame, and her resolve to work harder to please Charles.

Sometimes the arguments, which were seldom, and also minimized by Pamela ("We had a small disagreement, but all in all it was a very nice day and evening"), left her feeling confused and agitated. Often sexual activity ("love" or "cuddling") dissipated the upset.

Pamela was also extremely well organized, if not compulsive. She paid great attention to detail, sometimes in a childlike manner, once writing a check for "98 cents." This often prevented her from seeing the forest for the trees, and probably facilitated her use of denial in relation to Charles's more nefarious characteristics.

His latest business venture had turned sour. During the several years before the murder, Charles ran a telemarketing operation that, at one point, was grossing over $200,000 per month and had fourteen offices throughout California. He would gain the permission of a disabled veterans' group to raise money for them, install a bank of phones in an office, hire "cold callers" at minimum wage, and give the veterans' group twelve cents on the dollar. The contributors got a tax deduction and garbage disposal bags delivered to their homes.

But the cash flow collapsed in mid-1986. Unbeknownst to Pamela, Charles had already embezzled $70,000 from her mother, Ginger, the year before, on the pretense that he would invest her money from a trust deed in a Merrill Lynch account and generate a handsome monthly income for her. She decided not to tell her children, since she could surprise them with large monetary gifts at Christmas. Rather than create a new account for his mother-in-law, Charles deposited the funds into his personal Merrill Lynch account and then transferred the funds into his business account the same day. These funds helped to cover a month of operating expenses and save his business. Later, when the business failed, he returned to Ginger and borrowed another $8,000, which he promised to deposit into her Merrill Lynch account. He didn't. He also used her good credit to purchase his new Mercedes.

Pamela's value was slightly different. Over the course of two years, prior to the murder, Charles took out $600,000 in three term life insurance policies on Pamela. Her signature was forged on the first policy, worth $100,000. As district attorney Mark Pettine would say in his closing argument, "What did Pamela mean to Charles on the day of her murder? She meant $5,000 per pound."

Charles began looking for another scam, and this time turned his attention to Hawaii and Australia. He made several trips there in 1986, and convinced Pamela that moving to Australia would be another great adventure. They planned a trip to the America's Cup race in early February, 1987, and Qantas reserved two first-class seats for them in a three-week tour package. Ginger would join them in Hawaii on their return. Unfortunately, Charles was broke. The tickets were never paid for, despite Qantas's attempts to secure such payment from Pamela. She told them Charles was taking care of it.

On January 31, 1987, Pamela was beside herself with excitement about their departure on February 2. She had lunch with a good friend in Cardiff and then was last seen heading for a hair appointment. She had spent the previous several days shopping and writing $4,800 in checks on her Bank of America account to cover the next month's expenses. Charles told her he made the deposit to this account to cover these bills. She and Charles ordered a pizza that Saturday night, and the delivery boy remembers Charles paying for the pizza at the front door of their condominium, which they rented, at 2200. At 0054, on Sunday morning, February 1, an inquiry was made into Pamela's Bank of America account at the automatic teller machine near her home, registering a $78.00 balance. Ten minutes later, a second inquiry, and withdrawal of $60.00, was made at another ATM about 10 miles south down the coastal road.

These are the facts of the case prior to the killing. Reconstruction of the events preceding her murder suggests that Pamela became aware of Charles's deceit, the lack of any money to pay the bills, his bankrupt status, and the cancellation of the trip to Australia. She probably left the condo in angry disbelief, and traveled south toward her art studio, where she sometimes stayed overnight. She may have returned to the condo later to confront Charles; no one knows. It is highly probable that she stopped at the first ATM machine to confirm what she already suspected–that there was no money–and then stopped to check again. Charles may have followed her in his own Mercedes, and they eventually stopped, talked, and argued at the scene of the crime overlooking Torrey Pines State Park. She probably got out of her car, and by the left rear wheel the first *affective* violence occurred (Meloy 1988a), with Charles taking her head and smashing it into the wheel. Pamela then stumbled out into the road, dazed and disoriented by the open wound to her forehead. Charles got into her car, started the engine, and began stalking her with the headlights of the automobile, first searching for her over the shoulder, and then swerving out onto the road to see her walking away from him in the distance. He accelerated, she turned to face the lights and the sound, and their eyes met for one last time as she impacted the windshield of the car. This second violent event is *predatory* (Meloy 1988a), since it was planned and purposeful, and probably emotionless. Charles made the decision to kill his wife with her auto during these moments, but may have actually been planning her death for months to collect the life insurance, as the district attorney successfully argued at trial.

What was submitted into evidence was testimony that two Mercedes automobiles were viewed parked near the crime scene by a woman who did not see any people at approximately 0400. The crime scene also revealed two different sets of tire tracks, from two different Mercedes autos, and the shoe print of a Reebok sneaker. Charles's Mercedes, however, chemically analyzed three weeks later for blood stains, was clean.

Charles was not so grief-stricken that he didn't attempt to claim the insurance policies. The companies balked, and Charles waited. There was not enough evidence to charge anyone with the murder, and five months after the killing, Charles disappeared. He was eventually arrested almost two years later in Hollywood, Florida, living under the alias of Patrick Donovan with a new girlfriend at the North Beach Motel. His case had been broadcast on "America's Most Wanted" on two occasions during the summer of 1989, and this television program led to his capture.

When a positive identification was made, the arresting officer, William Zito, poked his head into the police car where Charles was detained and greeted him by his real name. He looked at Zito and said, "My real name is Patrick Donovan and I didn't kill my wife." A pair of Reebok sneakers was found in a storage locker in a box labeled "Patrick's Shoes." The FBI was able to say that this shoe was consistent with the shoe print at the crime scene, including the wear pattern on the heel. They also found a partially completed movie script in a trash bin behind the motel concerning a man who was unjustly accused of killing his spouse.

I first became involved in the case when I was asked by the district attorney's office to do a psychological autopsy of the victim to determine her mental state at the time she was murdered, and her habitual patterns of behavior. Although not unheard of (Jubes et al. 1986), the psychological autopsy has been used over the past twenty-five years, generally to reconstruct the motivation for suicide in both criminal (*Bartram* v. *State*, 33 Md. App. 115 [1976], 364 A. 2d 1119) and civil cases (*Campbell* v. *Young Motor Co.*, 211 Mont. 68, 684 p 2d. 1101 [1984]).

The fundamental question in such cases is whether sufficient evidence exists to render a reliable and valid opinion concerning an individual's psychology without a clinical evaluation, and to what degree of certainty can that opinion be rendered. In this matter, a wealth of information existed. I proceeded to take the case, and over the course of a month, began to know and understand Pamela in ways I found both deeply touching and disconcerting. I reviewed television and newspaper accounts of the incident, all the evidence in the case, and the preliminary hearing transcript. I was welcomed by her family, who gave me access to all her life's productions: from schoolwork, to letters home, audiotapes, notebooks, artwork, and extensive photographs of her throughout her life. I also interviewed one of her brothers, her mother, two friends who had been with her and Charles during the last week of her life, and her closest female friend from childhood.

And then there was the diary. This 744-page tome was a very important source of information, particularly concerning her relation with Charles. Unfortunately, only 6 percent of the entries addressed her internal psychological state at the time she was writing. This was disappointing, but also characteristic of a personality that was not particularly psychologically minded, and much more interested in activities and objects in the real world.

My method of investigation was to review as many of the direct products of Pamela's life as I could, and to learn from others who had known her about her behavioral patterns over time. Such data would provide the most salient material from which to form hypotheses concerning her personality and behavior, in the absence of direct clinical contact and psychological testing. Out of this mass of information, and interviews done independently of each other, I began to formulate hypotheses concerning Pamela and then would look for information that might disprove the hypotheses. I also was keenly aware that whatever my final opinions were, my confidence in those opinions would be less than "reasonable psychological certainty" given the secondhand data base.

My emotional reactions to this investigation were surprising and curious. I found myself forming an idealized attachment to this woman, which was both pleasant and a potential source of bias that I had to control. I also found myself to be very uncomfortable when I reviewed the most personal products of her life. I felt like a voyeur, which I was, who had no business invading this woman's privacy after death. I reconciled this, perhaps rationalized it, by knowing that the work I was doing would at least enhance the accuracy of her memory in the minds of others at trial, and at best would protect her from a litigious assault against her character at trial by defense counsel, even if I was never called as a witness.

The outcome of my investigation was a report that I submitted to the deputy district attorney, Mr. Pettine. It is reproduced here in full with the permission of Pamela's family.

Research Methodology

A postmortem psychological evaluation eliminates a major source of data for determining an individual's psychology: a standardized interview and psychological testing. In this case, there was also no history of psychological or psychiatric evaluations prior to Pamela's death. The absence of such data makes any conclusions drawn from other sources of data more tentative. The findings of my evaluation, therefore, should be viewed as having a reasonable psychological probability of being accurate. They should not be viewed as certain or absolute.

My methods were chosen to maintain the highest validity and reliability in the face of the limitations noted. I began by studying materials that were personally generated by the victim. From this voluminous material I developed hypotheses concerning her psychology, which I attempted to disprove. The source of data against which to test these hypotheses were individuals who personally knew Pamela, namely, both friends and family members. The purpose of this selection of data was to access individuals who had observed her behaviors over an extended period of time; and from these individuals' reports, inferences could be made concerning her thoughts, feelings, and relational behaviors. Measurement of the original hypotheses against the information provided by individuals who personally knew the victim would result in support, or lack of support, for the hypotheses, or generation of new hypotheses. Once all the data had been exhausted from these categories, findings emerged which are listed below. All of these findings have been supported by multiple sources of data to ensure some reliability, and should be interpreted as being reasonably psychologically probable.

Findings

1. There are no data that suggest that Pamela had a diagnosable mental disorder, drug abuse or dependency disorder, or personality disorder.

2. It is estimated that Pamela's intelligence was in the average to bright normal range (IQ 100–119).

3. Pamela was extraverted, or extratensive, by personality type. This is a largely heritable characteristic which is marked by behavior that is outgoing and gregarious, and a dependency on objects in the environment for stimulation, problem solving, and gratification. Pamela's predominant conscious focus was on external experience—that is, what one perceives through the senses—rather than internal experience—what one thinks, feels, or imagines. Despite her extraversion, she was not inclined toward the personal disclosure or probing of her feelings or thoughts with anyone.

4. Pamela's favored and habitual modes of sensory experience were visual and somatosensory (tactile). This is evidenced by her affectional activity, sexual patterns, devotion to her art, physical exercise, photography interests, Polynesian dance, and attraction to pets.

5. Pamela was extremely organized, traits manifested in childhood and expressed consistently through adulthood. Such traits would be described as compulsive, and would compel conscious attention to detail in her daily life. There is some evidence that this compulsive focus on detail functioned as a defense against awareness of the "big picture"; that is, Pamela had a limited capacity to organize into a meaningful whole current events, others' behavior, her own behavior, or the long-term implications of such behavior. In common parlance, she would tend to miss the forest by focusing on the trees. There is also a suggestion that her compulsive, detailed attention would occasionally fail, such as not being able to balance the small numbers in her checkbook, and not being able to effectively use her cataloguing system of photographic negatives which she kept at the condominium.

6. A predominant and conscious psychological maneuver that Pamela employed was minimization of negative experience or unpleasant affect. This means that she would attach less significance than others would to internal or external stimuli that would be felt as unpleasant, uncomfortable, foreboding, or hopeless by her. She would consciously work to maintain a positive attitude toward self and others.

7. A predominant and unconscious psychological defense operative within Pamela was rationalization. This is not a conscious mental task, such as minimization, but is an unconscious defense that supports minimization. It is the use of faulty reasoning or illusory explanation to understand a particular event or series of events. It also serves the defensive purpose of reducing anxiety or unpleasant feelings that might be evoked if rationalization was not used. This is a common defense in normal individuals who are not mentally impaired or disabled.

8. A second predominant and unconscious psychological defense operative within Pamela was denial. This is considered a more pathological, and developmentally earlier, defense. It is the disavowal in fantasy of certain aspects of reality, either within the self or outside the self. It is the chief defense, for instance, utilized by the alcoholic individual who, in the face of overwhelming evidence and confrontation by others that he has a drinking problem, denies it. In Pamela's

case, denial was suggestively more apparent in the last year of her life, and is usually a more regressed and obvious defense that emerges when an otherwise healthy individual is under increased stress.

9. The third predominant and unconscious psychological defense operative within Pamela was idealization. This is the attribution to self or others of ideal, positive, or unrealistically grandiose character- istics to defend against the more ambivalent, unpleasant, and negative aspects of self and others. Pamela manifested this most obviously in her relation to her husband, Charles, whom she first met, and ideal- ized, at age 16. She did not manifest idealization toward herself and, in fact, was prone to projective content as the vehicle for this defense, that is, her husband's behavior.

10. Pamela had a characteristic mode of processing and ex- pressing angry affect. First, she seldom felt angry, a conclusion that is consonant with her defenses outlined above and supported by the data. Second, there would be a period of buildup, or incubation, before Pamela would express her anger. The length of time for this buildup would positively correlate with the affectional-dependent bond that she had with the object of her anger. The defenses outlined above would mitigate the buildup and expression of anger unless they were overwhelmed by a variety of possible factors: an aggregation of facts that sharply contrasted with prior beliefs, fatigue, or other stressors. When the anger would be expressed, it would be verbalized without any physical assault. It would be accompanied by both crying and frustration, and preceded by a period of sullenness. It would be "blurted out."

11. There is evidence that her processing of anger with Charles had a distinctive pattern during the last year of her life. She would express negative feeling toward him on rare occasions, would then internalize blame for the problem, and then resolve to "try harder" in the future. When the intensity of the disagreement would overwhelm her coping mechanisms, she would leave for a period of hours. At times, confused thoughts would be indicated, which she would at- tribute to both herself and Charles, sleep or sexual activity would follow, and Pamela would then revert to her usual focus on activities outside herself. This pattern is more frequent during the calendar

year 1986 than 1985, when the frequency of recorded disagreements also increased. The presence of "confused thoughts" is a state characteristic, rather than a personality trait, of Pamela.

12. Pamela formed an intense affectional bond to Charles from age 16 until her death. This was her primary emotional attachment, superseded only by her attachment to her mother, Ginger. There is the suggestion of some symbiosis in her relation to her husband, that is, a sharing of the same affect states with little boundary separation or delineation. The developmental motivation for this attachment to her husband has several aspects: this was Pamela's first romantic relationship as an adolescent; sexual pair bonding occurred for the first time for Pamela, and there is no evidence that she was polygamous; Pamela had a developmental yearning to separate from her biological family, which was facilitated through her independence and individuality with her husband; and she fell deeply in love.

13. A source of internal conflict for Pamela was her belief that Charles wanted a very closed and contained relationship, in which no disagreements or problems between them were shared with others. This was in marked contrast to her internalized value from her family that feelings and problems should be openly aired, discussed, and resolved. This containment appeared to become more pronounced during the last several years of her life.

14. Pamela's chief conscious motivating values, that is, ideals that guided her daily activities, were honesty, integrity, her belief in "family," and her pursuit and development of her skills as an artist.

15. During the last year of her life, Pamela experienced occasional and intense upsurges of frustration, anger, and sadness over her social relationships and the use of her time. This appears to be a conflict between her usual task-oriented expenditure of time and demands to socialize and just "play." Pamela mentally resolved these affective crises through a conscious commitment to "try harder," a manifestation of her compulsive personality features and use of rationalization.

16. There is evidence that Pamela was excited during the afternoon of January 31, 1987, concerning her trip to Australia and Hawaii.

Results

This is the extent to which I can develop in a reliable and valid manner, given the methodological limitations, a psychological evaluation of the victim. Although the findings cannot be considered inclusive of all her psychological operations, they should provide a reasonably accurate construction of her psychology prior to, and at the time of, her murder on February 1, 1987.

The district attorney attempted to have this report, and my expert testimony, submitted into evidence at trial. The defense objected on the grounds that insufficient foundation existed for the rendering of the opinion; the findings were inadmissable expert opinions according to the California Evidence Code, § 720 and 801; and they lacked sufficient relevancy to be admissable.

The prosecution countered with arguments that evidence concerning the victim's state of mind at or near the time of the crime was admissible when relevant to issues in dispute at trial (California Evidence Code § 1250); the so-called "Kelly-Frye" rule did not apply to psychological evaluations and opinions of a victim's past state of mind (*People* v. *McDonald* [1984] 37 Cal. 3d 351, 373); and there was sufficient foundation for the admission of such expert testimony concerning the psychological autopsy of a victim (*Bartram* v. *State* [1976] 33 Md. App. 115; *Beaver* v. *Hamby* [1983] 587 F. Supp. 88; *Campbell* v. *Young Motor Co.* [1984] 211 Mont. 68, 684 P. 2d 1101; *Thompson* v. *Mayes* [1986] 707 S.W. 2d 951; *Harvey* v. *Raleigh Police Department* [1987] 355 S.E. 2d 147; *State* v. *Lewis* [1987] 533 A. 2d 358; *Matter of Estate of Skulina* [1988] 168 Mich. App. 704, 425 N.W. 2d 135; *State* v. *Montijo* [1989] 160 Ariz. 576, 774 P. 2d 1366; and *State* v. *Marchesano* [1989] 162 Ariz. 308, 783 P. 2d 247).

The court ruled that my report and testimony could not be used at trial as long as defense did not raise any questions concerning the victim's character or state of mind at the time she was murdered.

Nevertheless, Charles Ross was found guilty by a jury of two counts of forgery, two counts of grand theft, and one count of first-degree murder with a special circumstance of financial gain. He was subsequently sentenced to life in prison without the possibility of parole. The probation officer recommended such punishment, and closed his report, "Therefore, it is believed that the primary punishment of the defendant is his being committed to the state prison, but secondarily while incarcerated there, time will forever be the defendant's imprisonment, remaining unchanging and unforgiving."

CONCLUSIONS

The three cases of Karen, Sara, and Pamela provide the first published clinical records and objective psychological data of women who have formed enduring attachments to males whose behavior is consistent with psychopathic character. Although this research is only anecdotal, the first two cases suggest that such women are also quite psychopathological and have both complementary and concordant identifications that bond them to the psychopath (see Chapter 4). These identifications can be accurately described as sadistic, masochistic, histrionic, or psychopathic. Chemical abuse and dependency are also expected, with physical and sexual abuse of the mate also likely.

For those who, like Pamela, are not in such virulent psychopathic relations, it appears that the psychopathy would be more banal, not expressed in physical violence, and masked by higher level defenses in the mate, such as denial, rationalization, and minimization. Such a relationship might endure for years without the mate being consciously aware that she is deeply attached to a primary psychopath and is consequently at great risk.

9

Revisiting the Rorschach
of Sirhan Sirhan[1]

And yet it goes on, and on, and on . . . why?
— Robert Kennedy on the murder of
Martin Luther King, Jr., April 1968

It has been said that one act by one unknown individual may change, on occasion, the course of history. Such may have been the case when Sirhan Bishara Sirhan, a 24-year-old Palestinian immigrant, assassinated Democratic presidential aspirant Robert F. Kennedy on June 5, 1968.

Kennedy had just won the California Democratic Primary and finished his victory speech when he entered a poorly lit food-service corridor leading from the Embassy Ballroom in the Los Angeles Ambassador Hotel. It was 12:15 A.M. Sirhan stepped from behind a food tray rack and pointed his .22-caliber Iver-Johnson revolver within an inch of the back of Kennedy's head. The first and fatal Mini-Mag hollow-point bullet shattered his right mastoid bone and lodged in the right hemisphere of his cerebellum. The second and third bullets entered his back right armpit. Five other rounds were rapidly fired. There were seventy-seven people in the pantry. Six of them,

---

1. This chapter was originally published as a scientific paper in *Journal of Personality Assessment*, 1992, 58:548–570.

including Kennedy, became victims. Sirhan was wrestled onto a steam table, where police handcuffed him and immediately took him from the hotel. Kennedy died twenty-five hours later (Clarke 1982, Kaiser 1970).

During the summer and fall of that year, the defendant underwent unprecedented psychiatric and psychological examination by eight different clinicians. The defense team included Bernard Diamond, M.D., Eric Marcus, M.D., Martin Schorr, Ph.D., and Roderick Richardson, Ph.D. Steven Howard, Ph.D. and William Crain, Ph.D. consulted with the defense doctors. The prosecution team included Seymour Pollack, M.D., Georgene Seward, Ph.D., George De Vos, Ph.D., and Leonard Olinger, Ph.D.

Sirhan Sirhan was administered the Rorschach Inkblot Test on two occasions, first by Dr. Richardson and then by Dr. Schorr. The Rorschach test data were entered into evidence at trial and discussed in detail. The first Rorschach protocol, including miniature inkblots and location scoring, was published by Kaiser (1970). The second Rorschach protocol was administered several months later by Dr. Schorr in the presence of a team of deputies, an attorney, a writer, and a legal assistant. It was not published.

The purpose of this study was to generate and test clinical hypotheses from the first Rorschach protocol through the use of reliable and valid interpretive systems unavailable in 1968. Although an idiographic study does not substantially contribute to nomothetic scientific knowledge, this individual's psychology does find importance in the historical event of the Robert F. Kennedy assassination, given the small number of American assassins that are available for study in any one generation.

METHODOLOGY

The Rorschach protocol posed three difficulties (Table 9-1). First, the examiner did not limit the number of responses, yielding a protocol with R = 63. This tends to disproportionately increase the number of D and Dd location responses, and X + % may be lower than average

Table 9–1.

The Rorschach Protocol of Sirhan Sirhan.

Card I

1. I've seen it before. I still don't know. Looks like the back part of a chicken. You fry a chicken. That's the only thing I can—

2. A butterfly in flight.

3. A frog.

4. Two birds—doves.

5. Coastline.

6. Mountains.

7. Clouds.

8. Cliffs.

9. A bowl.

Card II

10. A crown.

11. A diamond.

1. It's the whole thing, this being the center. I've eaten some chicken. I never used to like that part, if I could avoid it. It's very bony.

2. The body is here and here are the wings.

3. Looks like the internal dissection of it. From the little of what I remember, this looks like the cloaca.

4. (Top dd.) (How does it appear?) As though they have just landed.

5. From a top view like from an airplane. Looks like both a photo and an aerial view could be either. I can see islands.

6. Looking down from a plane, the darker areas.

7. Is very dark. Just about ready to start to rain. Dark clouds.

8. This reminds me of cliffs looking far away. The space is the water.

9. It looks like the top of a bowl, like it's curved here.

10. It's in the space here, a crown for a queen or a king.

11. It looks like a diamond or the top of a mosque. A minaret up here. It's the same space, the cut of it.

(continued)

Table 9-1. (*continued*)

Card II (*continued*)

12. A satellite, you know, space.

13. A blood smear on a microscope thing.

14. A cross.

15. Blood! (Looks intently at the blot.)

16. A face of a person. Glass.

17. An elephant or a bear.

Card III

18. A couple of dancers.

19. Lungs.

20. Cauliflower.
21. Sternum. This is the sternum, isn't it. (Long pause.)
22. A rooster.

12. It's the same area, you know, just the shape of it.

13. In here looks like blood smeared around. (Red shading in the dark area, lower right.)

14. It's at the top, a Rosicrucian cross is the way I think of it.

15. All of the red especially here (lower D) looks like mixed with other liquids (W).

16. Profile (red, at top). It projects no feeling to me. (?) Madness (?), anger—the teeth are showing, they look more like women than men.

17. The GOP elephant (popular area). Maybe it could be just a bear.

18. A jovial bunch of Negro drum players—Watusi—although up here—this much looks like foxes—more animal than human—looks like a werewolf (sex?). Oh, men.

19. (Center D lower.) Looks like a cauliflower really. I see all the fine edges—the edge of it looks like a cauliflower. Also looks like the trachea, leading to bronchial tubes.

22. (Side d.) Maybe a turkey—Red made me think of it.

(*continued*)

Table 9-1. (*continued*)

Hell!

23. Underwater plantations—Plant life—kelp (grimace).

23. Looks like seeing through kelp, this depth thing here. I see it? Looking through it all. (Additional comment.) Now I feel like saying it looks like a casket to me. It represents death.

24. A medieval castle, abandoned.

24. (Top dd.)

25. An x-ray of the chest (grimace).

25. Well, going down the center here (top ⅓) in the shading it looks like the muscles around the neck.

26. (Points at own stomach.) I see these muscles, the abdominal muscles.

26. (Center line just above center.) The shading in here looks like the abdominal muscles. (Additional comment.) This much here is way out beyond. It goes beyond. I can't describe it.

27. Very dark—serpents (grimacing). (Blinks.) (?) Looks ready to strike.

28. An animal on hind legs.

28. (Center D) Say a penguin.

29. The hoof of an animal.

29. (dd at the bottom of D.)

Card V

30. A bird. A big eagle like. Flying head-on.

30. (W, FM, A, P.)

31. A chicken leg. Fried chicken.

31. You know these advertisements for fried chicken. Some old man has all these franchises for fried chicken.

32. Horns, look like the ears of a kangaroo.

32. Looks like horns and ears of a kangaroo, looking straight at me. Right in here.

(continued)

Table 9-1. (*continued*)

33. A ballet dancer.

33. The legs are here, the skirt and all that floating around. (Gestures.) Just the legs and standing on the toes. Just the center bottom legs.

34. A seal.

Card VI

35. A cat.

35. (Just the tip of the top d.) Eyes, whiskers.

36. This chicken comes in here again.

36. No inquiry.

37. A lamp.

37. It's the brightest spot in the blot. (dd on center line.)

38. A rocket.

38. The center line, (lower $\frac{2}{3}$, F +)

39. An owl.

39. No inquiry.

40. I have a feeling of high altitude.

40. From the cliffs. Very high. Looks like looking very high and from a high altitude.

41. The bust of a female from the chest up.

41. (Tip of outer top extension dd.)

42. The claws of an eagle or predatory bird.

42. Just these claws here.

43. Walking in a very dense forest, a lot of foliage.

43. Looks like an aerial view what you might see around the equator. (Center, both sides in shading.)

44. Vertebrae.

44. No inquiry. (Limits.) Can you find anything of a sexual nature in this particular blot? "Yeah, you mean this being the vagina?" What about an animal skin or a hide that's often seen on this card? "Oh, yeah, the whole thing. That's beautiful. Looks like the fur side–" Again this foliage.

(continued)

Table 9-1. (*continued*)

Card VII

45. Monkey with tail.

46. Bears. Stuffed bears.

47. A jigsaw puzzle.
48. A dam.

49. A canal.
50. A map of Egypt, you know the boundaries.
51. The Delta River, no, a delta, a river.
52. Towers (very ruminative, here).

45. Heads, playful. The heads and the tails (tail is the usual ear).

46. A bear's head. The expression is wicked, mean, mad.

47. A jigsaw puzzle (W no inquiry).
48. A dam. Inquiry—a canal, more like in Egypt.

(One side of lower D.)

52. The towers very distant. (At top of the center.) Very mountainous—might be a church on a cliff.

Card VIII

53. The California bear.
54. Flags.

55. The spine. The vertical column. Is it vertical?
56. I don't know, it's a desert plant. Grows very tall—not a cactus. I don't know the name.

53. (D, F, A, P.)
54. (Blue area.) Is that blue or green—like the United Nations flags at the top of the buildings.

55. The spine, the center line—the spinal column.
56. (Patient suddenly verbalizes) The colors shock me—no—I don't know—I feel very jittery— I can't hold still—it stirs me. I read this magazine article on the 20th anniversary of the State of Israel. It was in color— that color—I hate the Jews. There was jubilation—I felt that they were saying in the article, we beat the Arabs—it burns the shit out of me, there was happiness and jubilation.

(*continued*)

Table 9-1. (*continued*)

Card VIII (*continued*)
57. Guns—mortars.
58. Boats.

Card IX
59. In school class—in biology—plant life under a microscope—I don't remember the name of this plant.

59. The smear of a botanical slide (W). The color clashes—I am not used to it—too many of them at the same time—it confuses me. It just increases in degrees.

60. Apples.
61. Fire. It's weird (shakes head). Whew! It has depth—it's too deep. Whew!

Card X
62. This whole color—it throws me off! Monsters! (60 second interval.) It's really about all on this one? (You seem upset.) It's frightening—it frightens me—they all seem the same—wickedness! Too many entanglements!

62. It's a cacophony of colors, a hodgepodge. All those legs! This here looks like some kind of rat (brown area). No, not a rat—it flies—a bat. The whole thing looks like monstrosities. It's more vulgar—I'd avoid it. Everybody wants to catch on to you—with all those legs! The minute you're within reach you're in their clutches.

63. Blood! (Grimace, puts card away quickly.)

63. (What about the blood?) I seem to associate the whole thing negatively with blood. (What about the red area?) It looks like liver to me—some kind of meat. (Grimace.) I'd rather not even discuss it—I'd rather not even discuss it. All those legs.

owing to a higher frequency of unusual answers (Exner 1986a). Second, the examiner failed to inquire on nineteen, or 30 percent, of the responses. Ritzler and Nalesnik (1990) found that with no inquiry, color and shading determinants are reduced, pure F is therefore inflated, and blends decrease. Special Score (Exner 1986a) categories measuring formal thought disorder are also difficult to determine. All these scores would affect several composite scores, including distortion of EB in the introversive direction; the attenuation of EA and es; and increased Lambda. The Suicide Constellation, Depression Index, and Schizophrenia Index (Exner 1986a) would also be less sensitive to pathology. Ritzler and Nalesnik (1990) concluded, "Subjects whose protocols have no inquiry may appear more introverted, less emotionally expressive, more rigid and controlled, less suicidal and depressed, and/or less psychotic" (p. 652). They also found, however, that only six of thirty-three essential Comprehensive System indices demonstrated significant differences without inquiry across four groups of subjects. I addressed this problem by applying the Ritzler and Nalesnik (1990) liberalized scoring rules to the responses without inquiry. I assumed this application would restore the validity of overall scoring for these responses, except for Special Scores. The inability to ferret out Vista (V) from Form Dimension (FD) responses with the liberalized scoring rules would also obscure the former and increase the latter. The third problem was a "testing of the limits" for sex and texture done by the examiner to response number forty-four (Card VI). Although both a sex response and implied texture response were elicited, I did not score them, and subsequent responses did not yield a sex content or texture determinant.

The protocol was scored using the Exner (1986a) Comprehensive System, and interpretive hypotheses were generated with the Rorschach Interpretation Assistance Program, Version 2 (Exner 1990b). Interrater agreement was determined by a second independent scoring of the protocol. The protocol was also scored for defense mechanisms (Cooper and Arnow 1986, Cooper et al. 1988); primitive object relations (Kwawer 1980); and Mutuality of Autonomy responses (Urist 1977). Our aggression scores (Meloy and Gacono 1992a) and Gacono's (1990) Impressionistic response were also scored. The

Rorschach was then compared to results of a study by Miner and De Vos (1960) concerning Algerian males and the Rorschach acculturation hypotheses of Meyers (in press). The question of malingering was also considered. Rorschach data were then compared to psychiatric and psychological diagnoses at trial, major developmental events in the childhood and adolescence of Sirhan Sirhan, and his behavior around the time of the assassination.

RESULTS

Psychostructural Data

The Comprehensive System (Exner 1990a) sequence of scores and structural summary for the Sirhan protocol are listed in Tables 9-2 and 9-3. Interrater agreements for five scoring categories were: 98 percent for Developmental Quality, 83 percent for Determinants, 100 percent for Form Quality, 87 percent for Content, and 87 percent for Special Scores (Average = 91 percent). Differences were resolved through discussion between the independent raters (myself and Dr. Phil Erdberg). The protocol was positive for both the Depression Index (Score 7) and the Suicide Constellation (Score 8).

The Rorschach Interpretation Assistance Program, Version 2 (Exner 1990b) generated forty-three hypotheses, which are summarized according to each psychological operation.

Affect

Characteristics common to those who have attempted or effected suicide; frequent and intense experience of affective disruption; probable major affective or dysthymic disorder; a tendency to merge feelings and thinking during trial-and-error problem solving; serious emotional modulation problems; will convey impressions of impulsiveness; less mature psychological organization for age; tendency to avoid emotional stimuli; currently experiencing distress or discomfort;

excessive introspection focusing on negative features; irritated by testing; confused and intense feelings experienced; difficulty bringing closure to emotional situations.

Capacity for Control and Stress Tolerance

Unusually good capacities for control, considerable tolerance for stress, pervasive stabilization, and ready ability to formulate and give direction to behaviors.

Situational Stress

Significant increase in stimulus demands owing to situational stress; some decisions and behaviors may not be as well organized as usual; potential for impulsiveness is considerable; vulnerable to disorganization in complex situations; added psychological complexity and confused feelings are results of current stress condition.

Self-perception

Regards himself as less favorable when compared with others; engages in more introspection than is customary, and focuses on perceived negative features of the self-image; frequent painful feelings concerning negative self-value, which is largely based on imaginary rather than real experience; issues of self dealt with in a detached and overly intellectualized manner that tends to distort reality; unusual body concern and preoccupation.

Interpersonal Perception and Relations

Does not experience needs for emotional closeness; maintains distance and safety in relations, but prefers dependency on others, creating conflict; normatively interested in others; takes a passive, but not necessarily submissive, role in relationships; insecure about personal integrity, and will tend to be authoritarian when relations appear to challenge the self; regarded by others as rigid or narrow, and will have

Table 9–2.

Comprehensive System Sequence of Scores for the Sirhan Protocol.

Card	No	Loc	#	Determinant(s)	(2)	Content(s)	Pop	Z	Special Scores
I	1	Wo	1	Fu		Fd		1.0	PER
	2	Wo	1	FMao		A	P	1.0	
	3	Do	4	F–		A, An			
	4	Ddo	28	FMp–	2	A			
	5	Ddv	99	FDu		Ls, Sc			
	6	Ddo	99	FD.YF–		Ls			
	7	Ddv	99	Y		Cl			
	8	DdSo	32	FDu		Na		3.5	
	9	Ddo	99	Fu		Hh			
II	10	DSo	5	Fu		Art			
	11	DSo	5	Fu		Art		4.5	
	12	DSo	5	Fo		Sc			
	13	Ddv	99	C.Y		Bl			
	14	Do	4	Fu		Art			
	15	Wv	1	C.Y		Bl			
	16	Do	2	Mp–	2	Hd, Hx, Art			AG
	17	Do	1	Fo		(A), Art	P		
III	18	D+	1	Mpo	2	(H), Ay	P	3.0	INC2, COP
	19	Do	7	F–		An			
	20	Do	7	Fu		Fd			
	21	Do	8	Fu		An			
	22	Do	2	CFo		A			
IV	23	Ddv	99	FV–		Bt			AB, MOR
	24	Ddo	21	Fu		Ay			
	25	Ddo	99	FYu		Xy			
	26	Ddo	99	FYu		An			PER
	27	Do	4	FY.FMao	2	(A)			
	28	Do	1	FMp–		A			
	29	Ddo	99	Fu		Ad			
V	30	Wo	1	FMao		A		1.0	
	31	Do	1	Fo		Fd			DR
	32	Do	6	FMpo		Ad			INC
	33	W+	1	Ma.mpo		Hd, Cg		2.5	
	34	Wo	1	F–		A		1.0	

(continued)

Table 9-2. (*continued*)

Card	No	Loc	#	Determinant(s)	(2)	Content(s)	Pop	Z	Special Scores
VI	35	Ddo	99	Fu		Ad			
	36	Ddo	99	F–		A			PSV
	37	Ddo	32	Fu		Hh			
	38	Do	12	Fu		Sc			
	39	Do	3	F–		A			
	40	Ddv	99	FDu		Ls			
	41	Ddo	25	Fu		Hd, Sx			
	42	Ddo	21	Fo		Ad			
	43	Wv	1	FD.YFu		Ls			
	44	Do	5	Fo		An			
VII	45	Do	1	FMpu	2	A			
	46	Do	3	Mpo	2	(Ad)			AG, INC
	47	Wv	1	Fu		Id			
	48	Do	4	Fu		Ls, Sc			
	49	Ddo	99	Fu		Ls, Sc			
	50	Ddo	23	Fu		Ge			
	51	Wv	1	Fu		Na			
	52	Do	8	FDu	2	Ls, Sc			
VIII	53	Do	1	Fo		(A), Art	P		
	54	Do	5	FCo	2	Art			
	55	Ddo	21	Fo		An			
	56	Wo	1	FCo		Bt		4.5	DR2
	57	Ddo	99	Fu	2	Sc			
	58	Wo	1	F–	2	Id		4.5	
IX	59	Wv	1	CF.YFu		Bt, Sc			PER, DR
	60	Do	6	Fo	2	Fd			
	61	Dv	3	C.V		Fi			
X	62	Wo	1	CF.Mp–		(H), Hx, A		5.5	AB, AG, DR2
	63	Wv	1	C		Bl, Fd			MOR, DR

Summary of Approach

I :W.W.D.Dd.Dd.Dd.Dd.DdS.Dd		VI :Dd.Dd.Dd.D.D.Dd.Dd.Dd.W.D	
II :DS.DS.DS.Dd.D.W.D.D		VII :D.D.W.D.Dd.Dd.W.D	
III:D.D.D.D.D		VIII:D.D.Dd.W.Dd.W	
IV:Dd.Dd.Dd.Dd.D.D.Dd		IX :W.D.D	
V :W.D.D.W.W		X :W.W	

Table 9-3.

Comprehensive System Structural Summary for the Sirhan Protocol.

Location Features	Determinants Blends	Single	Contents	S-Constellation
				YES..FV + VF + V + FD > 2
			H = 0, 0	YES..Col-Shd Bl > 0
Zf = 11	FD.YF	M = 3	(H) = 2, 0	YES..Ego < 0.31, > 0.44
ZSum = 32.0	C.Y	FM = 6	Hd = 3, 0	NO ..MOR > 3
ZEst = 34.5	C.Y	m = 0	(Hd) = 0, 0	NO ..Zd > ±3.5
	FY.FM	FC = 2	Hx = 0, 2	YES..es > EA
W = 14	M.m	CF = 1	A = 10, 1	YES..$CF + C > FC$
(Wv = 6)	FD.YF	C = 1	(A) = 3, 0	YES..X + % < 0.70
D = 27	CF.YF	Cn = 0	Ad = 4, 0	YES..S > 3
Dd = 22	C.V	FC' = 0	(Ad) = 1, 0	NO ..P < 3 or > 8
S = 4	CF.M	C'F = 0	An = 5, 1	YES..Pure H < 2
		C' = 0	Art = 4, 3	NO ..R < 17
DQ		FT = 0	Ay = 1, 1	8.....TOTAL
...........(FQ−)		TF = 0	Bl = 3, 0	
+ = 2 (0)		T = 0	Bt = 3, 0	SPECIAL SCORINGS
o = 49 (11)		FV = 1	Cg = 0, 1	Lv1 Lv2
v/+ = 0 (0)		VF = 0	Cl = 1, 0	DV = 0x1 0x2
v = 12 (1)		V = 0	Ex = 0, 0	INC = 2x2 1x4
		FY = 2	Fd = 4, 1	DR = 3x3 2x6
		YF = 0	Fi = 1, 0	FAB = 0x4 0x7
		Y = 1	Ge = 1, 0	ALOG = 0x5
Form Quality		Fr = 0	Hh = 2, 0	CON = 0x7
		rF = 0	Ls = 7, 0	SUM6 = 8
FQx FQf MQual SQx		FD = 4	Na = 2, 0	WSUM6 = 29
+ = 0 0 0 0		F = 33	Sc = 3, 5	
o = 18 8 3 1			Sx = 0, 1	AB = 2 CP = 0
u = 28 19 0 3			Xy = 1, 0	AG = 3 MOR = 2
− = 12 6 2 0			Id = 2, 0	CFB = 0 PER = 3
none = 5 – 0 0		(2) = 11		COP = 1 PSV = 1

(continued)

Table 9–3. (*continued*)

Ratios, Percentages, and Derivations

R = 63	L = 1.10		FC:CF+C = 2: 7	COP = 1	AG = 3
			Pure C = 4	Food	= 5
EB = 5: 10.0	EA=15.0	EBPer = 2.0	Afr = 0.21	Isolate/R	= 0.27
eb = 8:11	es = 19	D = −1	S = 4	H:(H)Hd(Hd)	= 0:5
	Adj es =11	Adj D = +1	Blends:R = 9:63	(HHd):(AAd)	= 2:4
			CP = 0	H + A:Hd + Ad	= 16:8

FM = 7 : C' = 0 T = 0
m = 1 : V = 2 Y = 9

		P = 4	Zf = 11	3r+(2)/R = 0.17	
a:p = 4:9	Sum6 = 8	X+% = 0.29	Zd = −2.5	Fr+rF = 0	
Ma:Mp = 1:4	Lv2 = 3	F+% = 0.24	W:D:Dd = 14:27:22	FD = 6	
2AB+ Art+Ay = 13	WSum6 = 29	X−% = 0.19	W:M = 14:5	An+Xy = 7	
M− = 2	Mnone = 0	S−% = 0.00	DQ+ = 2	MOR = 2	
		Xu% = 0.44	DQv = 12		

SCZI = 3 DEPI = 7* CDI = 3 S-CON = 8* HVI = No OBS = No

difficulty maintaining relations; likelihood of forceful and aggressive behaviors, but may not be obvious or direct because of passive tendencies; less involved in social interactions, probably because of timidity.

Information Processing

A marked tendency to narrow or simplify stimulus fields; a form of psychological economizing that can create a potential for behaviors that do not coincide with social demands or expectations; preference for less complex stimulus fields; little effort made to organize and integrate fields of information in a complex or sophisticated manner.

Cognitive Mediation

Likelihood of less conventional responses and behaviors; may reflect individualism, social alienation, or more serious mediational or affective modulation problems; will likely result in a strong orientation to distance from an environment that is perceived as threatening, demanding, and ungiving; tendency to overpersonalize stimuli; perceptual inaccuracy; and mediational distortion.

Ideation

Thinking is usually merged with feelings during problem solving, which may give rise to more elaborate patterns of thought and acceptance of imprecise or ambiguous logic systems; feelings can be put aside in favor of an ideational approach; ideational sets and values are well fixed; chronic and higher than expected levels of ideational activity outside the focus of attention; excessive use of fantasy to deny reality and avoid responsibility in decision making, creating a self-imposed helplessness; a longstanding pattern of limited concentration and interruptions in deliberate thinking; intellectualization a major defense in affectively stressful situations; vulnerable to disorganization during intense emotional experiences because this pseudo-intellectual process becomes less effective; presence of seriously disturbed thinking, marked by flawed judgment, conceptualization, and disorganized patterns of decision making; promotes distortions of reality and a marked predisposition toward pathology.

In summary, the Comprehensive System interpretive hypotheses suggest that Sirhan Sirhan, at the time of testing, was suicidal and profoundly dysphoric, confused by intense and painful affective disruptions. His considerable stress tolerance and control were being tested by intense and complex situational demands that created a potential for impulsiveness. His self-perception was negative, and although he maintained a rigid distance from others, he preferred dependency. His cognitive processing was characterized by simplification, major impairments in reality testing marked by the perception of personal threat, and seriously disturbed thought organization suffused with unpleasant affect.

Psychodynamic Data

The Cooper and associates (1988) Rorschach Defense Scale scoring is listed in Table 9–4. The Sirhan protocol evidenced thirty-five score-

Table 9–4.

Rorschach Defense Scale Scoring of Sirhan Protocol.

Level of Personality Organization	Defense	Frequency
Neurotic	Higher level denial	1
	Intellectualization	1
	Isolation	7
	Reaction formation	0
	Repression	0
	Rationalization	0
	Pollyannish denial	3
Borderline	Devaluation	4
	Omnipotence	0
	Primitive idealization	5
	Projection	5
	Projective identification	2
	Splitting	5
Psychotic	Hypomanic denial	0
	Massive denial	2
	Total scored	35

able responses. According to the categorizing of their fifteen defenses as neurotic, borderline, or psychotic (Cooper et al. 1988, Kernberg 1984), there were twelve (34 percent) neurotic defenses utilized, the most common being isolation; twenty-one (60 percent) borderline defenses utilized, the most common being primitive idealization, projective identification, and splitting; and two (6 percent) psychotic defenses utilized. There were no apparent trends in the sequential use of the grouped defenses across the time of examination. For instance, isolation, a neurotic defense, was used on Card I and Card VII (e.g., Card I: "Cliffs. [Inquiry] This reminds me of cliffs looking far away. The space is the water"). Projection, a borderline defense, was used on Card II and Card IX (e.g., Card II: "A face of a person. Glass. [Inquiry] Profile. It projects no feeling to me. [?] Madness [?] anger–the teeth are showing, they look more like women than men").

There was only one scoreable primitive object relations response

(Kwawer 1980) to Card X: "This whole color. It throws me off!
Monsters! It's really about all on this one? It's frightening. It frightens
me. They all seem the same. Wickedness! Too many entanglements!"
[Inquiry:] "It's a cacophony of colors, a hodgepodge. All those legs.
This here looks like some kind of rat. No, not a rat, it flies, a bat. The
whole thing looks like monstrosities. It's more vulgar, I'd avoid it.
Everybody wants to catch on to you, with all those legs! The minute
you're within reach you're in their clutches" (Kaiser 1970, p. 608). This
would be categorized as engulfment (Kwawer 1980). Mutuality of
Autonomy (Urist 1977) scoring yielded five scoreable responses, with
a most adaptive score of 1 (reciprocal acknowledgment) to Card III: "A
couple of dancers. [Inquiry] A jovial bunch of Negro drum players—
Watusi—although up here—this much looks like foxes—more animal
than human—looks like a werewolf. [Sex?] Oh, men"; and a most
pathological score of 5 (coercion, hurtful influence, or threat) to three
responses (Card VII: "Bears. Stuffed bears. [Inquiry] A bear's head.
The expression is wicked, mean, mad.") The average MOA score was
3.6.

The aggression scores (Exner 1986a, Gacono 1990) and impressionistic score (Gacono et al. 1990) are listed in Table 9-5.

These Sirhan protocol scores are descriptively compared to data
from a small sample of borderline personality disordered outpatient
males ($N = 18$) previously described in Gacono and colleagues (1992).

Table 9-5.

Comparison of Aggression Response and Impressionistic Response
Frequencies of Sirhan Protocol to Male Borderline Personality
Disordered ($N = 18$) Protocols.

Category	Sirhan Protocol	Male BPD Patients		
		Mean	SD	Frequency
Aggression (Exner 1986)	4.0	1.39	1.33	13
Aggressive content	6.0	2.89	1.88	18
Aggressive past	0	0.83	1.46	8
Aggressive potential	1.0	0.89	2.16	6
Impressionistic	1.0	1.78	1.35	16

The protocol yielded eleven scoreable aggression responses and one impressionistic response: the same Card X response scored with the Kwawer (1980) criteria above (the impressionistic response is scored when a chromatic or achromatic color determinant and abstraction special score occur together). The most common aggression score was Aggressive Content (Gacono 1990), followed by Aggression (Exner 1986a), and Aggressive Potential (Gacono 1990).

Cultural Data

The protocol was compared with the Rorschach data provided by Miner and De Vos (1960) and De Vos and Boyer (1989) on Algerian males, and the Rorschach cultural adaptation hypotheses of Meyers (in press). Miner and De Vos (1960) reported Rorschach data collected in 1950 from sixty-four Algerian Arab males, aged 20–50. They divided the group into "oasis" and "urban" samples. The proportion of unpleasant content was significantly higher among the urban Arabs, most notably content indicative of body preoccupation and hostility. Two patterns of adjustment were frequent in the urbanized Arabs: greater rigidity and internalization of aggression, suggested by anatomical responses; or a more complex, flexible ego that perceived the external environment as hostile and dangerous. Human figures were rarely seen and were usually not moving or engaged in positive activity. When movement was perceived, it was attributed to foreign or supernatural figures. Often humans were incomplete or mutilated, and the latter responses usually involved a reference to the genitals. The Arab men were also loath to see women; only twelve of the entire eighty-two human percepts in all the Rorschachs were female. They were not perceived to move and attention was focused on their sexual organs. Human figures were usually attached to each other in a passive and immobile manner.

Most of these findings are consistent with the Sirhan protocol (see Tables 9–1 and 9–2). There were no Pure H responses and a paucity of (H), Hd, or (Hd) responses. There was one Sex (female) response, six Anatomy responses, and three Blood responses. Of the five Human Movement (M) responses, one had no human content (46).

Unlike the Arab sample, the Sirhan protocol evidenced no human figures either passively attached to each other or mutilated.

Meyers (in press) contended that the Rorschach is a useful predictor of cross-cultural adaptability, and hypothesized a number of Rorschach variables that measure the lack of flexibility and openness (Lambda, EB), poor perceptual acuity (X + %, X − %, Zd), decreased personal autonomy (T, Fd, Egocentricity Ratio, Morbid, Vista), and decreased emotional resiliency (FC:CF + C, Afr, S, Blends, AdjD) as predictive markers of pathological adjustment to a new culture. The Sirhan protocol is generally consistent with her predictions, except for AdjD.

Malingering

The question of malingering was considered and ruled out during the initial phases of this study for the following reasons: first, throughout trial Sirhan Sirhan adamantly opposed the use of a mental disability defense and did not want to be labeled as mentally ill (Kaiser 1970); second, despite his objections, he cooperated with psychological and psychiatric procedures and produced other valid test data (Minnesota Multiphasic Personality Inventory [MMPI], Wechsler Adult Intelligence Scale [WAIS], Thematic Apperception Test [TAT], Bender-Gestalt); third, he met only one (medicolegal setting) of the four *DSM-III-R* contexts for suspected malingering; and fourth, a *reduction* in R appears to be the most prominent finding in the Rorschach malingering literature, despite the overall inconsistent and inconclusive results (Perry and Kinder 1990).

DISCUSSION

The Sirhan Rorschach protocol, when analyzed with technology unavailable in 1968, strongly suggests a depressed and suicidal individual whose personality is predominately organized at a borderline-level (Kernberg 1984), with some adaptive neurotic, and occasionally psychotic, defenses. The protocol presents a mixed characterological picture with hysterical, paranoid, and dependent features all evident.

To what degree are the Rorschach findings of this study consistent with historical data concerning Sirhan Sirhan? A review of psychiatric findings at the trial, significant developmental events in the childhood and adolescence of Sirhan, and his behavior around the time of the assassination, should answer this question.

Psychiatric and Psychological Opinion at Trial

All of the psychologists independently evaluated the Sirhan Rorschach protocol and agreed, except for one, with a diagnosis of paranoid schizophrenia. Dr. Olinger dissented, and rendered a diagnosis of "pseudoneurotic schizophrenia" (Kaiser 1970).

The Rorschach data in this study, however, do not support a schizophrenic diagnosis. The Comprehensive System (Exner 1990a) Schizophrenia Index score of 3 suggests the unlikelihood of such a mental illness. Only 18 percent of Exner's normative inpatient schizophrenic sample scored less than 4 on this Index (Exner 1990a). There is likewise a 13 percent false-positive rate for borderline personality disorder on the Schizophrenia Index (Exner 1986b). The Cooper and Arnow (1986) defenses also do not support a psychotic diagnosis, but rather a personality organized at a borderline level of psychopathology (Lerner 1990; see Table 9–4). Lerner and colleagues (1987) found that the Cooper and Arnow defenses of splitting, devaluation, and omnipotence had the most power in discriminating borderline from schizophrenic patients. Both the Kwawer (1980) and Urist (1977) measures also suggest a borderline level of pathology. Blatt and associates (1990) found the Urist Mutuality of Autonomy Scale a better measure of psychopathology than interpersonal relations.

Nevertheless, the defense team, led by Dr. Diamond, concluded that Sirhan Sirhan had paranoid schizophrenia, and had killed Robert Kennedy in a dissociative state, a self-induced trance brought on by the lights and mirrors in the Ambassador Hotel lobby. His political views were considered delusional fantasies (Kaiser 1970). Dr. Diamond later found his own testimony an "absurd and preposterous story, unlikely and incredible" (*People* v. *Sirhan*, Vol. 24, p. 6998).

The prosecution team, led by Dr. Pollack, disagreed. In his February 5, 1969 report, he diagnosed the defendant as "borderline schizophrenia with paranoid and hysterical features, but I do not believe that he was clinically psychotic" (Pollack 1969a, p. 3). He also noted the complete absence of any hallucinations or delusions. He wrote, "Sirhan's motivation in killing Senator Kennedy was entirely political, and was not related to bizarre or psychotic motivation or accompanied by peculiar and highly idiosyncratic reasoning" (p. 3). In a March 21, 1969 supplemental report, Dr. Pollack considered the defendant a "developing paranoid personality whose assassination of Senator Robert Kennedy was motivated by political reasons which were highly emotionally charged" (Pollack 1969b, p. 1). These Rorschach findings are consistent with Dr. Pollack's diagnosis of "borderline schizophrenia" and Dr. Olinger's diagnosis of "pseudoneurotic schizophrenia," terms that described what we would today consider Borderline Personality Disorder (Stone 1980).

Developmental Events

The childhood and adolescent pathogenesis of Sirhan's personality was shaped by two psychological themes, trauma and loss. He was born into a large Arab family in Jerusalem on March 19, 1944, and by the age of 5 had experienced a number of traumatic events during the war-torn prelude to Israel's statehood: he witnessed a bomb explosion at the Damascus Gate that left mutilated Arab corpses in the street; he observed his older brother run over and killed by a Zionist truck trying to avoid sniper fire; he discovered the body of an Arab neighbor; he observed portions of a British soldier's body dangling from a church tower; and he fled from a driverless truck, which then exploded. When he was 5 years old, his family left their home in the middle of the night and moved into a 15-by-30-foot room in the Old Walled City of Jerusalem (Clarke 1982).

His Christian mother refused to let the children play in the street and his father's hostility resulted in physical abuse of the children, including Sirhan. Sirhan attended a Lutheran school from ages 7–12 and was described as mature beyond his years (Kaiser 1970). On December 14, 1956, he emigrated with his family to the United States. He was 12 years old. They settled in Pasadena in a lower-middle-class neighborhood but resisted acculturation. One year later, Sirhan's father abandoned the family and returned to Jordan. Neighbors described him as a mean and self-centered man (Clarke 1982). Sirhan, however, appeared to make a good adjustment. He learned English quickly, received above-average grades, and graduated from John Muir High School. He was not reclusive, joined the officer cadet corps, and was elected to the student council. He was viewed as cooperative and enthusiastic (Kaiser 1970).

When Sirhan reached the age of 20, however, his object world began to fall apart. His sister, Aida, whom he revered, died of leukemia. Two of his brothers were arrested. He was dismissed from Pasadena City College for not attending classes. He tried to pursue a career as a jockey, but fell from a galloping horse at a ranch in Corona when he was 22. His blurred vision and pain complaints were compensated through a suit that paid him two thousand dollars. He was now 24 years old, and in March 1968, he quit his job at a health food store (Clarke 1982), three months before the assassination.

Sirhan had fostered his identity as an Arab throughout his adolescence, and was quite vocal in his hatred of the Zionists, whom he equated with Nazis. Following the Six Day War, which began June 5, 1967, he often repeated his belief that the wealthy American Jews controlled the politicians and the media. His conscious hatred of the Jews is captured in this DR response to Card VIII: "I don't know, it's a desert plant. Grows very tall – not a cactus. I don't know the name. [Inquiry] The colors shock me, no, I don't know, I feel very jittery. I can't hold still. It stirs me. I read this magazine article on the twentieth anniversary of the State of Israel. It was in color – that color – I hate the Jews. There was jubilation. I felt that they were saying in the article, We beat the Arabs. It burns the shit out of me, there was happiness and jubilation."

The repetitive developmental experiences of trauma and loss

condensed into a conscious hatred (Terr 1991) for the perceived aggressor, the (father) Zionists, which was then generalized to all Jews. Structural characteristics of his depression (S-CON, DEPI, MOR, Isolate/R, Egocentricity, V, Y, T) and aggression (Ag, Ag Content, Ag Potential, S, Pure C) are amply evident in the Rorschach data (see Table 9–3). The inference that pathological mourning accounts for the depression is reasonable, given the plethora of his actual object losses: brother, first Jerusalem home, Palestinian cultural milieu (Levy-Warren 1987), father, sister, career opportunity, freedom after arrest, and Robert Kennedy as a persecutory object. Sirhan's depression would be considered anaclitic, rather than introjective (Blatt 1974), and the psychopathology is primarily oral aggressive with feelings of helplessness, weakness, and depletion in the face of a continual abandonment threat or a more annihilatory intent by the object.

Psychological trauma is also linked to mourning (Krystal 1984) and begs the question of the presence of Post-Traumatic Stress Disorder (PTSD; *DSM-III-R*) in Sirhan at the time of the examination. Two studies of inpatient and outpatient Vietnam veterans with PTSD (Hartman et al. 1990, Swanson et al. 1990) provide some comparative Rorschach data. Both studies indicate that the Sirhan protocol is more different than similar to the average PTSD Rorschach. Similarities include tenuous reality testing (X − %), high suicide risk (S-CON), devaluation of self (MOR), little interest in others as whole and real objects (Pure H), and a simplistic problem-solving style (Lambda). In contrast to the PTSD subjects (combined $N = 91$), the Sirhan protocol shows much more formal thought disorder (WSum6), an extratensive style (EB), no stimulus overload (AdjD), severe depression (DEPI), no pathological narcissism (Rf), and high aggression (Ag, S). However, comparison between an immigrant Arab who was subjected to combat as a child and indigenous soldiers subjected to combat as adults is only suggestive.

Other authors (Herman and van der Kolk 1987) have seen a similarity between PTSD and Borderline Personality Disorder (BPD) and have argued for the importance of assessing for actual childhood trauma in all borderline patients. Despite the organization of the

Sirhan data at a borderline *level* of personality (Kernberg 1984), the differences, once again, are greater than the similarities when his Rorschach is compared with a sample (Exner 1986b) of male and female borderline personality disordered patients. The Sirhan protocol is similar to this sample ($N = 84$) in poor modulation of affect (FC:CF + C), impaired reality testing (X − %), and extratensive problem solving (EB). It is different from the BPD patients in the absence of stimulus overload (AdjD), severe formal thought disorder (WSum6), abuse of fantasy (Ma:Mp), negative self-worth (Egocentricity Index), and avoidance of affect (Afr).

The hysterical character pathology of Sirhan is suggested by a number of Rorschach indices. The computer-based test interpretation hypotheses (Exner 1990b) emphasize the merging of thinking and affect and intense affective disruption. These hypotheses are based upon the variables of EB, eb, Y, FC:CF + C, Afr, Pure C, V, S, and three blends that have no form, two of which are C.Y (color and shading). These latter blends infer the experience of unmodulated affect followed by anxiety. The Cooper and Arnow (1986) defenses of denial and primitive idealization (31 percent of the scoreable defenses) are also consistent with hysterical character (Shapiro 1965). The impressionistic response suggests affect that is rapidly split off through the use of symbolization (Gacono et al. 1990). And the first and last responses to the Rorschach are food ambivalence responses (P. Erdberg, personal communication, May, 1991), perhaps regressive traces of early dependency frustrations and consequent oral rage. Card I: "I've seen it before. I still don't know. Looks like the back part of a chicken. You fry a chicken. That's the only thing I can−" [Inquiry] "It's the whole thing, this being the center. I've eaten some chicken. I never used to like that part, if I could avoid it. It's very bony." And the last response to Card X: "Blood!" [Inquiry] "I seem to associate the whole thing negatively with blood. It looks like liver to me − some kind of meat. I'd rather not even discuss it."

Hysterical character has historically been linked with dissociation (Breuer and Freud 1893–1895, *DSM-III-R*), and ego-dystonic dissociative states are found in BPD (Kernberg 1975), perhaps as a result of childhood trauma (Terr 1991). Sirhan was easily hypnotized on several occasions by Dr. Diamond, and abreacted his traumatic childhood experiences in Jerusalem (Kaiser 1970).

Despite the differences between the Sirhan protocol, the BPD sample, and the PTSD samples, the Rorschach data are somewhat consistent with the theme of psychic trauma, very consistent with the theme of recurrent loss and pathological mourning, and validate a characterological distrust and hatred of, yet hysterical dependence upon, the object world. The witnessing of extreme violence outside his home, and physical abuse by his father in his home, would disrupt the safety necessary for autonomous striving, the normative flowering of grandiosity, and the rapprochement subphase of separation-individuation (Mahler et al. 1975) during his preoedipal years. Hence, the predominance of borderline level defenses and object relations, and the absence of object constancy.

Predation and Assassination

On January 9 and 10, 1968, *The New York Times* reported Kennedy's proposed sale of fifty Phantom Jet fighter-bombers to Israel. Sirhan was enraged; an idealized paternal object for whom he hungered was shattered. Evidence suggests that he made the conscious decision to kill Kennedy on January 31, when he wrote in his diary, "RFK must die" (Kaiser 1970, p. 549). He had joined the Ancient Mystical Order of the Rosae Crucis that month and repeatedly used his diary as a form of self-hypnosis. As he later testified, "how you can install a thought in your mind and how you can have it work and become a reality if you want it to" (*People* v. *Sirhan*, Vol. 17, p. 4905). The defense considered this automatic writing.

When Kennedy announced his candidacy and President Lyndon Johnson announced his decision to not seek another term, Sirhan began practice shooting. On April 6, a few days after the Martin Luther King assassination, he told a Black trash collector that he was going to shoot Kennedy. He wrote in his diary on May 18, "My determination to eliminate RFK is becoming . . . more of an unshake-able obsession" (*People* v. *Sirhan*, People's Exhibit 71). He vowed to complete the act before June 5, the day after the California primary and the first anniversary of the Six Day War.

There were probably four stalking attempts to assassinate Kennedy before the actual June 5 killing. On May 20, he was seen with a woman at Robbie's Restaurant in Pomona, where Kennedy was dining and speaking. On May 24, he was observed at a Kennedy rally at the Los Angeles Sports Arena. On Saturday, June 1, he purchased two boxes of .22-caliber hollow-point cartridges and practiced shooting. On Sunday, June 2, he practiced shooting again, and then went to a Kennedy campaign rally at the Ambassador Hotel. And on Monday, June 3, he travelled to San Diego to see Kennedy speak at the El Cortez Hotel, and returned that night (Clarke 1982).

The day of the assassination, Sirhan practiced rapid-fire shooting at the San Gabriel Valley Gun Club and left the range at 5 P.M. He ate at Bob's Big Boy, went to the Ambassador Hotel, and had four alcoholic drinks over several hours. He then asked two people if the Kennedy bodyguards were with him all the time and if he would be coming through the kitchen pantry. Just before he shot Kennedy, he was heard to say, "Kennedy, you son of a bitch." (Clarke 1982, Kaiser 1970).

The assassination of Robert F. Kennedy was a paranoid conden-sation of hatred for the Jews onto an object with whom Sirhan projectively identified, a previously idealized, and then homicidally devalued, introject (Meloy 1988a). Kennedy was not only a projective vehicle, but also a malevolent object by whom Sirhan felt increasingly controlled and threatened. The operation of projective identification as a defense in Sirhan's object world is captured in the two Cooper and Arnow (1986) projective identification responses to Cards VIII and X (responses 56 and 62) noted above. The degree to which these Rorschach percepts both carry malevolent objects and are felt to control the subject is evident. In the Sirhan protocol, projective identification is used as a borderline, rather than psychotic, defense, since the object, rather than the self, representation is being projected and controlled, and the boundary between self and other is maintained (Goldstein 1991, Meloy 1991).

Although the motivation to assassinate Kennedy was suffused with intense affect, the stalking and killing closely fit the criteria for a predatory mode of violence (Meloy 1988b). The act was planned, purposeful, carried out over the course of five months, and involved rehearsal in both fantasy and deed.

Certain structural characteristics of the Rorschach data support this capacity for predatory violence. Both the elevated Lambda (1.10) and AdjD (+1) suggest an individual who was highly defended against his own affect with better than average stress tolerance and control, despite a proneness toward unmodulated affective outbursts (FC < CF + C). The absence of T suggests a chronic emotional detachment that would attenuate any feelings of empathy toward the proposed victim. The absence of Pure H responses would also facilitate the representation of others as part-objects suffused with imaginary, in this case grandiose, malevolent, and overpersonalized characteristics.

The Ma < Mp ratio in the Sirhan protocol is also suggestive of a capacity for rehearsal fantasy prior to an act of predation (Meloy 1988b). Instead of an abuse of fantasy (Exner 1986a), this passive ideational mode, which found its real-world correlate in the repetitive diary writings, may have facilitated the practicing of the assassination in fantasy. Sirhan's hysterical propensity to self-hypnotize, a voluntary form of dissociation learned from the Rosicrucians, may also have facilitated this process.

Content analysis is also suggestive of predatory violence. Objects of violence (Card VI: "a rocket," Card VIII: "guns–mortars") comprise several items of his aggressive content; and his one aggressive potential response (Card IV: "very dark–serpents [grimaces]. Looks ready to strike") is consistent with our finding in Rorschach protocols of psychopaths who are prone to predatory violence (Meloy and Gacono 1992a). Is the Sirhan protocol psychopathic? None of the Rorschach variables that discriminate between psychopathic and nonpsychopathic criminals, other than an absence of T, are present (Gacono et al. 1990, Gacono and Meloy 1991).

CONCLUSIONS

The archival study of a Rorschach protocol of an American assassin yields a wealth of data when subjected to current technology. The structural and psychodynamic characteristics of the Sirhan Sirhan protocol, although not supportive of the majority of psychiatric and psychological opinion at his trial, are quite consistent with known historical information concerning his development and the assassination of Robert F. Kennedy.

Appendix I

Erotomania, Culture, and the Insanity Defense

Mr. Jack Smith
Smith and Jones
646 9th St.
San Diego CA. 92101

RE: *People* v. *Hossein*

Dear Mr. Smith,

Pursuant to the order issued by Judge John J. Ryan dated January 30, 1991, I am submitting the following evaluation concerning Mr. Hossein. The purpose of this evaluation is to determine whether Mr. Hossein, by a preponderance of the evidence, was incapable of knowing or understanding the nature and quality of his act, or of distinguishing right from wrong at the time of his offense (California Penal Code § 25[b]).

SOURCES OF DATA

The following sources of data were used in the preparation of this evaluation: Transcript of a preliminary examination dated August 14–15, 1990; Copies of medical records from the San Diego County Jail concerning Mr. Hossein from February 3, 1990 until October 3, 1990; Report of Vehicle Examination dated February 2, 1990; Followup

Criminal Investigation Reports dated February 15, 1990; February 2, 1990; February 3, 1990; February 7, 1990; February 14, 1990; Fire Investigation Report dated February 5, 1990; Crime Scene Investigation Report dated February 2, 1990; Autopsy report of Manija dated February 3, 1990; Interview of Roghieg, undated; Interview of Ahmadreza Rhamin, undated; translation of a letter written by the defendant dated February 2, 1990; summary of an interview with Jeff Hossein by Daniel B. Webster dated January 3, 1991; a consultation with Dr. Shaul, on September 7, 1990; a telephone consultation with Dr. Mahmoud; review of the crime scene and autopsy photographs of the victim; a review of the relevant psychology and psychiatry literature concerning Iranian individuals from 1967 to October, 1990; results of the following psychological tests administered to the defendant: the Minnesota Multiphasic Personality Inventory, the Millon Clinical Multiaxial Inventory II, the Rorschach, portions of the Wechsler Adult Intelligence Scale-Revised, the Rey Dissimulation Test, the Quick Screen for Dementia; and four clinical interviews with the defendant and the translator, Mr. Farzan, on September 29, 1990 (5 hours), October 20, 1990 (6 hours), November 24, 1990 (1 hour), and January 6, 1991 (5 hours), for a total of 17 hours.

INSTANT OFFENSE

The defendant is charged with the murder of 35-year-old Manija, an Iranian female, on February 2, 1990 at approximately 0845. The crime is alleged to have occurred at 12345 Via Lomas, San Diego, California. Summary of the police investigation and witness reports indicate that the defendant drove his own car into the victim's car, hitting the driver's side at approximately 26 miles per hour, forcing both cars onto the lawn. The defendant then threw sulfuric acid and poured a flammable liquid onto the victim. He ignited it and the victim burned to death inside her car. The defendant then ran to the victim's house, yelling "I killed her" in Farsi to her mother, and banged his head on their door. He wrestled with the victim's cousin, Ramin, who ran to the car and tried to open it. The defendant then ran and threw himself in front of two trucks in succession, the second one hitting him. He then climbed aboard a third truck, but the driver ejected him. Mr. Hossein was arrested without resistance by the police.

The cause of death to the victim was fourth-degree burns over 90 percent of her body with smoke inhalation; also blunt force trauma with laceration of her left lung and intrathoracic hemorrhaging.

Comments by the defendant as remembered by witnesses at the time of the crime were as follows: in response to Steven M. telling him that he was pretty crazy, "I know." In response to Manuel M. telling him he was crazy for jumping in front of cars, "Yea, I know I am." To Officer Thompson when arrested: "I want to die. If I escape will you kill me . . . I wanted to hurt her. I got the car up to about 60 and crashed the car . . . I poured acid on her face and then gasoline and torched the car." In response to Officer Berney's comment that he killed someone, "Good, I wanted to kill her, she bothered me." In response to Officer Smith's Miranda rights reading to the defendant, "She died?" To Ramin, "I killed her, I killed her (in Farsi, *Man koshtamesh*)." To Roghieh, "I killed the girl." To Paramedic Adams, he rambled about a green card and a girl in Germany. He said that he paid a girl $7,000 to marry him and she backed out. He told him that he poured sulfuric acid on her face and killed her. He referred to the victim as his girlfriend and called her a motherfucker. He said the defendant said that if you saw the movie, *War of the Roses*, that would explain it. To Paramedic Kenny, "We were going to marry for $7,000 and didn't. I killed her." He was seen by witness Mulvaney to be moving about in a confused manner at the scene of the crime.

BACKGROUND OF VICTIM AND RELATION TO DEFENDANT

Manija was born in Tehran, Iran on January 4, 1955. She eventually moved to Vienna and married her first husband, 37-year-old Ardeshir. They moved to the United States in 1983 and divorced in 1988. She had no children, worked as a nurse, and frequented Iranian nightclubs, such as the Tea Room and the Oceanside Prime Restaurant. At the time of her death she had been dating an Iranian chiropractor named Mohammed who lived in southern San Diego County. He stated he was engaged to the victim, but did not know Hossein and was never told of any problems with him by the victim. She was living with her mother and cousin in San Diego at the site of her death. They had arrived in the United States during 1989.

Manija told her sister-in-law, Zari, one year before the homicide, that she was frightened of an Iranian male who lived in Germany. She told her that if she married someone else other than him, he would kill her. The victim also told her mother that she was having problems with a male Iranian who was in the cabinet business. The mother spoke with the defendant 20 days before the homicide, when he told her that his mother was looking for a wife for him. He told the victim's mother that he would marry her or die. He suggested that his mother and the victim's mother get together and discuss the issue. He also requested to come to the home and talk to her mother. She refused. She told him he should give up. The defendant insisted she not tell her daughter about the call, and she agreed.

The mother remembered the defendant calling the victim on the telephone the night before the homicide, but the victim hung up. She told her mother, "No one, just that nerve wrecker." She also reported that the victim would insult and curse him to leave her alone. He would cry and scream, "Come and marry me." He would call the victim at her own apartment before she moved in with her mother and cousin six months before her death. He would call three to four times a day. The victim never said that he threatened her, but always said he was madly in love with her. He said to her, "I am not going to let you go, times have changed." The victim reported to her mother that if she sweetmouthed him, he would call her from morning to night; if she screamed at him, he didn't call for a few days.

Other family members of the victim report knowing nothing of the relationship.

Mohammed, a cousin of the defendant, reported that a woman called the defendant from time to time, but he didn't know who it was. Jafar, the brother of the defendant, reported that Hossein had a girlfriend named Manija since he was in Germany, and he would show

Jafar photos of her. He reported that they broke up two months before the homicide for two weeks. He reported that Hossein dressed up for a dinner date with Manija either Tuesday or Wednesday prior to the homicide, but then was seen walking alone in a mall without her. He denied his brother had mental or physical problems, but states he was upset and depressed during the breakup.

The victim was seen by a Mrs. B. driving the defendant's car one to six months before the homicide. The victim told her she had borrowed the car from a friend.

The victim reportedly introduced her cousin to the defendant to get the former a job about four months before the homicide. The defendant reportedly got the victim's current address from the cousin's driver's license when they went to get insurance. The defendant reported to the cousin that his relationship to the victim was "just friends."

CLINICAL INTERVIEWS WITH THE DEFENDANT

Hossein was interviewed on four different occasions in the San Diego County Jail. All of the interviews were conducted in an interview room with Mr. Farzan, an Iranian private investigator retained by defense counsel, providing translation between this examiner and the defendant. A portion of the interview time was also devoted to psychological testing. The interviews will be discussed in sequence, sir.ce they provide a chronology of events leading up to the homicide from the defendant's perspective. The psychological testing will be analyzed in a subsequent section of this report.

September 29, 1990

The defendant reported that he was born in Mshad, Iran, a small town east of Tehran, on March 13, 1955. He was the fourth child of his parents, and they subsequently had four more children. One brother died in an auto accident in 1983. His father died in 1984 when he was 65 years old. He had diabetes and heart problems and had worked in the government. His mother was a housewife. The defendant and his brother Jafar are the only family in the United States.

Hossein was raised by both parents. He states "It was a good" childhood. Injuries as a child included several burns with boiling water, a broken hand, and some head blows. He remembers being unconscious one time for 10–15 minutes owing to paint fumes when he was 21. He also remembers having food poisoning on one occasion.

He was educated at the University of Tehran and attended the architectural college for two years. He received his AA degree in 1976–1977. He lived with his brother, Mehdi, while attending school, and then moved to Germany following his military duty from 1977–1979. In the military he was a corporal, and did mostly paperwork. During the final 3–4 months of military service, there was martial law in Iran prior to the February, 1979 overthrow of the Shah.

He moved to Germany "to go to school and have a better life." He returned to Iran once for his brother's funeral in 1983. He reportedly lived in Frankfurt by himself and sold cars and appliances.

He reports that he saw a psychiatrist once or twice after he was in the military. His brother suggested this, since he "was angry a lot" in 1979. He said, "people would give me orders that were unnecessary. Someone I knew had a higher rank, so they didn't bother me much. I don't recall exactly what." He states, however, that he doesn't get angry often, "less than other Iranian men."

He denies any prior criminal history.

When asked about his mother, he is reluctant to speak (an Islamic and cultural taboo). He reports that she "was nice to me, shorter than me." He reports that his father "never bothered me, a very nice man." Punishment would consist of slaps on the face and the use of a belt.

He reports that his sibling relations were good. He states they had arguments, but "I've never had a fist fight with anyone before; only one fight in jail, but he started it."

He states that he is a Shi'ite Moslem, and used to pray five times a day. His mother and father have both been to Mecca. He denies that he currently prays. "I don't have the ability here, my mind is too busy, I think a lot about my life now, the life I wanted with Manija in the past." He is able to demonstrate a fundamental knowledge of the Shi'ite Moslem faith.

He reports that his first girlfriend was at the University of

Tehran when he was 19 years old. She was named Behnaz. They did not have sex but reportedly kissed and touched. "I didn't like her enough to marry her, she liked me. She would go with me, go steady. After the Shah left, it was not OK to kiss in public, but OK in private. My brother was arrested for being out with his girlfriend." Hossein reported that his girlfriend touched his genitals, but he did not reciprocate. His first sexual intercourse reportedly occurred in Tehran when he was 22 years old. He reported that masturbation was not allowed as a Shi'ite. "If I had pressure I'd go to a whorehouse in Germany with friends. Shi'ites shouldn't even think about it."

He reports German girlfriends with whom he would have sex, and one Australian girl named Fariba. He defines girlfriend as "one conversation, I'd get her number, name, and address. If she's a good girl, I like her sure, why wouldn't I?" When asked how he would know if she was a girlfriend, "The way she talks, the things she says." When asked about Persian women, he says, "I can understand them. They can understand me. I prefer Persian girls. Sex is important; for other girls sex is normal, they don't care." He stated that all Persian girls are virgins before they are married, but states that Manija was not a virgin since she had been married. He states that Persian males are not virgins, "but no one will find out."

He reports that his drug and alcohol history is as follows: caffein – he uses Coca-Cola; alcohol – he reports his first drink in 1987, but after Manija, every time he'd think about her he'd drink, 2-4 times a week, 6-7 beers; nicotine – one time; cocaine – denied; opiates – one time in Germany; sedatives – Manija would give him these and he used them every night from December 1990 through January 1991 until the homicide; amphetamines – denied; cannabis – once or twice; hallucinogens – denied; inhalants – denied; phencyclidine – denied.

His first contact with the victim, Manija, occurred via telephone in February 1987. She was in the United States and he was in Germany. He had a friend from Germany, Vahid, who was then living in San Francisco, who told him he would find somebody for Hossein to marry so he could come to the United States. Vahid gave him numbers, and Manija was the second call. Vahid told him she would marry him for $5,000, and if she liked him, she might stay with him. "The minute I talked to her I had a different feeling, never before. Her voice was the type . . . I knew she could make me happy in life, grow in life. Nobody ever made me to get this type of feeling before." Hossein began to cry at this point. "I'm remembering all those feelings I had, at the time. I feel bad that she's not here, that she's gone. I really was in love with her. There are nights that I dream about her, and wake up crying, but not loudly. I'm walking with her on the street, and we're talking to each other, things like that. Sometimes she says nothing, sometimes she talks to me. I keep dreaming that we are still together."

He reports that they began talking each night; he would call. Manija flew to Germany on May 18, 1987. Hossein sent her $5,000 and she bought her ticket. Before this she had sent him her photo. "The feeling got stronger when I saw her picture, but her looks didn't matter, it was her voice. I kept the photos." Their first physical meeting was a "different feeling than ever before, I found someone I'd been looking for. An ideal person that has always been in my head, my heart, I knew she was the one. We said, 'Hi, how are you?' and then we hugged. I was very, very happy. We went home. She stayed until June 6 or 7." They would shop, have fun, go out, and went to most German cities. He reported that they slept together, but no sex. He reported that she let him touch her breasts and genitals. Then Manija called the United States and left, saying she didn't want to marry. "I bought her a ticket and gave her $1400. I knew she doesn't know what she's doing. She likes me, I don't know. But I was waiting for her to realize she was making a mistake, that's why I didn't push her. I know that she liked me 100 percent, but I don't know why she wanted to return home." When asked if she loved him, he said, "Yeah, from the way she looked and talked, but she never told me she did. I kissed her on the face, she left, I didn't . . . I fainted for a moment, fell to the ground, I couldn't see, a couple of people picked me up. I went home after an hour. I couldn't see anything, so I fell." He then started drinking to forget she was away. "I couldn't accept the fact she wasn't in my house."

Hossein resumed his talking to her by telephone. He sent her another $500. He reports other flowers and gifts sent to her. "I was in love with her, for her happiness I'd do anything." He denied any other contacts with other women, and continued to work in Germany, attempting to secure forged papers to get to the United States.

In 1988, he reported, he bought her $1500 in jewelry for her birthday. "I trusted her, I don't think she was the type of girl who would date others." Why not? "Because she didn't have sex with me." He states he gave her between $12,000–13,000 over the course of his involvement with her, and on May 26, 1988, secured a fake passport to travel to Canada for $6,000. He did not inform Manija he was coming for her. "She knew it, I didn't need to tell her. I always wanted to come to U.S., but not as bad as after I met Manija." He lived in Calgary on $600 from the government per month. Hossein continued to call Manija and urged her to come to Canada. She refused, then consented to visit for a week on September 4, 1988. She stayed with him for two nights in Edmonton. She told him her brother was in a hospital and her parents didn't know she was in Canada. "I knew she wanted to stay, but she couldn't make up her mind, she left after five days." He said they had slept in separate rooms. She returned to California and he went to Vancouver. On November 6, he tried to cross the border and was arrested. Manija told him by telephone she needed surgery, and he sent her $1800. He then paid $600 and was illegally transported to Seattle on January 15, 1989.

He immediately flew to Los Angeles, and moved in with his brother and cousin in Oceanside. When he called Manija, "She didn't believe it. She was happy and upset. She came to the mall. She was angry I hadn't told her when I left Canada. We had coffee, and she gave me a ride home. She was living in San Diego." He reports they went to a movie once during this first month. Hossein worked as a valet parking cars beginning in February 1989.

He states they dated once a week. They'd walk in the mall, he'd buy her things, and have dinner. There was no sexual contact. He worked for two months as a carpenter in September 1989. Manija changed her phone number in March 1989. "I don't know, she said someone was bugging her. She said she'd call me, but she didn't." Manija's mother and nephew arrived in September 1989 and she moved in with them. He reports she gave him her new phone number, and asked him if he could find a job for her cousin. "I bought her a VCR, and her mother asked me why."

Mental Status Exam on September 29, 1990

Hossein is a 35-year-old, small Iranian male with a crewcut, dressed in a San Diego County Jail jumpsuit. He is oriented to person, place, and time. His affect is blunted and his mood is dysthymic, but he is cooperative. He is also guarded and anxious with me. His fund of information is normal. His concentration skills are normal (math). His attention is mildly impaired (digits forward and backward). His short-term memory is normal. His concept formation is normal. He denies auditory and visual hallucinations. He denies depersonalization and derealization. He denies thought broadcasting, stealing, insertion, and control. He shows no indication of formal thought disorder to the translator. He reports suicidal ideation and intent. He reports sleeping normally, but losing weight. He reports being depressed most of the time.

October 20, 1990

At the beginning of this interview, the defendant tells me that he lied about his other girlfriends. He reports no sexual experience with any of them, and that the girls he mentioned before never existed, or he only saw them in class. He asks me if his prostate troubles have anything to do with masturbating. We start where we left off.

Hossein states that Manija became mad at him in October 1989. "She wouldn't return my calls, she wouldn't see me. I'd buy her things and she would ask me why. She'd take them if I pushed, I helped her pay off her car." He estimates spending $5000 on her in 1989. Hossein left the valet parking job in October 1989, and tried to start his own cabinet making business. "I wanted to open a business so she could see I had a better job and she would introduce me to her family." She refused to see him from December 1989 forward. Hossein reported drinking a mixture of Jim Beam and beer. "I'd drink till I didn't know what I was doing." He reported some blackouts, and taking "headache" pills. She continued to refuse to talk to him. He then called her mother in January and told her he liked Manija so much he would give his life for her. He states that Manija then called him at the same time. "No one can take Manija away, not even death can separate me and her."

He reports a meeting with her on Monday, January 22, 1990. He brought her flowers, and he was shocked when she asked him why. They had dinner in a Japanese restaurant, and then she needed to leave. "I kept thinking, Why did she ask that? I began to work, feel better, I decided to go to her school." He reports drinking 10–12 beers a day, one bottle of whiskey a week. On January 25, 1990, he went to her school and saw her with another man. "I saw her with another guy, she looked at me and said, 'Don't come and talk to me.' I left. I felt I'm gonna lose her, something's happening, I went home and called her. She told me that guy was her friend, a family friend. I knew he was not really just a friend. She told me 'He wants to marry me,' but she didn't sound happy. Her family was pushing her to marry him. Her family wasn't letting her talk to me. I told her she was making a mistake, she told me not to talk to anyone about this. I told her we were meant to be together and no other alternatives. I knew she wanted to be with me but her family was pushing her. I could recognize the way she talked, I'd been with her for 3 years, her tone of voice. She told me she wasn't making a mistake." Hossein then began to call her every day, 4–5 times. "I was angry and telling her, begging her, I just drank, to come up with something to stop her from making a mistake, sleeping 3 hours a night. My brother and cousin would see me, and ask me why I was drinking so much. I wouldn't tell them. I was hardly eating. I would throw up. I'd take a shower once a week, my cousin would tell me to. I needed to do something, to stop Manija, she would ruin her life."

On January 30 or 31, 1990, Hossein decides to buy some acid. He states, "I'll buy acid and throw on her face, and when she becomes ugly she'll realize that guy doesn't love her and I still do; but I didn't want to hurt her. If a girl's ugly, a guy won't like her, but it wouldn't matter to me, I'd like her, not the way she looked. She'd be stopped from making a mistake."

He reported that this happens in Iran. He remembers a singer named Daruosh who had acid thrown on him by a woman. "She really liked the singer, that's why she did it." He smiles slightly. He states he was drunk when he bought the acid. He also denied any auditory or visual hallucinations during these two weeks prior to the homicide.

On Thursday, February 1, he drank so much, he states, he passed out. He reports eight beers and whiskey. On the morning of Friday, February 2, 1990, he awakens about 5 or 6 A.M. His cousin and brother leave at 7. "I have to do something before it's too late to stop her from making mistake. I decided suddenly to go and burn myself in front of her house. She'll realize how much I love her, because my life wouldn't have any meaning. So I started writing a letter, saying goodbye to my family."

Excerpts from the letter are as follows: "The thing I will so today, I am fully aware of that it destroy my life for ever. However, I am willing to accept it. No one is allowed to cry for me, if I die. However, I if live and remain in jail for few years, addition revenge only can make me feel releaved . . . don't worry because I wanted this and by this revenge I feel better . . . there was no time, that I could sleep with out strong liquor . . . I wish I could of have die like my younger brother [Sadegh] because I was never interested in living . . . our family has the most bad luck than any one else. I don't think that god did not create a bad luckier people then us. I think I talked to much. . . ."

Hossein went to the gas station and bought gasoline. "I want to make a point by burning myself, I'd rather kill myself, I liked her enough to kill myself, I didn't care." He denied anger and depression. "I parked my car, other things on my mind, they kept changing, changing. What would be the right thing to do? Different ideas every minute. Should I talk? No, better to burn myself. Acid on her first, I don't know, I saw her get in her car. I decided to hit her car so we can both die, we'd be together in the other world. I went towards her." He denies memory for anything further until he is taken to the hospital by the paramedics.

When asked if further evidence would help him remember, he states, "I've read police report, it didn't help, people testified, I don't remember, maybe it would, maybe something else would help me out." He remembers his comment about the movie *War of the Roses*. "They both decided to die and be together." He denies a history of blackouts, except when drinking. He states his first thought of her dying was when he drove toward her car. He reported racing thoughts like never before. He stated the self-immolation idea "was to make a point, strongest way of showing your love to someone." When asked if he killed Manija, he says, "She died, but the decision I made was to be together. Her death was cause of my action. But I thought it would be good. If I was dead it would be better." When asked if he would be judged by Allah, he says, "depends on how you look, I did it for her and me, God knows how much I love her, it was not happy for her, we had to be together." When asked about Iblis, he smiles. "I never thought about it. I'm sad because I'm alive and she's not with me. When I remember, I can't stop." When asked about suicide, he says, "I think, but no way. I don't care, I wish to die. I tried to get life insurance for her if I die in Canada, I couldn't get it."

His mental status during this second interview evidenced increased depression and decreased sleep and appetite. He was hopeless. He denied a suicidal plan, but ideation was present.

November 24, 1990

The defendant was tearful and crying throughout this abbreviated interview (one hour). He reports the anniversary of his meeting with Manija for Thanksgiving one year ago. He states he has only slept intermittently for three days and eating "a little." He reports acute depression for a week and dreaming. "We're walking around and talking. When I dream, I'm happy, then I wake up and she's not here. How come she's by herself alone, and I'm here? I can't see her, I can feel that she's with me, I still see her, I dream about her every week, I don't believe she's dead. I don't know, maybe she's not. We still communicate, a little bit." He denies seeing or hearing her when awake. He reports talking to his brother and cousin, and phoning his mother. He denies me permission to talk to his mother. He demonstrates suicidal ideation and intent, but no plan.

Mental status indicates an anniversary reaction to their last contact before she rejected him. His clinical depression has increased in symptoms, he is passively suicidal and compliant, but wants to end the session. He then apologizes. His affect is labile, he is tearful and sobbing, he is not psychotic.

January 6, 1991

The last clinical interview refocused on the homicide and his cognitive processes at the time. He was asked about his different thoughts before the homicide the morning of February 2, 1990. "I wanted to leave the country, but she'd be here alone. If I left, I couldn't help her. One idea was to kill myself in front of her. Maybe it would make her realize that someone took their life because of her. She wanted to make her own family happy by marrying someone else. But it would destroy her life, I wanted her to realize this. To make her realize so she can realize." Hossein said, "She did not want to marry him, I knew she wanted me, the way she talked, I could just read it in her eyes. It was obvious." When asked about the acid, he says, "I was thinking of on myself or on her, if she was ugly the family would know I loved her. I had no other way of proving I loved Manija, no other way." In the parking lot by the house he had three plans: pour acid over himself, pour acid over her, or set himself on fire. How was he feeling? "Tingling in my hands, stomach turning, hands cold, legs numb and tingling. . . . As soon as she got in her car, I thought it would be better for us to die, no problems, and we could be together, never in my mind before." Did that change your feelings? "Better, a little bit." Memory? "I remember approaching her car. I don't remember impact." Did you kill her? "The way you guys say, yes. I don't want to, I regret how come I didn't die myself." Would Manija rather die and be with you than be with another man? "She liked life cause of being with me more than anything else." Is there another life? "Other worlds—we'd be there together. We'd be together alone. Her family wouldn't bother us, no one else." Would she rather be with you in another world than in this one without you? "Yes." Are you certain? "Yes. She never showed me otherwise, that she didn't want to." Is she happy now? "She laughs and is happy in my dreams." Are you together? "Yes. She's with me when I dream." She's actually alive and with you? "Yes.

Yesterday was her birthday (January 5) and I dreamed a lot about her the night before. The first January she's not with me." What did you do in the dream? "I bought some flowers for her, seeing her, always the same." Was it wrong that she died? "What do you mean? Unnecessary? It's wrong because I didn't die with her, if I died it would have been good, we would have been together." What does wrong mean? "Wrong means for no reason." Are there reasons for killing that aren't wrong? "What I did would be right if I died too." Since you're alive and she's dead, is it wrong? "It's wrong, 'cause she's there by herself." What is your legal definition of wrong? "Sometimes the law says you're wrong, but it doesn't know the stage you're in. Law isn't applied individually, but to the group, that's why it can be wrong." What are the wrongs in Islam? "Things that God doesn't like." Like killing Manija? "God put me and Manija together. That was our destiny to be together."[1] When did you realize this? "First time I met her, over the phone it starting, as days went by, it became stronger and stronger."

Should you be punished for killing her? "What is important is why I did it; when I thought of doing it, it wasn't bad thought, not a wrong decision." Will the law judge you wrong? "General." What will acid in the face do? "She would be ugly." What will gasoline and a match do? "She can be alive, she can die." If you run into someone with your car? "They can both die or both be injured." Is it acceptable to kill? "Only the person who makes the decision." Should laws protect potential victims? "If it's money or angry, then he shouldn't do it. If two people want to be together, someone interferes, it is better they both die and be together."

Did you violate United States law? "Yes, you guys say it." Did you violate Iran law? "You have to look at facts. If judge in Iran listened to facts, he would realize it was benefit of both of us, it would be no problem if I would have died too." Why are you alive now? "I don't have a choice." If I gave you a gun would you shoot yourself?

---

1. One of the central beliefs within the Islamic faith is predestination: Allah has determined everything in advance, that is, "It is God's will." This is quite similar to Calvinist doctrine, contemporarily seen in Christianity among Presbyterian theologians (Patai 1983).

"Yes, that is one of my hopes so I can prove to you." Will you have a future love? "Never." Were you moral in killing her? "I'm against violence. If you look at the reasoning and my act, it wasn't violent." So you can kill someone, and if the reasoning is OK, it's not violent? "Yes." Who decides? "The person." Does the victim have any say? "Victim could be happy or sad." Is Manija happy you killed her? "Only angry for one reason, she's alone and I'm not with her, she's not angry about my decision, the only way we could be together. If she was angry I wouldn't dream about her being happy."

PSYCHOLOGICAL TESTING

Hossein was administered the following tests: the Minnesota Multi-phasic Personality Inventory (computer scored and interpreted through the Caldwell Report); the Rorschach (invalid protocol due to R = 10); the Millon Clinical Multiaxial Inventory II (computer scored and interpreted through National Computer Systems); the performance subtests of the Wechsler Adult Intelligence Scale-Revised (scored by the examiner); the Rey Dissimulation Test (scored by the examiner); and the Quick Screen for Dementia (scored by the examiner). All tests necessitated translation by Mr. Farzan and were completed over the course of the four interviews at the San Diego County Jail. Each test will be analyzed in turn.

WAIS-R

The performance subtests of this instrument were administered on January 6, 1991. His scaled scores were:

Picture Completion	8
Picture Arrangement	7
Block Design	10
Object Assembly	9
Digit Symbol	5

Results of this intelligence test indicate a performance IQ of 85. This places the defendant in the low-average range of intelligence, one standard deviation below the mean. The significant finding within the subtests is the Picture Arrangement score of 7. This is one standard deviation below average, meaning that about 84 percent of the population would score *better* on this subtest than he would. The clinical significance of this test is that it measures an individual's ability to quickly and accurately understand a social situation and its consequences. The lowest score, Digit Symbol, is probably measuring psychomotor coordination and anxiety in this subject.

Rey Dissimulation Test

This is a measure of faking or exaggerating memory impairment. The test showed no indication that during the exam the subject was faking or exaggerating memory impairment.

Quick Screening for Dementia

Results of this screening test indicated no signs of dementia, and no need for further testing.

Rorschach

The defendant produced only ten responses to the Rorschach inkblots, rendering the test invalid.

MMPI

Each of the 566 questions of this test was read by the examiner, translated by Mr. Farzan into Farsi, and the defendant responded. Although this affected the testing procedure, it is the examiner's opinion that a valid protocol was produced. The Caldwell Report interpretive summary is as follows:

"The profile shows a moderate to severe depressive disorder. This may prove to be a psychotic depression or a schizoaffective schizophrenic decompensation. He tests as markedly fearful of emotional closeness with severe frustrations in his close relationships. He is apt to have many ways of keeping others at a distance. Multiple anxieties, ambivalences, and obsessive self-criticisms are suggested, along with such possible symptoms as confusion, inability to concentrate, loss of interest, inefficiency, compulsive habits, and phobic fearfulness. Others would see him as disengaged and as very slow to involve himself in changing his current circumstances. Disturbances of sleep are common with this pattern. He would be threatened by a loss of control, unable to let go even when appropriate. Severely shy, introverted, and socially panicky, he could become grossly withdrawn. His current functioning appears severely decompensated.

"The profile has often been associated with physical symptoms that are secondary to the patient's anxiety and are displaced expressions of current conflicts. Conversionlike symbolizations of unreleased resentments, tensions, and aggressive impulses are particularly common. In similar cases such symptoms have included odd muscular symptoms, dizziness, fainting, anorexia, weakness, and paralyses. In addition, the numerous somatic preoccupations that he expressed on this test suggest a wide variety of chronic physical complaints lacking a sufficient organic basis. Gastrointestinal distress, headache, and fatigue would be typical, as would be concern about poor or declining health and overreactions to minor physical dysfunctions. He is likely to attribute many of his current difficulties to his health problems.

"He may have been repeatedly hurt in his past close relationships and as a result quick to be distrustful and resentful. His considerable underlying anger could be expressed through negativistic, ill-judged and inappropriate behaviors. Lacking in stable, solid, long-term goals, his tolerance of frustrations and ability to handle pressures and demands on him appear poor. Underneath his self-blame or when less depressed, he appears prone to rationalize resentments and to feel that his difficulties cannot really be relieved unless other people or circumstances change.

"He obtained the so-called 'burnt child' pattern type, for which the phrase 'The burnt child fears the fire' has aptly characterized the chronic fears of emotional closeness and involvement. Many men with this pattern enter suddenly and impulsively into marriages or other man–woman relationships. This then reactivates their mother–son dependency struggles, especially as they want and invite maternalistic behavior from the women in their lives. Typical histories associated with this pattern have included uneven past achievements that were poor relative to the patient's intelligence and general potentials. Lacking in acceptance of his self-centered impulses, he tests as having many sexual fears and inhibitions. His overall balance of masculine and feminine interests tends mildly toward verbal or aesthetic interests rather than mechanical and outdoor activities.

"The psychiatric diagnoses associated with this profile are mixed, but most commonly reflect severe depression. The disturbance is apt to be borderline if not overtly psychotic, such as a psychotic depression or schizoaffective schizophrenia. It should be reemphasized, however, that his extreme self-favorableness makes his profile much more ambiguous than most."

MCMI II

The Millon Clinical Multiaxial Inventory II was also translated for the defendant by Mr. Farzan, following this examiner's reading of each question. The answer sheet was scored and interpreted through National Computer Systems, and their report follows:

"This patient's response style may indicate a broad tendency to magnify the level of experienced illness or characterological inclination to complain and to be self-pitying. On the other hand, the response style may convey feelings of extreme vulnerability, which are associated with a current episode of acute turmoil. Whatever the impetus for the response style, the patient's scale scores, particularly those on Axis I, may be somewhat exaggerated, and the interpretations should be read with this consideration in mind.

"The behavior of this man is typified by an introversive, colorless, dependent, and timid way of relating to others. Preferring to remain in the background, he lacks social initiative and displays little stimulus-seeking behavior. Notable also is his impoverished affect and his unclear thinking about interpersonal matters. His anger and discontent rarely surface. Reluctant to accept help from others, he readily sacrifices his own interests, tries not to be a burden, and acts in a compliant and placating manner. His easy fatigability and slow personal tempo are compounded by a general weakness in expressiveness and spontaneity. Although he prefers a peripheral role in social and family relationships, he also has a strong need to depend on others. These conflicting attitudes stem from his feelings of low self-esteem and his deficiencies in autonomous and competent behaviors. Quick to self-blame, he is strongly inclined to belittle himself, possessing a self-image of being a weak and ineffectual person.

"Life for this patient is experienced as uneventful, with periods of passive solitude interspersed with feelings of emptiness and occasional depersonalization. He is indifferent to social surroundings, is minimally introspective, and is generally insensitive to the subtleties of emotional life, exhibiting weak affectionate or erotic needs. His thought processes are unfocused and tangential, particularly in regard to interpersonal matters. As a result, his social communications are often strained and self-conscious. His hesitation to express affection may stem from an inability to experience enthusiasm or pleasure. Moreover, for extended periods, he may exhibit a pervasive dysthymic mood that is punctuated occasionally by unanchored and ill-defined anxiety.

"This man prefers to follow a simple, repetitive, and dependent life pattern. He actively avoids self-assertion, abdicates autonomous responsibilities, and is indifferent to conventional social aspirations. Disengaged from, and disinterested in, most of the rewards of human affairs, he often appears apathetic and asocial. Although lacking in drive, he is nevertheless fearful of rebuff. Therefore he restricts his social and emotional involvements, which consequently perpetuates his pattern of social isolation and dependency on others.

"Preoccupations with matters of personal adequacy and chronic feelings of worthlessness and guilt appear to predominate in the major depression evident in the clinical picture of this socially awkward and introverted man. Timid, shy, and apprehensive, he is especially sensitive to public humiliation and rejection. Worthy of note is his toleration of daily unhappiness and emptiness, a willingness to accept his feelings of worthlessness and guilt. Plagued with self-doubts and thoughts of death, he may be notably saddened by the view that he is both socially unattractive and physically inferior. Fearful of expressing his discontents to others who might thereby reject or humiliate him, he deals with his frustration by turning it inward, becoming intropunitively depressed.

"Evidence indicates the presence of a prominent anxiety disorder syndrome in this man. Widely generalized symptoms would be consistent with his overall general personality makeup: pervasive social disquiet, behavioral edginess, apprehensiveness over small matters, and worrisome self-doubts, the most frequent of which may relate to feelings of masculine inadequacy. Specific psychosomatic signs may be present in addition to the more general anxious state. These signs include fatigue, insomnia, headaches, and an inability to concentrate. Especially sensitive to public reproval, yet lacking the confidence to respond with equanimity, he may be experiencing more discomfort than usual, particularly if his resentments have poured forth against someone with whom he rather would have maintained peace or a safe distance."

CURRENT *DSM-III-R* PSYCHODIAGNOSIS

Axis I: 296.33 Major Depression, recurrent, severe without psychotic features
             297.10 Delusional (Paranoid) Disorder, erotomanic type
             305.00 Alcohol abuse, in institutional remission
Axis II: 301.20 Schizoid Personality Disorder with additional dependent traits
Axis III: Chronic prostatitis (diagnosed by physician)
Axis IV: Stressors–5: extreme. Death of love object and incarceration for her murder
Axis V: Global Assessment of Functioning, Current: 50; Highest in Past Year: 50

FINDINGS

The following clinical findings and opinions have been formed on the basis of the available data. Subsequent data unknown to this examiner at this time could alter these findings and opinions:

1. The defendant at the time of examination had three diagnosed mental disorders and a personality disorder. Psychological testing also indicates that he exaggerated his symptomatology.

2. The Axis I disorders were both present at the time of the homicide, in addition to an alcohol abuse diagnosis, which is currently in remission owing to incarceration. Evidence indicates that the major depression began 6–8 weeks prior to the homicide (probably in December 1989), and was precipitated by the rejection of the defendant by Manija and the continual ingestion of large amounts of alcohol. The major depression prior to the crime is confirmed by reports of the brother, Jafar, who witnessed the deterioration in hygiene, sleep patterns, and eating patterns of the defendant during the month of January 1990. The delusional (paranoid) disorder, erotomanic subtype, began in February 1987, when the defendant had first telephone contact with the victim. It developed in intensity, and was intermittently reinforced by her approach–avoidance of him through her visit to Germany and Canada. It appears, however, that the defendant's recollection of his contacts with her (frequency and intensity) were grossly exaggerated, especially during the year preceding the homicide. This would be a product of both his wishful fantasy and denial, his refusal to acknowledge that she did not love him. The paranoid dimension of the erotomania was exacerbated when she overtly rejected him in early December 1989, and refused to see him. At that point he consciously believed that her family was forcing her to leave him and marry someone else.

3. The psychodynamics of this case are instructive. Hossein formed an immediate, erotomanic attachment to the voice of the victim on first telephone contact. He believed she was the ideal person for him, and they were destined to be together. Because of his inherently conflictual schizoid and dependent personality traits, he

took great pleasure in the feeling of being mesmerized by her and wanting only her, and also fantasized that they would be together as a couple, ideally isolated from all others: a paired schizoid existence. He also had virtually no heterosexual experiences with women prior to this, owing to his upbringing in an isolated city in a sexually very conservative Shi'ite culture.[2] His relationship with her was asexual and primarily based upon wishful fantasy. It was also the product of a primitive defense called projective identification, in which he attributed to her certain qualities, and also needed to control her, and be controlled by her.

When she rejected him in December 1989, he was filled with abandonment rage, but could not consciously tolerate such feelings toward his idealized love object. Instead, he became depressed, drank, and displaced his rage onto her family. This triangulation allowed him to view her family as a malevolent, destructive force that would take her away from him. He also lost control of her, and felt she no longer controlled him, a source of dependent and maternal reverie. The genetic roots of his erotomania probably lie with his attachment to his mother in what we would consider a very symbiotic relationship. Little is known of this relationship, however, so this is only speculative.

At this point in time, December 1989 to January 1990, Hossein also consciously began to think that there was only two choices: the relationship or death for him. This is a form of defensive splitting, and is consistent with his borderline personality organization. The defendant sees the world, and experiences it, in black and white terms, all or nothing. He has little tolerance for ambiguity or complexity.

The actual homicide began with the conscious desire to disfigure the victim so she will love him, a logical absurdity. It then shifted to, and included, a desire to suicide. The means to these ends was acid throwing and self-immolation, two forms of violence toward self and others deeply rooted in the Persian culture–although illegal, to my knowledge, in Iran–and in the honor of martyrdom in the reformed

---

2. His brother showed the investigator photos of himself after he had been flogged by the police; he and friends were caught dancing to "western music."

Shi'ite tradition of Islam. It suddenly shifted seconds before the homicide to a conscious wish and impulse to die together so that they could be united forever and not be bothered by threats from the outside. Of course, the most obvious homicidal threat at this point in time was the defendant himself. He was awash in his own projections. The homicide followed, and the suicide, foretold in the note written several hours before, was attempted, and failed. This formulation appears to be supported by evidence and witness accounts of the defendant's behavior immediately after the killing of Manija.

4. The defendant genuinely appears to have no memory for the homicide. Attempts to establish malingering were not successful (Rey test, reinterviewing, deceptive questioning). This can be psychodynamically understood as a defensive use of psychogenic amnesia to not remember, and therefore not feel, the rage involved in this homicide that was verbally communicated to witnesses at the scene. It also may be due to the head blow received by the defendant either in his car or when he banged his head on the door of the victim's home. This abandonment rage continues to be split off and is intolerable to the consciousness of the defendant. His dissociative personality traits as measured by testing, and the "fainting" and "blindness," perhaps a brief conversion reaction when he first left Manija at the Frankfurt airport, are also consistent with a propensity to split off angry, unpleasant affect.

5. He currently is mourning the loss of the victim, and is experiencing active suicidal ideation. He also has many psychosomatic complaints, but these do not rise to the threshold of criteria needed to diagnose somatization disorder.

6. Parodoxically, his relationship with the victim has been renewed through her death. He now experiences her, once again, as an idealized object in his mind, when in sleep he can suspend the "reality-tested" knowledge of her death and can be with her in a pleasant, isolated place. He has intrapsychically come full circle: he initially idealized her, she rejected him, he devalued her and killed her, and now, once again, he can idealize her. The limits to this, however, are obvious. When he is awake, the dictates of reality, and absence of a

florid psychosis, force him to remember she is dead. Hence his wish to sleep at night, or in death.

7. Hossein knew the nature of his act. He knew that he had gasoline to burn himself and acid to throw on the victim. He also knew he was driving his car to hit the victim in her car.

8. Hossein knew the quality of his act, if quality is understood to mean immediate consequences. He knew that by throwing acid on the victim he would disfigure her. He knew that gasoline would injure or kill himself or the victim. He knew that driving his car into the victim's car would injure or kill himself and the victim.

If quality is understood to mean other consequences, he did not know the quality of his act. He believed the victim would rather die if she could not be with him. He believed they would be united, and could be together in an isolated, romantic fantasy in another world. He believed that through his violence, the victim and her family would know that he loved her. He now believes she is happy and with him, and only angry that she is separated from him by death. These are fixed and false, and therefore delusional, beliefs.

9. Hossein did not understand right from wrong at the time of the crime. In his subjective beliefs, he was morally justified to kill her, and the only wrong is that he did not die. He believes that others would understand and accept his act if they knew his reasons. He believes that United States law is trying him because it is normative law, and it does not take into consideration individual differences. He believes that an Iranian judge would understand and accept his act if he knew his reasons and the facts of the case. He believes that Allah would understand and accept his act because he put him and Manija together and it was their destiny.

OPINION

It is my opinion that Hossein meets the legal criteria for insanity in the State of California, pursuant to Penal Code § 25(b).

Thank you for this most interesting and complex case, and if you have any questions, please telephone me.

Sincerely,

J. Reid Meloy, Ph.D.
Asst. Clinical Professor of Psychiatry
    University of California, San Diego
Diplomate, Forensic Psychology,
    American Board of Professional Psychology

POSTSCRIPT

Hossein's defense attorney pled him guilty to the crime of first-degree murder with the special circumstance of torture (California Penal Code § 190.2[a][14]). Because insanity trials are bifurcated in California, a jury only heard the sanity phase of the trial. The defense strategy was to present all the prosecution evidence to the jury, demonstrating how "crazy" Hossein must have been to commit such a crime. I testified as an expert witness called by the defense for a day and a half. The prosecution called no experts. Their retained psychiatrist had agreed with me in his report filed with the court.

The jury believed that he was mentally ill, but not legally insane. They found him sane at the time of the crime. Immediately following the verdict, Hossein asked his attorney if he could address the jury. He rose and said, "Thank you for finding me sane. You have shown me your belief that what I did was right." The jury looked on dumbfounded as Hossein sat down. Several weeks later he was sentenced to life in prison without the possibility of parole.

Appendix II

Weapons History Assessment Method

I. History

1. Have you ever owned or possessed a weapon?
2. If so, what weapons have you owned or possessed?
3. How did you get the weapon?
4. How old were you?
5. What did you do with your weapons?
6. Did you ever threaten, injure, or kill a person or an animal with your weapon?
7. Were you ever criminally charged with illegal possession or use of a weapon?
8. Did other family members own or possess weapons? Who?

II. Skill

9. Were you ever trained in the use of weapons?
10. If so, who trained you and under what circumstances?
11. How old were you when trained?
12. What did you think of the training you received?
13. Do you continue to practice your weapons skills?
14. If so, how often and what do you do to practice?
15. How skilled do you believe you are with your weapons?

III. Conscious Motivations-Beliefs

16. Should people be allowed to have weapons?
17. If so, for what purpose and when?
18. What is your main reason for having/wanting a weapon?
19. Do you have any other reasons for wanting a weapon?
20. What do your family and friends think about weapons?
21. Do you have any feelings when you have or use your weapon?

IV. Self and Object Representations

22. Can you describe your weapons to me in sufficient detail so that I can picture them and understand how they work?
23. How do you feel about yourself when you are possessing/using your weapon?
24. How do you feel about others when you are possessing/using your weapon?

V. Approach Behaviors and Correlates

25. Do you like to visit gun shops?
26. If so, how often, and when was the last time you did?
27. Do you like to visit shooting ranges?
28. If so, how often, and when was the last time you did?
29. Do you like to read gun magazines, such as *Guns and Ammo* or *Soldier of Fortune*? Do you subscribe?
30. Do you have friends that possess/use weapons?
31. Are there any movie stars that you like that often use a gun?
32. If so, what movies have you seen with them, and what did they do in the movie?
33. Any movie that you've seen more than twice?
34. Any television shows that you watch and like that have weapons in them?
35. Do you like to be around policemen?
36. If so, do you do anything to make this happen?
37. Do you have any camouflage clothes? When do you wear them?

38. Do you have any other military equipment, like holsters, belts, boots, survival gear, canteens, food items?

VI. Unconscious Motivation (This material may, or may not, be able to be solicited through questions)

39. Do you ever dream about weapons, using them, or having them used against you?
40. Do you ever wish that you had a weapon when you get upset?
41. Observations of the patient during this assessment:
    a. Pleasant affect when talking about weapons
    b. Parapraxes, or slips of the tongue
    c. Intrusions of primary process, such as primitive spontaneous associations to weapons or illogical, tangential responses concerning weapons
    d. Symbolic utterances that associate weapons to certain religious or political beliefs, or magical powers
    e. Behaviors that imply narcissistic enhancement when responding to these questions
    f. Behaviors that imply paranoid or suspicious mentation when responding to these questions

VII. Other Diagnostic Information that Increases Lethality Risk

42. Does patient have a personality disorder, especially narcissistic, antisocial, histrionic, borderline, or paranoid personality disorder?
43. Does patient have a mental disorder that includes paranoid symptoms or delusions?
44. Does patient have a poor or absent attachment history?
45. Has patient been violent without weapons in the past?
46. Does patient use, or did patient use, alcohol or psychostimulants?
47. Does patient have weapons in close proximity to him?
48. Has the patient moved his weapons closer to him in the recent past (such as from the closet to under his bed, from the garage to

inside the home, occasional illegal concealment on his person, recent attempt to get a concealed weapons permit)?
49. Does patient show evidence of manifest anger or fear, emotional lability, or poor impulse control?
50. Are there any psychological test indicators that suggest an increased risk of violence?

Cautionary Note to Examiner: This is a structured interview, not a reliable and valid psychological test instrument. It has been constructed from data available in the current psychological and psychiatric research literature and my own clinical experience with individuals in both criminal and mental health settings (custody, inpatient, and outpatient). It has not been subjected to any tests of reliability or validity. Any inferences concerning violence risk made from the results of this interview are solely those of the examiner using this interview.

References

Aber, J., and Slade, A. (1987). *Attachment theory and research: a framework for clinical interventions.* Paper presented at the regional scientific meeting of the Childhood and Adolescent Division for Psychoanalysis of the American Psychological Association, New York, January.

Abraham, K. (1923). Contributions to the theory of anal character. *International Journal of Psycho-Analysis* 4:400–418.

——— (1925). The influence of oral erotism on character formation. *International Journal of Psycho-Analysis* 6:247–258.

Ainsworth, M. (1962). The effects of maternal deprivation: a review of findings and controversy in the context of research strategy. In *Deprivation of Maternal Care: A Reassessment of Its Effects*, no. 14. Geneva: World Health Organization.

——— (1985). Patterns of infant–mother attachments: antecedents and effects on development. *Bulletin of the New York Academy of Medicine* 61:771–791.

——— (1989). Attachments beyond infancy. *American Psychologist* 44:709–716.

Ainsworth, M., Blehar, M., Waters, E., and Wall, S. (1978). *Patterns of Attachment: A Psychological Study of the Strange Situation.* New York: Wiley.

Ainsworth, M., and Bowlby, J. (1954). Research strategy in the study of mother–child separation. *Courr. Cent. int. Enf.* 4:105.

Allen, W. (1976). *Starkweather.* Boston: Houghton Mifflin.

American Psychiatric Association (1987). *Diagnostic and Statistical Manual of Mental Disorders.* 3rd. ed., rev. Washington, DC: American Psychiatric Association.

Anderson, A., Ghali, A., and Bansil, R. (1989). Weapon carrying in a psychiatric emergency room. *Hospital and Community Psychiatry* 40:845–847.

Arboleda-Florez, J., and Holley, H. (1991). Antisocial burnout: an exploratory study. *Bulletin of the American Academy of Psychiatry and the Law* 19:173–184.

Arndt, W. B., Jr. (1991). *Gender Disorders and the Paraphilias.* Madison, CT: International Universities Press.

Beebe, B., and Stern, D. (1977). Engagement-disengagement and early object experience. In *Communicative Structures and Psychic Structures*, ed. N. Freedman and S. Grand, pp. 35–55. New York: Plenum.

Bergler, E. (1961). *Curable and Incurable Neurosis–Problems of Neurotic vs. Malignant Masochism*. New York: Liveright.

Berke, J. (1988). *The Tyranny of Malice*. New York: Summit Books.

Berliner, B. (1940). Libido and reality in masochism. *Psychoanalytic Quarterly* 9:322–333.

_____ (1942). The concept of masochism. *Psychoanalytic Review* 29:386–400.

_____ (1947). On some psychodynamics of masochism. *Psychoanalytic Quarterly* 16:459–471.

_____ (1958). The role of object relations in moral masochism. *Psychoanalytic Quarterly* 27:38–56.

Bion, W. (1959). Attacks on linking. *International Journal of Psycho-Analysis* 40:308–315.

Blacker, K., and Tupin, J. (1991). Hysteria and hysterical structures: developmental and social theories. In *Hysterical Personality Style and the Histrionic Personality Disorder*, ed. M. Horowitz, pp. 17–66. Northvale, NJ: Jason Aronson.

Blackman, N., Weiss, J., and Lamberti, J. (1963). The sudden murderer III. Clues to preventive interaction. *Archives of General Psychiatry* 8:289–294.

Blatt, S. (1974). Levels of object representations in anaclitic and introjective depression. *Psychoanalytic Study of the Child* 29:107–157. New Haven: Yale University Press.

Blatt, S., Tuber, S., and Auerbach, J. (1990). Representation of interpersonal interactions on the Rorschach and level of psychopathology. *Journal of Personality Assessment* 54:711–728.

Blos, P. (1991). Sadomasochism and the defense against recall of painful affect. *Journal of the American Psychoanalytic Association* 39:417–430.

Blum, D. (1986). *Bad Karma: A True Story of Obsession and Murder*. New York: Atheneum.

Blum, H. (1991). Sadomasochism in the psychoanalytic process, within and beyond the pleasure principle: discussion. *Journal of the American Psychoanalytic Association* 39:431–450.

Bonaparte, M. (1952). Some biophysical aspects of sadomasochism. *International Journal of Psycho-Analysis* 33:373.

Bowlby, J. (1946). *Forty-four Juvenile Thieves: Their Character and Homelife*. London: Bailliere, Tyndall and Cox.

_____ (1953). Some pathological processes set in train by early mother–child separation. *Journal of Mental Science* 99:265–272.

_____ (1958). The nature of a child's tie to his mother. *International Journal of Psycho-Analysis* 39:350–373.

_____ (1960). Separation anxiety. *International Journal of Psycho-Analysis* 41:89–111.

_____ (1969). *Attachment and Loss*. Vol 1, *Attachment*. New York: Basic Books.

_____ (1973). *Attachment and Loss*. Vol 2, *Separation, Anxiety, and Anger*. New York: Basic Books.

_____ (1980). *Attachment and Loss*. Vol 3, *Loss, Sadness, and Depression*. New York: Basic Books.

———— (1984). Violence in the family as a disorder of the attachment and caregiving systems. *American Journal of Psychoanalysis* 44:9–27.

———— (1988a). Developmental psychiatry comes of age. *American Journal of Psychiatry* 145:1–10.

———— (1988b). On knowing what you are not supposed to know and feeling what you are not supposed to feel. In *A Secure Base*, pp. 99–118. New York: Basic Books.

Bradford, J., and Pawlak, A. (1987). Sadistic homosexual pedophilia: treatment with cyproterone acetate: a single case study. *Canadian Journal of Psychiatry* 32:22–30.

Brenman, M. (1952). On teasing and being teased: and the problem of moral masochism. *Psychoanalytic Study of the Child* 7:264–285. New York: International Universities Press.

Breslow, N., Evans, L., and Langley, J. (1985). On the prevalence and roles of females in the sadomasochistic subculture: report of an empirical study. *Archives of Sexual Behavior* 14:303–317.

Breuer, J., and Freud, S. (1893–1895). *Studies on Hysteria*. Reprint. New York: Basic Books, 1957.

Bromberg, W. (1951). A psychological study of murder. *International Journal of Psycho-Analysis* 32:117–127.

Browne, A. (1987). *When Battered Women Kill*. New York: Free Press.

Bruhn, A. (1990). Cognitive-perceptual theory and the projective use of autobiographical memory. *Journal of Personality Assessment* 55:95–114.

———— (1990). *Earliest Childhood Memories: Theory and Application to Clinical Practice*. Vol. 1. New York: Praeger.

Bruhn, A., and Davidow, S. (1983). Earliest memories and the dynamics of delinquency. *Journal of Personality Assessment* 47:476–482.

Buhrich, N. (1983). The association of erotic piercing with homosexuality, sadomasochism, bondage, fetishism, and tattoos. *Archives of Sexual Behavior* 12:167–171.

Campion, J., Cravens, J., and Covan, F. (1988). A study of filicidal men. *American Journal of Psychiatry* 145:1141–1144.

Campion, J., Cravens, J., Rotholc, A., et al. (1985). A study of 15 matricidal men. *American Journal of Psychiatry* 142:312–317.

Caplan, L. (1987). *The Insanity Defense and the Trial of John W. Hinckley, Jr.* New York: Dell.

Carrier, L. (1990). Erotomania and senile dementia [Letter to the editor]. *American Journal of Psychiatry* 147:1092.

Chasseguet-Smirgel, J. (1984). *Creativity and Perversion*. New York: W. W. Norton.

———— (1991). Sadomasochism in the perversions: some thoughts on the destruction of reality. *Journal of the American Psychoanalytic Association* 39:399–416.

Chelkowski, P. (1980). Iran: mourning becomes revolution. *Asia*, May-June, pp. 30–45.

Chodoff, P. (1982). Hysteria and women. *American Journal of Psychiatry* 1399:545–551.

Chomsky, N. (1957). *Syntactic Structures*. The Hague: Mouton.

Clarke, J. (1982). *American Assassins*. Princeton, NJ: Princeton University Press.

———— (1990). *On Being Mad or Merely Angry*. Princeton, NJ: Princeton University Press.

Cleckley, H. (1941). *The Mask of Sanity*. Reprint. St. Louis: C. V. Mosby, 1976.

Coe, C., Lubach, G., and Ershler, W. (1989). Immunological consequences of maternal separation in infant primates. *New Directions for Child Development* 45:65–91.

Coen, S. (1988). Sadomasochistic excitement: character disorder and perversion. In *Masochism: Current Psychoanalytic Perspectives*, ed. R. Glick and D. Meyers, pp. 43–60. Hillsdale, NJ: Analytic Press.

Coid, J. (1983). The epidemiology of abnormal homicide and murder followed by suicide. *Psychological Medicine* 13:855–860.

Cooper, A. (1981). Summary of panel discussion on "masochism: current concepts." *Journal of the American Psychoanalytic Association* 29:673–688.

_____ (1988). The narcissistic-masochistic character. In *Masochism: Current Psychoanalytic Perspectives*, ed. R. Glick and D. Meyers, pp. 117–138. Hillsdale, NJ: Analytic Press.

Cooper, S. H., and Arnow, D. (1986). An object relations view of the borderline defenses: a Rorschach analysis. In *Assessing Object Relations Phenomena*, ed. M. Kissen, pp. 143–171. Madison, CT: International Universities Press.

Cooper, S. H., Perry, J., and Arnow, D. (1988). An empirical approach to the study of defense mechanisms: I. Reliability and preliminary validity of the Rorschach defense scales. *Journal of Personality Assessment* 52:187–203.

Cornell, D., Benedek, E., and Benedek, D. (1987). Characteristics of adolescents charged with homicide: review of 72 cases. *Behavioral Sciences and the Law* 5:11–23.

Davidow, S., and Bruhn, A. (1990). Earliest memories and the dynamics of delinquency: a replication study. *Journal of Personality Assessment* 54:601–616.

Davis, M., Savitz, D., and Graubard, B. (1988). Infant feeding and childhood cancer. *Lancet* 2:365–368.

de Bary, H. A. (1879). *Die Erschienung der Symbiose*. Strassburg: Karl J. Toubner.

de Clerambault, C. G. (1921). Les psychoses passionelles (The passionate psychoses). In *Oeuvres psychiatriques*, pp. 315–322. Paris: Presses Universitaires de France, 1942.

Deutsch, H. (1926). Occult processes occurring during psychoanalysis. In *Psychoanalysis and the Occult*, ed. G. Devereux, pp. 133–146. Madison, CT: International Universities Press, 1953.

_____ (1942). Some forms of emotional disturbance and their relationship to schizophrenia. *Psychoanalytic Quarterly* 11:301–321.

De Vos, G., and Boyer, L. B. (1989). *Symbolic Analysis Cross-Culturally: The Rorschach Test*. Berkeley: University of California Press.

Dietz, P. (1988a). *Threats and attacks against public figures*. Paper presented at the meeting of the American Academy of Psychiatry and the Law, San Francisco, October.

_____ (1988b). *Interview with Arthur Jackson*. Presented at the meeting of the American Academy of Psychiatry and the Law, San Francisco, October. Videotape.

Dietz, P., Hazelwood, R., and Warren, J. (1990). The sexually sadistic criminal and his offenses. *Bulletin of the American Academy of Psychiatry and the Law* 18:163–178.

Dietz, P., Matthews, D., Martell, D., et al. (1991b). Threatening and otherwise inappropriate letters to members of the United States Congress. *Journal of Forensic Sciences* 36:1445–1468.

Dietz, P., Matthews, D., Van Duyne, C., et al. (1991a). Threatening and otherwise inappropriate letters to Hollywood celebrities. *Journal of Forensic Sciences* 36:185–209.

Di Maio, V. J. M. (1985). *Gunshot Wounds: Practical Aspects of Firearms, Ballistics, and Forensic Techniques.* New York: Elsevier.

Dorian, B. J. (1979). Monosymptomatic hypochondriacal psychosis. *Canadian Psychiatric Association Journal* 24:377.

Doust, J. W. L., and Christie, H. (1978). The pathology of love: some clinical variants of de Clerambault's syndrome. *Social Science Medicine* 12:99–106.

Drevets, W., and Rubin, E. (1987). Erotomania and senile dementia of Alzheimer type. *British Journal of Psychiatry* 151:400–402.

Dubinsky, A. (1986). The sado-masochistic phantasies of two adolescent boys suffering from congenital physical illnesses. *Journal of Child Psychotherapy* 12:73–85.

Eidelberg, L. (1959). Humiliation and masochism. *Journal of the American Psychoanalytic Association* 7:274–283.

El-Assra, A. (1989). Erotomania in a Saudi woman. *British Journal of Psychiatry* 155:553–555.

Enoch, M. D., and Trethowan, W. H. (1979). De Clerambault's syndrome. In *Uncommon Psychiatric Syndromes,* 2nd ed., pp. 15–35. Bristol, England: John Wright.

Epstein, A., and Ervin, F. (1956). Psychodynamic significance of seizure content in psychomotor epilepsy. *Psychosomatic Medicine* 18:43–55.

Esquirol, J. E. D. (1838). *Mental Maladies: A Treatise on Insanity.* Trans. E. K. Hunt. New York: Hafner, 1965.

Eulenburg, A. von (1911). *Sadism and Masochism.* Reprint. New York: Bell, 1984.

Evans, D., Jeckel, L., and Slott, N. (1982). Erotomania: a variant of pathological mourning. *Bulletin of the Menninger Clinic* 46:507–520.

Ewing, C. P. (1987). *Battered Women Who Kill: Psychological Self-Defense as Legal Justification.* Lexington, KY: D.C. Heath.

_____ (1990). Psychological self-defense: a proposed justification for battered women who kill. *Law and Human Behavior* 14:579–594.

Exner, J. (1986a). *The Rorschach: A Comprehensive System.* Vol. 1, *Foundations.* 2nd ed. New York: Wiley.

_____ (1986b). Some Rorschach data comparing schizophrenics with borderline and schizotypal personality disorders. *Journal of Personality Assessment* 50:455–471.

_____ (1990a). *A Rorschach Workbook for the Comprehensive System.* 3rd ed. Asheville, NC: Rorschach Workshops.

_____ (1990b). *Rorschach Interpretation Assistance Program,* version 2. Asheville, NC: Rorschach Workshops.

_____ (1991). *The Rorschach: A Comprehensive System.* Vol. 2, *Interpretation.* 2nd ed. New York: Wiley.

Fairbairn, W. R. D. (1936). The effect of the King's death upon patients under analysis. *International Journal of Psycho-Analysis* 17:278–284.

_____ (1963). Synopsis of an object-relations theory of the personality. *International Journal of Psycho-Analysis* 44:224–225.

Fast, I. (1985). *Event Theory.* Madison, CT: International Universities Press.

Feder, S. (1973). Clerambault in the ghetto: pure erotomania reconsidered. *International Journal of Psychoanalytic Psychotherapy* 2:240–247.

Federal Bureau of Investigation. (1989). *Uniform Crime Reports.* Washington, DC: Federal Bureau of Investigation.

Felthous, A., Bryant, S., Wingerter, C., and Barratt, E. (1991). The diagnosis of intermittent explosive disorder in violent men. *Bulletin of the American Academy of Psychiatry and the Law* 19:71–80.

Fenichel, O. (1945). *The Psychoanalytic Theory of Neurosis.* New York: W. W. Norton.

Fintzy, R. T. (1971). Vicissitudes of the transitional object in a borderline child. *International Journal of Psycho-Analysis* 52:107–114.

Fletcher, G. P. (1988). *A Crime of Self Defense.* New York: Free Press.

Flynn, J. (1967). The neural basis of aggression in cats. In *Neurophysiology and Emotion,* ed. D. Glass, pp. 40–59. New York: Rockefeller University Press.

Flynn, J., and Bandler, R. (1975). Patterned reflexes during centrally elicited attack behavior. In *Neural Basis of Violence and Aggression,* ed. W. Fields and W. Sweet, pp. 41–53. St. Louis: Warren H. Green.

Foreman, M. (1988). *Psychopathy and Interpersonal Behavior.* Ph.D. diss., University of British Columbia.

Forth, A., Hart, S., and Hare, R. (1990). Assessment of psychopathy in male young offenders. *Psychological Assessment* 2:342–344.

Freeman, T. (1990). Psychoanalytical aspects of morbid jealousy in women. *British Journal of Psychiatry* 156:68–72.

Freud, A. (1936). *The Ego and the Mechanisms of Defense.* Rev. ed. New York: International Universities Press, 1966.

Freud, S. (1905). Three essays on the theory of sexuality. *Standard Edition* 7:135–243.

_____ (1911). Psycho-analytic notes on an autobiographical account of a case of paranoia. *Standard Edition* 12:2–82.

_____ (1919). A child is being beaten. *Standard Edition* 17:179–204.

_____ (1924). The economic problem of masochism. *Standard Edition* 19:159–170.

_____ (1931). Female sexuality. *Standard Edition* 21:221–243.

_____ (1938). Splitting of the ego in the process of defense. *Standard Edition* 23:271–278.

Freund, K. (1976). Diagnosis and treatment of forensically significant anomalous erotic preferences. *Canadian Journal of Criminology & Corrections* 18:181–189.

Gabbard, G. (1990). *Psychodynamic Psychiatry in Clinical Practice.* Washington, DC: American Psychiatric Press.

Gacono, C. (1990). An empirical study of object relations and defensive operations in antisocial personality disorder. *Journal of Personality Assessment* 54:589–600.

Gacono, C., and Meloy, R. (1988). The relationship between cognitive style and defensive process in the psychopath. *Criminal Justice and Behavior* 15:472–483.

_____ (1991). A Rorschach investigation of attachment and anxiety in antisocial personality disorder. *Journal of Nervous and Mental Disease* 179:546–552.

_____ (1992). The Rorschach and the *DSM-III-R* antisocial personality: a tribute to Robert Lindner. *Journal of Clinical Psychology* 48:393–406.

Gacono, C., Meloy, R., and Berg, J. (1992). Object relations, defensive operations, and affective states in narcissistic, borderline, and antisocial personality disorder. *Journal of Personality Assessment* 59:32–49.

Gacono, C., Meloy, R., and Heaven, T. (1990). A Rorschach investigation of narcissism and hysteria in antisocial personality disorder. *Journal of Personality Assessment* 55:270–279.

Galenson, E. (1988). The precursors of masochism: protomasochism. In *Masochism: Current Psychoanalytic Perspectives*, ed. R. Glick and D. Meyers, pp. 189–204. Hillsdale, NJ: Analytic Press.

Garnett, E., Nahmias, C., Wortzman, G., et al. (1988). Positron emission tomography and sexual arousal in a sadist and two controls. *Annals of Sex Research* 1:387–399.

Gayral, L., Millet, G., Moron, P., and Turnin, J. (1956). Crises et paroxysmes catathymiques. *Annales Medico-Psychologiques* 114:25–50.

Geberth, V. J. (1990). *Practical Homicide Investigation: Tactics, Procedures, and Forensic Techniques*. 2nd ed. New York: Elsevier.

Gedo, J. (1988). Masochism and the repetition compulsion. In *Masochism: Current Psychoanalytic Perspectives*, ed. R. Glick and D. Meyers, pp. 139–150. Hillsdale, NJ: Analytic Press.

Geffner, R., and Rosenbaum, A. (1990). Characteristics and treatment of batterers. *Behavioral Sciences and the Law* 8:131–140.

Gero, G. (1962). Sadism, masochism, and aggression: their role in symptom-formation. *Psychoanalytic Quarterly* 31:31–42.

Gharagozlu-Hamadani, H. (1970). Psychiatric evaluation of 100 cases of suicidal attempts in Shiraz, Iran. *International Journal of Social Psychiatry* 17:140–144.

Glenn, J. (1981). Masochism and narcissism in a patient traumatized in childhood. *Journal of the American Psychoanalytic Association* 29:677–680.

Glick, R., and Meyers, D., eds. (1988). *Masochism: Current Psychoanalytic Perspectives*. Hillsdale, NJ: Analytic Press.

Goldstein, R. L. (1986). Erotomania in men [Letter to the editor]. *American Journal of Psychiatry* 143:802.

_____ (1987a). More forensic romances: de Clerambault's syndrome in men. *Bulletin of the American Academy of Psychiatry and the Law* 15:267–274.

_____ (1987b). What is de Clerambault's syndrome? *Harvard Medical School Mental Health Letter* 3:1.

Goldstein, W. N. (1991). Clarification of projective identification. *American Journal of Psychiatry* 148:153–161.

Gosselin, C., Wilson, G., and Barrett, P. (1991). The personality and sexual preferences of sadomasochistic women. *Personality and Individual Differences* 12:11–15.

Greyson, B., and Akhtar, S. (1977). Erotomanic delusions in a mentally retarded patient. *American Journal of Psychiatry* 134:325–326.

Griffith, E., Zonana, H., Pinsince, A., and Adams, A. (1988). Institutional response to inpatients' threats against the President. *Hospital and Community Psychiatry* 39:1166–1171.

Grolnick, S., Barkin, L., and Muensterberger, W. (1978). *Between Reality and Fantasy: Transitional Objects and Phenomena.* New York: Jason Aronson.

Gross, M. D. (1991). Treatment of pathological jealousy by fluoxetine [Letter to the editor]. *American Journal of Psychiatry* 148:683–684.

Grossman, W. (1991). Pain, aggression, fantasy, and concepts of sadomasochism. *Psychoanalytic Quarterly* 60:22–52.

Grossmann, K., Grossmann, K., and Schwan, A. (1986). Capturing the wider view of attachment: a reanalysis of Ainsworth's strange situation. In *Measuring Emotions in Infants and Children,* vol. 2, ed. C. Izard and P. Read, pp. 23–64. New York: Cambridge University Press.

Grotstein, J. (1978). Inner space: its dimensions and its coordinates. *International Journal of Psycho-Analysis* 59:55–61.

———— (1980). A proposed revision of the psychoanalytic concept of primitive mental states: I. An introduction to a newer psychoanalytic metapsychology. *Contemporary Psychoanalysis* 16:479–546.

———— (1981). *Splitting and Projective Identification.* New York: Jason Aronson.

———— (1982). Newer perspectives in object relations theory. *Contemporary Psychoanalysis* 18:43–91.

———— (1990). Invariants in primitive emotional disorders. In *Master Clinicians on Treating the Regressed Patient,* ed. L. Boyer and P. Giovacchini, pp. 139–163. Northvale, NJ: Jason Aronson.

Hambridge, J. (1990). The grief process in those admitted to regional secure units following homicide. *Journal of Forensic Sciences* 35:1149–1154.

Hamilton, N. G. (1990). The containing function and the analyst's projective identification. *International Journal of Psycho-Analysis* 71:445–453.

Hare, R. (1980). A research scale for the assessment of psychopathy in criminal populations. *Personality and Individual Differences* 1:111–117.

———— (1985). *The psychopathy checklist.* Unpublished Manuscript. Vancouver: University of British Columbia.

———— (1991). *Manual for the Revised Psychopathy Checklist.* Toronto: Multi-Health Systems.

Hare, R., Hart, S., and Harpur, T. (1991). Psychopathy and the *DSM-IV* criteria for antisocial personality disorder. *Journal of Abnormal Psychology* 100:391–398.

Hare, R., and McPherson, L. (1984). Violent and aggressive behavior by criminal psychopaths. *International Journal of Law and Psychiatry* 7:35–50.

Hare, R., McPherson, L., and Forth, A. (1988). Male psychopaths and their criminal careers. *Journal of Consulting and Clinical Psychology* 56:710–714.

Hare, R., and Schalling, D. (1978). *Psychopathic Behavior: Approaches to Research.* Chichester, England: Wiley.

Hare, R., Williamson, S., and Harpur, T. (1988). Psychopathy and language. In *Biological Contributions to Crime Causation,* ed. T. E. Moffitt and S. A. Mednick. Dordrecht, Netherlands: Nijhoff Martinus.

Harpur, T., Hakstian, R., and Hare, R. (1988). Factor structure of the psychopathy checklist. *Journal of Consulting and Clinical Psychology* 56:741–747.

Harpur, T., Hare, R., and Hakstian, A. (1989). Two-factor conceptualization of psychopathy: construct validity and assessment implications. *Psychological Assessment* 1:6–17.

Harris, G., Rice, M., and Cormier, C. (1991). Psychopathy and violent recidivism. *Law and Human Behavior* 15:625–637.

Hart, H. (1952). Masochism, passivity and radicalism. *Psychoanalytic Review* 39:304–321.

Hart, S., and Hare, R. (1989). Discriminant validity of the Psychopathy Checklist in a forensic psychiatric population. *Psychological Assessment* 1:211–218.

Harter, S. (1983). Developmental perspectives on the self system. In *Handbook of Child Psychology*, vol. 4, *Social and Personality Development*, ed. M. Hetherington, pp. 275–385. New York: Wiley.

Hartman, W., Clarke, M., Morgan, M., et al. (1990). Rorschach structure of a hospitalized sample of Vietnam veterans with PTSD. *Journal of Personality Assessment* 54:149–159.

Hayes, S., Brownell, K., and Barlow, D. (1978). The use of self-administered covert sensitization in the treatment of exhibitionism and sadism. *Behavior Therapy* 9:283–289.

Heilbrun, A., and Seif, D. (1988). Erotic value of female distress in sexually explicit photographs. *Journal of Sex Research* 24:47–57.

Herman, J., and van der Kolk, B. (1987). Traumatic antecedents of borderline personality disorder. In *Psychological Trauma*, ed. B. van der Kolk, pp. 111–126. Washington, DC: American Psychiatric Press.

Hinckley, J. (1985). *Breaking Points*. Old Tappan, NJ: Chosen Books.

Hofer, M. (1983). On the relationship between attachment and separation processes in infancy. In *Emotion: Theory, Research, and Experience*, vol. 2, *Emotion in Early Development*, ed. R. Plutchick and H. Kellerman, pp. 199–219. New York: Academic Press.

_____ (1984). Relationships as regulators: a psychobiologic perspective on bereavement. *Psychosomatic Medicine* 46:183–197.

_____ (1987). Early social relationships: a psychobiologist's view. *Child Development* 58:633–647.

Hoffman, J. L. (1943). Psychotic visitors to government offices in the national capital. *American Journal of Psychiatry* 99:571–575.

Hollender, M., and Callahan, A. (1975). Erotomania or de Clerambault syndrome. *Archives of General Psychiatry* 32:1574–1576.

Hopfe, L. (1987). *Religions of the World*. 4th ed. New York: Macmillan.

Horner, A. (1984). *Object Relations and the Developing Ego in Therapy*. New York: Jason Aronson.

Horner, T., and Rosenberg, E. (1991). The family romance: a developmental-historical perspective. *Psychoanalytic Psychology* 8:131–148.

Horney, K. (1937). *The Neurotic Personality of Our Time*. New York: Norton.

Horowitz, M., ed. (1991). *Hysterical Personality Style and the Histrionic Personality Disorder*. Rev. ed. Northvale, NJ: Jason Aronson.

Hucker, S., Langevin, R., Dickey, R., et al. (1988). Cerebral damage and dysfunction in sexually aggressive men. *Annals of Sex Research* 1:33–47.

Insel, T., Gelhard, R., and Shapiro, L. (1991). The comparative distribution of forebrain receptors for neurohypophyseal peptides in monogamous and polygamous mice. *Neuroscience* 43:623–630.

Insel, T., and Winslow, J. (1991). Central administration of oxytocin modulates the infant rat's response to social isolation. *European Journal of Pharmacology* 203:149–152.

Jablensky, A., Sartorius, N., Gulbinat, W., and Ernberg, G. (1981). Characteristics of depressive patients contacting psychiatric services in four cultures. *Acta Psychiatrica Scandinavia* 63:367–383.

Jackson, L. (1949). A study of sado-masochism attitudes in a group of delinquent girls by means of a specially designed projection test. *British Journal of Medical Psychology* 22:53.

Jacobson, E. (1964). *The Self and the Object World*. New York: International Universities Press.

———— (1971). *Depression*. New York: International Universities Press.

Jacoby, S. (1983). *Wild Justice*. New York: Harper & Row.

Joseph, B. (1982). Addiction to near-death. *International Journal of Psycho-Analysis* 63:449–456.

Jubes, D., Berman, A., and Josselson, A. (1986). The impact of psychological autopsies on medical examiners' determination of manner of death. *Journal of Forensic Sciences* 31:177.

Kagan, J. (1981). *The Second Year: The Emergence of Self Awareness*. Cambridge, MA: Harvard University Press.

Kaiser, R. (1970). *"R. F. K. must die!"* New York: E. P. Dutton.

Karol, C. (1980–1981). The role of primal scene and masochism in asthma. *International Journal of Psychoanalytic Psychotherapy* 8:577–592.

Karpman, B. (1954). *The Sexual Offender and His Offenses*. New York: Julian Press.

Katz, A. (1990). Paradoxes of masochism. *Psychoanalytic Psychology* 7:225–242.

Keller, C., Peele, R., and Sorrentino, E. (1965). White House cases. *Proceedings of the 28th Annual Medical Society of Saint Elizabeth's Hospital.*

Kelley, K. (1980). Stress and immune function: a bibliographic review. *Annales Recherche Veterinaire* 11:445–478.

Kernberg, O. (1975). *Borderline Conditions and Pathological Narcissism*. New York: Jason Aronson.

———— (1976). *Object Relations Theory and Clinical Psychoanalysis*. New York: Jason Aronson.

———— (1984). *Severe Personality Disorders: Psychotherapeutic Strategies*. New Haven, CT: Yale University Press.

———— (1988). Clinical dimensions of masochism. *Journal of the American Psychoanalytic Association* 36:1005–1029.

———— (1991). Sadomasochism, sexual excitement, and perversion. *Journal of the American Psychoanalytic Association* 39:333–362.

Kissen, M., ed. (1986). *Assessing Object Relations Phenomena*. Madison, CT: International Universities Press.

Klassen, D., and O'Connor, W. (1988). A prospective study of predictors of violence in adult male mental health admissions. *Law and Human Behavior* 12:143–158.

Klein, M. (1930). The importance of symbol formation in the development of the ego. *International Journal of Psycho-Analysis* 11:24-39.

——— (1945). The oedipus complex in the light of early anxieties. *International Journal of Psycho-Analysis* 26:11-33.

——— (1946). Notes on some schizoid mechanisms. In *Envy and Gratitude and Other Works, 1946-1963*, pp. 1-24. New York: Free Press, 1975.

——— (1957). Envy and gratitude. In *Envy and Gratitude and Other Works, 1946-1963*, pp. 176-235. New York: Free Press, 1975.

Koch, J. L. (1891). *Die Psychopathischen Minderwertigkeiten*. Ravensburg: Maier.

Kohut, H. (1971). *The Analysis of the Self: A Systematic Approach to the Treatment of Narcissistic Personality Disorders*. New York: International Universities Press.

——— (1972). Thoughts on narcissism and narcissistic rage. *Psychoanalytic Study of the Child* 27:360-400. New Haven, CT: Yale University Press.

Kosson, D., Smith, S., and Newman, P. (1990). Evaluation of the construct validity of psychopathy in black and white male inmates: three preliminary studies. *Journal of Abnormal Psychology* 99:250-259.

Kraepelin, E. (1915). *Psychiatrie: Ein Lehrbuch*. 8th ed. Leipzig: Barth.

——— (1921). *Manic-Depressive Insanity and Paranoia*. Trans. R. Barclay. Ed. G. Robertson. Edinburgh: E. & S. Livingstone.

Krafft-Ebing, R. von (1906). *Psychopathia Sexualis: A Medico-Forensic Study*. New York: G. P. Putnam's Sons, 1965.

Krystal, H. (1984). Psychoanalytic views on human emotional damages. In *Post-traumatic Stress Disorder: Psychological and Biological Sequelae*, ed. B. van der Kolk, pp. 2-28. Washington, DC: American Psychiatric Press.

Kulcsar, S. (1976). De Sade and Eichmann. *Mental Health and Society* 3:102-113.

Kurtz, I. (1987). Envy. *The New York Times Magazine*, Feb. 22, p. 42.

Kwawer, J. (1980). Primitive interpersonal modes, borderline phenomena, and Rorschach content. In *Borderline Phenomena and the Rorschach Test*, ed. J. Kwawer, H. Lerner, P. Lerner, and S. Sugarman, pp. 89-105. New York: International Universities Press.

LaBarba, R. (1970). Experiential and environmental factors in cancer: a review of research with animals. *Psychosomatic Medicine* 32:259-276.

Lamberti, J., Blackman, N., and Weiss, J. (1958). The sudden murderer: a preliminary report. *Journal of Social Therapy* 4:2.

Lane, R. C. (1990). Successful fluoxetine treatment of pathologic jealousy. *Journal of Clinical Psychiatry* 51:345-346.

Lang, A., and Sibrel, P. (1989). Psychological perspectives on alcohol consumption and interpersonal aggression. *Criminal Justice and Behavior* 16:299-324.

Langevin, R., Bain, J., Wortzman, G., et al. (1988). Sexual sadism: brain, blood, and behavior. Conference of the New York Academy of Sciences: Human sexual aggression: current perspectives (1987, New York). *Annals of the New York Academy of Sciences* 528:163-171.

Laudenslager, M., and Reite, M. (1984). Loss and separation: immunological consequences and health implications. In *Review of Personality and Social Psychology*, ed. P. Shaver, pp. 40-48. Newbury Park, CA: Sage.

Laudenslager, M., Reite, M., and Harbeck, R. (1982). Suppressed immune response in infant monkeys associated with maternal separation. *Behavioral Neural Biology* 36:40–48.

Laws, D., Meyer, J., and Holmen, M. (1978). Reduction of sadistic sexual arousal by olfactory aversion: a case study. *Behavior Research & Therapy* 16:281–285.

Lerner, H., Albert, C., and Walsh, M. (1987). The Rorschach assessment of borderline defenses. *Journal of Personality Assessment* 51:344–354.

Lerner, H., and Lerner, P., eds. (1988). *Primitive Mental States and the Rorschach.* Madison, CT: International Universities Press.

Lerner, P. (1990). Rorschach assessment of primitive defenses: a review. *Journal of Personality Assessment* 54:30–46.

Levy-Warren, M. (1987). Moving to a new culture: cultural identity, loss, and mourning. In *The Psychology of Separation and Loss*, ed. J. Bloom-Feshbach and S. Bloom-Feshbach, pp. 300–315. San Francisco: Jossey-Bass.

Lewis, D. O., Moy, E., Jackson, L., et al. (1985). Biopsychosocial characteristics of children who later murder: a prospective study. *American Journal of Psychiatry* 142:1161–1167.

Loewenstein, R. (1957). A contribution to the psychoanalytic theory of masochism. *Journal of the American Psychoanalytic Association* 5:197–234.

Loftus, E. (1979). *Eyewitness Testimony.* Cambridge, MA: Harvard University Press.

Lorenz, K. Z. (1935). Der kumpan in der umvelt des vogels. *J. Orn. Berl.*, 83. Eng. trans. in *Instinctive Behavior*, ed. C. H. Schiller. Madison, CT: International Universities Press, 1957.

Low, P., Jeffries, J., and Bonnie, R. (1986). *The Trial of John W. Hinckley, Jr.: A Case Study in the Insanity Defense.* Westbury, NY: Foundation Press.

Luisada, P., Peele, R., and Pittard, E. (1974). The hysterical personality in men. *American Journal of Psychiatry* 131:518–521.

MacCulloch, M., Snowden, P., Wood, P., and Mills, H. (1983). Sadistic fantasy, sadistic behaviour and offending. *British Journal of Psychiatry* 143:20–29.

MacDonald, J. (1968). *Homicidal Threats.* Springfield, IL: Charles C Thomas.

Mahler, M. (1968). *On Human Symbiosis and the Vicissitudes of Individuation.* Madison, CT: International Universities Press.

_____ (1979). *Selected Papers of Margaret S. Mahler.* New York: Jason Aronson.

Mahler, M., Pine, F., and Bergman, A. (1975). *The Psychological Birth of the Human Infant.* New York: Basic Books.

Maier, H. (1912). Ueber katathyme wahnbildung und paranoia. *Ztschr. f.d.ges. Neurol. u. Psychiat.* 13:555.

_____ (1923). Ueber einige arten der psychogenen mechanismen. *Ztschr. f.d.ges. Neurol. u. Psychiat.* 82:193.

Main, M., and Westen, D. (1981). The quality of the toddler's relationship to mother and to father: related to conflict behavior and the readiness to establish new relationships. *Child Development* 52:932–940.

McConnell, B. (1970). *The History of Assassination.* Nashville, TN: Aurora.

McCord, W., and McCord, J. (1964). *The Psychopath: An Essay on the Criminal Mind.* Princeton, NJ: Van Nostrand.

McGinnis, J. (1989). *Blind Faith*. New York: G. P. Putnam's Sons.

Meissner, W. W. (1978). *The Paranoid Process*. New York: Jason Aronson.

Meloy, J. R. (1985). Concept and percept formation in object relations theory. *Psychoanalytic Psychology* 2:35–45.

_____ (1986). Narcissistic psychopathology and the clergy. *Pastoral Psychology* 35:50–55.

_____ (1987). The prediction of violence in outpatient psychotherapy. *American Journal of Psychotherapy* 41:38–45.

_____ (1988a). *The Psychopathic Mind: Origins, Dynamics, and Treatment*. Northvale, NJ: Jason Aronson.

_____ (1988b). Violent and homicidal behavior in primitive mental states. *Journal of the American Academy of Psychoanalysis* 16:381–394.

_____ (1990). Nondelusional or borderline erotomania [Letter to the editor]. *American Journal of Psychiatry* 147:820.

_____ (1991a). The decision to criminally prosecute the psychiatric inpatient. *American Journal of Forensic Psychiatry* 12:69–80.

_____ (1991b). Further comments on projective identification. [Letter to the editor]. *American Journal of Psychiatry* 148:1761–1762.

Meloy, J. R., and Gacono, C. (1992a). The aggression response and the Rorschach. *Journal of Clinical Psychology* 48:104–114.

_____ (1992b). A psychotic (sexual) psychopath: "I just had a violent thought . . ." *Journal of Personality Assessment* 58:480–493.

_____ (in press). *The Rorschach and Psychopathy: A Structural and Psychoanalytic Investigation*. Hillsdale, NJ: Lawrence Erlbaum Associates.

Meloy, R., Haroun, A., and Schiller, E. (1990). *Clinical Guidelines for Involuntary Outpatient Treatment*. Sarasota, FL: Professional Resource Exchange.

Meloy, J. R., and Singer, J. (1991). A psychoanalytic view of the Rorschach Comprehensive System "Special Scores." *Journal of Personality Assessment* 56:202–217.

Meltzer, D. (1975). Adhesive identification. *Contemporary Psychoanalysis* 11:289–310.

Menaker, E. (1953). Masochism—a defense reaction of the ego. *Psychoanalytic Quarterly* 22:205–225.

Menninger, K., and Mayman, M. (1956). Episodic dyscontrol: a third order of stress adaptation. *Bulletin of the Menninger Clinic* 20:153–165.

Metcalf, A. (1991). Childhood: from process to structure. In *Hysterical Personality Style and the Histrionic Personality Disorder*, ed. M. Horowitz, pp. 69–145. Northvale, NJ: Jason Aronson.

Meyers, J. (in press). Assessing cross-cultural adaptability. *Journal of Personality Assessment*.

Meyers, J., and Meloy, J. R. (1992). Erotomania in a male immigrant from a traditional Islamic culture Manuscript submitted for publication.

Millon, T. (1981). *Disorders of Personality; DSM-III: Axis II*. New York: Wiley.

Miner, H., and De Vos, G. (1960). *Oasis and Casbah: Algerian Culture and Personality in Change*. Ann Arbor: University of Michigan Press.

Mintz, I. (1980–1981). Multideterminism in asthmatic disease. *International Journal of Psychoanalytic Psychotherapy* 8:593–600.

Monroe, R. (1981). Brain dysfunction in prisoners. In *Violence and the Violent Individual*, ed. R. Hayes, T. Roberts, and K. Solway, pp. 75–86. New York: Spectrum.

———— (1989). Dyscontrol syndrome: long term followup. *Comprehensive Psychiatry* 30:489–497.

Montgomery, J., and Greif, A. (1989). *Masochism: The Treatment of Self-Inflicted Suffering*. Madison, CT: International Universities Press.

Moravesik, E. (1894). Das hysterische irresein. *Allg Z für Psychiatrie* 50:117.

Morse, S. (1990). The misbegotten marriage of soft psychology and bad law. *Law and Human Behavior* 14:595–618.

Moser, C., and Levitt, E. (1987). An exploratory-descriptive study of a sadomasochistically oriented sample. *Journal of Sex Research* 23:322–337.

Munro, A. (1984). Excellent response of pathologic jealousy to pimozide. *Canadian Medical Association Journal* 131:852–853.

Novick, J., and Novick, K. (1972). Beating fantasies in children. *International Journal of Psycho-Analysis* 53:237–242.

———— (1987). The essence of masochism. *Psychoanalytic Study of the Child* 42:353–384. New Haven, CT: Yale University Press.

———— (1991). Some comments on masochism and the delusion of omnipotence from a developmental perspective. *Journal of the American Psychoanalytic Association* 39:307–332.

Ogden, T. (1982). *Projective Identification and Psychotherapeutic Technique*. New York: Jason Aronson.

———— (1986). *The Matrix of the Mind*. Northvale, NJ: Jason Aronson.

Ogloff, J., and Wong, S. (1990). Electrodermal and cardiovascular evidence of a coping response in psychopaths. *Criminal Justice and Behavior* 17:231–245.

Omidsalar, M. (1984). Invulnerable armour as a compromise formation in Persian folklore. *International Review of Psycho-Analysis* 11:441–452.

Ophnijsen, V. (1929). The sexual aim of sadism as manifest in acts of violence. *International Journal of Psycho-Analysis* 10:139–144.

Osofsky, J. (1988). Attachment theory and research and the psychoanalytic process. *Psychoanalytic Psychology* 5:159–177.

Packer, I. (1987). Homicide and the insanity defense: a comparison of sane and insane murderers. *Behavioral Sciences and the Law* 5:25–35.

Palmer, S., and Humphrey, J. (1980). Criminal homicide followed by offender's suicide. *Suicide and Life Threatening Behavior* 10:106–118.

Patai, R. (1983). *The Arab Mind*. Rev. ed. New York: Charles Scribner's Sons.

Patrick, C., and Lang, P. (1989). *Psychopathy and emotion in a forensic population*. Paper presented at the meeting of the Society for Psychophysiological Research, New Orleans, October.

Pearce, A. (1972). De Clerambault's syndrome associated with folie a deux [Letter to the editor]. *British Journal of Psychiatry* 121:116–117.

Peaslee, D. (1992). *An explication of female psychotherapy*. Dissertation. California School of Professional Psychology. Fresno, CA.

Pekowsky, J. (1988). "Say you're sorry": a sadomasochistic transference. *Psychoanalytic Review* 75:459–468.

People v. *Sirhan*, No. 14026, Los Angeles County Superior Court, State of California.

Perry, G., and Kinder, B. (1990). The susceptibility of the Rorschach to malingering: a critical review. *Journal of Personality Assessment* 54:47–57.

Pfohl, B. (1990). *Histrionic Personality Disorder: A Review of Available Data and Recommendations for DSM-IV.* Unpublished paper.

Piaget, J. (1954). *The Construction of Reality in the Child.* New York: Basic Books.

Pollack, S. (1969a). Psychiatric report to the Honorable Evelle J. Younger, District Attorney, February 5, 1969. *People* v. *Sirhan*, People's Exhibit 111.

_____ (1969b). Supplemental psychiatric report to the Honorable Evelle J. Younger, District Attorney, March 21, 1969. *People* v. *Sirhan*, People's Exhibit 111.

Pollock, B. (1982). Successful treatment of pathological jealousy with pimozide. *Canadian Journal of Psychiatry* 27:86–87.

Prentky, R., Burgess, A., Rokous, F., et al. (1989). The presumptive role of fantasy in serial sexual homicide. *American Journal of Psychiatry* 146:887–891.

Racker, H. (1968). *Transference and Countertransference.* New York: International Universities Press.

Raine, A., and Dunkin, J. (1990). The genetic and psychophysiological basis of antisocial behavior: implications for counseling and therapy. *Journal of Counseling and Development* 68:637–644.

Raine, A., Venables, P., and Williams, M. (1990). Relationships between central and autonomic measures of arousal at age 15 and criminality at age 24. *Archives of General Psychiatry* 47:1003–1007.

Ramchandani, D. (1989). The concept of projective identification and its clinical relevance. *American Journal of Psychotherapy* 43:238–247.

Raschka, L. (1979). The incubus syndrome: a variant of erotomania. *Canadian Journal of Psychiatry* 24:549–553.

Reich, W. (1933). *Character Analysis.* Reprint. New York: Simon & Schuster, 1972.

Reid, W. H., ed. (1978). *The Psychopath: A Comprehensive Study of Antisocial Disorders and Behaviors.* New York: Brunner/Mazel.

Reik, T. (1963). *The Need to be Loved.* New York: Farrar, Straus.

Reiser, D. (1963). Observations of delinquent behavior in very young children. *Journal of the American Academy of Child Psychiatry* 2:50–71.

Ressler, R., Burgess, A., and Douglas, J. (1988). *Sexual Homicide: Patterns and Motives.* Lexington, MA: Lexington Books.

Revitch, E., and Schlesinger, L. (1978). Murder: evaluation, classification, and prediction. In *Violence: Perspectives on Murder and Aggression*, ed. I. Kutash, S. Kutash, and L. Schlesinger, pp. 138–164. San Francisco: Jossey-Bass.

_____ (1981). *Psychopathology of Homicide.* Springfield, IL: Charles C Thomas.

Rice, M., Harris, G., and Quinsey, V. (1990). A follow-up of rapists assessed in a maximum security psychiatric facility. *Journal of Interpersonal Violence* 4:435–448.

Richards, A. (1989). A romance with pain: a telephone perversion in a woman? *International Journal of Psycho-Analysis* 70:153–164.

Rinsley, D. (1982). *Borderline and Other Self Disorders*. New York: Jason Aronson.

Ritzler, B., and Nalesnik, D. (1990). The effect of inquiry on the Exner Comprehensive System. *Journal of Personality Assessment* 55:647–656.

Robertson, J., and Bowlby, J. (1952). Responses of young children to separation from their mothers. *Courr. Cent. int. Enf.* 2:131–142.

Rogers, R., ed. (1988). *Clinical Assessment of Malingering and Deception*. New York: Guilford.

Roheim, G. (1934). The evolution of culture. *International Journal of Psycho-Analysis* 15:387–418.

Rosenbaum, M. (1990). The role of depression in couples involved in murder–suicide and homicide. *American Journal of Psychiatry* 147:1036–1039.

Rosenbaum, M., and Bennett, B. (1986). Homicide and depression. *American Journal of Psychiatry* 143:367–370.

Rosenberg, M., and Mercy, J. (1986). Homicide: epidemiological analysis at the national level. *Bulletin of the New York Academy of Medicine* 62:376–399.

Rosenfeld, H. (1963). Notes on the psychopathology and psychoanalytic treatment of schizophrenia. In *Psychotic States*, pp. 155–168. London: Hogarth Press, 1965.

_____ (1988). On masochism: a theoretical and clinical approach. In *Masochism: Current Psychoanalytic Perspectives*, ed. R. Glick and D. Meyers, pp. 151–174. Hillsdale, NJ: Analytic Press.

Rothstein, A. (1984a). *The Narcissistic Pursuit of Perfection*. New York: International Universities Press.

_____ (1984b). Fear of humiliation. *Journal of the American Psychoanalytic Association* 32:99–116.

_____ (1991). Sadomasochism in the neuroses conceived of as a pathological compromise formation. *Journal of the American Psychoanalytic Association* 39:363–376.

Rudden, M., Sweeney, J., and Frances, A. (1990). Diagnosis and clinical course of erotomanic and other delusional patients. *American Journal of Psychiatry* 147:625–628.

Rule, A. (1980). *The Stranger Beside Me*. New York: W. W. Norton.

Ruotolo, A. (1968). Dynamics of sudden murder. *American Journal of Psychoanalysis* 28:162–176.

Russell, D. H. (1982). *Rape in Marriage*. New York: Macmillan.

Rutter, M. (1981). *Maternal Deprivation Reassessed*. Middlesex, England: Penguin Books.

Sacher-Masoch, L. von (1870). *Venus in Furs*. New York: William Faro, 1932.

Sander, L. W. (1983). Polarity, paradox, and the organizing process in development. In *Frontiers of Infant Psychiatry*, ed. J. D. Call, E. Galenson, and R. Tyson, pp. 315–327. New York: Basic Books.

Satten, J., Menninger, K., and Mayman, M. (1960). Murder without apparent motive: a study of personality disorganization. *American Journal of Psychiatry* 117:48–53.

Schafer, R. (1968). *Aspects of Internalization*. Madison, CT: International Universities Press.

_____ (1988). Those wrecked by success. In *Masochism: Current Psychoanalytic Perspectives*, ed. R. Glick and D. Meyers, pp. 81–91. Hillsdale, NJ: Analytic Press.

Schrenk-Notzing, A. von (1895). *The Use of Hypnosis in Psychopathia Sexualis.* Reprint. New York: Julian Press, 1956.

Searles, H. (1961). The evolution of the mother transference in psychotherapy with the schizophrenic patient. In *Collected Papers on Schizophrenia and Related Subjects*, pp. 349–380. New York: International Universities Press, 1965.

_____ (1963). Transference psychosis in the psychotherapy of chronic schizophrenia. *International Journal of Psycho-Analysis* 44:249–281.

_____ (1986). *My Work with Borderline Patients.* Northvale, NJ: Jason Aronson.

Sebastiani, J., and Foy, J. (1965). Psychotic visitors to the White House. *American Journal of Psychiatry* 122:679–686.

Sedlak, A. (1988). Prevention of wife abuse. In *Handbook of Family Violence*, ed. V. Van Hasselt, R. Morrison, A. Bellack, and M. Hersen, pp. 457–481. New York: Plenum.

Sedman, G. (1966). A comparative study of pseudohallucinations, imagery and true hallucinations. *Journal of Psychiatry* 112:9–17.

Seeman, M. (1978). Delusional loving. *Archives of General Psychiatry* 35:1265–1267.

Segal, J. (1989). Erotomania revisited: from Kraepelin to *DSM-III-R. American Journal of Psychiatry* 146:1261–1266.

_____ (1990). Dr. Segal replies [Letter to the editor]. *American Journal of Psychiatry* 147:820–821.

Shapiro, D. (1965). *Neurotic Styles.* New York: Basic Books.

_____ (1981). *Autonomy and Rigid Character.* New York: Basic Books.

Shore, D., Filson, R., Davis, T., et al. (1985). White House cases: psychiatric patients and the Secret Service. *American Journal of Psychiatry* 142:308–311.

Shore, D., Filson, R., and Johnson, W. (1988). Violent crime arrests and paranoid schizophrenia: the White House case studies. *Schizophrenia Bulletin* 14:279–281.

Shore, D., Filson, R., Johnson, W., et al. (1989). Murder and assault arrests of White House cases: clinical and demographic correlates of violence subsequent to civil commitment. *American Journal of Psychiatry* 146:645–651.

Sims, A., and White, A. (1973). Coexistence of the Capgras and de Clerambault's syndromes: a case history. *British Journal of Psychiatry* 123:635–637.

Slavney, P. (1990). *Perspectives on "Hysteria."* Baltimore: The Johns Hopkins University Press.

Smith, S. (1984). The sexually abused patient and the abusing therapist: a study in sadomasochistic relationships. *Psychoanalytic Psychology* 1:89–98.

Smith, S., and Newman, J. (1990). Alcohol and drug abuse-dependence disorders in psychopathic and nonpsychopathic criminal offenders. *Journal of Abnormal Psychology* 99:430–439.

Socarides, C. (1974). The demonified mother: a study of voyeurism and sexual sadism. *International Review of Psycho-Analysis* 1:187–195.

Solnit, A. (1986). Introduction. In *Self and Object Constancy*, ed. R. Lax, S. Bach, and J. Burland, pp. 1–7. New York: Guilford.

Spalt, L. (1980). Hysteria and antisocial personality: a single disorder? *Journal of Nervous and Mental Disease* 168:456–464.

Sperling, M. (1973). Conversion hysteria and conversion symptoms: a revision of classification and concepts. *Journal of the American Psychoanalytic Association* 21:745–771.

Spielman, P. M. (1971). Envy and jealousy: an attempt at clarification. *Psychoanalytic Quarterly* 40:59–82.

Spitz, R. (1945). Hospitalism: an enquiry into the genesis of psychiatric conditions in early childhood. *Psychoanalytic Study of the Child* 1:53–74. New York: International Universities Press.

Sroufe, L. (1985). Attachment classification from the perspective of infant–caregiver relationships and infant temperament. *Child Development* 56:1–14.

Stein, R. (1990). A new look at the theory of Melanie Klein. *International Journal of Psycho-Analysis* 71:499–511.

Stekel, W. (1929). *Sadism and Masochism: The Psychology of Hatred and Cruelty.* New York: Liveright.

Stern, D. (1983). The early development of schemas of self, other, and "self with other." In *Reflections on Self Psychology,* ed. J. Lichtenberg and S. Kaplan, pp. 49–84. Hillsdale, NJ: Analytic Press.

———— (1985). *The Interpersonal World of the Infant: A View from Psychoanalysis and Development Psychology.* New York: Basic Books.

Stone, E., Bonnet, K., and Hofer, M. (1976). Survival and development of maternally deprived rats: role of body temperature. *Psychosomatic Medicine* 39:242–249.

Stone, M. (1980). *The Borderline Syndromes.* New York: McGraw-Hill.

Straus, M. (1987). State and regional differences in U.S. infant homicide rates in relation to sociocultural characteristics of the states. *Behavioral Sciences and the Law* 5:61–75.

Sugarman, A. (1979). The infantile personality: orality in the hysteric revisited. *International Journal of Psycho-Analysis* 60:501–513.

———— (1991). Developmental antecedents of masochism: vignettes from the analysis of a 3-year-old girl. *International Journal of Psycho-Analysis* 72:107–116.

Sullivan, H. (1953). *The Interpersonal Theory of Psychiatry.* New York: W. W. Norton.

Swanson, G., Blount, J., and Bruno, R. (1990). Comprehensive System Rorschach data on Vietnam veterans. *Journal of Personality Assessment* 54:160–169.

Swanson, J., Holzer, C., Ganju, V., and Jono, R. (1990). Violence and psychiatric disorder in the community: evidence from epidemiological catchment area surveys. *Hospital and Community Psychiatry* 41:761–770.

Swenson, J. (1985). Martyrdom: mytho-cathexis and the mobilization of the masses in the Iranian revolution. *Ethos* 13:121–149.

Symonds, M. (1984). Discussion of "violence in the family as a disorder of the attachment and caregiving systems." *American Journal of Psychoanalysis* 44:29–31.

Tarasoff v. *Regents of the University of California,* 17 Cal. 3d 425, 131 Cal. Rptr. 14, 551 P. 2d 334 (1976).

Taylor, P., Mahendra, B., and Gunn, J. (1983). Erotomania in males. *Psychological Medicine* 13:645–650.

Terr, L. (1991). Childhood traumas: an outline and overview. *American Journal of Psychiatry* 148:10–20.

Trevarthen, C. (1979). Communication and cooperation in early infancy: a description of primary intersubjectivity. In *Before Speech* ed. M. Bullowa, pp. 321–346. New York: Cambridge University Press.

Urist, J. (1977). The Rorschach test and the assessment of object relations. *Journal of Personality Assessment* 41:3–9.

Vaillant, G. (1975). Sociopathy as a human process. *Archives of General Psychiatry* 32:178–183.

Valenstein, A. (1973). On attachment to painful feelings and the negative therapeutic reaction. *Psychoanalytic Study of the Child* 28:305–392. New Haven, CT: Yale University Press.

Walus-Wigle, J., and Meloy, J. (1988). Battered woman syndrome as a criminal defense. *Journal of Psychiatry and Law* 16:389–404.

Waters, E., and Deane, K. (1985). Defining and assessing individual differences in attachment relationships: Q-methodology and the organization of behavior in infancy and early childhood. In *Growing Points in Attachment Theory and Research*. Monograph of the Society for Research in Child Development Serial 209, ed. I. Bretherton and E. Waters, pp. 41–65. Chicago: University of Chicago Press.

Weber, C., Meloy, R., and Gacono, C. (1992). A Rorschach study of attachment and anxiety in inpatient conduct disordered and dysthymic adolescents. *Journal of Personality Assessment* 58:16–26.

Weideranders, M. (1991). *The Effectiveness of the Conditional Release Program: A Report to the Legislature*. Sacramento, CA: Dept. of Mental Health, Program Development and Evaluation.

Weinberg, T. (1987). Sadomasochism in the United States: a review of recent sociological literature. *Journal of Sex Research* 23:50–69.

Weiner, I., and Exner, J. (1991). Rorschach changes in long-term and short-term psychotherapy. *Journal of Personality Assessment* 56:453–465.

Weiss, J., Lamberti, J., and Blackman, N. (1960). The sudden murderer: a comparative analysis. *Archives of General Psychiatry* 2:669–678.

Wertham, F. (1937). The catathymic crisis. *Archives of Neurology and Psychiatry* 37:974–978.

_____ (1966). *A Sign for Cain*. New York: Macmillan.

Westen, D. (1989). Are "primitive" object relations really preoedipal? *American Journal of Orthopsychiatry* 59:331–345.

_____ (1991). Clinical assessment of object relations using the TAT. *Journal of Personality Assessment* 56:56–74.

Westen, D., Ludolph, P., Block, M., et al. (1990). Developmental history and object relations in psychiatrically disturbed adolescent girls. *American Journal of Psychiatry* 147:1061–1068.

Widiger, T., Frances, A., Pincus, H., et al. (1991). Toward an empirical classification for DSM-IV. *Journal of Abnormal Psychology* 100:280–288.

Wiggins, J. S. (1979). A psychological taxonomy of trait-descriptive terms: the interpersonal domain. *Journal of Personality and Social Psychology* 37:395–412.

Williamson, S., Hare, R., and Wong, S. (1987). Violence: criminal psychopaths and their victims. *Canadian Journal of Behavioral Sciences* 19:454–462.

Williamson, S., Harpur, T., and Hare, R. (1990). *Sensitivity to emotional polarity in psychopaths.* Paper presented at the meeting of the American Psychological Association, Boston, August.

Wilson, C. (1980–1981). Parental overstimulation in asthma. *International Journal of Psychoanalytic Psychotherapy* 8:601–621.

Winnicott, D. W. (1965). *The Maturational Processes and the Facilitating Environment.* New York: International Universities Press.

Winslade, W., and Ross, J. (1983). *The Insanity Plea.* New York: Charles Scribner's Sons.

Winslow, J., and Insel, T. (1991). Social status in pairs of male squirrel monkeys determines the behavioral response of central oxytocin administration. *The Journal of Neuroscience* 11:2032–2038.

Woddis, G. (1957). Depression and crime. *British Journal of Delinquency* 8:85–94.

Wolf, E. (1988). *Treating the Self.* New York: Guilford.

Wood, B., and Poe, R. (1990). Diagnosis and classification of erotomania [Letter to the Editor]. *American Journal of Psychiatry* 147:1388–1389.

Zeanah, C., and Zeanah, P. (1989). Intergenerational transmission of maltreatment: insights from attachment theory and research. *Psychiatry* 52:177–196.

Zelnick, L., and Buchholz, E. (1990). The concept of mental representations in light of recent infant research. *Psychoanalytic Psychology* 7:29–58.

Zetzel, E. (1968). The so-called good hysteric. *International Journal of Psycho-Analysis* 49:256–260.

Credits

The author gratefully acknowledges permission to reprint the following material:

Index